A FEW TALES

*Dramatic Incidents Over The Winter Of Discontent
In The UK*

By

Valukalam Anthony Thomas

Dedication

All those numerous friends who have trusted me with the memories of their lives, I gratefully remember them here. Some of these memories were humorous at times when I laughed with them, some sad when I tried to reassure them about an approaching dawn of happiness, and some lonely when I hugged them. I don't think I am at liberty to disclose their identity, but they know who they are and the energy of the story.

My friends, I never forget you!

I also kindly remember my wife, who never had any faith in me, even on the wedding day, but stood beside me day and night all these decades and silently encouraged me to succeed in everything I had wanted to achieve, including the writing of this story. I salute her wholeheartedly.

And my daughter Lynnette, who was angry and aggressive throughout the writing period to see this story succeed. She read the drafts several times and advised me strongly about her opinions as a young person. Lyn, I quietly see your love and respect!

About the Author

When V A Thomas arrived in the UK, the country faced political turmoil from all fronts, such as an unstable government in power. Union disputes in every industry, a high level of national unemployment and, still soaring, unprecedented inflation, and numerous refugees from Uganda. Due to the Arabian embargo on oil and gas, the energy cost to the households and the haulage sector increased intolerably. It was dark and cold throughout the region.

However, Anthony managed to enrol in Hammersmith College for English courses and then picked up a job as a trainee accountant.

He continued to work in various business until 1985, then set up his own company, Thomas Enterprises Ltd, which is still running successfully. At the height of his business career, he bought a nursing home in Plymouth, next to Cornwall where this story is set in.

He wrote stories in his teenage days in Kerala, a South Indian state where he was born and grew up, but failed to make a successful breakthrough.

Anthony Thomas lives in London with his wife and a daughter. They also have other three children, two daughters and one son. They live apart; the eldest daughter is in the USA, the other two are in London, and all three are teachers.

Acknowledgment

John Andrew and Alex Paul, and those backroom staff of Writer Cosmos who kindly received my story and edited and published it. I like to give a "BIG THANK YOU ALL" because you have been marvellous to me.

Katherine Chaveli taught my children English in school years ago. Now, she has read my book, corrected it, and encouraged me to have hope in my writing. Thank you!

Susan Cranberry, you are very busy with your poetry writing, but you read my story and gave me a good review. Thank you!

Father William Johnstone, you have been very enthusiastic about my story. Thank you, Father, for your moral support.

I also remember everyone in my family who continuously assisted me in writing this story. Your tireless encouragement hasn't gone wasted. I thank you all!

Table of Contents

Chapter 1

Emma to St Ives

Part 1: Sunday, the 11th of December 1988

The intensity of lightning literally struck her blind, and the thunder crashed simultaneously close to her. Emma jolted up violently in her seat. She held the steering wheel tightly – blinking desperately to open her eyes while trying to quickly regain composure. She was on the motorway and traveling around 70 miles per hour through a heavy downpour. In all fairness, this trip should have been postponed. However, there was no advanced forecast about this horrendous weather. Anyway, there was no comfort in worrying about it now. She reduced the speed to under 40 miles per hour as per the safe driving instructions that were announced frequently on the local radio.

And, despite the thick presence of moisture in the view, Emma had managed to see the name Exeter on the destination and also find the information that the dual carriageway A30 would take her to Cornwall. Well, she was en route, and not very much behind the time regardless of this difficult condition on the way. "Emma, don't panic," her own thoughts reminded in her mind. "You're late. But it isn't the end of the world if you're not dying."

"Dying?" Emma shouted half crazily and half-jokingly and into the noise of the speeding traffic. "In this weather? And in this motorway? She smiled, whispering, 'Not a chance!'"

Emma had already seen a few accidents and long delays related to rescue services. Obviously, she had no time for any of these. She got an appointment for which she had genuinely struggled to get, and she didn't want to miss it at all. It was very vital to her future and life. But her life was more important.

Emma bypassed Exeter and easily got into the A30 dual carriageway, and she was on her way to the Great Atlantic Hotel, which was practically on the other end of this road. It would take just over 2 hours to reach her target.

When Emma was a good while on this route, the radio bulletins came through the air that the A30 dual carriage was closed entirely between Launceston and Bodmin due to the numerous trees that fell on the road during the storm in the early morning that smashed the local area, mainly the North Devon regions. The bulletins went on to urge people to avoid the area if possible and advised them to use the A38 dual carriageway instead in order to travel to Cornwall. Everyone was reminded to make sure there was enough fuel in the tank if they were setting out to this destination.

She glanced at her petrol gauge and noticed that half of the tank was full. She took the petrol at Bristol before she started the journey. Mercedes cars normally had larger tanks than some of their competitors. She saw a service station rather soon and drove in. Firstly, she needed some guidance, and secondly, she wanted to top up the petrol. A police car was parked off the driveway, and she parked behind it. She walked over to them. The officer in the driving seat lowered the window. "Hello love, you're alright?"

"Not really, officer," she replied politely. "I need to go to St Ives in Cornwall."

"I know St Ives," he said rather easily. "I worked ten years in Cornwall. But it's a long way from here. And in this treacherous weather, it's a real struggle."

Absently, Emma shot a glance into the road and beyond. Huge clouds hung low and rolled over to the horizon that appeared nearer. It was still raining lightly, though. A gentle gust of wind was blowing against the huge oak trees which were on a slope further up the road. It might be the last gasp of the storm that terrified the region earlier, or there might be another danger brewing up. The sky was very low, with massive clouds that stretched to the horizon. And the horizon looked nearer. Somehow, the world had shrunk in every way.

She looked back at the policeman. "It's very important. I ought to go."

"What's your name?"

"Emma Wilford."

He caught her eyes steadily for a moment. "Emma, where are you coming from?"

"This morning from Bristol."

"You have got a clear London accent?"

She smiled pleasantly. "That's my city."

"Why didn't you use the train, Emma? It could have been a relaxing journey. And safer in this treacherous weather."

"Trains are on strikes, sir."

"Strikes? What on earth for?"

"To be honest, I don't know!"

A policewoman who was in the passenger seat, talking on the phone, turned to her. "This man on the phone tells me that they are striking against the weather," she said, sounding rather serious. "And who wouldn't be if they are noble?"

Without speaking, Emma smiled.

"Don't bother with my colleague. She only comes to duty when she isn't well."

The policewoman pulled his face comically. "What can I do? He's my mentor."

The smile on her face grew broader, but, for her credit, she didn't make any comments.

The policeman waited as if visualizing the routes to Cornwall in his mind. "You go down a mile to the next junction," he said, gesturing the direction with his hand. "Take the first left to A386, which takes you to Plymouth. You heard of Plymouth?"

"Yes, officer! I've been in Plymouth."

"Good. And when you're approaching Plymouth, watch out for A38."

"I think I saw A38 at Exeter?"

"Yes, you would have. But you don't go to Exeter. You go to Bodmin, which is in the opposite direction. And then you get back to A30 that takes you towards St Ives."

The policewoman said helpfully. "When you're in Bodmin, you're in Cornwall."

"I know, officer," she replied respectfully. "I've been learning the maps in the last couple of days."

"Shame, it's a long way because a section of A30 is closed," he explained slowly, looking at his side mirror and spotting a Mercedes car behind them. "Well, you have a good car there. You have no problem."

She said, smiling. "But it's on-hire."

"Our car is also hired," the police said, pulling her face rather amusingly, "from the police station."

Now, they all laughed.

In the end, the policewoman said, "Look out for signs posted. And you will be alright."

"Thank you."

The woman looked at her caringly, "A word of advice, if you don't mind?"

She met her eyes. "Not at all, officer. What's it?"

She hesitated. "You're a beautiful young lady,"

The man stared at his colleague, then turned to her. "She seldom gets her conversation right," he chuckled teasingly. "Anyway, be careful if you've to ask strangers for help."

The policewoman explained, this time more seriously, "You pass lots of open countryside. And you never know who you may come across."

Emma smiled, "Oh, I know officer. London is no exception either."

"So be careful!"

"Thanks, both of you."

"Alright. And drive carefully."

Emma went around her car, checking the tires. She moved the car to the pump and topped up the petrol, then paid the money at the till before she got into her car. The police were still there. She waved them goodbye, then drove off.

It was a long struggle to the St Ives. The roads were covered under heavy snow or slushy water – either remaining like ponds or flowing over the surfaces. It was over one hundred and twenty miles to the destination, which took almost four hours. She was absolutely shattered when she arrived at the hotel.

Part 2: Emma Reaches the Hotel

Two reception staff, a male and female, rushed to her. Emma rolled down the window and looked at them. "Good afternoon, young lady," the female staff greeted her first. "My name is Philomena. You are alright?"

She looked at them nervously. "Good afternoon," she said. "This is the arrival point?"

"Yes, Ms, for the VIP guests."

The look of nervousness increased on her face. "My God, am I in the wrong place?" Emma asked, her voice was clearly exhausted. "Where is the entrance for the ordinary guests?"

"That's at the Main Hall in the front," Philomena replied courteously. "What's your name, Miss?"

"Wilford. Emma Wilford." She paused and sighed quietly.

"That's okay, Miss Wilford," both staff members answered unanimously. And then, the male staff continued gently, "I am Collin. And we've been expecting you."

"Have you? Oh, I am so sorry. The weather hampered my travel."

"Yes, Ms Wilford," Philomena responded quickly. "And you're okay with us here."

"Guests are always late on a day like this," Collin said reassuringly. "What a stormy day! But we are glad you arrived alright."

Emma waited. Obviously, she needed a breath of fresh air. "In fact, I'm supposed to be meeting Mr Mark Windrush."

"No problem, Miss," Philomena replied. "Mark is here."

"He advised me to come here."

Philomena nodded as if for an answer, and then she turned to her colleague. Without a word, he hurried to the building and disappeared behind the foyer. Swiftly, she turned her face and, stooping slightly towards the car window, whispered respectfully, "While we wait for Mark, shall I assist you to a room?"

"Shall I stay here, please? I need a little rest."

"That's fine, Ms Wilford, if you're perfectly happy here." She paused briefly as though unsure of herself. "Or I can take you to a room, and you can rest there more comfortably."

She smiled. "No problem, dear. I'm fine here."

"Shall I offer you something? Something hot, or cold? Or anything you may like, Miss Wilford?"

"You're very kind. I am okay at the moment."

"It might have been a terrible drive, I believe."

She nodded to answer with a tired face. "Mark will take long?"

"Yes, I'm here," Mark said as he was coming towards the car. He came close to it. "Good evening, Emma," he said cheerfully, meeting her gaze through the window. Suddenly, he froze as if a chill shot up his spine. Somehow, he managed to sustain his composure. "You…you Miss… Emma…. Wilford?" He asked, obviously his voice breaking.

Emma smiled easily. "Good evening, Mark?"

Mark wanted to take off his eyes from her steady gaze. But he wasn't successful with his effort as his eyes seemingly glued to her stare.

She chuckled. "You're alright, Mark? You seemed to be struggling?"

"Sorry, Emma," he grinned nervously. "I had a busy day." He managed to make an excuse and then coughed tactfully for a couple of moments to regain his confidence. "Shall we go to the reception, please," he asked, still rather nervously.

"Alright, Mark."

He didn't say anything immediately but looked away into the garden and then the ocean beyond. In the end, he turned back slowly. "I think we better go into my office."

"Of course," Emma answered clearly, "if that's okay." She stepped out, and then stood in front of him. "What about the car?"

He held his breath steadily for a moment, meeting her eyes before he was able to reply, "We'll take it to our car park."

"It's a hired car. They will come for it in the morning."

"That's fine, Emma."

"And my luggage. Two suitcases!"

"That's fine, Emma. The porters will bring them to your chalet."

Emma noted the word 'Chalet' and smiled. "Chalet? I never stayed in a chalet."

"It's a pleasure!"

She handed the car key to him.

"You need to take anything from the car now, Emma?"

"Oh, my handbag." Emma turned back to the car and picked up a leather bag from the passenger seat. Slowly, she slung it on her left shoulder.

He closed the car and gave the key to Collin, who was on his side. "Miss Wilford will be in chalet No 5, in Gemma House."

The attendant nodded for an answer.

He turned to Emma. "Let's go."

"Okay."

His office was at the back of the Great Atlantic Hotel and was on the ground floor. In fact, it was a small room with a desk in the middle and two additional chairs at the front. Emma took a seat, and he sat down on his chair behind the back. "I know you're a tea addict, Emma," he said nervously, looking at her across the desk.

"Yes, you're right," she said cheerfully. "But I'm okay now, Mark. I had tea and pasties when I was at the service station in Penzance."

Mark grinned. "And, of course, the Cornish pasties. I missed out on that."

Emma laughed. "I can't forgive that."

He joined in her laugh. "We've freshly baked Cornish Steak pasties. Shall I order it with a glass of homegrown wine?"

Emma refused politely. "Maybe later, Mark."

"Not even a tea?"

She giggled quietly. "Later. Thanks."

He waited, staring at her rather strangely. "I've a form to fill up. Just a few questions! It's an insurance requirement."

"Let's do it now. Anyway, what kind of questions, Mark?"

"Your personal details, mostly!"

Emma giggled innocently. "You know them all, except the finance."

He sat, smiling quietly. To be honest, he was strangely uncomfortable with her presence. "That's true," he readily agreed. Obviously, he was avoiding lengthy conversations. "Okay, I'll complete the form. And you can sign it when you're free."

"And regarding the payment for the stay, I'll pay...... "

"Oh no," he interrupted her gently. "You're Mr. Atkinson's guest. He'll write it off."

Emma chuckled happily. "I can pay if I've to!"

"Absolutely no. Mr Atkinson won't have it."

"That's very kind of him."

"You can thank him when you see him."

"I will."

He waited awkwardly for a moment. "I checked your application thoroughly. But I didn't see your parents' names or contact details. It's important for the insurance requirements."

A shadow of concern crossed over her face. "I'm sorry," she said uneasily, meeting his eyes steadily. "Mark, I can't help you with that."

Mark moved in his chair and leaned against the back of the chair. "You are not in speaking terms?"

Emma turned her eyes away from his face and looked out the window. The ocean was in her view, which extended to the distance. Slowly and reluctantly, she met his eyes again. "I grew up with my adopted mother. She died a few years ago."

Mark remained silent.

"I've no knowledge about my biological parents." She paused uneasily and looked at the sea again before she spoke quietly, "The sixties were a colourful decade, and some unwanted children were born. And I am one of them."

He waited for her to continue,

"It doesn't worry me, Mark. I always face this issue."

"I am sorry to hear this, Emma."

"When this sort of situation comes up, I tell them to put me as an orphan."

"I didn't wish to give you a hard time, Emma," he said finally. "And I am sorry."

Emma watched him quietly for a moment. "You have a problem with that, Mark?"

He appeared more puzzled. "Not really."

"If you have a problem, I can go back."

Mark leaned forward and put his elbows on the desk and his face in his hands while his eyes stared at her steadily. In fact, he was deep in shapeless thoughts.

"Mark? You're alright?"

"Sorry, Emma," he replied in the end. "I don't know what came over me. I lost my mind for a moment."

"Is it because of me?"

He smiled clearly to ease the expression on his face. "Of course not, dear."

"Well, Mark. We spoke on the phone five or six times?"

"True."

"And you saw my application and my photo?"

"The answer is: yes and no."

"What do you mean?"

He waited. "The personnel office received your application and passed it to the training department. they should have made a decision then and there." He paused briefly, recollecting the incidents in the right order. "But they didn't. In the end, they directed it to the chairman, Mathew Atkinson. And this is rather unusual, I must admit!"

"Why did they do that?"

"No idea whatsoever. But, maybe, you can ask Mr Atkinson."

"I will!"

"Anyway, he wanted to help you on this. And he put me in charge of your project. And that's why I kept in touch with you regularly."

She looked at him in amazement. "Thank you, Mark."

"That's okay."

"This opportunity is very important for my studies. And when we talked on the phone, I knew I was safe with you." Emma paused briefly. "Can I meet Mr Atkinson in the morning?"

"No."

"Why?"

"He couldn't leave on time."

Without speaking, she waited for him to explain.

"He should've left two days ago. He was in Atlantica."

"Atlantica?"

"Yes. Atlantica in Africa. And when he arrived at the airport, violence broke out."

"My God! Is he safe?"

"Yes, yes. He is safe."

"What happened?"

"Shooting. Fatalities. Burnings. Lootings. Just the normal pandemonium there!"

"Why?"

"It was a military affair this time. One major general in the army had a bad sleep. In the morning, he's seeing dreams in his mind. And he wanted to take over the country."

Emma waited carefully.

"And yesterday, everything was back to normal. They reopened the airport in the capital. By the way, the capital is also called 'Atlantica or Atlantica City in full.'"

Emma continued to be silent.

"Mr Atkinson is on his way now. And he'll be home about midnight, our time. I hope our weather won't cause further trouble. And he will be here tomorrow. In the early afternoon, I suppose. Or maybe earlier than that, because you're here. He's dying to meet you."

13

Emma giggled gently. "I heard the weather is fine for days."

"Good!"

"Mark, if it's okay, I want to see my room. I like to rest a bit. To be honest, I'm exhausted after the drive."

"Well, I take you now. And you have a fine chalet."

"Chalet?" Emma asked in an excited voice.

"Yes, a chalet in Gemma House!"

"In Gemma House? What's that?"

"It's part of the hotel, but a different building named Gemma House. The name Gemma was Atkinson's grandmother's…"

"Gemma!" she interrupted him. "Do you know I love that name?"

"Oh, tell Mr Atkinson when you see him tomorrow. He will be pleased." Mark stopped talking briefly. "The grandmother, Gemma, had several wonderful years in this house."

"That's nice!"

"Mathew Atkinson's father, Albert, built this beautiful house. And he built it close to his hotel so the staff could look after her when Albert and other relatives were away on business."

"Wonderful!"

"Until recently, only the Atkinson family members were allowed to stay there – in this particular top floor. Now, Mathew Atkinson lets you have a chalet there. Maybe he's considering you as a family member!"

She hesitated for a moment, then giggled quietly, "Am I that lucky?"

Philomena entered quietly. "Miss Wilford's suitcases are in the chalet now," she told him. "And the car is in the private car park."

"Thanks, Mena."

She handed the chalet's key to Mark. "Is there anything else I can do for Miss Wilford?"

"No Mena. If anything, I will let you know."

Philomena left the office. He turned to Emma. "We go?"

"Okay."

Part 3: Gemma House

"How many floors are here in Gemma House?" Emma asked as they were climbing up the stairs.

"Two floors and the ground floor. Your chalet is on the second floor. I choose it deliberately."

"Why?"

"It's very peaceful up there."

Emma kept silent as she expected him to continue.

"Yours is the last chalet in that end. And very spacious. Though another staircase is there, which is actually in front of Chalet 5, nobody tends to use it. It's mostly considered as a fire escape route."

"Good!"

They came to the second floor of the Gemma House and outside her accommodation. Mark opened the door and held it wide for her. Emma entered first, and he followed her to the hallway. He went with her to the lounge. Please have a look around and tell me how you see it." She went to the bedroom, bathroom, and the dining room by the side of the lounge. She turned back, her eyes gleaming with excitement. "I feel like I am a princess."

Mark smiled lightly. "You like it, I take it?"

"I love it. And thank you, Mark. And I can't wait to see Mr Atkinson to thank him."

"You will see him tomorrow."

"I hope so," she whispered, moving to the huge window of the lounge. "Where is the sea? You have been promising the view of the sea."

"I don't think anyone could smuggle the Great Atlantic Ocean as easy as you say," he chuckled as he moved over to her and turned to the way she was looking out. "She is definitely there," he said more hilariously. "But the mist and fog are blocking your view."

Emma laughed innocently, meeting his eyes. "I got the direction right."

"Of course. And you will see the sea when the air is clear."

"Thank you for telling me," she said mockingly.

He laughed quietly, then asked, "Can I get you some drinks? Hot? Cold? Strong? Anything?"

She grinned. "Tea, if you tempt me badly?"

"It's my pleasure!"

Emma grinned again, steadily meeting his gaze.

"Anything else, like biscuits, cakes or chocolates or anything."

"Oh! You're tempting me indeed, aren't you?"

"I have to. You are the guest of our chairman, Mr Mathew Atkinson. We've to make sure you are enjoying every minute of your stay with us."

Emma stopped laughing, but her mouth remained open as if in a laugh. A moment later, she spoke rather gratefully, "Alright, Mark. A tea will do. And for anything else, I leave it to your choice."

"Excellent. And another thing, if I may say to you."

"What's that?"

"If anybody rings your doorbell, you are not obliged to answer if you don't want to!"

"Thank you. And I hope you can help me on another thing?"

"Yes, young lady?"

"I noticed some of your staff are crowding at doorways and staring at me. Why is that?"

"No harm intended, Emma. But you are very rare, very precious, and stunningly beautiful."

She smiled faintly. "Rare?"

"Have you seen anybody with your complexion in this area, young lady?"

"You mean mixed race? Yes. I am looking at one."

Mark felt rather embarrassed. "But I mean, a young lady like you?"

"I don't know, Mark. I have never been to Cornwall."

"And precious?"

"My answer is the same. I don't know. Anyway, I don't think I'm any precious."

17

"You are an extremely elegant lady if you allow me to say so."

Emma laughed loudly. "Wow, you're something else. Now I can see what your wife looks like."

Mark didn't speak. Instead, he started walking out. He stopped before the door and stood, turning half-away towards her. "The tea will be with you in ten minutes, Emma."

"Thank you!"

"What time would you prefer dinner?"

"I will tell you later."

"Please do so!"

"Thank you."

"You're welcome," he said, pacing towards the door.

"Mark?"

He turned back. "Yes, Emma?"

"Did I upset you when I talked about your wife?"

"Of course not," he replied politely. "But it bubbled up so many memories."

"I am sorry."

"I was crazily in love with her. And so was she! But we didn't marry."

"Very sad."

"Fate was cruel to us."

Without speaking, Emma stared at him.

He caught her eyes constantly, then went out and closed the door behind him.

Emma stood there a few more minutes, absolutely quietly as if lumbered with thoughts. Slowly, she sat down on a chair by the window. She looked again into the garden and the Ocean beyond. She didn't see anything. The air was filled with dense fog. However, she didn't know she wasn't seeing anything. A feeling of restlessness surged inside her. A moment or two ticked away lazily when she thought she was about to burst out to cry. She didn't cry, though.

Three keys of a soft music drifted into the room as somebody pressed the switch on the doorbell. Quickly, Emma grabbed a tissue from her jeans pocket and freshened her face. She reached out to the door. "Who is it?"

"It's the room service, Ms Wilford. My name is June Murphy."

She looked out through the peephole. A young woman dressed in the hotel uniform stood by a food trolley. She opened the door.

"Thank you, Ms Wilford." June slowly entered with the trolley in front. "Shall I take this to the dining room?"

"Please."

June pushed it further to the dining room and left it by the table. Emma's eyes ran over the shelves of the trolley. Steaming teapot, fresh milk in a stainless flask, and sugar in a glass jar were placed on the top shelf in addition to empty cups, saucers, and spoons. The second and third shelves were full of snacks such as a variety of chocolates, biscuits, sliced cakes, and whatever snacks one could fancy. "June, is it all for me?"

June laughed merrily. "I'm afraid this is all I could bring now." She giggled a little. "I can bring some more if you allow me."

Emma stared at them obviously bewildered. "Is it a punishment?"

"If I've to suffer this punishment, I thank the good Lord for it."

Emma smiled mischievously.

"Can I mix a tea for you, Ms Wilford, before I go."

"No, dear. I will do it in a minute."

"Anyway, I leave everything. And you enjoy it." She gestured to a switch on the wall, saying, "By the way, if those items are not enough, please press that switch. I will rush back with another trolley full of food."

"You better do that if you've a death wish."

"Miss Wilford, that'll make my fellow very happy?"

"What are you saying?"

"If I die now, he will be singing jingle bell all day on Christmas day with his new girlfriend."

She smiled pleasantly. "Can you blame him?"

She laughed cheerfully. "Please switch on the alarm if you need help."

"Quite a difficult job, but I try."

And June went smiling.

Emma made tea and sat down by the bay window. She sipped on her drink rather absently as the tension inside her surged viciously. She finished the tea, got up to put the cup back on the trolley, and then the door music wafted again. She went over to the front door. "Who is this?"

"Emma?"

"Yes, I am Emma."

"My name is Berney Smith," he said politely. "Tomorrow, you are having some induction courses with me."

"I know," Emma said pleasantly, opening the door.

Berney entered into the hallway, meeting her eyes.

"I meant to see you this afternoon. But I was awfully late. The weather delayed my journey."

"That's not a problem," he said, his eyes steadily on her. He stopped talking as if he was nervous in her close presence. "I finished for today," he went on somewhat uneasily, moving back a step or two. "But I thought to see you before I go home."

Emma grinned lightly. "Am I that important?"

"Well, duty matters," he said naively. "I like to do things properly."

"Thank you," she appreciated, standing slightly out of the doorway. "Please come in."

Berney came in rather hesitantly. She shut the door, then turned to him. "You are alright?"

"Yes, yes," he reacted hurriedly, pacing up the hallway, and then moved back to the door as though he was going out. "I'm alright, but a bit tired."

"Come to the lounge," Emma said courteously, "and sit down. I like to talk with you if you have a minute."

Without saying anything, he moved to the lounge but stood by the side of a chair, obviously unable to decide whether to sit or not.

"Shall I make a tea? Or coffee? I've the stuffs for it."

He sat down half-heartedly. "I'm okay. I just had tea before I left. Anyway, thank you."

Emma raised a friendly smile and sat in her usual seat at the window. "What sort of day you had today, Mr Smith? A lovely day, I suppose."

"I don't get such days. Always hectic."

"Oh! That's not good."

Berney waited, watching her studiously. "You look different from the impression I got from your photo in the application," he said abruptly.

She shrugged helplessly, still smiling. "I didn't have a better photo to enclose at the time. Anyway, what sort of difference, you see?"

He seemed to be confused. "I don't know, really. I think you looked bigger and stronger in the photo."

Emma chuckled amusingly. "I hope it's true." She stopped talking for a moment and laughed. "Maybe I am too shattered after the long drive through the atrocious weather."

Silently, Mr Smith sat there, staring at her tensely.

"You sure I can't offer you a tea?"

"How do you know I drink tea?"

She smiled uncomfortably, "That's all I've, Mr Smith!"

He waited helplessly for a moment. "I saw your certificates in the application."

"Are they okay?" Emma asked politely, moving back in her chair.

He struggled to speak as words were harder to come by. "I can't remember. But don't worry about it."

22

"Thank you. And I know it wasn't a good picture. But that's the only one I had at the time."

He looked at her steadily. "You might have noticed the way I looked at you. And I am still looking at you."

She smiled trivially. "You mean staring?"

"Yes. No. I mean…."

She interrupted him. "I don't worry about that, Mr Smith. I am quite used to it now."

"No, no. I didn't mean that."

She waited patiently.

"I meant to say that I was trying to recognize something."

"Oh? What is that?"

"You're a young, beautiful lady. But that's not what I have in my mind. I'm sorry if I gave you any wrong impression."

"That's okay."

He hesitated. "Your picture reminds me of somebody."

"My God! Who is that?"

Berney hesitated, seemingly unsure of himself. "Her name was Daniella."

She stared at him apparently confused. "Daniella? Who was she?"

"I adopted Daniella."

She was silent.

"She was very tall and strong for her age. And very beautiful."

"Where is she now?"

He didn't speak for a long while, as if painful memories lapping up on his conscience.

"We had to separate in the end. I am sorry."

"Why did you say 'sorry,' Jeffrey? Sorry, I meant Mr Smith?"

"Jeffrey?" he asked, staring at her, completely shocked. "How did you get that name?"

Emma appeared puzzled. "What name?"

"Jeffrey?"

"Did I call you that?"

"Yes!"

"Maybe I thought you said, Jeffrey when you came in?"

He was obviously annoyed. But he replied as calmly as possible. "I never said, Jeffrey."

"Sorry, Jeffrey. No, I meant Berney. I am getting confused now."

"I believe so."

"Did you hurt her? I mean, Daniella?"

"I don't know."

Emma waited for him to speak.

"The adoption didn't work out for her and for us. In the end, she went back to the social care."

"Very painful for you, of course!"

"No, it wasn't painful."

She didn't speak. Instead, she stared at him sympathetically.

However, Berney didn't have the expression of sympathy on his face. "It was the right outcome for both of us."

"Why? You didn't love her?"

"No."

"Did she love you?"

"It's immaterial."

Emma caught his eyes gently. "It must have been very disappointing for you," she said deliberately to please him. After all, she had to do the induction for his courses the next day.

"This is life. And nobody knows what is best for anyone."

"I suppose Daniella is feeling very bad about this outcome."

"What do you mean?"

"I just thought so. That's all, Mr Smith."

"What?"

"She accepted you as her own father. And she did everything that you asked her, whether she was capable of doing it or not. And she may be thinking, you treated her like a slave child. And abused her badly. And you discarded her as a bag of garbage when it suited you."

He looked at her with raging eyes. "How do you know? You were there?"

She lightly smiled in order to ease his temper. "I was only saying what she must be thinking. Anyway, it's none of my business. If you don't like talking about Daniella, we change the subject. That's all, Mr Jeffrey Smith."

An expression of fear and increased anger was displayed on his face. "Why are you still calling me Mr Smith?"

"Sorry, maybe I am confused now."

He hesitated. "How did you get that name? You better tell me!"

She looked at him, bewildered. "I don't know. I thought you said, 'Jeffrey 'was your name. Oh God, it's getting pure torture. And now, can you imagine how much Daniella was scared when she lived with you?"

He didn't answer. Instead, he asked as if he was possessed, "Why did you call me Jeffrey?"

"When you came in!"

"I didn't. Tell me how did you know it?"

"Know what, Mr Jeffrey? Oh! I'm sorry, Mr Smith. I'm completely lost!"

"You're taking me for someone else," he retorted. A shadowy expression of anger and humiliation darkened his face. "And stop calling me with someone's name. It's making me upset."

"Sorry, Mr Smith. I've no desire or intention to upset you."

"You're playing games with me," he shouted, getting to his feet. "Now, I'm beginning to wonder who you're?"

"You're frightening me, Mr Jeffrey? Oh! Sorry, Mr Smith. I will scream if you don't calm down."

"Who's going to hear you from this top floor?" He stood with a shivering temper. "Who'll know even if I kill you?"

"Please don't come near to me," she begged, still sitting in her chair, and tears bubbling up behind her eyelids. "Now I know you are Jeffrey Smith."

Trying to move towards her with his trembling legs, he shouted with seething rage, "You're Daniella?" he paused, staring at her with an evil eye. "I've nowhere to go. I should have killed you a long time ago."

"Please stop where you are, Mr Smith. I won't disclose your identity to anybody. Please go back."

However, he came close to her. She was in the corner, and there was no way to escape. Emma moved steps away from where she was and made herself enough space. And then, like a flash, she swung around on her legs, and her right fist pounded on his mouth. He staggered for a moment, then fell on the sofa with dripping blood on his face. Suddenly, he struggled to get back on his feet, holding onto the arm of the chair. His hand slipped, and he tumbled down to the carpet. But frantically, he writhed away while trying to get back to his feet. At the inner doorway, he managed to stand up but banged his face on the door.

"Look where you are going, Jeffrey," she said in a caring voice. She moved closer to him. "Don't hurt yourself. Wait, let me help you."

Berney didn't listen to her. Her words petrified him even further, and that she was coming closer. He forced himself forward to the front door but failed to figure out the mechanism of the lock. "Move to the side, Mr Jeffrey, please. Let me open it for you."

He moved a step or two to the side, deeply frightened. "Please don't hurt me."

"I don't know what you're talking about," she said politely, opening the door. "You're taking me for someone else."

Berney hurried out to the passage, and Emma shut the door and locked it, then watched him through the peephole. The stairway was almost in line with her door, and she saw him climbing down. He kept staring back rather frequently, obviously petrified, and checking whether or not she was chasing him. In one of those moments, he missed one step and tumbled down the staircase. He ended up on the landing space below on his head, and then the body slipped down, and finally, the hands and leg.

Emma turned around and stood leaning against the door. A shivering fear sprang up inside her, though she was absolutely convinced she had no part in his accident. However, she continued to stay there, almost frozen, before she started to get her senses back. She turned around and looked through the hole in the door. The man was still there, lying in the same way. She wasn't ready to alert anyone. She couldn't go through the various interrogations of the police if she let it out. She came back to the dining room and mixed a tea. She sipped it as she filled the bath. She felt the water with her hand, and it was nice and warm. Slowly, she lowered herself into it and let the heat soak her body, mind, and soul.

Emma stayed in the bath for a good twenty minutes and then got up. Her hair hung low and loose. She dried them in a cotton towel before she scooped them up to the back of her head and rolled them into a knot. She picked a short dress, slipped into it, and then pulled a house gown over it. It was five minutes to 7. The time went rather fast. She settled in the lounge and turned on the telly. BBC 1 was screening a movie, BBC 2 was showing a cartoon, and sports was on ITV. She chose the sport and sat down on the sofa.

Part 4: Emma Learns More

The doorbell music drifted suddenly and made her jump out of fear. In fact, Emma had forgotten about the music bell. In her mind was the thought of fatality and the possible outcome of it. She went to the door and said as calmly as possible, "Hello!"

"It's June, Ms Wilford."

Emma unbolted the door and pulled it inwards.

"We are very sorry," June apologized quickly. "The dinner is delayed on Gemma House side. "

"Oh?" She exclaimed innocently. "Why?"

"I don't know. Ask Mark Windrush. He might say."

"Is it that bad?"

She shot a glance onto her sides and down the stairways. Nobody was around in the vicinity. "An employee died!"

"How?"

"Heart attack. The hospital doctor says."

"Very sad!"

She waited vaguely. "Would you like the dinner in the dining room downstairs?"

"Can I have it here, darling?"

"Of course. I will bring it for you?"

"Thank you. What is the main course?"

"Roast Lamb and …"

"Good."

"What time would you like the dinner?"

"About eight, I would say."

"Okay, Ms Wilford, I will bring your dinner at 8."

"Thanks."

Before she could say anything, June left hurriedly.

Emma sat down at the desk by the bay window and opened the local newspaper she had bought at a service station. It was called Cornwall News. It had pages of property adverts for buyers and renters along the sea and across the country. She flipped those sections rapidly, as she wasn't interested in properties. Then she found what she had wanted to know, such as cafes, restaurants, and eating stalls. What dishes they would make normally, and where they got the ingredients. Suddenly, she stopped reading as Mark called in. "Sit down, Mark, if you've a few minutes."

"In fact, I'm on my evening break now," Mark said, taking a seat facing her. "But I have to return to work a bit early. One of our staff members died."

"Staff?" Emma asked in a curiously concerned tone. But her heart was pounding with tension uncontrollably, "What happened?"

"He suffered a massive heart attack. He collapsed on the staircase just outside here."

"Very sad. Was he ill?"

"I didn't know the man that well. His name was Berney. He didn't socialize with anybody." He paused thoughtfully. "The undertakers will come shortly and take the body away."

Emma sighed fairly easily. "No relatives?"

"The personal department deals with his case. But I heard he was a loner."

Emma cast her eyes down in an expression of respect for the dead man. "He was supposed to give me some induction course tomorrow if it was the same person."

"It must be him. We've only one person with that name. And he used to give training to the new staff."

A brief period ticked away quietly. "What's my program for tomorrow, Mark?" Emma asked finally, changing the subject discreetly.

"Haven't you got a schedule from us?"

"No. And I was hoping you would tell."

"Well, Berney was the man. But don't worry. Other staff can give you the induction."

"Thanks!"

"I suppose you've to meet the Helena Roscoe if she's available."

"Who is she?"

"And the girl who is getting married on Saturday."

"I know about the wedding. And my main intention was to witness a wedding of this kind."

"That's fine! If Helena isn't available for a day or two, you can meet her mother, Isabella Roscoe."

"Okay."

"But Isabella is always a very busy lady. And with her daughter's wedding's so close, you may not see her either that easily."

"Well, Mr Atkinson is coming. He will help me."

He grinned faintly. "It's not as easy as that."

Without speaking, she looked at him.

"Mr Atkinson has no role to play in this marriage."

"What do you mean? His daughter is getting married?"

He hesitated. "Helena isn't his daughter."

"No?"

"No!"

"But Isabella is Mr. Atkinson's wife?"

"Only for the business's sake and tax regulations."

"Quite confusing!"

"Let's hope Isabella knows him. But you shouldn't ask Isabella about him."

"I'm stupid. But not that level."

"Thank you. I can relax now."

Emma smiled sarcastically.

"One more thing."

"What is that?"

"You've to meet Tanya Roberts. Tanya will help you meet Isabella and Helena."

"Where do I find Tanya?"

Mark waited a moment. "Tomorrow, I start at twelve. But I can come early for your sake. Say, about 10. Can you meet me at about ten-thirty?"

She nodded lightly. "Fine. I don't see any danger. You don't look like a dangerous man."

He smiled. "Okay. one more thing."

"What's that?"

"Helena has a brother, Jacob. And I hope you won't ask him anything personal."

"No. Not a word."

"Good. You're learning fast."

"Thank you."

"Jacob is Tanya's boyfriend."

"I see."

"She's the head of the division called the 'staff coordination unit'."

Emma nodded.

"You will be alright with her."

"And you're around, aren't you? If I need any help!"

"I'm mostly in Gemma House. Or in the store room."

"Where will I be?"

"You will be mostly in the Great Hall, which is mainly run by Isabella. But you'll have many chances to come to the Great Atlantic Hotel, which is primarily run by Mr Atkinson." He glanced at his watch. "Well, I've to get back. If I can, I will come and see you before I go home."

"Thanks."

Mark went out, and Emma locked the door. Slowly, she moved back to the dining room and checked the tea jar. It wasn't hot. She always liked steaming hot tea. But it was a different time and a difficult situation. She poured the tea into a fresh cup and sipped a small bit of it. It wasn't fairly warm. She drank a large sip and settled by the window.

Emma heard the music again and went to the door. "Hello?"

Part 5: Dealing with the Police

"Hello. We're from the local police station. Can we have a talk with you?"

A shiver shot up her body. However, she couldn't remain inactive. She looked through the peephole. Yes, there were two police officers outside the door, a male and a female. She took a deep breath and blew out. "Of course," she said, then opened the door.

"Good evening," the male officer said.

"Good evening."

Abruptly, they stared down over the stairs before the policewoman asked softly, "Can we come in and talk with you, please?"

"Oh! I am so sorry," Emma replied, opening the door fully and allowing them to enter. "I had a terrible day today. I haven't got the balance right."

Without speaking, they stepped in.

Emma shut the door and then turned to look at them. "Would you like to sit in the lounge?"

"No," the woman answered. "Here is fine."

"What's it you like to talk?"

"They found a dead body of a male," he explained calmly. "In fact, the body was at the bottom of the stairs in front of your door."

As she looked at them, her eyes grew wide as an expression of shock. "Sad to hear, officers! Who was he?"

"I don't think we can give you the details yet," he answered politely. "We're making enquiries."

"Did you hear any voices or sounds?" The female officer asked quietly.

"No. I didn't!"

"Any sounds?"

"Sounds? No."

"People frequently use the main stair at the other end," he said calmly. "But nobody comes around on this end. And I suppose this stair is a fire escape route."

"Sorry, I can't answer that. I moved in only two hours ago."

Silently, the officers shot a glance at each other before he asked, "Seen anybody in those two hours?"

"Sorry, I was inside and resting. I had an atrocious journey. Severe storm along the way, plus road blockage due to tree falls. A two-hour journey took five hours or more."

"Where did you come from?" She asked.

"From Bristol!"

"Good gracious. You made it! I don't think I would have."

"Why didn't you use the train? Stress-free travel!"

"I love train travel. But today, they are on strikes."

"Why?"

"Solidarity strikes, I heard. I could've been killed today. They don't care."

"Sorry, we don't hear these things very much in this corner of the country. Anyway, let's go back to our mission. I noticed CCTV surveillance is everywhere here. We should get the information from it."

"But if you hear anything about it, please let the management know about it."

"I will."

"Sorry for troubling you while you were having your rest."

"No problem!"

The officers left, and Emma shut the door. She ran to the room and slumped into the bed. There was no answer she could find *'Why is it the troubles follow her wherever she goes? And each trouble is stronger than the previous, and harder to solve than the last.'*. She cried silently. But there wasn't anyone around to hear her cry.

Exactly at 8 pm, June arrived with the dinner. Roast lamb, potatoes grand mere, and red wine. "Lovely! I promise I am going to enjoy it."

"I chose the side dishes. I hope you like it."

"Like it? I love it."

36

"This is Ribera Del Shero, the best wine in Italy."

"Good Lord, I don't believe it," she exclaimed enthusiastically. "That's my favourite."

"Please enjoy it. And I'm leaving the dinner trolley with you here. But I take back the Tea trolley."

"Fine!"

"And you've fresh tea in the new trolley."

Laughing, she started towards the front door. Suddenly, she stopped walking and turned to look at her. "Can I ask you a simple question, my princess?"

"Yes?"

June left the trolley behind and stepped closer to her. "You sure you don't mind?"

"I'm settled with a man."

June giggled nervously. "I didn't mean it."

"Please ask."

She waited cautiously. "Have you been in this hotel before?"

"No."

"Not even for a day?"

"No."

June stared at her silently.

"Why you asked?"

"People are talking in the kitchen."

"Maybe they may have seen somebody. But definitely, I've never been here."

June stood there, unsure of herself, then moved towards the exit door.

"June?"

She stopped and turned back. "Yes, princess?"

"Can I ask you…?"

"Of course. What is it?"

"It's secret."

"Of course. Cross my heart."

"Do we have CCTV camera system everywhere here?"

She smiled trivially. "Yes. But it lasts only for 28 days. And then it expires."

"I see!"

"But you don't worry. You've never been here in the last 28 days, I am sure."

"Shut up, you fool!"

"What do you want, princess?"

"The police were here. They asked me about the man who died."

"Oh, that thing? What did you say?"

"I know nothing about it."

"That's right."

"In case he was hanging around outside my chalet?"

"It's a hotel, princess. These unfortunate incidents happen. But none of us got any control over them."

"The police asked me."

"They shouldn't do that, I suppose. But they have duty sheets to fill up. And for that, they are wasting your time."

"Oh?" She sighed with relief. "I just want to know."

June went back to the door again. "Can I go now, please?"

"Yes, please."

June giggled, then went out, pushing the trolley.

Emma had her supper quietly. In fact, she didn't eat anything at all, even the lamb roast, which used to be her favourite. She was not in the mood for food. Her mind was revolving outside her power to restrain it. She wanted to relax completely, and in order to do that, she had to do away with her past. How on earth could it be possible?

She took a book from her suitcase and settled in the chair by the window. She was a good reader and enjoyed any kind of story, whether it was great or not. However, right now, she was having no fun of it. She dropped the book down on the table and continued to sit there, gazing out. The garden was fully lit, and the sandy shore beyond. However, it was dim and dark in the distance as the fog rose like cliffs. The lamps on the posts appeared to be floating like whitish scruffy balloons in the air.

The doorbell played its music once again, and she opened the door. It was Mark Windrush! "I thought you had gone?"

"I haven't said goodnight yet," he replied as he started to cross the floor towards the window.

Emma was on his side. "You can't see the Ocean now," she said, clearly to make something to talk.

He smiled pleasantly. "I don't think it's that easy for anyone to steal the ocean."

Emma laughed deliberately to restore her composure.

He looked out the window. "Oh, it's the fog," he said, in an amazed tone. He paused thoughtfully. "But I should say I've never seen this sort of fog before. It must have come from the ocean. Anyway, I'm glad to say that the ocean is safe, Ms Wilford."

A faint smile sprouted on her face. "That's great news," she said, her eyes still staring into the direction of the beach. "Anyway, I don't need it after all the mist and fog I drove through on my way here."

Mark interrupted her gently. "Oh, I can imagine! You are exhausted. You need a proper sleep. I better go."

"I don't normally go to bed before ten."

Without replying, he started moving back towards the front door. However, he stopped in the middle of the lounge. "Alright. I won't be long."

Emma came away a couple of steps from the window. She didn't say anything, as if she wasn't sure what to say.

"Well, my life has never been great, Emma," he added rather listlessly. "It never happens what I dearly wish to." Mark stopped talking. Covering his mouth with the back of his hand, he coughed quietly for a moment, apparently trying to change the subject. "Alright, Emma," he paused, seemingly unsure of himself. "I want to ask you something?"

"Of course!"

"Have you been in this hotel before?"

Emma laughed mildly. "The room service girl, June, asked me the same thing."

"Did she?"

"She didn't mean any offence."

"I know."

"What did you say, Emma?"

"The truth. I've never been here."

He nodded his head vaguely.

Emma laughed again. "What is it?"

He joined in her laughter. "Have I seen you before?"

She was silent, thoughtfully, before she replied, "Where do you think we could've met?"

"Somewhere. Anywhere. Or wherever God had intended to."

Emma smiled. "Mark, I have never been in this hotel. As a matter of fact, I have never been in Cornwall."

Mark absently picked up a cigarette packet and a matchbox from his trouser pocket. "I knew a girl who was a spitting image of you."

She giggled happily. "Which means I have a double somewhere."

Mark threw a cigarette into his mouth and lit it. He inhaled heavily on it and blew it out through his nostrils. He inhaled again and blew out hurriedly. "I hope I'm not boring you at all. Forgive me if I am!"

Emma shook her head before she said, "Very interesting! Please continue."

He looked out into the stagnate fog which hovered over the garden. The Great Atlantic Hotel soared majestically on the left side from the rugged mist and seemed like the palace in the sky. 'Beautiful," he thought to himself, then turned to her. "I didn't have friends," he whispered as if he was reading through his own thoughts. "My work and the colleagues at the workplace. Then come home and shut the door to every form of existence."

"Why, scared off fresh air?" Emma laughed jokingly.

He noticed the humour in her question. "More than that. I was scared of life itself."

"This is not the Mark Windrush I used to capture in my imagination when we talked on the phone."

"True, but I'm talking about my lonely life before I met this girl."

Emma didn't speak. Instead, she waited for him to continue.

"I loved my mum. She was a graceful lady. And I loved my dad. He was from Jamaica in the Caribbean Island and my best friend." He lit a new cigarette from the butt of the old one. "But my mum and my dad couldn't love each other," he said, drawing a puff on the new cigarette and leaving the butt in a dustbin by the side of the dining table.

"Long story, dear. Maybe another time. But my mum died when I was nine. My dad died when I was twelve. And I grew up in a rotten care home until I was sixteen." He smoked his cigarette and blew out the smoke away. "When I came out of the care home, to be honest, I had no desire to live."

"I am sorry to hear, Mark. I am genuinely sorry."

"And then I met this girl. Suddenly, I started to dream."

Without speaking, Emma stared at him. However, she suspected she had traced tears bubbling up in his eyes.

Abruptly, he whispered, walking to the exit door, "I see you tomorrow. And Goodnight!"

Before she could pull herself together and say goodnight, he had gone. And the door shut behind him.

Absently, Emma went to the door and locked the door from inside. She stood there, leaning against the door. She wasn't sure how long she had stayed there. Slowly, she came back to the room and got into bed. Very slowly, she fell into sleep.

Traces of dried tears remained on her face.

Chapter 2

Emma Receives a Great Welcome

Part 1: Mathew's Office

Monday, the 12th of December 1988

The office was very spacious, with a large oval-shaped oak desk in the middle. Behind the desk was a high semi-circular window with numerous panes that were almost as wide as the office floor and finished stunningly in oak wood. The window overlooked into the beach gardens and the wavy ocean beyond. A single chair remained at the back of the desk for Mathew Atkinson, while four chairs were at the front – all chairs were made of oak and finished inside with black leather. The floor and walls were covered in wood panels. There were some wooden carvings in alcoves on the side walls. Mathew was in his chair and flipping through a file. Apparently, he was busy searching for something. It was a few minutes before two o'clock, and Mark came into the office, with Emma by his side.

"Please sit down," he said, obviously happy, while his eyes rolled over to Emma, and then they stuck on her.

Emma came round a chair and sat on it.

Mark didn't sit down. Instead, he moved closer to the desk and stood virtually facing both of them. "I'm an escort of this lady, Emma Wilford. She was dying to meet you."

"So was I," he whispered breathlessly. Clearly, he was frozen in thoughts and memories. *'Who is she?'*

Mark realized his boss's predicament quickly. "I suppose you had a bad flight?" He said, obviously assisting him with something to talk about and a few minutes to return to the real world. "You are shattered, Mr Atkinson."

Mathew knew exactly what was the intention of Mark's question. "More chaos than certainty," he replied gratefully, still looking at her face. "I meant to fly by Air Montingo. Just one stopover and one transit. That was fine. However, this flight was cancelled due to the military coup and the anticipated violence. Who wants to fly the aircraft to a volatile country? In the end, Air Africa came, and to my surprise, it came three hours early."

"How did it happen, Mr Atkinson?" Emma asked easily. "Normally, planes arrive late."

He tried to raise a smile, and he succeeded to his own amazement. "It was the previous day's flight."

Mark laughed. "It should be a joke."

"No, it's the truth," he replied. "They've a saying in that part of the world. *Cela Afrique.*"

"What does it mean?" Mark asked.

He caught his staff's stare briefly, then turned to her, "Do you speak French, Emma?"

Emma smiled shyly. "Not a word, Mr Atkinson."

He shot a knowing glance at Mark before he explained, "Which means, this is Africa. And in this context, it means anything can happen in Africa."

She laughed amusingly. "How was the flight? Any Cele Afrique in the flight?"

"Thank God, nothing, Emma. Just the normal two stopovers and a transit flight from Paris to New Quay." He paused and looked at Mark before he continued. "In a way, it was a blessing. I didn't have to go to London. And then pick up a flight to New Quay."

"Good. I've to go," Mark said cheerfully. "You two are getting on well. And I've one or two things to attend urgently."

"What time you're coming back? We've this young lady here to take care of."

Without speaking, she laughed rather shyly.

"True. Very true. I've to see Tanya Roberts. She will be assisting Emma with her course."

"Alright, busy man. We see you later."

"Okay," he answered, meeting Emma's gaze, and then left the office.

Emma turned to Mathew. "I was hoping to see you yesterday."

"And I wanted to see you too. But Atlantica is not a politically stable country. And I couldn't leave on time."

"I know. Mark told me."

"It used to be a peaceful country, with courteous and hardworking loving people. And still they are. However, after independence, the tyrants regularly took over power. Now, nobody knows where the country is heading. And a lot of countries in Africa are in the same situation."

An anxious silence engulfed them as though they had other thoughts on their minds. A moment later, she said, meeting his eyes across the desk and smiling, "I like your office."

He smiled back. "Thank you."

Emma sat there with her mouth partially open, but no voice came out. "I'm nobody to judge, but I think you have achieved a wonderful quality in wood carving," she added finally.

He didn't answer immediately. Instead, he watched her eyes wander around. "In fact, I only maintained it, Emma."

She looked at him. "What do you mean?"

Mathew paused thoughtfully, "It's my great-grandfather who built this. And, quite proudly, I should add, that his descendants succeeded in keeping its beauty intact."

The office girl brought in two cups of tea and put one cup on the desk for Emma and the other in front of Mathew. They both thanked the girl, and she left.

Emma stared around the office, drinking her tea. "Wonderful craftsmanship on each panel."

"As a matter of fact, it's designed by the Atlantican tribes' men, known as Atlantis." He took another sip hurriedly. "They carved all these panels and shipped them over here. And then a few of them came over and fitted them together."

"Wow, it's amazing," Emma exclaimed. "Really Amazing." She picked up her cup and took a sip. "Where are these Atlantis tribes in Africa?"

"They are in Atlantica – one of the provinces of Nyanbique."

"I think I've heard of Nyanbique."

"Yes, you must have, I'm sure. They are always on the news. Because something happens every day that draws the attention of the world."

47

Emma took another sip before she put the cup back on the desk. "Any particular reasons?"

"All sorts of reasons, I am afraid."

She waited silently.

Mathew explained that Atlantica province was a large region that spread along the Atlantic coast and was overwhelmingly inhabited by the local tribe known as the Atlantis. The provincial capital, also known as the Atlantica City, is the biggest city in the country. The State Assembly House there is always run by the Atlantis Peoples Party, a political wing of the Atlantis tribes, also known as APP in brief. To make matters better or worse, the Atlantic City is also the national capital of Nyanbique country, where the National Parliament House stands proudly on the shore of the Atlantic Ocean, half a mile away from the State Assembly Hall.

Besides these settings, the national airport, harbour, medical college, and university college were clustered here. So were the overseas embassies, banks, commercial and industrial investment bodies, and the like. And here, Atlantis, also known as Atlans, picked up the best job opportunities while other tribes were pushed around for menial labours.

Against this political setup and daily existence, each and every tribe looked over the shoulders and checked who was following, obviously angrily. Trusting was a difficult practice to follow. Survival was the name of the game. Some would adopt violence, which was the only acceptable salvation for them. Some were forced to accept violence to protect what they had. So, violence broke out anytime and anywhere. In violence, like anywhere else, some fell dead, some disabled, some destroyed. Unfortunately, this was the day-to-day life in the capital city and the country.

However, their elected representatives to the parliament had one policy in common, and that was to stand together against the APP and command a majority under some coalition or alliance and assume power. It was one city with two governments, each one of them had its own agenda, manifesto, and policies. However, none of them had been discussed, negotiated, or agreed with the other government or parties, and hence, the outcomes were stagnation, starvation, and bloodshed.

"Oh, Mathew!" Emma cried, completely surprised, staring at him with admiring eyes, "You know so much about Nyanbique."

Without speaking, he caught her eyes. "I was born there," he said finally. "I was a Nyanbique citizen until I was 23."

She waited. "Why did you change it?"

He hesitated. "In that year, it wasn't the usual riots." He paused vaguely. "It was a revolution called, *'Quit Nyanbique.'*"

"Meaning?"

"Go back to your country of origin."

Silently, Emma moved in her chair and leaned against the back. "Really frightening."

"It was more than frightening. They burned our ancestral home in the night. My great-granddad built this property. My granddad and grandma used to live there whenever they came for holidays or business meetings."

She stared at him without saying a word.

He was quiet for a moment. "My dad was born in this house. And in fact, I was also born in it."

"Very sad. I am sure it meant the world to you."

"And the worst to come, Emma." Mathew stopped talking and puffed deeply on his cigar. Slowly, he blew out the smoke towards the window. He turned back to her. "When they burned this house, my grandma was there. They burned my grandma, too."

Without a word, she stared at him, her eyes full of horror.

A silence sprang up for a brief period.

He finished his tea and put the cup back on the desk. Emma also drank her tea.

After a few minutes, he said, clearly breaking the silence and changing the subject. "Emma, I wanted to talk about you when we met."

She grinned lightly. "About me?"

"Yes, love. And I've a reason for it."

"Allowing me for my course work?"

"That's nothing, Emma. As a matter of fact, I don't get involved with recruitment matters."

"Then what, Mathew?"

He hesitated. "I lost somebody who was very special to me. In fact, she was more special to me than my own life."

Emma listened to him carefully.

"When the recruitment staff opened your application, they saw your photo."

"It wasn't a good photo of mine, Mathew. Sorry, that was the only one I had at the time."

"The photo is fine, but the staff thought this is the picture of the girl I lost."

Emma stared at him with her mouth partially open. She was more confused than the look on his face. "I'm so sorry. I don't know what it means. If you don't mind, can I ask you who she was?"

Mathew looked out to the back garden and then to the sea beyond. His face registered mixed expressions of sadness and misfortunes and downfalls. Slowly, he turned back his face and met her staring eyes. "Please don't, Emma," he replied. He had wanted to say why he refused to talk on the subject, but suddenly, he became speechless, as if words were getting tangled inside him.

Emma waited silently for a moment before she said, "Oh, I am sorry."

Mathew hesitated again. "I don't talk about these painful memories. In fact, nobody talks about it. It hurts badly."

"My apologies, Mathew. Silly of me to ask. I promise it will never happen again."

"Thank you."

Awkwardly, Emma sat silently.

As if to bring her to a pleasant mood, he asked amiably, "How are your parents?"

Emma grinned faintly. "I hope they are alright?"

He waited, silently watching her face. "You get along well with your parents?"

"Dear Mathew, I don't know who they are."

51

He didn't speak. Instead, he waited for her to continue.

"My memories could go back to the days when I was four or five. I had never met anybody who had told me, 'You are our daughter. Or we are your parents."

Mathew didn't speak.

"I got Wilford as my surname. I don't know if it was my biological father's name. Or someone else chose it for me."

Mathew remained silent before he said, "I am sorry. I put you through lots of memories."

Emma didn't answer immediately. "That's okay. I've outlived all these sad thoughts. They don't worry me anymore."

The interconnecting door on the flank opened, and his secretary entered. He turned to look at her. "This is Kathrine Williams," he said, clearly proudly. "And Kathrine is my secretary. However, she is much more than that. She carries a huge weight of my responsibilities, especially when I am not here." He waited hesitantly but spoke quickly, "This young lady is Emma Wilford."

Kathrine moved further and took a seat by the side of Emma. She looked at her with an expression of welcome and warmness. "Emma, you look exactly as pretty as your picture," she said, tapping her shoulder.

Emma chuckled pleasantly, "Next time, I'll send a good photo. And thanks for telling me."

They laughed. In the end, Kathrine said, "Mark told you had a terrible time in the bad weather when you were coming."

The girl looked at them intermittently, rather amazed, "It sounds like I am a celebrity here. Everybody is talking about me."

She patted on Emma's shoulder. "You are. You're Mathew's guest."

She looked at him. "Thank you. I don't think I can appreciate your kindness enough."

He smiled quietly.

"I was off for this morning. In fact, I just got into my office." She stopped talking and shot a glance at Mathew, then looked back at Emma. And the first is first, and you are the first."

Emma laughed, "You're embarrassing me."

"Not at all," the secretary said, joining in her laugh.

Part 2: Meeting Tanya

The office door opened this time, and Mark and Tanya walked in. They walked further to the desk. Tanya sat down on the other side of Emma while Mark stood behind the girls. Mathew gestured to a corner of the office floor where a few chairs had been clustered around a low-level desk, saying, "Pull a chair and sit down, Mark."

"I'm fine here, boss. Anyway, I must be going soon."

"Take a seat, Mark," Mathew repeated. "You can go soon."

Mark moved a chair nearer to Emma and sat on it. "Thank you, boss."

All the while, Tanya's eyes were on Emma without even a blink. "I am very pleased to meet you, Emma," she said somewhat uncomfortably. "We were supposed to meet at 11 o'clock but was held up in Isabella Roscoe's office." She held Emma's hand as a way of saying sorry. Or maybe she was feeling her body as if Emma was real. "You're very beautiful," she said quite shyly.

Emma felt awkward and smiled shyly. In the end, she replied, "We've plenty of time for the coursework."

Tanya was still holding her hand in a caring way. "Alright, Emma. You should pick up a job here after your course."

Everyone laughed softly. However, Mark whispered jokingly, "It's all Mathew's fault. He came late. And Emma was waiting for you."

"I accept the blame," Mathew murmured with a mock guilt.

"Don't blame my boss," Kathrine retorted softly. "He's got a genuine excuse. His plane let him down."

"Blame is mine," Emma insisted. "You know, my middle name is blame."

They laughed. While laughing, Mathew and his secretary shot a discreet glance at each other before she said, "I'm taking our guest to my office for a few minutes. And then Tanya, you can take her."

"Okay, Kathrine."

Kathrine rose to her feet and so did Emma. They went through the interconnecting door, and the door shut automatically behind.

Mathew stared at Mark and Tanya alternatively. "What do you think?" He whispered softly as possible.

Without answering, they caught his eyes. Obviously, they couldn't answer.

Impatiently, Mathew repeated the question

This time, Mark and Tanya stared at each other, then turned to their boss. Mark spoke first, quite nervously. "I don't know," he said uneasily. "It's absolutely impossible!"

Mathew met his eyes for a moment. "What do you mean, Mark?"

"I don't know," he said nervously. "It could be her. Or it couldn't be her."

"Good lord! What an answer, Mark? You knew her before anyone on earth."

"I know, Mathew. But it's a difficult question."

"Alright, what do you think, Tanya? She was your closest friend."

Tanya hesitated fearfully. "Yes, she was my best friend. But this girl, I can't say anything." She stopped talking and took a heavy sigh. "One moment, yes, she is. And the next moment, I am losing my confidence."

"Tanya is absolutely right," Mark cut in thoughtfully. "Probably, we need more time."

Without speaking, Mathew stared at them intermittently.

"Emma talks exactly in the same way," Mark said, looking rather helpless. "Same words and same phrases!"

"She moves in the same way," Tanya whispered. "But I don't know!"

"Know what, Tanya?"

"I don't know who Emma is?"

He looked at her and then at Mark. "She's fake?"

They both looked at him silently. In the end, Mark answered sadly, "We're having the same difficulties you're facing, Mathew." He paused briefly, staring at Mathew. "Hard to say, no. Or, yes!"

55

"Well, we've to wait, I think. But what do you think, Mathew?"

"I'm petrified to say yes or no."

Without speaking, Mark and Tanya stared at each other. Just then, the interconnecting door opened, and Emma came to the view in front of Kathrine. "Beautiful office," she said cheerfully, meeting the others' stare gently. "I wish I would have an office like that one day."

Mathew, covering his mouth, coughed to clear his voice before he asked in a mock cheerful voice, "I'm sure you've a thing or two to tell Kathrine about her office?"

Everybody laughed briefly, then Emma replied, coming close to the desk, "Cleverly organized. I've lots to learn from Kathrine."

They discreetly looked at each other.

"What's your agenda for this afternoon, Emma?" Tanya enquired. "I want to introduce you to a couple of people. One of them can give you the induction courses." She stopped talking briefly. "Poor Berney Smith would have done a better job."

"Berney's body is still in our mortuary?" Mathew enquired. "Or taken to any funeral home?"

"It's gone," Tanya answered.

"It's sad the way he's gone. But we hope he's in a safe place now."

"I don't know the man very much," Tanya added. "But he never talked to me about anything other than his duties here."

"I worked with him," Mark mentioned. "But he hardly spoke about his private life."

56

"Very private man, I would say," Tanya added.

Emma looked at them eagerly as they spoke. But she never made any remarks.

"Anybody else knows him?" Mathew wondered helplessly.

"I doubt it," Tanya spoke softly. "He never kept any friendship with anybody."

Kathrine tactfully moved over to Mathew. She shot a glance at Emma before she whispered subtly, "Hard to say anything."

Mathew threw a cigarette into his mouth, cleverly in an attempt to hide his mouth moving. He lit it and drew a puff on it. "What do you say?" He asked softly, blowing out the smoke to his side.

"We saw our girl three years ago," she murmured. "That's quite a long time in the growing of a girl."

"She has no memories of us."

"No. Maybe the accident caused it."

He smoked again.

"Take her home tonight. See whether it makes any difference."

He lightly nodded his head while he swung back in his chair to face the others. "This evening, you are coming to my house, Emma. And you're staying with me until you go back."

Everybody cheered except Emma, who said, certainly happily, "That's very kind of you, Mathew. But not tonight."

"Why not?" They shouted jointly.

Emma laughed rather embarrassed, "I loved Gemma House. I slept like a child last night."

"One more night, alright, I think," Tanya giggled. "And I'll visit you."

"Come, come. You're more than welcome."

"And Tanya, you can come, by all means, to Abigale House when Emma is there."

"Definitely, I will come."

"Tanya, you know, one time you used to stay there."

Without saying anything, she looked at him.

"And going back to your induction, Emma," Mark intervened quietly. "Can you start this afternoon? Well, this is already afternoon. I mean, as soon as possible?"

"Of course! Can I start right now?"

"Yes. I put Brian Jenkins to cover some of Berney's duties," Tanya said. "We can go and see him. Probably, he will have a talk with you about the hospitality industry."

Emma smiled happily. "Oh! I am looking forward to it."

Shortly, the meeting was closed, and Tanya took Emma to Brian Jenkins' office. "Hello, hello," Brain welcomed her warmly. "I thought you're not coming."

She laughed, somewhat embarrassed. "Anyway, we're here."

He stared at her vaguely. "Mr Atkinson mentioned you to me. Berney also talked about you." He paused for a moment and smiled broadly, "I gather you are a very intelligent young lady."

Emma smiled, meeting his eyes. "Mr Atkinson gave you that impression, I suppose?"

He nodded for an answer.

"It's Mr Atkinson, isn't it?" She whispered rather courteously. "He doesn't talk badly about others. And I am sure you know him more than I do."

Without speaking, he watched her as if he was focusing on something beyond her and the present time. After a brief while, he spoke quickly, clearly woken up. "I wish people would talk about me in that manner."

"I hope so."

"Have you been trying to join us for a while?"

Her smile faded out slowly. "How did you know, Mr Jenkins?"

"I am not sure. Maybe, Berney might have said."

The smile faded completely from her face. "Sorry, Mr Jenkins. Many things happened."

"In the hotel calendar, this is the busiest time. On top of that, as you know, Jacob's wedding is in days."

"I'm really sorry."

He was quiet for a moment. "You are writing up a project for the degree course."

"Absolutely!"

"Why didn't you try in one of the hotels in London?"

"I've spent some time in Hilton. And Savoy. And Ritz. But I also want to know how they run outside the capital. And I chose the South West, oddly enough."

"And Mr Atkinson replied?"

"Yes. And he responded very positively." Emma waited while trying to remember. "In fact, I didn't know him in the beginning. The majority didn't bother with a response. They were frightened to let somebody go over their trade secret."

"I wouldn't blame them."

Emma smiled confidently this time. "Mr Atkinson was absolutely helpful. I couldn't thank him enough."

He was silent before he asked, "Can I offer you something hot? Coffee, tea? Strong stuffs are forbidden during duty hours. Work ethics!"

"Please don't bother, Mr Jenkins. I'm quite alright."

He moved back in his chair and looked at her across the table. "What exactly do you want to know?"

Emma caught his eyes. "Perhaps, about your way of ordering your stocks and the method of storing. How do you keep the stock fresh? And how do you take the stock list accurately?"

Mr Jenkins laughed loudly. "That's lots of questions in one breath."

She joined him in laughing but didn't add anything further.

He pulled out a cigarette packet from the drawer and, opening it, asked, "You smoke?"

Emma shook her head gently.

He stuck a cigarette between his lips and lit it with a lighter. He drew a puff. "Keep off it if you can," he said quietly, blowing away the smoke on his side. "Bad habit, I can swear. But I am committed to it. And I've to suffer with it."

She grinned faintly, then said, "Perhaps you can tell me later if you don't want to answer now."

"Later is good. I need some time to think about it."

Emma waited for a moment. "My subject is called '*Hotel Management.*'"

"Brilliant subject! You will be delighted that you chose it. This industry has lots of potential. It's growing beyond imagination and recognition."

Emma looked at him, obviously pleased. "With a title like Operation Manager, what are your responsibilities, if I may ask?"

Mr Jenkins leaned back in his chair and looked at her across the table, puffing heavily on his cigarette. "Regardless of my job title," he replied, blowing out the smoke upwards, "I'm more like a troubleshooter."

She didn't speak. Instead, she waited for him to continue.

"Three years ago, when I was recruited," he continued slowly, "I was in the restaurant and was a chef. Six months later, the manager left due to ill health, and I was promoted. I loved the job. And, fairly quickly, I brought in lots of changes."

"Changes? What kind of changes?"

Mr Jenkins puffed heavily. "On various matters. But I'm not supposed to disclose them."

She waited. "Staff members and management agreed to these changes?"

"Not always and not in everything," he retorted, smiling and blowing the smoke through his nostrils. "But the staff getting the extra wages and the management getting the extra income, they started to love me."

"Good. I hope you will tell me about those changes one day."

"I will."

"How are you valued with your tasks?"

He smiled broadly. "Not greatly, I can assure you. I don't think either the staff or the management appreciate it. And all my friends become my worst enemies."

"I hope they are paying you well."

Mr Jenkins laughed loudly. "The management will always say they pay their workers more than they deserve. The workers will say that management abuses the staff. There are no happy parallels between the two."

Emma giggled. "Thank you. That's something new to me."

"And the management happily tolerated me."

"What makes you say that?"

"When a senior manager's position came up in the hotel about a year and a half ago, they readily offered it to me. Why? Because they knew I was worth their money and trust."

"Great. Definitely great! I don't normally see an employee who talks unselfishly and greatly about the employer."

"True. Because Great Atlantic Hotel is exclusively different," he laughed loudly, blowing the smoke. "That's why it outlived two hundred years easily and proudly."

Emma sat quietly with an amazing sparkle in her eyes. "I am proud to be here."

"Hang around, Emma. One doesn't know one's future! Maybe you have a wonderful life in this hotel."

"Thank you. And I'll be grateful for your advice."

"You are welcome."

"You took your studies in the hotel business, I believe?"

Mr Jenkins laughed jokingly. "My education? There is nothing I can boast about. I didn't even finish my primary schooling."

"Why?"

He lit another cigarette and puffed heavily on it. "It was the year nineteen forty-three, the worst time of the Second World War for Great Britain. British soldiers were getting massacred in Europe and the Far East."

"An atrocious time," Emma said quickly. "I learned about it."

"I was nine at the time and living in the Aldgate area of London. You know the area?"

"Not much. I'm from Harrow."

He took a couple of puffs. "Very dangerous area at that time. Lots of villains and thugs everywhere. Their siblings aren't any better, either. Many bullies in the classrooms, causing nothing but trouble."

She didn't speak. Instead, she waited for him to continue.

"One day, some bullies turned on me. Big fight, but I stood for my ground."

"Didn't the teachers do anything?"

"They were frightened to death. These bullies come from very violent families. In the end, the teachers dismissed me from the school."

"Why?"

"These thugs were known as Cockney Brothers. And they could smash up the teachers. Or anyone they didn't like."

"I see."

"And they could smash up my parents as well."

"Terrible."

He shook his head silently for an answer. "We got into our food van in the night and fled the area."

She stared at him, almost in disbelief. "Are they that nasty?"

He smoked on his cigarette. "My dad always feared that they would come after me."

Emma waited silently.

A minute elapsed before Mr Jenkins continued, "In a way, that helped my future."

She looked at him quizzically.

He met her eyes. "My mum and dad rented a small house in one of the back streets of Willesden and continued their mobile catering. And I've no school to go to. So, I helped my parents in the catering."

"And that's where you started your career in the food industry?"

"Absolutely," he replied proudly. "And ever since, I served this industry day and night."

Silently, Emma stared at him respectfully. He didn't speak either. A silence crept in for a while. In the end, she broke the silence. "I am very honoured to have this conversation with you."

"My pleasure," Mr Jenkins said curtly.

"Now I know you. I know you have great knowledge in the catering, hospitality, and holidaymaking industry. And I admire it."

"Thank you."

"Now I know what I should ask you in our next meeting. I will……"

He interrupted. "It will be after the wedding. Until then, I need to utilize every second for the wedding preparation."

"That's fine, Mr Jenkins."

He drew the last puff on his cigarette and blew out the smoke. He ground the butt in an ashtray and put it in the bin under his desk. "You are lucky, Emma. We don't normally entertain students, or reporters, or any other outsiders. We are too busy for it."

"I am sorry."

"You've to be very grateful to Mr Atkinson. He asked us to help you."

"I know."

"He is very kind to you."

"I'm very grateful."

Mr Jenkins obviously hesitated. "Do you know why he's very kind to you?"

"No idea, to be honest."

He hesitated. "He had a girl. She was a spitting image of you, Emma."

"Who was she?"

"I can't talk about it."

"What was her name?"

"I don't talk about it, as a respect to the Atkinson family. Nobody talks about."

"I am sorry."

"Can I ask you something very important?"

"Of course, Mr Jenkins."

"Remember, it's very secretive?"

"I promise I won't tell a single soul."

"Are you Emma Wilford or someone else?"

She giggled amusingly. "I am Emma Wilford."

"Do you have a sister in your complexion?"

She giggled again more amusingly. "No, I wasn't lucky to have a sister or brother."

Wordlessly, he looked at her.

"I would have been absolutely thrilled if I had a man like Mr Mathew Atkinson as my father."

"I am sorry. Please don't say to anybody that I talked about it."

"No. I won't. I promise."

Part 3: Understanding Business

This time, his intercom rang, and he picked up. "Hello?"

"Hi Brian," Tanya's voice came through the wire. "How's your meeting progressing?"

"Alright. We had a lovely chat. And it should also be added that Emma is a very intelligent lady."

"I thought so, too. Anyway, what's your next plan?"

"I wanted to take Emma into the store room. But I won't be able to do that right now."

"Alright. Can I bring her into my office?"

"No problem."

Tanya turned up shortly and took Emma to her office.

"Very nice," Emma said happily. "It's a nice place."

"Nice. But a bit small."

Emma took a seat at her desk. "To me, it looks big."

"I see lots of agency staff. But I manage with the space I have."

"Why the agency staff?"

"You probably know the hospitality industry depends on the locations and seasons."

Emma didn't speak.

"In London, people are everywhere. Because it's the capital city, and efficiently managed businesses flourish all year round. But Cornwall is a county in the far corner of the South West. We've the average trade; it's okay, but not very busy. And then, we've the busy periods, like the Christmas seasons, Easter breaks, and the long summer holidays. And we've enough staff to meet our requirements. During busy periods, we recruit casual laborers through the agencies. Major portions of my duties, along with other staff, are interviews and recruitments, which means, I conduct group interviews frequently." She paused, slightly alarmed, "Oh, Emma! What do you like to drink? Sorry, I didn't ask you."

"Thanks, dear. I'm okay."

"No. You must have something, dear."

"Shall I get a tea? I heard you drink a lot of tea."

"Maybe later, Tanya."

"We don't have much time now, Emma. I've to see Isabella in 20 minutes. Isabella is off tomorrow."

Emma looked at her face intently.

"Alright, I choose tea for you."

"Alright, Tanya. That's fine."

Picking up the intercom phone, she dialled three digits. Shortly, a female voice arrived through the line. "Yes, Tanya?"

"Two teas."

"Milk and two Sugars?"

"Okay."

She hung the receiver on the phone.

"You've a good position in the company?" Emma said, looking very pleased.

Tanya met her stare steadily. "Yes, you could say," she said quite proudly. "But I've to carry lots of responsibilities with it."

Emma grinned lightly. "I hope you don't mind me asking."

"Please do."

"You are such a young lady, Twenty-one, twenty-two?"

"I am twenty-one, in fact,"

"How did you come to the top in such a short time."

"Sheer hard work," Tanya answered quickly. "And honesty and loyalty to the authorities."

Emma sat staring at her, an admiration in her eyes.

"If you allow me, can I give you a word of advice, please?"

"Oh, thank you. I will cherish that."

She waited for a moment, meeting her eyes constantly. "Atlantic Hotel Holdings (PLC) is the parent company with three subsidiary establishments."

Emma continued to stay very attentively.

"You don't need to know many details about them, but I want you to know this."

"What is that, Tanya," Emma asked quickly and nervously.

"Two families control most of the shares, and they are Atkinsons and Roscoes."

Emma remained silent, but her eyes steadily on Tanya's face.

"They cooperate in running the business wherever they have to. But outside the business, they are bitter enemies."

"Why are you telling me, Tanya?" She asked finally. "I'm here today. And gone in four to five days' time."

"I know."

"And my graduate course only involves the catering and caring side. Not about the shareholders and dividends!"

Tanya laughed tactfully. "The wedding belongs to the Roscoe family. And they're allowing you to go through the preparations and allowing you to witness the solemn ceremony."

"And I am absolutely grateful to them, Tanya."

She waited as if unsure of herself. "The chances are that you'll talk to Isabella or Helena or Jacob or Adam, or anybody from these circles."

Emma didn't speak.

"And when you talk with them – hopefully you'll get the opportunity, you shouldn't talk anything unless you are answering their questions. And you answer them as simply as possible."

"Thank you, Tanya. I will remember that."

"And another thing."

"Yeah?"

"You never mention anything about Mr Atkinson or his cars or home. Nothing at all."

"Thank you. I've a habit of talking too much."

A woman staff brought the tea in a tray.

Tanya collected them and thanked the staff who then left.

Emma picked up her cup and had a quick sip. She held it in her mouth for a second, tasting, before she swallowed. "Very nice tea."

"Thank you. And………"

She was disturbed as the intercom rang. She took the receiver and held it closer to her mouth. "Hello?" she whispered into the mouthpiece.

"Isabella here," the words arrived clearly.

Her eyes shot a glance across the desk at Emma before she said very politely, "Hello, Isabella. I can come now if you want to see me early?"

"No. Come at your time. But have you seen the girl?"

Her eyes shot another glance at Emma. "I will be with you soon."

"Alright. I got the message. She is with you." And the line went dead in her hand. Slowly, she put the receiver back on the hook.

"Am I bothering you?"

Tanya raised a laugh. "No, Emma. But I am a bit busy now. I'll meet you in the morning."

"That's okay."

"And I take you to Mark's office now?"

"That's fine. And I know where his office is."

"Where will I meet you in the morning, Emma?"

"I will be in Mark's office."

Emma immediately left.

Mark was on the phone when she reached his doorway. He acknowledged her presence with a nod of the head, and then he gestured her to a seat at his desk. However, she hung around in the corridor.

"I will get back to you tomorrow," he said, looking at her gladly. "I need to attend to something urgent. I'm very sorry." And before the other person could speak a word, he cut off the line and put the receiver back on the phone.

Emma smiled, slightly embarrassed. "Am I that urgent?" She asked, stepping into the office.

"Definitely," he chuckled. "And I was wondering what had happened to you?"

"Well, I am here."

"I know. Please sit down."

She sat down,

"It's supper time now. Let me order a nice meal for you."

She smiled lazily. "Not now, Mark. My room attendant, June Murphey, is very good. She knows exactly what I need and how I like it."

"June Murphy knew all that in less than a day?"

She chuckled. "Very smart girl!"

"Very glad to hear that."

"And I like to eat alone in my own privacy."

He waited, then grinned cleverly, "Two people too many for your privacy?"

"Not necessarily!"

"That sounds great. Which means I can join your meal tonight?"

She giggled happily. "When I said, 'not necessarily,' I meant my boyfriend."

Mark made a mock expression of bitter sadness, "I was soaring with my dream a moment ago. Now, you pulled me right down into the fire."

"At least I gave you the fire, which is better than nothing at all."

He laughed heartily. "You are a killer queen!"

"Sorry, I can't help."

Mark stopped laughing quickly and stared at her, a fear twinkling in his eyes. Moving forward in his chair, he dropped his head into his hands and the elbows on the desk, then didn't move a single tiny muscle in his whole body.

"You dead?" Emma laughed heartily now.

"Dead!" he exclaimed, springing back to himself. "I'm alive now. For the first time in three years, I feel like I am flying."

"Good lord, I must be a magician."

"You are indeed! Baby, you're indeed." He stopped to inhale a heavy breath of air. "What's your boyfriend's name?"

Emma took her eyes away from his face. She looked out the window at the greenery outside and a narrow view of the Atlantic Ocean beyond. The water surface was rough as the waves rolled over one by one towards the shore. She turned her face and caught his eyes. "I don't know."

"Why?"

"I don't call his name."

He waited. "Why don't?"

"We don't meet."

Without speaking, he stared at her.

"He can't see me."

He remained silent.

"Blind."

"Blind of love."

"You are reflecting the truth. Thank you."

"Which means he has no sight of direction."

"Yes, for the time being."

"How long you can go on, Emma?"

"As long as he needs it!"

He waited as if bewildered. He picked up a cigarette packet from the drawer and extended it to her. She refused. "I don't smoke. Anyway, thanks."

He lit a cigarette with his gas lighter and puffed deeply. He blew out the smoke through his nostrils. "This waiting is a sacrifice of love."

Emma retorted proudly. "Not at all. It's the grace of love."

Mark wanted to say something, and he even opened his mouth, but no voices came out.

She said quietly, "Mark, I need to write up my journal. I'm going to my room."

He managed to find his voice. "No supper with me?"

"Another time, Mark. I see you tomorrow."

He stared at her intently for a moment. "Okay. See you tomorrow."

Part 4: June Brings Food

Emma lay on the bed. Nothing moved since then except the tears sprouted out through the slits of her tightly closed eyes. Again, the moments ticked away silently until the beating music of the doorbell drifted through the air. 'Go away," she whispered in her mind. Suddenly, she wondered who the caller could be.

A couple of minutes passed by, and the music played again. This time, Emma opened her eyes and sat up. She grabbed a towel from the dresser and cleaned the moisture from her face. She could see herself in the mirror behind the dresser. Her face looked alright. She came to the door. "Who is it?"

The reply arrived quickly. "It's June, dear. June Murphy."

She opened the door. "Hi, June."

"Hello, Emma. I was worrying about you?"

"Oh! Thank you."

"What do you prefer for supper, Emma?"

She giggled. "Supper?"

"Yes, dear. Did you eat?"

"No. You didn't give me anything?"

June laughed. "My god, what would you like this evening?"

"I like anything you like for me."

She was thoughtfully silent for a moment. "Well, leave it with me, dear. And you wait for minutes. I will give you a surprise indeed."

"A tea will be nice before your surprise."

"Okay. I'll be back in five minutes with your tea."

"Alright. I'm waiting right here. You can trust me on that."

June laughed loudly before she went away. And before the waves of laughter settled, she came back rushing and carrying a tray with teapot, sugar, and fresh milk.

"June, this is not room service."

She was about to laugh. "No?"

"This is magic."

Now, she burst into laughing. "Wait, Emma. You will have the absolute magic when I bring your supper."

"Why, nothing in it?"

"You'll see it."

"How can I see if nothing is in it?"

June went back, suppressing the surging laughter.

Emma drank the tea quietly. And a few minutes later, the supper arrived with delicious dishes. She didn't eat much of them. Her mind revolved around the past – the defeats faced by friends and the desire for revenge with equal force!

June returned at about 8 o'clock, cleaning the dining table and clearing the crockeries into a trolley. "Did you like the food I chose for you?"

"If I tell the truth, will you hate me?"

With a puzzled expression on her face, June stared at her face. "I hope you liked it?"

She held her shoulders and gave her a gentle shake. "I loved it, you stupid."

June sighed a long breath. "I chose the best for you."

"To be honest, that was the best food I ever had."

June laughed happily. Emma joined in her laugh. Suddenly, they hugged each other. "You're my greatest friend," June whispered in her ear.

"Because you're a liar!"

June turned to the trolley, giggling. "You want another cup of tea?"

Emma looked at the table with searching eyes. There were jars of different fresh juices and three bottles of wine in addition to fresh water bottles. She grinned in amazement. "No, dear. I got enough to open up a quality stall."

June pushed her trolley towards the door, her eyes still on Emma's face. "I'm on duty until eleven."

"I have made a note of that."

"You ring the alarm any time. Somebody is always there."

"Okay, teacher. I make a note of that as well."

She stood behind the trolley for a moment as if unsure of herself. "Well," she said rather sadly, "good night then."

"Good night. And thank you for everything."

She nodded for an answer, still smiling, then went to the door. Emma followed her. Slowly, she went out, then disappeared through the dim light in the corridor.

Emma stood on the door, leaning against the door frame and staring into the narrow way the girl disappeared.

Slowly, Emma returned to her room. She had a thing or two in her mind to do, and yet she was sure about how to do stuff. She stood idly by the side of the bed, thinking and planning. In the end, she poured a glass of wine and drank it rather hurriedly. She went to the bathroom and had a shower.

That was not in her plan but a way of passing the time. She slipped into a denim trousers and a polo neck jumper, then a suede jacket over it. She grabbed a pair of light boots and pulled up over her feet. She checked her wristwatch. It was 5 minutes to 9. She left her flat and discreetly passed through the corridors. At 9, she was outside Tanya's room. She gently knocked on the door and waited for the response.

No response arrived.

She knocked again.

No response!

She knocked again, and this time, she did it hard.

A couple of minutes later, a carefully guarded voice was heard from inside. "Who is this?"

"Tanya, this is Emma."

"Emma?"

"Yes, Tanya."

"I can see you through the peephole. You don't look like Emma."

Emma laughed. "Your view is distorted, I suppose. You need to clean your glass panel."

The door opened partially with the security chain on. "Hi?" She greeted Emma with a surprised expression. "What's it, Emma? I'm a bit busy now."

"I'm sorry, dear."

She removed the chain and opened the door fully. Emma came in and then shut the door behind.

"I am about to go and meet Jacob." She paused still with a surprised expression. "We're meeting some entertainers for Helena's reception."

"Wedding reception?"

"Yes. We've two receptions. One on this Friday, the 16th. All friends and staff and neighbours are invited for this. And it will be held at the Lands End Hotel. The entertainers for this are going to meet me now."

Emma listened quietly.

"And the main reception is on Saturday the 17th, after the wedding?"

"Where is it going to be, Tanya?"

"In our hall. Only the relatives and business associates are invited for this occasion."

"Wow, that will be great."

Tanya paused for a moment. "How did you get my room number?"

"You gave me. Why?"

"No. I don't give my room number to anybody."

She shrugged lightly. "I can't remember it now."

"Somebody always troubles me for something. I don't get a single free moment."

"Sorry!"

"It's okay. You are special. I can afford a few minutes with you."

They both laughed.

"It's a nice place you have got here."

"I won't be here long."

"What do you mean?"

She smiled with a sparkle in her eyes. "I will be moving in with Jacob after this wedding."

"Good Lord! That's great."

They walked further into the room and then sat down at a small desk.

Tanya turned to look at her. "Well, what do you want to talk about?"

"A small chat and laugh were my intentions. But I can see you're very busy."

"December is our busiest period. Plus, the weddings and two nights' parties."

"Time for fun, girl. Enjoy it."

"And Jacob is refurbishing a house for us to move in."

"Wonderful. I'm pleased to hear about it."

She smiled. "Just for your information only. Don't say a word to anybody."

She giggled. "Do I look like that sort?"

"Jacob and I are getting married soon."

Emma literally screamed with excitement. "When? I'll have to come back for the occasion."

"We are planning for the spring."

"Oh God! I was planning to travel to Australia. Now, I've to postpone the trip."

"You've no other choice, Emma."

"I do not have any other choice either."

They both laughed rather hysterically. Suddenly, Tanya's voice froze in her mouth as her face darkened with a shadow of fear.

Emma noticed the changes that were seizing her breathless. "You alright, Tanya?"

Tanya couldn't answer straightaway. She struggled visibly for her breath, but the fear inside her was getting the better of her. Her hands and legs were trembling irrepressibly, and the muscular tissues on her face twitched. However, holding tightly to the desk, she tried to speak, and the voice burst out even before she realized, "You are not Emma."

Emma laughed hysterically again. "I am not Emma? Then who am I?"

She held her staring eyes steadily. "Please go."

"Why are you getting so awkward? What have I done to you?"

"Go."

Without replying, Emma continued to sit there, though.

Tanya shouted while struggling to breathe, "If you don't go, I will call the security men."

Emma chuckled, "Is it necessary, Tanya?"

"It is," she retorted in a mixed voice of anger and fear. "Please go. Get out."

Emma giggled calmly. "Why are you so frightened of me, suddenly?"

"You're fake," she retorted while trying to rise up to her feet.

"We are good friends, aren't we? How can you say that?"

Tanya was holding on to the edge of the desk in an effort not to stagger and tumble to the floor. She wanted desperately to get to the alarm switch on the side of the bed. But she couldn't move, though. Her legs had gone completely paralyzed. She breathed heavily, taking as much air as she could into her lungs, and opened her mouth to scream as loud as she could. But before the sound of a scream came out, Emma's right hand poked into her neck. She fell down on her back by the side of the alarm switch. On the floor, she writhed while her hands and legs threw up into the air frantically. She tried again to scream, but Emma's right leg landed on her neck with the full weight of her power. "How are you feeling, my dearest friend."

Tanya couldn't answer. A kind of froth was foaming in her mouth. She kept turning her face to the side in an attempt to free herself. However, her strength was diminishing by the second. Her windpipe to the lungs was completely blocked as Emma's leg jammed her neck flat.

"Tanya, my friend, how are you feeling now?"

Tanya didn't reply. She was dead.

Emma moved back to the door. She opened it gently and partially. She looked outside and down the corridor. Nobody was out there. She turned off the light inside and stepped out.

Once again, she surveyed the view down the corridor. Nobody was in sight. Anyway, she walked quietly as if nothing ever happened.

Emma came back to her room. For a moment or two, she hung around in the room as if she had completely lost her mind. And, then, she slumped into her bed and cried.

Chapter 3

Mathew in Atlantica

Part 1: The Next Day

Tuesday, 13th December 1988 and other days

The door music played exactly at six.

Emma heard it through her subconscious mind. She was having a sound sleep. In fact, she had been wide awake until about 2 am, or even later than that. The scenes of Tanya's murder kept fluctuating in her view. She closed her eyes tighter and tried harder to restrain her mind, but the scenes, challengingly, zoomed clearer and unbearably torturous. She couldn't imagine what would happen or who would turn up. The thought woke her up instantly, with a chilling terror gripping her heart.

Suddenly, the music soared again. Emma sprang up at a terrifying speed and sat on the bed with fear gleaming in her eyes. There was no time for logical reasoning. Her nightgown was right in front of her on the chair. She grabbed it and slipped into it, and then, moving lightly as a butterfly, got behind the door. "Who…. is this?" She asked in a shaky, broken voice.

"It's me, June!"

Emma was stooping with her hands on her knees in order to support her body over her hips. She opened her mouth and, breathed in a lungful of air, and blew out easily. It had nothing to do with last night's incidents. She sighed again before she managed to retort sullenly, "You mad girl, what's your problem? You want to kill me?"

"I want to," June said, laughing. "But you're secured behind the door."

Emma took another heavy puff before she spoke. "Alright. Wait a moment."

Without waiting for her reply, she returned to her bedroom. She grabbed a moist tissue from a packet and, stepping closer to the dresser, looked at herself in the mirror. The eyes and cheeks were obviously dark and tired due to the lack of sufficient sleep. Other than that, the image in the mirror looked alright. She quickly freshened her face with the tissue and then went and opened the door. "Are you still there, Ms Murphy?"

"Open the door, you rude woman."

Emma opened the door. "What's this emergency?" She asked with a mock, angry voice. "Don't you let people rest a bit?"

"This is the wakey, wakey call," June replied, glancing down at the trolley on her side. "I've your tea here."

"Thank you, my angel. But I prefer a coffee, if I can, when I wake up."

The room attendant gaped at her. "I knew you're a difficult client to please."

"Thank you."

So, I have it down in the bottom self."

Emma smiled. "You're a sweetie."

She pushed the trolley in. "How long do you know I've been ringing the bell?"

"Sorry, sweetie. I couldn't sleep until early morning."

"Liar!" She pushed the trolley to the dining table.

"White, black?" She retorted while she was fixing the coffee.

"White, please," she replied, taking a seat.

She made it and put it on the desk in front of her. "Like a biscuit? Or a slice of cake?"

"What are you doing? Trying to fatten me?"

"I don't think I will succeed."

"Why not?" She smiled, drinking a sip of coffee.

"The shape of your body. And the height."

"What about them?"

"You're very slim. And tall and very strong. And I can assure you you'll never put on weight."

"What are you? A doctor? Painter? Sculptor? Writer?"

"What do you think I am good at?"

"I am not very sure. But I can honestly say that you make a nice cup of coffee."

June laughed pleasantly. "That means a lot."

Emma joined in her laugh. "Why don't you have a drink with me?"

"Don't ask," she chuckled, sitting on the opposite. "I'm having it."

"I normally charge five pounds to my friends. But to you, because I am a kind friend of you, June. So, I charge only 10 pounds."

"If I've a kind friend like you, do I need an enemy?"

"Oh! That's harsh!"

June started sipping her coffee. "We shouldn't be laughing."

"Why?"

"You know Tanya Roberts?"

"Of course. I met her two or three times yesterday."

"Did you?"

"Yes. And she's taking me around the kitchen today, hopefully in the morning. And then introducing me to Helena Roscoe and Adam Aylesbury, if they are free."

June didn't speak. Instead, she stared at her.

"Anyway, why did you ask?"

She hesitated a moment. "Tanya died last night."

Emma held her breath, bewildered. "I hope you are joking."

"It's true."

Without saying anything, she stared at her. Even her breathing stalled for moments. "If you're lying, I will kill you."

"I cross my heart."

A couple of minutes elapsed uneasily. "Tragic," Emma whispered in a sad voice. "Very tragic. Anyway, how? I meant, what happened?"

June didn't answer immediately. Obviously, she wasn't sure about the answer. She made another cup of coffee for Emma and one for herself. While sipping her drink, she replied carefully, "Jacob found her body by her bedside. They meant to go out somewhere. Tanya didn't turn up. So, he went to her room."

"I can't believe it, June. What a sad news!" She continued to stay in her chair, almost immobile. In the end, she whispered again, "I liked her. She was lovely."

June cast down her eyes thoughtfully. "We'll talk when I come back. Probably, I'll know how she died. And when I come back, what do you like for breakfast?"

"Anything you choose."

"Okay. I see you in half an hour. Or later?"

"Later."

"7.30?"

"Okay."

June left, and Emma stood behind the door, leaning her back on it. Two days had gone since she arrived at this hotel, and in this small span of time, two people had died. However, she didn't want to go too much into them. Slowly, she returned to the dining table and checked the coffee in the cup. It was still warm. She drank it all in one go, then went back to the room. And a moment or two later, she got into the bath and lay submerged under water up to her neck. The warmth nurtured her troubled mind and soul and soothed her resolves. Suddenly, she shut off her mind and kept the memories at a distance.

Emma returned to her dresser. In fact, it was a room of its own, at the far end of the bed, with an open door. She put on a jeans and polo-neck jumper, which she used in freezing weather, and pulled over a denim jacket over the jumper. They were her usual outfit, and she could already feel warm.

Today, she needed something like this outfit as the weather outside ought to be freezing. Inches of snow were shrouding the garden meadows, and the bars of icicles were looming down on the trees. Anyway, it didn't bother her at all. She got the right stuff on. Today, she should be going in and out of various offices and meeting different managers and officers with a little bit of luck. Jeremy Smith was supposed to help her, but he wasn't alive. And Tanya was the other person who wasn't around either. Who would guide her with her project? Of course, she could go to Mathew Atkinson or Mark Windrush for guidance. She tried to calm her thoughts for the time being.

The door music played, and Emma approached the door cautiously. "June, is it you?"

"Emma, It's Mark."

Part 2: Mark is Stunned

Emma opened the door.

Mark came in quietly with a gentle smile on his lips. However, the moment he saw her, he stepped back completely stunned. "I don't believe it," he exclaimed breathlessly.

Emma laughed softly. "It's only the clothes."

Without speaking, he watched her face and her clothes.

"What's wrong with you, man? Haven't you seen girls before?"

Silently, Mark moved on to the lounge and sat down swiftly as if his legs were failing to support him. He opened his mouth and drew a breath of air in front of her. "I was right when I said it," he managed to speak finally.

She chuckled. "What?"

"I don't believe it."

Emma rolled her eyes sarcastically. "Please tell me what it is that you don't believe?"

Mark breathed in again and again before he replied with a stammering voice, "You .... you look like somebody....... I .... I knew... knew.... so well."

She giggled rather spontaneously. "I'm only an ordinary girl. Nothing special about me!"

He didn't speak immediately. "But to me," he replied after a few moments, "she was special to me."

"Did you love her?"

"It wasn't love."

"Then what?"

"Sheer adoration."

"What a blessed girl she was."

"It was me who was blessed."

"Was she beautiful?"

"Yes. She was the nature's greatest creation."

"Heaven forgive me! This man can talk."

"I'm telling the truth."

"If she was that beautiful, what have I got to do with her."

"You're her."

She giggled loudly. "What drugs are you on?"

A few moments ticked away. "I came here to tell you just two things, and you're making me gasp."

"What are those two things, anyway."

He waited. "June told you that Tanya Roberts died?"

She nodded lightly. "Very sad news indeed. I had a good chat with her yesterday."

"She was a lovely girl."

"What happened?"

"Nothing confirmed yet. But the rumours are that she died of an overdose of drugs."

"Good gracious! She didn't look that type."

Mark waited reluctantly. "And you're not sleeping here tonight."

"No?"

"Mathew Atkinson is taking you to his house."

"Wow. What have I done to deserve this?"

"I'd say you're born under a lucky star."

"Oh, thank you."

"So, keep your clothing in the suitcase."

"Definitely. But I like this chalet very much."

"I am glad to hear that."

"You chose this chalet for me."

"Not me, dear. Mr Atkinson chose it for you."

"Alright. I thank him."

The door music played.

Emma opened it, and June came in with her food trolley.

Mark watched her come through the hallway. "Thanks for bringing my breakfast," he chuckled. "It smells nice."

"Because I made it!"

Mark got up. "Let Emma enjoy it. Let me go to my duty."

"Have some," June chuckled. "I've enough here."

"I know. But I can't eat good food. My stomach is allergic."

The women giggled.

Mark moved to the front door. Suddenly, he stopped turning back to Emma. "Now it's 8 o'clock. Can you see me at 9? Or 9.30."

"I will be at your office at nine."

"Okay." And he went out and shut the door behind him.

"I've Froot loops, Cocoa puffs, and Cap'n Crunch for cereals. I have hot milk and cold milk. I have sandwiches and toast. Whatever do you prefer?"

Emma stared at her blankly. "Do you know what you are?"

"To be honest, I haven't looked at myself in the mirror."

"You are an angel."

"Many people have called me several names. But nobody ever dared to call me an angel."

"They are honest people, not like me. I am a liar."

They laughed before June started making a bowl of cereal and a couple of sandwiches. "Can I trust you, Emma?"

"What for? I'm not marrying you."

"Thank you for that. But please tell me. Can I trust you?"

Emma nodded slowly. "Only for a few minutes."

She held her mouth close to Emma's ears and whispered like a gust of breeze. "Tanya is a devil woman."

Emma gawked into her eyes, then whispered, "I give you a slap right on your mouth if you don't shut up."

"Later, darling. But now, listen."

"My god, what's next?"

"She was a clever bed-jumper."

"What's this? A new sport?"

"She sleeps with anybody if she can get promotions of one kind or another."

"Nothing wrong with that. Or is it?"

"You're beautiful. But you're a dump."

"My boyfriend also calls me that."

"You got no brain at all."

"Very true in times like this. Anyway, she got promotions?"

"Yes, several times! She rose to the post of staff recruitment manager."

"Then what happened?"

93

"She jumped to Jacob's bed. And would you believe it? They decided to get married."

"Good, June. And this is what you'd call marriage made in heaven."

"And Jacob is pleased with it as well. It will keep his name intact."

"Intact? You're using difficult words, June. Tell me in simple words. Something wrong with it?"

"Yes!"

"Yes? A man is marrying a woman. Is it wrong in your book?"

"Yes. Jacob is gay."

"That's quite common in hidden circles. And they call it a marriage made on earth."

June laughed, covering her mouth with a hand. "You're terrible." She turned back to the dining table. "Enjoy your breakfast."

"Thank you."

"I'm going to leave the trolley here, Emma."

"Why?"

"If you fancy something, they're all there."

"Like?"

"Sausages, chips, baked beans, fried eggs, soups, cereals, milk......"

"Enough, enough. You are not as bad as I thought, June."

June laughed, then moved towards the door. "If you need me, you know where the switch for the alarm is."

"What I need is a police alarm to grab you away."

Laughing, she moved further to the door.

"Hello, beautiful."

She stopped looking back.

"I'm going to stay in Mr Atkinson's house."

"Good Lord! When?"

"This afternoon."

"That will be like a dream come true."

Emma looked at her silently.

"That is called Abigale House. It's a gorgeous, beautiful mansion. It may be the best house in the country. You'll cherish every second you live there."

Emma was still looking at her, really puzzled. "How do you know this?"

"I worked there on and off for a while. And Tanya used to stay there, too."

"Is that so?"

"Well, Tanya was the friend of Atkinson's daughter."

"What was her name?"

"I can't tell her name. But I can tell you this much. You are absolutely her image. And that's why we are giving you all this care."

"What was her name?"

"Please don't ask me."

"What was her name?"

"Gemma."

"Thank you. And thank you for everything."

"Please don't say to anyone that I told her name."

"I cross my heart."

"When you are in Abigale House, don't go to the room Tanya used to stay. I think it must be haunted by her spirit."

Emma laughed happily. "Anyway, I'm not saying goodbye yet. I will be coming here every day for my course until Saturday."

"Make sure you see me."

Emma laughed. "As if I've no other choice!"

June didn't laugh. She was sad. Slowly, she walked out and disappeared into the corridor.

Part 3: Learning Exploration

Daylight was fading when Mathew and Emma left the cemetery.

They started to move up the lane slowly towards the dual carriageway about a mile away. The lane was very narrow, with hugely overgrown hedges on either side. The view looked treacherous and dark. But he was alright with his driving; he had been through these tracks several times and in all seasons. Again, on this occasion, he had the company of an elegant girl whom he adored very preciously for reasons he had no explanations. Emma appeared to be very enthusiastic about knowing everything. She said, looking at his face. "It's more than a cemetery. It's actually a real garden."

He smiled without meeting her eyes. He was driving carefully through a bumpy road with lots of potholes and muddy puddles. "It's meant to be a resting place for the departed souls of the Atkinson family. Some of the headstones are as old as four hundred years or more."

"There are a good few headstones there," she said, looking ahead the route. They were passing under some oak tree canopies, and the headlights reflected on them. "Especially on the shore, where some angels stood high watching over the graves."

"True." He puffed on his cigarette and added as if he had just remembered, "There should have been a lot more. But the survivors buried the dead in the sea."

Her eyes stared at him. "Why?"

He puffed again. "Prior to the colonial days, or even during the colonial periods, the medical facilities were not great when you compare with our time. And we knew nothing much about the mighty Atlantic Ocean or any other great seas. No wireless communications existed or were known. In the beginning, colonial explorations also meant brave adventures into the unknown fantasy world."

She didn't speak. Instead, she listened to him carefully.

They came to an area where the road was submerged under muddy water. He reduced the speed to about twenty miles and drove more carefully as if he would come across a patch where there would be no ground underneath. And yet, the water was split under the tires and scattered to the thick hedges along the routes.

"Oh, Uncle Mathew, I never knew this."

"And here comes the tragical bits. Whoever died in the offshore waters, whether they were the masters or slaves, men or women, the survivors couldn't keep their dead bodies in the ship. They were thousands of miles away from the shores. So, they threw the bodies into the sea.

"My God, that was cruel. How on earth could they do that, throwing the dead bodies of fellow human beings into the sea."

"Dear Emma," he said, puffing on the cigarette, "we have to see the realities in the right order."

"What do you mean?"

"In the past, people were buried on the same day. Why – have you thought about it?"

"No. I thought it was some religious practice."

"Nothing to do with religion. But we didn't have the mortuary for the dead in those days."

"Why?"

"There was no technology to keep the body fresh. And the hotter the country, the quicker the body rots. And the faster they bury the bodies. And in most cases, they buried the dead in eight or nine hours."

"I didn't realize it in that manner."

"Otherwise, the decaying bodies spread illnesses like cholera and wipe out everyone on the ship."

Without saying anything, she stared at his face.

"And when they are on the land, they buried them on the land."

Emma remained silent.

"And when they were in offshore sea, they buried them in the water. And lots of my ancestors were buried in the sea." He stopped speaking and puffed the cigarette. "Now, we look back and blame one another. And it's true that lots of disgraceful incidents happened, such as the enforced human trafficking and the eventual slaveries and the colonial empires."

They came to a junction and waited at the traffic light to change. "I read about them. A shameful period of mankind when men traded men for glory."

"Yes, you are right, Emma. But if you widen the focus of mind on this period, you will see glorious achievements?"

She stared at him bewildered, "Glorious achievements?"

"Yes, dear."

"What are they, Uncle?"

"The discoveries of three continents we never knew existed before this period. And numerous islands!"

Emma was silent.

"These discoveries opened the door for a new world which is almost as big as the old world we were accustomed to." He lit a new cigarette and puffed heavily on it. "This new world inspired us to form new countries."

Emma hardly spoke a word as she was enthusiastic to listen to him.

"A country needs roads, railways, schools, hospitals, shops, farms, agriculture, etc. All these things need huge manpower to build, run, and maintain, which means the countries should generate huge income. Income depends on the workforce and the goods they produce."

Without making any opinions of her own, she sat quietly.

"And here comes the competition, better goods and cheaper prices and large open market. And the police force is needed to maintain the law; you need men. Each country should be protected from external aggression, which means more men for the military."

"Everything needs manpower," Emma said as if taking part in the conversation. "And suddenly, where is this manpower going to come from?"

"And that was the problem." He smoked and blew out the smoke into the clouded air. "This is where the human trafficking started. And I should immediately add that some of these men physically suffered where they were captured, or in the ship or in the country where they were sold to."

"Sad and brutal. And inhuman!"

"Absolutely, dear. You are right on it. No excuse for it. We hope it won't be repeated at any time in the future." He waited thoughtfully for a moment. "Sadly, we can't go back and correct the actions. But we can look at the brighter side of it now."

"What is it?"

"The descendants of these slave generations are everywhere in the world and settled as equal citizens as any other ethnic group. And some of them are great singers, or entertainers, or sportsman. Or hardworking common people. And let's hope one day we will find a solution to justify the offenses of the past."

"I sincerely hope so."

A couple of minutes ticked, and then she asked, looking into his face. "Uncle, where did you meet Abigale?"

He met her eyes and smiled immediately. "In Atlantica."

"How?"

He looked straight ahead as though he was seeing her right in front of him. He wasn't smiling this time. It was more like a shadow of sadness that spread over his face.

Emma looked at him through the corner of her eyes. She wanted him to continue as easily as he could. He steered around a pothole and managed the car back into the trails. "She was my cook," he continued, trying to recapture the times and scenes. Many decades passed by, while numerous episodes shot up and then withered to ashes.

"She was your cook for a long time?"

He turned his face and caught her eyes before he turned to look ahead the lane.

'Was she?' He repeated her question in his own mind. And with it, for one reason or another, his past began to unfurl in his mind.

Part 4: Back in Atlantica

It was the year 1957, during the struggle for independence

Mathew was a Nyanbique citizen living in the capital city, Atlantica City, at the time. He was a civil engineer, and his company, called 'Atkinson constructions Ltd', engaged with government policies for building constructions and road works. Most of the roads in Nyanbique, like in the neighbouring countries, ran towards the harbour, as they were built in the colonial days to ship goods to Europe but were not designed to link the local towns and cities. Now, the elected government urgently wanted to study the blunders the exploiters had brought about in their beloved country and then quickly modernize them good for the proud people. During the struggle for independence, which lasted almost ten years, the local leaders made promises that they would make the country great with roads and rails, schools and colleges, factories, and distribution centres. The crowd cheered them hysterically and assured their life long support.

On 14th June 1961, the country achieved independence. An elected government took the power for the people, and the national president, Kuladoo Michaels, moved into the State Palace. On the national broadcast on Independence Day, he announced, "The jobs in the country go to the countrymen. The transport systems will be revamped and more built for the good of the nation and the people. New international airports and major harbours will be constructed and operational in five years. A seaside road called National Marine Drive will be developed with numerous holiday resorts for the rich and famous. We will make our country great."

He went on and on with numerous projects and policies, and people crowded wherever there were radios and cheered with excitement. The country was heading towards greatness.

Two years ticked away slowly, and no developments were noticed. The opposition went berserk and organized protest marches for evidence of what was happening in the country. President Michaels organized a press meeting at Swampy Bay, near the Nyanbie River mouth, and asked the contractor Mr Abdhi Nalloo, mainly to satisfy the media men, to show where the constructions were going on for the sea barrier and also for the Marine Drive and resorts. The projects were intended to provide tens of thousands of well-paid jobs for the proud countrymen. Mr Abdhi was silent for a moment, apparently pondering how to reply, then pointed to the Atlantic Ocean.

A burst of crazy laughter erupted in the press corner. "Are you separating the Atlantic Ocean, Mr Abdhi?"

He held his breath. "It's a swampy area. Stones are sinking into the bottom of the sea."

"When do we intend to finish this senseless project?"

He replied quietly. "When the money runs out!"

Another laugher erupted from the media benches, more loudly and discourteously than before. "Are we losing any land to the sea here?"

He waited. "No."

"Then why the hell on earth do we need these barriers?"

Abdhi couldn't think straight. He said rather frightfully. "You need to ask this to the president."

Another laughter erupted from the media men and also from the members of the pubic who were standing behind the security marking. They were desperate to know why the country was squandering money and throwing stones into the great ocean. However, the president realized that people were getting angry, and the number of bodyguards who accompanied him there was not enough to restrain the crowd if the tension turned into nasty violence. He got up from his chair, tugging his earphone properly, and announced, "I hear that some foreign warships are approaching our shore. I have to stop this press conference now and get back to the Palace."

The next day, the Nyanbique Chronicles, the largest newspaper from Atlantica City, published a list of treasury funds looted by the president and his collaborators over a period of two years and transferred to various banks in to Switzerland, Paris, and London. All sorts of people - rich and poor, men and women - crowded outside the palace and chanted for the president to resign immediately. The size of the crowd grew and began to spill over to the parliament building, state assembly hall, secretariat houses, and the

Nyanbique party headquarters tower. A few hungry, destitute jumped over the massive Palace Gates and were about to open the main entrance door. But the state police fired live bullets and killed 29 people instantly. The news flared across the nation and brought the people to the streets, calling for the president's resignation.

In the small hours of the night, Kuladoo Michaels fled from the palace. Nobody knew his destination, but it was rumoured that he was on his way to Zurich, Switzerland.

Three days later, on the 19th of September 1963, the opposition leader, Chekund Kalideen, was sworn to be the president. He was a rousing political orator and promised the nation that he would deliver food, clothes, and homes for the needy. However, he stated there was no easy answer for the country's dreadful situation. The previous government under Kuladoo Michaels emptied the government treasure, and before it, the colonial masters had drained the nation's wealth over centuries. He pleaded with the people to be patient and wait for the national economy to grow, which he said would start sooner rather than later.

Three years passed, and the people continued waiting for the growth. However, President Kalideen kept his hands clean from fraud and promised his hands would always be clean until the day he would resign from power. Another few months passed by, and around this time, the World Bank declared that they would aid poorer nations with long-term loans at a very low interest rate for industrial developments. Atlantica country also qualified, and President Kalideen organized the loan into a London Bank. He told the World Bank authorities that there was no safe bank in Atlantica and no safe box was present in the country's treasury. Kalideen arrived in London shortly and transferred the funds to various banks. Then he drowned into the unknown.

People in Nyanbique went out on a rampage, destroying government properties and attacking the police. The general of the army, Frank Dumbanka, declared martial law in the country, and the army started patrolling streets and guarding the important town centres and buildings.

A week later, General Frank moved into the palace as the president of the country. In his inauguration speech to the nation, he pleaded with everyone to forget all those who had disgraced the country through fraud and let babies and mothers die through starvation. The truth was that it was the fault of the democracy. However, now, a new administration has achieved power based on love, trust, and care, not based on meaningless democracy. The new administration in power would change the crimes of the past and make our country great. And to achieve that, all men and women of this country – whether native or foreign, black or white – should respect each other and work hard for our beloved country.

Three days later, on the 22nd of October 1966, a police jeep arrived at the driveway of Atkinson Construction Ltd. The transport secretary of the new government, Ollan Mallu, and his personal secretary walked into the reception office, introduced themselves, and asked to see Mr Mathew Atkinson. The receptionist went to his office and passed the message. He rushed to the reception and met the visitors. "What on earth brought you here, Ollie? And your companion?"

"I am glad you remember me, Mathew!"

"Of course! We played volleyball a few times. And you're a cheat!"

"That's me," he laughed cheerfully. "And this personal secretary, a London graduate, Paul Nelson."

"Hi, Paul. Anyway, why are we standing here? Let's go to my office."

"Thank you, Mathew. But not now. I was passing by, and I thought of you. I never liked you very much on those days. You played well."

"I'm sorry about that!"

"Don't worry. I've already forgotten about it." He and Paul laughed for a moment. "Do you answer your phone?"

"Yes. When I know who is on the other end!"

"Good. In the next day or two, my office clerk will give you a call for an appointment."

"I see."

"I will come and see you here."

Mathew was silent.

"I've seen some of the houses you built for the previous government. Those houses look even better than your buildings."

"I haven't got a penny."

"I know. And I know you won't get anything soon either." He paused vaguely. "But listen, the country needs us. All of us got to work together and make the poor and the destitute survive at the least."

"Make the appointment. Let's talk."

"That's good. We'll talk."

And they went.

Part 5: Facts about Atlantica

Atlantica was considered a city, but it covered only a small area. The seafront was stunning, with excellent two to three-story houses, once owned or occupied by overseas business tycoons or government ministers in the colonial days. On the southern end of these sought-after zones, a few private properties clustered along two short roads, and this section was known as the colonial district. And here, Mathew had his home, inherited from his great grandad who bought this plot of ground with a detached timber shelter at the centre of it. A few years later, he demolished it and built a two-story stone house in classical English style and character.

His parents, Hugh and Elanor, stayed mostly in Kondakko, the capital of Madakka province, whenever they arrived from England. They owned a company that extracted copper and exported it to Europe. But the business hadn't been viable for a long time, and the mines were practically exhausted. Besides this, the pilfering, theft, and bad management pulled the company to its feet. Hugh was mostly in Cornwall and overseeing the businesses at The Great Atlantic Hotel and its associated companies. However, he tried to spend some time at Kondakko and invested further funds to reconstruct the business. Eventually, he learned his lesson that he couldn't sail the ship against the wind. The staff had showed no responsibilities, the local people showed no appreciation for the improvements he was achieving for the locality, and the local government ministers were after him for bribes. His personal safety was challenged several times, and the attacks on his properties increased, especially after the independence of 1961 from Britain. He sold his business for a very low price to his nephew, Peter Atkinson, who was an African mixed race, and his brother-in-law, Adai Kumasi.

Besides the fact that they hated the Europeans, the local tribes, known as the Madaks, didn't welcome the other national tribes either, who had settled in Kondakko and got blamed that they were 'stealing the jobs of Madaks.' However, most of the hatred was aimed directly at Atlantis, who had arrived from Atlantica province. The core issue for this hatred was that the national capital was in Atlantica City.

The Madaks believed that Kondakko should have been the capital city as Madakka was the largest out of all the seven provinces and that Kondakko was in the centre of the province and also in the middle of the country, which would have been a real blessing if anybody had to go to this capital city rather than going all the way to Atlantica in the southwest. Madaks were also a force to be reckoned with because they were the largest tribes, and their sizable presence remained in other prominences, too.

Germans were the colonial rulers until the end of the First World War. In the war, the Germans lost, and the League of Nations handed over Nyanbique to the British. As soon as Britain took over, the old gossip resurfaced that the capital city was going to be Kondakko. But nothing changed; everything remained exactly as it was under German rule. Changing the location of the capital city immediately wasn't realistic for the British. Kondakko had no airport and no credible network of roads, but it had a small harbour on the west coast, which was about 30 miles away. So, the capital remained in Atlantica as before.

When Hugh cleared the business and the stocks in 1961, their housekeeper, Hanna, wasn't happy to stay alone at Kondakko. She was an Atlantis woman. In the end, he brought her to Atlantica City, where she became Mathew's cook. Hugh didn't want his son to live in Atlantica anymore. The area was dangerous for his life. But Mathew loved Atlantica and that he wanted to live there. After all, he was a Nyanbique citizen. Hana was a good cook and a very good person. She would be like a mother to him, as she had promised Hugh. But Mathew continued to stay in the Colonial House. Whenever he wanted to visit his parents, he could fly and, in a few hours' time, he would be in England, and so could his parents if they had wanted to visit him. Travel facilities were improving fast all across the world.

However, Hanna died in 1966 in a car accident outside the parliament building while two police vehicles were chasing the driver of a stolen car.

Mathew brought in Chelangu Kulumga for cooking. He had some acquaintance with Chelangu beforehand because she had been in the colonial house a few times to see Hanna when the latter was in charge of the cooking. They were stepsisters. She was a good cook, and he enjoyed whatever she had made. To be honest, he was mostly out.

And then a girl, aged about 15 or 16, started coming for work in the house, mostly cleaning and washing or tidying up the yard. The girl worked in the kitchen as well, chopping vegetables or cutting meat or grinding spices or something. A few times, he watched her curiously. She had a pleasant voice for talking, lovely walking, and meeting others respectfully. To be honest, he thought he liked her and would promote her – one day, not right away – to handle the phone calls when he wasn't in. Anyway, it didn't happen for a long time. He was busy with his construction work for the government, and he didn't find time for little issues.

One morning, he had a meeting to attend and was about to go. She showed up at the doorway of his study room. "Good morning, sir."

He was at his desk and scribbling something on a loose sheet. "Yes?" He said mechanically.

She hesitated. "What time are you coming back, sir?"

"About 12. Or 1. Why?" He asked, still writing on the sheet.

"What do you like to eat when you come."

"I'm busy now. Tell your mother to make anything."

"She is home. She isn't well."

"She's a very nice cook."

She grinned. "What do you prefer?"

"Who is cooking."

"I am."

He swung his chair to look at her. "Do you know where the kitchen is?" He asked rather jokingly.

The girl didn't laugh. "I've cooked for you several times with my mum. Haven't you seen me?"

"Yes. I suppose."

She giggled lightly. "Did you like them?"

"Well, I am still alive."

"What do you prefer?"

"Alright. I prefer what you prefer. Let me see how good you're."

Her smile grew broader. "Good. Please tell me what you like?"

He stared at her sarcastically, then took the paper he was writing on and pushed it into his trouser pocket. He grabbed a set of car keys from one of the drawers in front of him and got up. He began walking to the front door. She was on his side, "I'm starting a new building today."

"What is it?"

"A girls' primary school. Eight classrooms, one teachers' room, one office, and three bathrooms. And a wide passageway. What do you think?"

"Quite big. What's going to be the name?"

"They haven't named yet. Probably, I've got to find a name. Do you know any nice names of girls?"

She was thoughtfully silent for a moment. "Abigale?"

He said with mock sarcasm, "I said a nice name for girls."

"You're getting nothing for lunch."

"Thank you. Plenty hotels here! And their food tastes like heaven on earth."

She laughed before she said, "I'm making fish stew for the main course."

"Don't worry. Eat it yourself. If you're alive, I'll have it in the end."

"What time you're coming?"

He looked over his shoulder at her face. "What's the problem?"

"I want to just finish cooking when you arrive. It tastes much better if it's nice and warm."

He stepped outside the door and then turned back to her. "Who decided I should eat fish today?"

She replied quickly, "I?"

"Why?"

"You eat too much meat. And every day. It's not good for you."

"Again, you decided?"

"Yes."

"Why?"

"I don't know why. Maybe I care about you."

Silently, Mathew went down the steps to the sandy ground. He stopped there and, half-turning back, looked up at her. Her face was emotionless. He walked over to his car and drove down the driveway. About one hundred yards, the driveway was straight, and he saw her reflection on the side mirror. She was at the door, leaning against the frame, staring down at him.

The days rolled on. Abigale managed the family routines neatly, just as her mother had done. She ordered the daily food and drinks, all fresh. She made sure he wore clean clothes every time he went out.

One night, at about 10 o'clock, Mathew was out in the family garden looking to the beach and beyond. The beach was deserted. The sea was invisible to the distance under the curls of darkness. However, the waves rolled over and hugged the shore, then slipped back to the sea, all the while drifting music of nature's symphony.

He was sitting on a low bough of a flowering tree. The night was beautiful; the abyss was clustered with gazing stars. Away in the eastern horizon soared a lazy crescent of the moon. Suddenly, he heard Abigale's voice behind, as audible as a whisper in the ears. "What are you watching, Mathew?"

Slightly startled, he looked at her. "The stars and the sea."

"They're all beautiful, I believe?" She whispered again.

"Of course!"

Abigale sank her body and sat down on the bough, close to him, her arm almost touching his. "What's most beautiful of all that you see?"

Mathew held her eyes quietly for a moment. "You don't need to hear!"

Her arm weighed against his as she slightly leaned on to him. "Tell me."

"Hard to say"

"Well, you've to try."

This time, she moved her body closer to his chest and put her slender hands around him and her chin on his shoulder. "Why is it so hard?"

Mathew lowered his face and rested it on her head. "Hard to say the truth." Suddenly, his arm fell around her slim waist.

"Try, please."

"What was the question?"

"What is the most beautiful of all that you see?"

"I can't see anything now."

"No? Why?"

"I am blind."

"Say it properly, please."

"I am blindly in love with you."

Her tender lips moved to speak, but no words were found.

Only the beats of their hearts tuned audibly into the music of the sea under the starry sky. A couple of moments passed silently, then a couple of minutes passed, and then time didn't have a word while the feelings of two hearts drifted, mingled, and engulfed.

In the end, Mathew whispered reluctantly. "I'm going to England."

She asked slowly, "When?"

"On Sunday."

"For holiday?"

Mathew didn't answer suddenly. "I'm getting married."

Abigale was silent for a while. "I will pray for you."

Part 6: Marrying Isabella

Mathew married Isabella and took her to Atlantica for the honeymoon. Unfortunately, it was a disastrous mistake. Somehow, they couldn't stay together for three days, even during their honeymoon times. They realized that the marriage between them wasn't tenable, so she settled back with her parents in England, and he continued to live in his beloved country, Atlantica. He wasn't lonely either; Abigale stayed even closer. "Didn't you know Isabella before your wedding?"

"Yes."

"How?"

"Six or seven generations of our ancestors were partners in their business at home and abroad." Mathew paused, staring at a cluster of stars gleaming brightly as a large band of clouds glided away in the western sky. The sea was fairly calm, although the waves ran quietly over the shore and sank into the sand, leaving the froth behind as a landmark. He turned to her, who was sitting on his side, and felt the coolness of the breeze coming over the waters. "In fact, we were neighbours at one time. And we went to the nursery together."

"What went wrong then? Is it me?"

He leaned over and kissed her. "You're not wrong at all. To be honest, you're the best thing that ever happened to me."

She held him close and kissed him. "Let's go in and sleep, darling."

They moved up to the house side by side, hands firmly clutched and bodies tenderly colliding.

They entered his room. The light was off, but everything there was visible in the starry light that sneaked through the side windows. There was a white sheet on the bed. She removed it. It was a hot night. "Don't bother to get up in the morning," she told him as they cuddled together.

Confused, Mathew stared at her.

"I'll call you up when it's necessary."

He chuckled, "Whatever you say."

Abigale giggled, "And whatever I do."

And the night rolled on silently as they fell asleep. This was the first night they slept together, then countless nights followed.

One night, she got up from his side. He was half sleepy and half-awake but turned over to his side. "What's the problem," he whispered with his eyes still shut.

"Nothing," she calmly replied, pulling her night rob over her. "But an emptiness is hurting me."

Mathew opened his eyes narrowly. "You want to marry me, darling?"

Abigale smiled cautiously. "Of course, that's my dream. But you are not ready yet."

She slipped to the hallway. She didn't turn on the lights there either; it was dimly bright by the stars. Hurriedly, Mathew sat up as if possessed, his eyes chasing her. He could see her go, her head held high, body straight up and drifting away symmetrically. She stopped at the staircase and glanced back into his room. Whether she saw him or not, she waved in his direction, smiling. Slowly, she disappeared as she descended down.

Mathew sat there, apparently frozen. A few moments ticked away, very slowly. And, suddenly, he got to his feet and ran along the hallway, then down the stairs. He found Abigale outside the servants' quarters at the back of the building and she had already slipped into a long pullover tunic. He rushed towards her. "Going home?"

She waited until he came nearer. "Mum alone," she replied, meeting his gaze and smiling. "She isn't well."

"This time of the night? Villains hanging in the street?"

"Some are my siblings, And the rest know me." She paused, still smiling.

Mathew didn't speak.

"My father was a Chief of our tribe. And he had eleven wives."

"Good gracious. Can I be a Chief?"

Abigale laughed. "Why you want to be a Chief?"

"I want eleven wives."

She laughed. "That's only half the story."

"What's the other half?"

"He had several concubines."

"Poor chap. Did he live long?"

"No idea. One early morning they found him dead."

"Can you kill me like that?" He cried, moving closer to her body.

Playfully, she pushed him back, still laughing and slightly embarrassed. A moment later, he stepped close. "If I say you are beautiful than any stars I've seen, will you love me?"

Abigale stopped laughing but caught his stare steadily.

Mathew stepped closer. "You're more beautiful than all the stars put together."

She looked into his eyes more intently as if she was seeing the whole of his heart, as if reading the writing on its cells. "What about Isabella?"

He sighed before he answered uneasily. "It's never been a marriage."

A brief silence.

"What is it then?"

Mathew waited to choose the right words. "It's a business arrangement. But it failed from the very beginning."

"What's the end?"

He took a long time to reply. "I need time, darling."

Patiently, Abigale waited for him to continue.

"In the wedding certificate, we're husband and wife. But she is not my wife, and I'm not her husband. We're just the directors of a large company. And that's all."

A few moments ticked away in an uneasy silence.

Abigale let her body lean on to him, her mouth close to his. She said in her usual soft voice. "I'm not interested in your wealth or reputation."

Mathew didn't speak. Instead, he extended his arms around her body and watched her speak.

Abigale put one hand on his shoulder and the other around his waist. "About two years ago, I saw you in the Marina, where you were building some flats. And………"

Mathew interrupted her gently. "What did you do there?"

"I was a cook, preparing food for your builders."

"Did I see you?"

"I don't think." She paused, seemingly memorizing the scene clearly, and then added, "But when my eyes fell on you, my heart stopped pounding."

"Oh God, I was that frightening?"

Abigale's hand that was around his waist squeezed him towards her while the other hand pushed down his face onto her. She kissed him in his mouth, tenderly at first, then passionately. Moments moved on to minutes; they lingered on in the kiss. Ultimately, she dropped her face on his chest, and he lowered his chin down on her head. She muttered, "I loved you ever since."

"Why didn't you tell me?" Mathew asked in a mock anger. "I could have paid you. I always carry a few pence for charities."

"Will you shut up?"

"Okay, order is taken."

Abigale was silent for a while. "Will you remember me if things go wrong tomorrow?"

"Ask me then."

She raised her head and watched the expression on his face. She grumbled, "Don't smile. It's not funny."

Mathew kissed her. A moment later, he said, "Let's go to your mum."

She looked at him astonished. "Where do you sleep?"

"Where you sleep!"

"I sleep a little with my mum."

"Alright. I sleep with your mum, as well."

She laughed.

Part 7: The Civil War

A few months passed, then the Atlantic Civil War broke out.

The violence started in the southern part of Atlantica province, known as the Kalinga bread baskets region. As the name suggested, the region consisted of thousands of agricultural plots that grew rice, wheat, barley, bananas, yams, olives, and other similar food products. Most of these plots were owned by European descendants, who had merged them into large-scale farms with strong fences built around them. They might not necessarily live on the farm, but they reside in their expensive houses in the posh locations of nearby towns or on the seafront. The laborers were mostly the local Atlantis or the Kalemins from the neighbouring Kaleminca province. These fertile lands gave great yield when the weather was good and dependable. So, the farmers were happy, and so were the laborers – they got regular work and wages.

But when the weather was dry, the overall situation was different. For a start, the farmers were under pressure. They couldn't afford many staff or any at all if the returns were not feasible, unless otherwise something was urgent. And in urgent cases, the farmers dictated the terms and brought the wages down. Literally, everyone was out in the street, desperate for work. The Kalemins would work for whatever the bosses prepared to pay. And the payment could be made much later. The Atlantis knew exactly what was going on around them. But they silently bore it for peace's sake, as had been for decades.

One summer day, the system changed terribly wrong. Three Atlantis men crawled over the border fence and climbed down to a farm yard. Lying flat on the stomach, they stared across the farm far and wide. They breathed rapidly, the look of terror intensifying in their eyes. After a brief period, they glanced at each other. The eldest man among the three murmured, fear sounding heavily in their voice, "No one anywhere. I told you, 'Sunday at two, they all go home.'"

The second man, who was the tallest whispered, "A car is there in the parking way outside the office building."

"That's the boss's car," The eldest man told; his eyes still scrutinizing the farm. He paused vaguely and then added, "He should have gone. Must be counting the cash-taking of the week. Anyway, it's good that he's there."

Confused, the other two stared at him.

"Heavy metal doors and hard to break."

The other two didn't speak.

"The door should be open now. Because he is there."

They ran a good few yards to the back of an olive tree and hid behind the foliage. They were still absolutely frightened and felt trembling throughout their bodies. They could see the farmhouse which was about a hundred yards away on the right side. The young olive trees stood in an orderly manner all the way to the parking bays in front of the farmhouse, and they would be safe behind the cover until the parking bays.

They safely moved up to the last tree and hid behind it.

"What do you think?" The eldest man murmured. "Fifty yards of open space, then we are in."

There was a brief silence.

"Hang Spears behind. Tuck machete in the trouser belt. And we'd be alright."

Another brief silence.

"If the man sees us, I'll say we're looking for work."

All of them glanced at each other for a moment and then nodded in unison. They came to the open and started to walk across the ground allocated for parking and loading. When they entered the open ground, the owner saw them coming in the security mirror. He got terrified and shouted through the window. "Stop there. It's a private property. You are trespassing."

They didn't stop. Instead, they continued to walk as normal as possible, saying loudly, "We're looking for work."

"Go away. Otherwise, I'll call the police."

The eldest man laughed in a rather friendly manner. "No need for that. We don't harm you."

VALUKALAM ANTHONY THOMAS

The boss suddenly disappeared at the window. And then, he reappeared within a moment and watched the men running towards the building with raised spears. He had the gun in his hands and pulled the trigger even before he had come to his senses.

All three men dropped dead at the front of the entrance door.

Shootings or killings were quite frequent in Nyambique. However, the Kalinga episode exploded into national politics and integrity, far more historic than ever before. The shooter was a white European, the victims were black Africans, and the killing took place in the heart of Africa -no further explanations required. The crowd massed through the streets, rioting, looting, and burning. And rampaging went on and on in all the towns and cities of Nyanbique. All parties named it universally the Bread Basket Murders, and NNP, the Nyambique National Party, immediately resurrected the call for land reformation. The NNP, which currently runs the national government, would pick up a massive swing of voters with this policy and probably take even power in the Atlantic State Assembly for the first time.

The Atlantic Peoples Party, known briefly as APP, started publishing more extreme programs to counteract NNP. Their current guidelines, which would be more precisely in the election manifesto, were that they would permit the owners to keep a maximum of twenty acres of land, which was definitely a drastic reduction, and that there were no compensations whatsoever. The funds available for compensations would be allocated to assist their dream ventures, such as schools and colleges and hospitals.

There were other parties calling for socialism and communism. These parties were not very insignificant in size, but they promised everyone heaven and earth as they knew they would never attain power. Their main propaganda was to chase out the Europeans or kill them on sight. In the last three months,

682 black Africans and 19 white European were either gunned down or stabbed to death. The four European whites who were included in the statistics had actually lived in the Colonial District – two German men, aged 39 and 61, a Scottish woman of 52, and a girl of 14. Mathew and Abigale had known them personally. Definitely, the killings were coming home. The country's political unity was at a breaking point; everyone was plotting against another and trying to accomplish the best out of the chaos.

Field Marshall Adloo Johnson had been surveying the scene and waiting in the wing for the right time to achieve his ambition, the presidency, which was the supreme power in the country. With the support of the military hierarchy, he carried out a military coup. The elected president, Beninu Milanku, fled the country for his life. At midday on Sunday, 27th July 1969, he addressed the nation and announced that he was the president of the country, and he took power to do justice for the three Kalemins who were shot dead at Kalinga and where their blood was crying out from the ground for justice.

Field Marshal Adloo was one of the Kalemins tribes, which were nationally only about 7% of the population. The Ex-president Beninu Milanku was a Madaks, and they consisted of 60%, who were, in fact, everywhere in the country, either as large groups or a few scattered families.

Adloo was fully aware that the Madaks wouldn't support him, and none of the other tribes would welcome him to power in large numbers. He was a notorious man all his life. He robbed several banks and raped several women, out of whom nine were killed in their own beds. But no case was won against him. He was a military man, first and foremost. He was 6 feet 4 inches tall and 18 stones in weight, and he was ruthless. It would take a battalion to conquer him. And he had stepped over everyone in his way and achieved the throne he had coveted all his life. He was a very happy man finally, but a very worried man, too. In fact, he was more worried than ever before. Now, all the countrymen were under him. His question was this, 'Who is coming after me for my throne?'

The new president was sweating all night. He couldn't sleep either. Whatever would happen, he couldn't care, but he would keep his throne until the end. By the time the next morning was breaking up in the East, he had ideas of his own. In public, he should pretend to be a kind, loving, caring democratic president. And he had to come up with ideas and policies such as liberty, equality, and fraternity.

On the next day, Monday 28th of July, after the prayer hour on the radio, he addressed the nation again at 4 pm and started by saying, "Atlantica was a proud nation where milk and honey used to flow sufficiently before the colonial masters arrived. Out of sheer jealousy, these animals destroyed our nation's infrastructure, such as transport systems, educational institutions, cottage industries, family farming, and the rest. But Atlantica people will make our nation great again." This address was concluded with the information that he would make further announcement at 4 pm on Tuesday, 29th of July, which was, in fact, the next day.

It was a full moon night, and the view through the window went to the distance. A gentle breeze floated in unscrupulously, carrying the sounds and music of the high waves that rolled onto the smooth sandy beaches or smashed cruelly against the stony cliffs. Somewhere in the nearby gardens, some sumptuous plants bloomed timely, drifting the intoxicating fragrance in the breeze.

Mathew propped his head in his hand and lay on his side, admiring Abigale's body constantly as if nothing else ever existed for his eyes. Looking out, she was by the side of the open window, her elegant body held high, and the crochet braided hair hung massively down to the shoulders. She appeared motionless and like a grand picture of a naked black girl against a picturesque scene.

He came off the bed and went to her.

Abigale didn't react to his presence.

He stepped nearer to her.

She didn't care.

He put his arms around her and held her close to him.

She didn't respond. Instead, she watched the beach under the moonlight and the view of the sea beyond.

Mathew turned her face towards him and kissed her. This time, she loosened her body onto him wholly, her hands around his neck clutching him even tighter, two bodies in one embrace and two hearts exploding to be merged.

After a few minutes, she pulled back her face and pulled back an inch at the most. She hung limply in his arms, her eyes slowly rolling on his face, studiously searching every tissue up there before they settled in his own eyes. She asked, mockingly angry, her voice audible under his breathing, "What's your problem, man?"

Mathew smiled softly. "You."

"Yea?"

"Very beautiful."

Abigale rolled her eyes friskily. "You took all this while to find out?"

"No, darling. But I was trying to find the right words."

Without speaking, she buried her face onto his chest. "The killings going to be here long time," she said in the end. "Let me take you to Kondakko."

"Don't worry. They won't find me."

"They know your house," she retorted quietly. "And the car. And your office and housing development sites."

"How we're going to cross the Nyanbie River Bridge? The militiamen are controlling the traffic."

Abigale thought for a moment. "We can go through the back of the city."

"What do you mean?"

"Through the country lanes outside the city to the river bank."

"I know. But that's a long way."

"We can make it in an hour. Or an hour and a bit. That's all."

Mathew didn't reply.

"The lanes are normally deserted in the evening. Nobody will know us."

"How do you know?"

"You have to wear my long robe and a face mask. No one disturbs the religious women."

He stared at her. "With my height?"

She laughed modestly. "When anybody comes along, you stoop a bit and walk with a little limp. Who is going to worry about a disabled woman."

He pulled a fake, angry face for a moment. "How we're crossing the river? Crocodiles are not going to help us?"

She giggled quietly. "We've a crocodile there. And you know him."

"Who?"

"My cousin's partner, Neilanku. He's the ferryman. And he lives close by if he isn't at the jetty."

"He's not a friendly man, is he?"

"That's for money. We give him some."

"Going to the river with him?"

"No. He's harmless."

Mathew didn't say anything. Instead, he held her close to his body.

"The vehicles will stay in the garage. The properties will be alright. My mummy is here. And some staff are always on the premises. So, nothing to worry about."

"Safe? Going through the country roads. No snakes?"

"That's nothing. I always carry something."

"Machete?"

"Don't worry. I won't use it on you now."

"Thank you," Mathew said sarcastically, lifting her face from his chest. They kissed.

On the next day, Tuesday, 29th of July, at 4 pm, Field Marshall President Adloo addressed the nation as he declared yesterday and laid out his plans for the restoration of the nation. "All Europeans must surrender to the military police by 6 pm today for their own personal safety. Those who refused to surrender would be picked up by the military forces and thrown behind bars.

The lands and properties of all foreigners will be confiscated and used by the nation for the development of the country."

Abigale stared out the window; the fear in her face narrowed her eyes. "You've to stay away for a while, darling," she said rather uneasily. "Until things get back to normal."

Mathew didn't reply.

"He's animal. And nobody would know what he would do next."

"He's a killer," Abigale's mother, Chelangu, reminded, tears running down her cheeks. "Son, you get moving."

Mathew waited thoughtfully.

"You've to go to Kondakko?" Abigale urged impatiently

"Why Kondakko?" Chelangu enquired hurriedly.

"Mathew's cousin, Peter, lives there."

This time, he whispered, "I can't leave you alone here, Abigale."

She turned to look at his face. "I won't send you alone, either."

Uneasily, a moment elapsed. "The Madaks hate the foreigners, usually," Chelangu said. "Careful, whatever you do."

"Not now, Muma. Adloo kicked out their leader, Beninu Milanku. They'll kill Adloo if they get him."

In an hour and a half or so, they reached the river jetty. Abigale's step-brother, Neilanku, was in the ferryboat, quietly sitting on the edge and drinking a locally made alcohol. He was happy to see Abigale and talked courteously with Abigale. However, he cleverly avoided eye contact with Mathew. He didn't even wish him 'Hello.' More than that, he kept the conversation deliberately in Atlantis language, which Mathew wasn't very fluent in.

In the end, Abigale repeated, somewhat annoyed, "I don't think you heard. This is Mathew."

He replied sullenly, in Atlantis, "I know."

She chuckled, "Why are you using Atlantis?"

He replied quickly, "That's my language."

"Mathew isn't very good with Atlantis."

"That proves he's a foreigner."

"What's the ......"

Mathew interrupted her gently. "Alright, Neilanku. Will you take us to the other side, please?"

He drank the last bit of drink from the aluminium flask and threw it under the board at the end of the ferry. He looked across the river diagonally before he replied, "Jetty on the other side is a mile up the river. Today, the current is strong. You've to pay 5 pounds. Lots of hard work to get there."

"Too much," she laughed annoyingly. "It's normally half a pound for a full ferry. And I'm your girlfriend's cousin. And you know that?"

He suddenly got annoyed. "I know who is who. And I know why you are running away. If ...."

Mathew disrupted him politely, "Neilanku, I will pay."

Abigale opened her mouth to say something. But Mathew glanced at her face and spoke quickly. "I agreed on the price. Can we go, please?"

"Get in," he said rudely.

Abigale got in first and sat in the middle of the boat on a seat-like frame, and then Mathew stepped in with the two lightweight bags he was carrying. He dropped them in front of her and sat down on the board at the front of the boat.

The ferryman, who was standing right now on the other end, pushed the boat out into the river and then, sitting down on his usual board, started to oar. The boat was not more than twenty feet long, but overall, it was quite fattish for its length, and it could accommodate about ten passengers. This section of the river was definitely wide, like a lake, and the banks were overgrown with trees and bushes.

Nobody spoke a word for a while, and the boat slipped further ahead. Abigale was rightly annoyed with her cousin's bad manners. Mathew didn't show any emotions on his face, though he was hurtful about the talking on the ferry and the political developments that made this trip necessary. He was calm and continued to watch the surges the boat was making on the water. And the boat moved on, diagonally upwards, cutting along the low waves that appeared randomly. When the boat was about midway to the jetty on the other side,

asked abruptly, "What are in the bags?"

Abigale and Mathew glanced at the bags and then at each other.

The ferryman repeated the question, more loudly this time.

Abigale turned her head and looked at him. "Why?" Her voice was a combination of fear and anger.

"You sit there," he retorted, looking past her. "Yes, man. Is it money? Gold? Diamond."

"Only clothes," Mathew replied, slightly startled.

"Let me see it." The ferryman put down the oar by the side of his seat and took a knife from under the seat.

Abigale sprang up and stood firm as if to block him. "Sit down and start paddling."

He stared at her. "This is the way you talk to me? I am a Kalemins. Women never talk to me like that?"

"Let's go. I'm asking politely."

Without speaking, he moved closer to her. Mathew hurried to her side. "Neilanku, I will open them," he said, calmly.

"No," she said helplessly. "No need for it."

Neilanku pushed her out of his way and moved further past her. Abigale staggered backward and one moment, she thought she was going to stumble into the floor. Nonetheless, she managed to steady down and stay up in a moment or two. And then, to her horror, she saw the two men squaring each other up – the ferryman holding the knife to strike Mathew and the latter standing firmly on his ground with empty hands. She stepped near them, balancing carefully as the boat was tilting. She grabbed the machete like a flash from the offside of her thigh and swung it on Neilanku's neck. He struggled to look back at her, but his massive body weight was faltering on his legs. The time was right; her long leg landed on his chest. He fell on the edge of the boat, the top half of him outside and the lower half inside. Suddenly, the body rotated in its own force; the head dipped down into the river water first, and then the rest slipped deeper until it disappeared completely.

Part 8: Running Away

Abigale stood there almost immobile. Her eyes kept staring into the water. Mathew was by her side, holding her close to him, and his fingers of one hand tapping on her back shoulder. Neither of them uttered a word. No voices or sounds rose from the background. Even the birds that flew over didn't chirp. Even the boat didn't move. Everything was at a standstill after everything had happened, like a thunderbolt right in front of their eyes. In the end, he sighed, saying, "Did you hurt yourself, darling, when you staggered?"

She shook her head gently for an answer.

"You sure?" He asked, staring at her growing belly.

Abigale nodded lightly.

I'm really sorry."

Her eyes rolled back to him, and she dropped her face on his chest. "Thank God you're alive."

Another long silence.

She sighed in relief. "Let's move before somebody sees us."

The daylight was fading, and they were away from the bank. "Can we paddle to the jetty he was talking about?"

"Dangerous. People may be there, waiting to cross."

Mathew was silent.

Abigale glanced across the waters to another length of the bank before the jetty. "Two or three low levels of shores are there. But we've to go up against the current."

He stared down at the water's surface. "I don't think there is any current at the moment. The tide in the sea is changing, I think. The boat is not moving at all."

"Just luck," Abigale sighed slowly. "Going up the hill behind these shores won't be easy."

"We worry about it when we get there," Mathew said, walking to the end where Neilanku used to sit. He picked up the roar, sat on the board, and then started to paddle. "You know this place anyway, don't you?"

"We used to live here a few years ago."

"Any other choices."

"None."

"Okay. Let me paddle."

It took about twenty minutes before they landed on the low shore. "Look anything in Neilanku's box. They may become handy for us in our way."

He couldn't open it, though. It was locked. Abigale moved over and shattered the lock with the back of her machete. There was a metal sword and a machete. "Take these, darling. We don't know what we are going to meet."

It was already night, but millions of stars were shining in the sky, and faint beams of brightness lingered in the air, which helped them to make their way out. They crawled up the steep bank to the flat ground above, and they were in front of a thick woodland. "Any life after death, darling?"

Abigale chuckled, "We'll talk about it when we have time."

"Very promising. By the way, any snakes?"

"All snakes stink. I can get it yards away."

"And if they bite?"

"You'll die."

"Very promising."

"Thanks."

They fought through the bushes and trees, grass and overgrowth, and ditches and bumps until they came out to a clearing. "It was absolutely dreadful."

"Yes, it was. But we were lucky. The moon rose and gave us some light."

She laughed happily. "That was nice. But one more forest area to go through."

"Bloody hell. Look like you are enjoying it."

"Learn from me then."

"If we make it, this is the final. Don't take me for another trip. I don't fancy it very much."

She laughed again. "This is Africa. Anything can happen, and you know it."

"Yes, my love. I know. I found you!"

"Before we start again, let me give you a piece of advice."

Mathew looked at her through the dim light.

"If you come across a tiger or lion or anything of that kind, don't scream and frighten them."

"No?"

"No. Just kill them with the long sword."

He chuckled, "Is that alright?"

"Of course!"

They went through another forest area, which was luckily smaller than the last, and came out to a country lane. "With a bit of luck, we might get something from here."

Abigale stood leaning to a tree and gasping for air. "Well," she replied finally, "this lane goes to the road that links Atlantica and Kondakko. And, with a little bit of luck, lorries or cars should pass by in any minute."

"Another wolf?"

She laughed, trying to breathe. "Cars, lorries, or trucks or anything?"

As they spoke, light like a big ball lit up on the other end of the road. She stared at it for a while before she said, "Looks like a lorry."

"Careful. It could be the junta's vehicles."

They stood behind a tree, staring at the vehicle carefully. As it came nearer, they became sure it was a builder's lorry. Mathew raised the hand quickly for a signal for help. But the driver didn't stop.

And there were no other lights from either end. However, they sat down on the ground and waited. They needed a bit of rest as well. "How far to the road from here?" Mathew asked in a disappointed voice.

"About four miles, darling, to the junction. Then fifty miles to Kondakko."

"Rather than wait here, can we slowly walk?" he suggested, gazing up and noticing the full moon on the eastern sky. "May be on the way, we might get a vehicle."

They started to walk. About five minutes later, a vehicle arrived, but it didn't stop. Another couple of cars came and went, they didn't stop for them.

Another fifteen minutes later, a light brightened up. "When it comes close," Abigale said, somewhat slightly cheerfully, "You hide, and I stop it."

"How? You got magic!"

"Wait and see," she laughed.

It was a car, and she stood on the driver's side. When it came close to her, she pulled up her long robe to the top of her thigh and raised one leg up in the air. The car gave out a loud noise as the break was applied before it went out of control and collided with an oak tree and stopped moving. They hesitated for a moment, as if unsure of themselves, then ran to the car. There was a middle-aged woman in it, with her face lying on the steering wheel – one hand hanging down on her side and the other holding the hand break. She stared at him breathlessly. "She dead?"

Mathew cast his eyes through the side window. He slowly opened the door and moved his face closer to the woman inside. "You alright? Are you alright?"

She didn't reply.

"Is she breathing?"

He looked at her carefully. "I don't think so."

"My god," Abigale cried quietly, "two deaths in two hours?"

Exactly at that moment, he saw her hand moving on her side. He asked quickly, more hopefully, "Are you alright, dear? Can you hear me?"

No voice was heard for an answer, nor did any other motions in her body appear.

"What happened, dear?" Mathew asked in utter frustration.

Again, her hand moved, and more than last time. He looked over the car and met her eyes. "Hand moving."

Abigale didn't speak.

At that time, she slowly raised her hand from the break and held the steering wheel. And again, slowly, she pulled back her head and stared at him, an inexplicable horror in those eyes. "You are real?"

"Yes, dear. My name is Mathew."

She waited a good minute. "My name is Thalami. I'm a doctor."

"I'm glad to hear that. And that you're recovering!"

"Thank you. But I don't know what happened. My mind went blank."

"You're tired, I think."

Dr Thalami hesitated. "I thought I saw a ghost."

He stretched back his body and looked over the car, pulling a ridiculing gesture at his partner. "Yes, Dr Thalami," he looked back at the doctor. "I always see a ghost. But I get away with it." He paused vaguely. "Anyway, dear, where are you going to?"

"Kondakko Hospital. Do you know the way, Mathew."

"How lucky you are!" He turned to look at Abigale. "Do you mind if I drive her to the Kondakko Hospital? I don't want her to see a ghost again."

"Petrifying it was," the doctor said, still feeling the effect of the shock. "A woman ghost pulling her clothes up."

"Disgusting. Absolutely disgusting! Even if a ghost, she needs her bloody manners." He looked at her, asking, "Don't you think so dear?"

137

Without saying anything, she laughed.

A moment later, the doctor asked quietly. "Do you know the way to Kondakko?"

"Not really. But my partner knows this area."

"Oh! Thank you."

Mathew checked the car. It was dented in front, but no problem for driving, and the petrol tank was reasonably full.

They reached Kodakko at about 11 o'clock. They parked the car at the doctor's parking bay, saw off Dr Thalami to a nurse at the hospital's front door, and then took a taxi to his cousin's house, which was less than a mile away.

When Peter Atkinson saw them outside their front door, he felt a tremble springing from the bottom of his abdomen. He screamed in a mixed voice of alarm and caution, "Get in quick."

They got in quickly. Peter picked up their bags from the taxi and paid the fare. He stood there watching the taxi go in the distance. He also watched whether any military vehicles were anywhere in sight. Everything was okay, so he ran in and shut the door behind. "You alright, Peter?"

"No," he replied quickly. "Yes, I am alright. But the army men came here three times this evening. We'll talk about it later."

"I don't believe it."

"Neilanku's wife saw him taking you across the river."

"That's mean we're not safe here."

"I've worked out the plan."

"What's it?"

"My brother-in-law, Adai, is waiting in a car at the back of the garden. He will take you to Makolo, where his sister lives alone. It's a hilly area. Margaret will hide you there as long as it's necessary."

"Okay," Abigale answered nervously. "We'll go right away."

"Please go. I don't want to see junta men taking you away."

"Where do we find Adai?"

"At the end of the garden door." He glanced out to the road fearfully. "Please go quick."

"The roads to Makolo are safe?"

"Adai won't use much of the road."

"What do you mean?"

"He drives through any open place, like parks, and you don't need to bother about it. You'll be alright. Come on, let us go to the garden."

They went to the garden.

"Adai lives on the way. You can pop into his house. Have something to eat and then continue the drive. Anyway, he knows all this."

"Can we meet a doctor here for Abigale?"

"Good. His sister Julia is a nurse. She will arrange all that."

Peter and Abigale hugged each other. "God will look after you. Go peacefully!"

"Thank you, Peter."

Peter hugged Mathew. "I'll come and see you when it's safe."

"Thank you."

They walked down the garden and then moved over to a car parked under some bushes. Adai had known Mathew and Abigale over the years. He came out and welcomed them, then opened the door for them. "Please drive carefully."

"Mathew, you know I will do that."

"Abigale is pregnant."

"Congratulations. We'll go to my house, which is quite near here. And you can have a little rest and eat something. And then we go to Julia."

"Thank you!"

"Go slowly. I know the roads are not good."

"We use open grounds, which are in most cases better than roads."

"Okay. And thank you."

About 2 o'clock in the night, they arrived at Julia's house.

"Thank God, you're here," she said gracefully. "No government officers know this area. We're safe."

Mathew and Abigale were tired, so they went to sleep straight away. Adai stayed there, too.

Julia got up early and made a lovely breakfast. They sat round in a corner on a mat and ate it together. "That was lovely," Mathew said gratefully. "I enjoyed every bit of it."

"You were hungry," Adai joked. "But I don't think it was any better than the cheap takeaway."

They all laughed in unison.

Julia grinned, feeling shy. "I wasn't sure what to make."

Mathew slowly cut in. "You weren't sure what to make. And then you made this."

"You're making me quite jealous, Mathew," Adai complained. "When you ate my supper I made, you didn't say a word."

Abigale laughed softly. "We were busy eating. And forgot to say anything."

After breakfast, the men sat in the veranda. And a few minutes later, the women joined them. "Abigale needs a medical check-up," Mathew raised the subject. "Any idea, Julia?"

"It's a miracle that you came out of the jungle alive. When Adai was telling me last night, I was petrified to death. Anyway, let's praise God. He was with you."

Adai asked seriously, "You can take Abigale to Dr Yoruba?"

She waited thoughtfully. "Dr Yoruba is a good doctor. I used to work with him. Now he's retired but runs a clinic from home."

"Where?"

"Not too far!"

"Can we go now?"

"Yes, Mathew. But you don't say much about your situation. We can't trust anyone; that's the political situation now. I will tell him Abigale is my sister. And you're a friend."

Adai drew them to the clinic. Dr Yoruba was there, and he examined Abigale thoroughly. In the end, he saw Julia and Mathew and said that Abigale and her child seemed to be okay now."

"Now? What d'you mean, doctor?"

Dr Yoruba looked down at the notes he had prepared while examining her. He looked up at them intermittently. "Our political reputation is terrible at the moment. Maybe it will be bad for a long time, as long as President Adloo Johnson is steering our country."

Mathew and Julia shot a glance at each other, then looked back at the doctor. "Is it as bad as that, doctor?" Mathew asked.

"Worse than that," he replied instantly. "Most of the foreign countries, especially European countries, are putting up sanctions against us. Did you know that?"

Mathew shook his head silently.

"That means we don't get medicines, food, clothes, oil and the rest. We'll be finished as a nation."

Julia or Mathew didn't speak.

"If Abigale needs English medicines, and our stock runs out in this country, what will we do?"

They remained silent.

The doctor stared at Mathew for a moment. "I think you're English?"

"I am born here, but my parents are English."

"Send her to England. She and her child will be safer there."

"Thank you, doctor."

142

A FEW TALES

After a few more minutes, Mathew listened to the doctor before he went to the reception and met Abigale. "Did he give you any prescription?"

"Yes. Julia is buying it at the chemist."

Another few minutes later, Adai drew them back to Julia's house. It was about 10.50. At 11.50, Peter Atkinson's wife, Edith, arrived discreetly. The military junta raided their house last night at 2 am. They arrested Peter and took him to prison. In addition to this, they raided the colonial house at 1 o'clock and seized Chellangu, Abigale's mother. They claimed that they had ground reasons for these actions. Kiadi, Neilanku's partner, saw him taking Abigale across the river. And she couldn't remember whether anyone else was in it. The ferry was away at the midway point of the river, and the light was fading fast. Now, there was no sighting of Abigale or Neilanku. So much blood was found in the ferry, scattered around on one side of the hull. How did it come about? They had to find out.

"Edith, please don't let Abigale know that her mother is in prison now."

"No, Mathew. I know that."

"This house is also not safe. They will find out."

"How soon can we get two tickets to London?"

"There are no flights to any countries. Our airport is closed."

"Good heaven. Alright, which is the nearest airport? I suppose it's Lusaka, the nearest."

"Yes. But it's 400 miles that we are talking about."

"As much as that?"

She nodded for an answer. "The roads to that place are terrible. She won't make it."

He was thoughtfully quiet.

"And they'll pick you up at the border security point."

"What's the solution, Edith?"

"There is a ship leaving tonight from Kavula Harbour, which is about 5 miles from here. I knew it from my aunty – my mother's sister."

"What about the security check-up?"

"We're a bit lucky on that at Kavula. Alkesh, my aunt's husband, is the harbour manager. And he should know one or two shortcuts to the ship."

"Thank you, Edith."

"Adai will take me to the harbour. I better see my uncle early."

"Okay!"

"The roads are very bad to there. It takes one hour to get there. But we'll be back as soon as possible."

"Thanks."

"Don't stay in the house. Hide behind some bush. They might come here looking for you."

"Julia knows the area well. We'll hide ourselves somewhere."

About 3 hours later, Edith and Adai returned when Mathew and Abigale were hiding in the bush about 500 meters away. Even if the junta managed to raid Margret's house, they wouldn't get any evidence that they had been there or where they were hiding.

Edith was absolutely pleased when she and Adai returned. The ship that would travel tonight was a cargo vessel with limited space for passengers. It was a blessing from the sky because only a limited number of passengers could be present for the voyage, which in turn reduced the customs officers significantly, and being the departure starting at 4 am, they must be in deep sleep even if on duty. In fact, this cargo ship should have departed last night but was delayed due to engine difficulties. And hence, the crew and the passengers were bored and tired and waiting to resume the journey. And Edith's uncle had already made the arrangement to take Abigale straight to her cabin as soon as she approached the checkpoint.

At about 2 o'clock in the morning, Adai and Julia brought Abigale and Mathew into the harbour car park. They stayed in the car and watched whether any uniformed policemen or military members were present. In the end, they agreed unanimously that none of them were anywhere there. Abigale said bye to them, and then she and Mathew got out. "Please wait here."

"Okay, Mathew," Adai replied, "I stay here. Julia will come with you."

The three walked up cautiously through the car park and into the harbour hall. They stood behind a heap of goods in bags. A clerk from the shipping office came to them. He glanced around, and when it was safe to talk, he whispered to Mathew, "Who are you?"

"Mathew."

"Yes."

He took a small envelope and gave it to Mathew. "It's the ticket. Manager Alkesh got his friends on duty. All okay. I will come to take Abigale in 30 minutes."

Without adding further, he left.

"Why is he taking only me, Mathew?"

He shot a meaningful glance at Julia before he said, "Please promise me, darling. You'll listen to me now."

"What is it?"

"You have to go alone."

"You brought me all the way to here to tell this?"

"Please listen. Militia men raided our house in Atlantica city."

"Yeah?"

"They took away your mum."

"What for?"

"Mum refused to answer."

"What?"

"They asked mum where we are."

Without saying anything, she stared at him.

Mathew caught her eyes uneasily. "He raided our factory. And the office. And last night, he also raided Peter's house."

Abigale continued to be silent.

"Adloo Johnson's father, Marvin, used to work in our factory when I was a little boy. Things will quieten in 3 to 4 weeks' time. Normally, it does. I will see Marvin secretly, and let me see how I can get mum out. Of course, money will do the talking. And at any cost, I will get mum out. Then, I will go to some other airport and come to you."

She started crying. "I love my mum."

146

He held her close to him. "I love mum, too. I will get her home as soon as possible."

"I love you."

"I love you, too."

"But you're forcing me to go away?"

"Because I love you. And our baby. And I want to make sure you are safe and sound wherever you are. And when mum is home, I'll sneak to some other airport and come to you like a flash."

Abigale waited, confused.

"This ship is going to London. But they have a stop at Plymouth. You get off there, and as you come out through the nationality checkpoint, you'll see my dad waiting at the door."

She waited as emotions clogged up in her throat.

"You've enough cash with you. Take care of it."

Silently, she nodded.

"And all your legal documents are in your hand luggage."

"I wish......." she managed to talk with difficulty. "I hadn't met you at all in my life."

"Tell me when I meet you in England."

Julia saw the clerk coming back. "Your time is getting ready, Abie," she said, moving closer to Abigale. "The clerk is coming."

The women hugged each other. "We'll pray for you."

"Thank you." And then she turned back to him. "Whatever happens," she said to him, tears trickling down her eyes, "remember, I will always love you."

"Remember, I will be with you sooner than you think."

They hugged again and kissed. "Be happy. You're going to England. Everything will be fine."

The clerk took her luggage and waited for her.

Abigale came off the hold of Mathew, saying, "Look after yourself. And I will be waiting for you."

Mathew nodded silently.

Abigale followed with the clerk. However, she kept looking back and waved goodbye. He and Julia were still behind the heap of goods, waving at her. Shortly, she arrived at the custom's door. She stood there for a moment and, looking at him, sent a goodbye kiss before she walked in through the door and disappeared.

They hung around and watched the ship moving away from the harbour and heading out into the sea. The clerk came back shortly. "Mr Mathew," he said happily, "everything went well. And Abigale is on her way to England."

Mathew thanked him and cautiously left the hall with Julia.

Adai was wide awake, sitting low in his chair and alertly watching who was coming into the harbour and going back. "Abie is gone?" He quickly asked.

"Yes, Adai," Julia replied sadly, getting into the car. Mathew followed her and sat down on the floor in between the front and back seats.

"You okay, Mathew?" Adai asked. "When we are out through the gate, we'll be alright and Mathew can sit up on the seat."

She said, "He's fine."

"Alright. Let's go," Adai said, obviously nervously. "This place is making me nervous."

Adai started the engine while they all checked the car park once more for safety. "All looking good," he said while driving forward quietly.

They came around the exit way to the gate. There were normally two securities in the cabin. Only one was there now. He didn't bother to come out and check. He was in a mixed state of sleepy and tired. He just opened his eyes narrowly and saw the driver and passenger. He waved the driver to go, and Adai moved the car out of the gate and then onto the road. "How are you, Mathew?" Julia asked caringly.

Mathew was literally on the floor with his head resting on her lap. "Okay."

"Let him stay there," Adai replied strongly. "I feel very nervous."

"Why?"

"I don't know. But when I feel like this, the omen isn't good."

"You and your omens!" she whispered, slightly annoyed. "Just drive carefully."

Adai didn't speak. Instead, he sped the car fast. He passed Kavula and was heading through the open countryside called Maruka wilderness. This zone was sparsely clustered with small trees and bushes and stretched all the way to Makolo village. Above the tree lines of Makolo, the colours of dawn were rising.

They came further up and passed the Maruka T junction, where a police van overtook them and asked them to stop. "Hoi. Hoi?" They shouted as they approached the car. "Are you having a lonely racing? Or World War Three broke out?"

Everyone in the car was silent.

Two policemen stood outside the driver's door. "You're coming from the harbour? Got smuggled items?"

"We've nothing," Adai replied, clearly petrified.

"Get out. We've to check the vehicle."

"My sister in the back. She's sick."

"I can see her there. What's in her lap? Gold?"

Another three policemen crowded on the other side of the car. "It's a white man's head," one of the three shouted, staring through the window. "How did this national thief get in this car?"

Margaret cried loudly. "This is my husband."

"A national thief, your husband?"

"He isn't well."

"Alright. You all are under arrest. We will take you to the station."

Chapter 4

Earlier Days and Darker Dawns

Part 1: Jeffrey and

The rain started about 9 o'clock in the morning. It was very light at first for a good while, then began to pour down heavy and constant. Suddenly, the water was everywhere, gushing down the gutters, filling the ground in front of the house, and flowing on the road right outside. The heavy pouring continued until one o'clock before it turned gradually to light drizzling. With it, a quiet atmosphere returned, and a view of the distance cleared. However, there wasn't much space. The clouds drifted above the tree lines, the horizon appeared black and frightfully close, and even the sky hung low. The world was shrinking, and everything else was diminishing.

The rain resumed at about four o'clock, this time severely torrential and backed by strong winds that howled as they passed the terrain. Occasionally, the gusts of winds lashed against the window, and the panes on loose hinges jostled. The worst was the front door, which had never aligned accurately against the frames, and at times like this, water found its way into the hallway. reminded Daniella a few times during the day to be careful of the wet floor and not to fall.

She looked at the clock on the wall; it was twenty-past six. Jeffrey should generally be home by four. 'Must be the weather keeping him late,' she reassured herself. She wouldn't like to see him arriving late after work because, in all honesty, he would be drunk and, sometimes, very drunk.

The rain sustained its hammering; the wind howled far and wide. A few times, lightning flashed the abyss without its usual peal of thunders. moved

151

the edge of the curtain and peered out the window. It was already dark, and the visibility didn't extend further than fifty yards along the terraced houses.

In the end, Jeffrey arrived. She rushed to the hall while he was entering the hall and said, somewhat concerned. "Wet floor, dear."

"I know," he replied in a frustrated voice. "What day!"

Suddenly, she breathed a sigh of relief. He wasn't drunk. She had a glimpse of the courtyard before he shut the door. She spoke quickly, "Good Lord. It's a pond outside."

He took the towel she was holding and began to wipe his head and face. "Strikes, strikes. No buses, no taxis, nothing. Where is this country heading to?"

She didn't speak immediately. "How did you come?"

"A colleague dropped me at the top. I had to wait until he finished his shift."

He returned the towel, then moved over to the hanger and put his coat and jacket on it. They came to the sitting room. "Where is your treasure?"

She smiled slightly nervously. "Went to bed."

He stared at her. "Early?"

"You're late?"

He waited. "Meaning?"

She waited this time, obviously choosing the right words to avoid an argument. "Get you a glass of wine? You look very tired, dear."

He repeated, still staring at her. "Meaning?"

She laughed vaguely. "Can we eat now, dear? And we can have this conversation some other time, please?"

He looked away deliberately, whispering, "Whatever!"

They went to the dining room. They had vegetable soup, baked fish, and chips. had pineapple juice to drink, and Jeffrey had wine.

"Daniella is a very intelligent girl," she said, looking at him across the table.

He caught her eyes silently for a moment. "She told you that?"

She pretended that she didn't hear him. She looked back silently at the glass of juice that she was holding between her fingers. She took a large sip and then put the glass on the table. "I can read her mind like an open book."

"She is only three."

"I know that. But Jeff, you don't talk to her, do you?"

"I don't laze around, do I?" He said clearly annoyed.

She noticed that he was getting upset and that she was not talking sensibly, either. When the atmosphere was tight with tension, she would always talk about the wrong argument and in the wrong way. "Jeff, what I meant was," she said intentionally, trying to please him, "you are always out for work."

Without speaking, he finished drinking the wine and went back to the sitting room. She hurriedly tidied up the kitchen and joined him. He was on the sofa, almost slumped. The television wasn't even on. She switched it on and sat on an adjustable chair, facing him. "Are you resting?"

He didn't answer immediately. "Does it matter?"

She tried to raise a smile. "Of course, Jeff."

"You got a refuge. Now I'm nothing to you?"

"Jeffrey, dear, we don't want to go into it again." She paused, seemingly struggling to contain the emotions. "She is our child, yours and mine. And that's all it matters now, please."

He moved around a bit on the sofa, searching for a packet from his trouser pocket, and pulled out a cigarette. He lit it up using a lighter, drew a deep puff, and blew out. The smoke rose in the still air, spreading like a stringless net, of which he was on one side, and she was on the opposite. He drew again and blew out. The strength of the net increased all the while, while the visibility between them was decreasing all the time. "I had a fine job in London," he finally spoke. "I worked over fifteen years there. And then I left it. What for?"

Without answering, she looked at him blankly. She had answered it several times years over, and the simpler she answered, the worse it clouded the air.

"I can't get a decent job over here. So, whatever comes my way, I take it. I worked in four places in the last three years." He stopped talking and puffed; his mind was interacting with the days he was thrown out or run away. "Doing cleaning the kitchens and toilets, or washing the crockeries or scrubbing the floors, or whatever. And what for?"

She didn't answer; her mind was completely devoid.

"Now I got this job at Mark's Transporting and Shipping. Well, in their hotel." He dragged a long puff and let out the smoke through his nostrils before he continued quietly, "I like it, the first job that I liked since I left London."

This time, she spoke quickly, though her voice was beginning to break. "Oh, I'm …. I'm glad to hear that."

"Definitely, you'll be," he retorted. "You want money." He angrily smoked the last bit of his cigarette and ground out the butt on an ashtray. "Money, money, and money. For you and your girl." He waited a moment and took a deep breath as though to say something unpleasant or painful. However, he wasn't in the mood to tell right now. He wasn't ready for it. Instead, he absorbed his thoughts and emotions.

In the end, she asked in a voice lower than a whisper. "Where do we go from here, Jeff?"

He cleared his throat and whispered back. "It doesn't matter anything now. I'll work as long as a job is there."

"I don't spend a penny unless it is absolutely necessary."

He was silent.

"What do you want me to do?"

"You always bring subjects about your precious girl. She wants shoes, clothes, or special food items. And on and on." He waited and stared at her to know whether she had anything to say.

She didn't say anything, though.

"But have you ever thought about the money? Or where is it coming from, my darling?" Again, he waited a moment, his eyes angrily meeting her gaze. "And you've nothing to talk about you and me. I mean, about us?"

"What do you…. you want me to say?"

"Oh, I don't know."

"You always find fault with me lately. So, I don't know what to ask or say. And I'm nervous." She paused and then started to sob, saying, "Then you drag my baby into everything. She is a lovely little child. What harm did she do to you?"

He sprang up and sat leaning against the back of the sofa. "That's correct," he retorted, pointing his hand at her. "It's your baby. I've nothing to do with her. And thank you!"

She stayed quietly for another few seconds before she got up and started walking towards the hall. His voice chased up her hauntingly. "Go. You can't face the truth. And sleep with your treasure."

She went up the staircase and entered Daniella's room. She closed the door and turned the lock in.

Jeffrey continued to sit there watching the telly, with another cigarette burning between his lips. A smoke could ease off the pressures of the mind, he whispered absently. It wouldn't be the first day she stayed away, and it wouldn't be the last, either. Recently, he couldn't talk to her about the difficulties of their lives. She would bring tension and tears into the conversation, then rush to hide in the second room.

Anyway, he was also waiting for the 9 o'clock news. It wasn't him alone; the whole country was desperate for some good news.

It was a period of economic troubles and political disputes. The unions after unions were calling out for general strikes almost every day for their grievances and better rewards. Their genuine concern was the record-high unemployment rate in the country since the 1930s, and they demanded huge investments in industries such as schools, hospitals, roads, railways, and coal fields. They adamantly argued that this would re-establish the progress in productivity and employment in the factory floors, shops, offices, travel sector, and building sites. No more factories or shop closures would be required, and they wouldn't dare shed staff but eagerly search for men and women to fill vacancies.

But the government took different solutions, as advised by the British Business organizations and the powerful media moguls, that investment in the economy would emerge into hyperinflation that would lead to major difficulties with overseas balance of payments, the sterling pound would deteriorate in the foreign money markets. To solve this mega-crisis, the Bank of England had to step in and increase the interest rate again, which would permanently pull shutters on shops and factories. The unemployment record, already the highest since the Great Depression of the 1930s, would head even higher, and the country couldn't afford to function properly. So, they chose the way out of it by more taxation and higher interest rates, which were known as the principles of austerity. The business units were closed down literally every day. Hard-working people like Jeffrey Smith couldn't find a regular job to bring home a steady income to feed the family. In the end, most of the ordinary workers were living with unpleasant work, unfriendly colleagues, trivial wages, and at home, unnecessary arguments.

Suddenly, he felt frustrated and got up, then turned off the telly and went upstairs. The bathroom was behind the landing space. A small bendy corridor completed the access to the rooms, a smaller room on the left side and then the front room at the end. He passed the corridor quietly, trying to listen to any voices from the smaller room. It was dead quiet up there, and he moved further to his room at the front.

He didn't go straight to the bed, neither did he turn on the light. Instead, he sat down on the edge, leaning against the headboard. The curtains weren't pulled in, and he could see the road outside and the hedges and fields to a short distance in the dim, dark night. Suddenly, like a silent lightening, the fragments of his life gleamed across his mind.

Part 2: The Couple's History

He was living in a semi-detached house in Ealing and working in Victoria, next to Victoria Station, London, in a restaurant called Mulberries. Debra grew up next door to his own house and worked for an insurance company, which was minutes' walking from Mulberries. There were days they travelled together to work or back. His shift varied, but she had a fixed time of Monday to Friday from 9 am to 5 pm. However, she would go to Mulberries for lunch with Jeffrey or for a chat. In the evenings, especially the weekends, they were always together, going to movies, some shows, or football matches. Otherwise, they would meet in one of their houses and spend time playfully arguing or fighting. Their gardens bordered a large meadow, and on a nice day, they'd creep in through the broken hedges, then run and run until they'd become completely exhausted. And they'd fall into each other's arms, hugging, laughing, and kissing. In a nutshell, they had enough time for each other.

They married in January 1953, and to be more precise, on Saturday 17th at 3 o'clock in St. Antony's Catholic Church in Ealing. All relatives and close friends of both families had been invited for the occasion and also for the reception at the parish community hall, a detached building on the right-hand side of the church. Debra was extremely tired but continued dancing, holding on to his neck, whispering into his ears. "We need a two-bedroom flat."

"Why, my darling?" He muttered back into her ears. "Are you too big for one room?"

"Shut up, will you! And listen, unless you don't want a smack."

"Darling, the parish priest is still here. He faints when he sees violence. So, be gentle, please."

She retrained the urge to giggle. Instead, she kissed his neck.

"Alright, two-bedroom flat. You want it now?"

She didn't answer directly. "I love children."

"Not now, darling. Your mother is at the dinner table."

"I want four children."

"All in one go."

"Yes, if you're man enough."

He glanced around in a mock annoyance. "Control your tongue," he said finally. "This is a church building. Dignity is paramount."

"Promise me you'll give me four children."

"My dearest honey pie," he said, meeting her gaze steadily, "I've had nothing more serious than this."

Jeffrey was twenty-three then, and Debra was three years his junior. Since the wedding, they have been dreaming about the day she would tell him she was pregnant with his child. She hadn't told him yet because she hadn't conceived. Hopefully, it won't be long. The time moved on slowly. The days circled around the weeks, the weeks rolled on to months, and the months returned in every new year. However, she hadn't borne a child, not even a pregnancy. In 1963, when Jeffry was 33 and Debra 30, her mother suggested to them to go for an adoption. She wasn't sure whether to accept the idea or refuse. The thought of adoption loomed over her head like tonnes of bricks. If a couple didn't have children, the blame would routinely go to the wife that she was not fertile. In Debra's case, she was prepared to accept any eventualities for a child, and if an adoption was the solution, let it be so. However, Jeffrey was against this idea – substitution wasn't a solution. If his wife couldn't have their offspring, sadly, they weren't meant for it. But he wasn't prepared for kissing someone else's baby.

However, in 1967, Dr Philippa Johnson moved into a salle of the hotel where Jeffrey worked at the time. This American doctor was very strict with the ingredients in her meals, and Jeffrey, amongst his duties, was put in charge of her diet and the condition and cleanliness of her accommodation. One day, while discussing the weekend arrangements, she asked him casually about his family. In his reply, it came out clearly that he wished he had a child, especially his wife, who was absolutely desperate for it. "Have you had a check-up?"

"No," he replied. "But Debra had many check-ups." He paused indecisively. "They say she's fine."

"They didn't check you?"

"No."

"No? Why?"

He stared at her, completely confused. "Men can also have problems?"

"Of course," she replied firmly. "I'm a gynaecologist. I've seen many men with infertility problems."

A week later, he saw his GP. Two weeks later, he had a thorough examination in Ealing maternity hospital. It took another fortnight or so before he finally got his result. It was heart breaking. He wouldn't be able to be a father. However, it didn't stop him there; he went on having numerous tests and check-ups. All in all, he had attended eleven hospitals, and seen sixteen doctors and consultants at various stages. In the end, they had come to the same conclusion that he couldn't become a father. He told Debra, "It's not a bad idea if we can adopt."

She caught his eyes. "Only if you are happy!"

He waited. "No other choices for us," he said slowly. "Everyone's calling me all sorts of names. I can't go on fighting with all of them."

"Of course not," she replied readily. "We adopt a child. "

He didn't speak; he was deep in thought.

"We'll move again to a new town," she added, clearly in an assuring tone. "Nobody will know us. And we say it's our child."

He hesitated for a moment, seemingly helpless. "I was thinking just the same. After all, it's a baby."

"Of course, darling," she said, hugging him. "And our baby."

They met the adoption agencies and discussed in detail their overwhelming desire to parent a child and become a family. The agency appreciated their approach and promised they would help them. In a month or two, they introduced four children with the option of adopting one child. Somehow, Jeffrey turned down the options; the children didn't look right. To be honest, one of them had a crossed eye, another child with one leg disabled, the third child of a foreign descendant, and the fourth with heart problems. Another three months passed silently, without any hope. And then, this call came from the South West, "Is it Mr Jeffrey Smith?"

"Yes, I am."

"Good morning, Mr Smith."

"Good morning. Who is calling?"

"This is Natalie Wilkes of Adoption Agency in Plymouth."

"Thank you." Suddenly, he could sense a tension creeping up his spine. "Oh, I hope you've some good news for me?"

"Yes, Mr Smith. We have a child for adoption."

He couldn't speak quickly. A gripping fear started to cripple him from toe to head. 'Is adoption going to be the heaven on earth for him?" A thought raced through his system. "Or is it the hell made in heaven?"

"Are you there, Mr smith?" Natalie asked, a faint trace of suspicion filtering into her tone. "Are you there?

He still couldn't find his voice or tell his decision. He knew very well that this was the time of his life to dictate the shape of his future. However, he was utterly helpless to decide or speak.

"Mr Smith, are you there?" she repeated the question, the trace of suspicion echoed clearly stronger than before.

"Yeh... yes," he managed to answer, his voice shaking.

"If you're not completely happy, please tell us honestly. There are other people who desperately need a child."

"Yes, I am completely happy."

"You're sure? I get the feeling that you have a change of mind."

"I'm very emotional. Please forgive me. I'm very happy. And my wife will be very happy, too."

"Good. You'll be happy. It's a sweet child."

"Thank you," he replied hurriedly. "It's a boy? A girl?"

"Does it matter?"

"Not at all. Just to know, that's all?"

"Well, it's a beautiful baby girl."

"Oh, my God," he said. "My wife will be over the moon."

"And you?"

"Absolutely thrilled."

"You like to see the baby?"

"Of course." He took another deep breath. "Sorry. I'm a little nervous and may be asking the wrong questions."

"That's okay. When can you come? Tomorrow?"

"No chance for today? We can leave right now."

"You may take four to five hours to get here. But we close in two hours."

"Alright, tomorrow, then?"

"12 o'clock, alright?"

"That's fine."

"I book the appointment for 12 o'clock."

"That's absolutely fine. And I also promise that my wife won't be sleeping tonight."

She said swiftly, in a pleased tone, "We'll see you at 12, and bye for now."

In normal road conditions, it would take about four hours to drive and two breaks at service stations, which meant adding another hour to the journey. But the hesitations kept playing up in the back of their minds whether it was worth taking the risk of driving all the way to Plymouth. They had wasted many hours before and faced many disappointments. "Why didn't you get more information?" Debra asked while they were getting into the car at six o'clock in the morning, which allowed another hour for delays due to possible road works or accidents.

Jeffrey took the car out of their driveway and then headed up the road. He briefly looked at her and said, "You can't ask lots of questions."

She stared at him, confused.

"We don't know how they take our questions."

"So what?"

He stopped talking and concentrated on the road as they approached a sharp corner. He pulled the car safely through and replied, "They study us through our questions and conclude what sort of parents we could be."

She stared at him rather concerned.

"We speak when we've to reply to something. Or speak when it is necessary."

"I know, darling. But it is not an easy matter adopting an unknown child."

"True!"

"We've to speak when we've to."

"Of course!"

"Hopefully, it will be alright. Now, you forget it and drive carefully."

He smiled cynically. "Order is accepted."

They went through a few more roads before they came to a dual-carriageway. They turned right and accelerated towards the motor way. Suddenly, she spoke in a mixed voice, tired, sleepy, and frustrated, "If we're not successful this time, that's it. No further frustration! We're not meant to have a child. And that's it."

An hour or so later, as they were going down the Motorway, known as M4, he said calmly, "I was thinking more or less on the same line."

"That's it, darling. This is too much to bear. And whatever happens, I've you, and you've me. And we live happily."

Smiling, he stretched his body and killed her on the cheek.

She kissed him back, then said, "Drive carefully."

At ten minutes to noon, they were at the door step of the Plymouth Adoption Agency, and they were certainly pleased that they were on time.

A young girl in the reception led them to the waiting room. "Please sit down," she said politely. "Someone will see you soon."

"That's fine," Jeffrey replied, sitting down on a chair. Debra sat down next to him.

"While you wait," the girl asked, "can I get you something to drink – coffee, tea?"

Debra shot a glance at her husband, then turned to the girl. "Coffee will be lovely."

Shortly, she brought the cups of coffee in a tray and placed it on a table in front of them. "Thank you," they said almost in unison. The girl smiled for an answer and returned to the reception.

They started to sip straightway. The warmth of the drinks pleasantly went down their throats. And they finished it before a middle-aged woman came up to them. "Good morning, Mr and Mrs Smith."

"Good morning," they said readily.

She took a seat on the opposite. "I hope the drive wasn't too bad?"

"No bad at all," he replied rather joyfully. "And we arrived on time."

"Good," she said, glancing down the corridor that led to the inner offices. She looked back at them. "My name is Gillian Moran. And I am in charge of the adoptions."

Without speaking, they looked at her.

"We've to go to the consultation room," She paused vaguely, then added quietly, "I don't take any decision of my own. I share it with the rest of the board. It helps if anything goes wrong. You never get everything right."

They continued to be silent.

"Besides me," she said, "four of my colleagues will participate in the meeting. Are you okay with this arrangement?"

They looked at each other for a moment before they looked back at her. "We're okay," Debra answered politely. "All we want is a child to love and cherish, and that's all we want to make our life complete."

"I'm very pleased to hear that," Gillian said, catching their eyes intermittently. "And on that note, let's go to the consultation room."

The consultation room was on the other end of the corridor. It was a spacious room with a large round table in the centre. Gillian Moran and her four colleagues sat down on one side and Jeffrey and Debra took their chairs on the opposite side. There were several questions about the total income of

166

the couples, the expenditures, and the long-standing debts. Some enquiries were based on their hours of work and their physical and medical conditions. The conditions of the house they had leased and the terms of the lease. All questions were set out to expose the truth that they could survive any natural difficulties and that the baby would be safe with them. They answered each question as accurately as possible and submitted relevant papers such as bank statements, pay slips, a copy of the tenancy agreement, and a letter from the parish church.

"I wonder what the baby's doing?" Gillian said finally, quietly laughing. "Shall we go and say 'Hello'?"

"About time," a female colleague joked. "We can't make her wait any longer. She gets annoyed."

They got up with their individual files and note books and came out, then entered into a room down the corridor. It was a small room, beautifully decorated in shades of pink and little flowers. In the middle, slightly near the window, in a cutely furnished cot bed, the baby lay silently. Her large black eyes appeared to be steadily staring towards the window. They moved closer to the cot and looked down gently at the girl. Her eyes slowly rolled back and met their gazes, strictly speaking, one by one, permitting a few seconds to each individual, and, in the end, landed on Debra's face and stayed stuck there. Her tiny little lips sprouted into a faint smile. Debra stood there, almost frozen, and then started sobbing. Jeffrey stretched his arms and held her to him. She dropped her head on to his chest, still sobbing, while whispering, "This is our child. I love her."

"Please, darling," Jeffrey murmured, "calm down. The child is watching you."

She couldn't stop sobbing. Instead, it grew faster and louder. "Let's go to the corridor," he suggested softly.

They started for the corridor. But at the doorway, she stopped walking and stood still, restraining her emotions. In a moment or two, her sobbing finished. She turned round and looked at the others. "I'm so sorry," she murmured, loud enough to be heard.

"We understand," Gillian replied, stepping towards her. "We know how you feel, dear."

"Thank you. Please, can I carry the baby for a moment?"

Gillian looked at the staff, then looked back at her. "Have you carried children before?"

"Many times, Miss Moran. Mainly my sister's children."

"Okay," Gillian said. "Please, be careful."

Debra came back to the cot and then stooped down. The child's gaze rose to her face. She took her very lovingly, her one hand holding the head and neck and the other supporting the waist and the legs. She lifted her up slowly close to her chest as she straightened up herself, watching her face all the while. She kissed her softly on her head and cheeks. And then she absently closed her own eyes. But she could see the baby more clearly now, in her heart and life.

After a moment, she opened her eyes and looked at Jeffrey standing by her side, "Would you like to hold the baby, darling?"

"Of course," he replied eagerly. He picked her up from her hand very carefully, kissed her cheeks, and then held her on his chest. "You're a priceless gem, aren't you, darling?"

Debra almost opened her mouth to speak, but Gillian's voice came out swiftly. "Well, you can stay here and play with the young lady," she informed politely. She gestured to an open door and added, "the carer is inside the room. You can see her if you need any assistance. And if you fancy something to eat, a couple of places are around the corner. The young girl in the reception will guide you."

They both answered immediately. "Thank you."

"And we'll see you in about an hour. We've some more work to do."

They repeated, slightly uneasily, "Thank you."

However, it took about two hours before they returned. And, again, they assembled in the consultation room. "Well," Gillian said, starting the meeting, "We spoke to our director, Ian Allely." She vaguely stopped as if searching for words. Jeffrey and Debra sat there, feeling a stiff sensation shooting up their spine. Luckily, Gillian continued quickly, "Ian has seen your papers, which you submitted to us early. He had made relevant enquiries, and he has received the results. He will shortly come and see you personally."

Debra and Jeffrey shot a glance at each other, then patiently waited for Gillian to continue.

Gillian stared at her colleagues impassively, then looked at them alternatively. "I can congratulate him on being very happy to trust you with the life of this amazing child."

Debra couldn't say anything. The sudden burst of emotions literally numbed her. But she felt the tears bubbling up behind her eyelids.

Somehow, Jeffrey managed to talk, with a breaking tone, "Thank you." He paused and moved in his seat to hold his wife. "Please give us a moment."

169

"Of course," Gillian replied. "We know how you feel."

After a short break, Debra managed to find her voice. "We……. we love you," she said in an emotionally frail voice. "We love you for this great kindness."

"Thank you," Gillian said, pleasantly laughing. "We have full faith in you that you'll raise our princess proudly."

Part 3: Finding Daniella

It was a strike's day. Jeffrey wasn't sure who was organizing it or the reasons for it. These days, strikes could erupt any time – whether it was an official protest supported by national unions or small groups that were creating local chaos to earn a few pounds on the side or achieve positions in the establishment, nobody knew. And nobody cared to know anymore either. The industry machines and services were put to halts even before the information would be sent out. In his case, the electricity was cut off, and the restaurant closed abruptly for the day.

He came home just before four in the evening. He found Debra in the small garden at the back of their maisonette with Daniella in a pink Moses basket. The four-month-old girl was well awake, and the mother was introducing her to various flowers and colours. She saw him as he came out through the back door and came towards them. She rushed with the baby and met him half way. "Our daughter is loved here," she said, laughing gleefully. "We're lucky to have this house."

Without saying anything, he bent a little and lifted the baby from the Moses basket. "Hello, cutie," he said finally, "how're you today?"

The baby looked at him silently and steadily for a moment, then turned to Debra. She picked up the baby's little hand and waved at him gently, whispering in a childlike voice, "I'm fine, daddy."

He glanced up at the sky, then looked back at the baby. "Isn't the sun a bit hot for the child?

"Oh no," she retorted, smiling pleasantly. "She's loving it. And the basket hood gives her the shade."

"Okay, then," he replied tersely. However, he stepped over to the shade of a pear tree that stood on the border; the child lay in his hands. Debra followed them with the Moses basket. "We've been here for an hour," she said, playfully biting the baby's cheek, and added, "You had your feeding. Didn't you, greedy girl?"

Whether the baby understood it or not, she laughed mutely. Debra watched her for a moment, as quietly as possible, then told her husband, "She got a beautiful laugh."

He didn't speak immediately. "Yes," he agreed. "I'm going in to lie down. You can stay here if you want to."

"I'm coming in, too. The young lady had a good wandering for today."

They went in through the back door and into the kitchen. He picked up a can of beer from the fridge and sat down on the sofa in the sitting room. Debra turned on the telly, and the channel BBC 1 was showing a children's show. She changed it to ITV, which showed a nursery serial. "What do you like?"

"Doesn't matter," he replied trivially, drinking from the beer can. "I'm going up soon."

He finished the beer and went up. He changed his clothes to a pair of shorts and a tee shirt and lay down on the bed. Debra gave a wash to Daniella, then fed her, and put her on the cot. She might go to sleep or stay awake, staring at the colours inside the cot. She went to the front room. He was flipping through a magazine. "What do you fancy for the supper, darling?"

He dropped it by his side and looked at her. "Whatever is there," he answered quietly. "If you want to, I can come down."

She burst into a gentle smile. "That's lovely!"

He got up. "I will make it. You can stay with the child."

"She's fine. If she cries, we'll hear it in the kitchen."

They made a chicken casserole, fried potatoes, and vegetable salad for supper. They served it on the dining table and sat down. They ate quietly in the beginning, then Debra asked, "Darling, what's wrong?"

He chewed the food slowly that he had in his mouth and swallowed it down. And then he looked at her. "Where have you been?"

Debra didn't answer immediately. Instead, she caught his eyes steadily. "We've a child now. We'd have liked two or three. But it doesn't matter any longer." She paused, seemingly searching for the right words. "Now we've a child, a beautiful child. Can't you see that? And be happy?"

He filled the wine glass and took a large sip. "It's more than that," he said calmly.

"What's that?"

"You want to tell everyone that it's our own child?"

"It's our child. We're the only two people she has. And who is going to know anything different if we don't tell them?"

172

"But our friends know that I can't father a child."

"That's why we left them all – and relatives, our jobs, and colleagues so we can have a new life. And most importantly, we can have a family life. That's all we wanted in our life."

He sipped mechanically and sipped again. "Since I left my Victoria job, I had three jobs and none any good," he whispered as if talking to himself. "And we got this little house in Harrow. And……."

She interrupted him. "It's a nice little place for our needs. And that's why we managed to adopt Daniella."

"But we can't afford it."

"We'll afford it. I'll find a part-time job."

"That will take years."

She hesitated, "Well, we'll get some family allowance soon, won't we?"

"That won't be much. They know we've some savings in the bank."

"Anyway, we'll manage."

He finished eating the food he had on the plate. He looked at the empty wine glass. He filled the glass halfway up and sipped a full mouth. "Do you know I came home early?"

"I didn't. I thought your shift finished early."

He shook his head. "Power cut," he said, somewhat annoyed. "The second one this week."

"That's not very good, is it?"

He nodded, his annoyance changing into depression. "If this pattern continues, they will close down."

Without saying anything, she stared at his face blankly for a moment. "Why is this happening?

"It's the fight between the unions and the government." He stopped talking and drank another mouthful of wine before he continued thoughtfully. "Inflation is rising, so union leaders want higher rates of wage increases. The government can't let it happen. Otherwise, inflation will go even higher. Ordinary people got no say but left out to bear the consequences."

She said, sighing heavily, "All miserable, frightening news every day."

There was a worrying silence. In the end, Debra said, "It won't be long."

She went up and had a quiet glance into the cot. The little girl was asleep. She threw a flying kiss to the little one and gently walked back from the room. She returned to the kitchen.

"You know my friend Kenny Jones? Well, not that much of a friend. But I know him.""

"I think so. Is the one who got a café in the city?"

"Yes. Actually, it was a restaurant."

"In Cannon Street?"

"Yes, that's the one."

"Which means he's Lizzy Jones's brother?"

"Yes, that's the one."

She stared at him, obviously angry. "You're going back to them?"

He caught her eyes silently.

"She's a bitch. Lucky, she didn't get pregnant with anybody. Otherwise, she would've said you were the father."

"Debra, it's totally unnecessary to talk about it now. And …."

She interrupted him angrily. "Is it? Lizzy is a whore. And you were one of her bastards."

He opened his mouth to speak, but he didn't speak. He looked outside through the small window behind him. She didn't speak either. A heavy silence engulfed them briefly. In the end, he said quietly, "Those days, we were young. And we made a few mistakes………."

Debra interrupted him again, but this time she wasn't as angry as before, "I didn't make any mistakes."

He turned back and caught her eyes. "Thank you, but I made!"

She didn't say anything.

"It was the sixties, a decade of wrong morals. The historians termed it, as 'the swinging sixties."

"What about Salome?"

"It was her father's fault?"

"Marcia?"

"Well, I'm not having this conversation, Debra. Because I've apologized for these over a million times, and that's that."

Debra remained silent.

A few minutes ticked away.

"I believe this is a good opportunity for us to go into business," he calmly said as if he was starting it fresh. "He closed down his restaurant in Cannon Street about six months ago. The landlord was nasty. He wanted a big rent increase."

She remained silent.

"He was working with me in Earls Court."

She didn't speak.

"Now he has found a new one." He reached out for a cigarette and lit it. He drew on it and blew out the smoke. "The current owners are retiring. Kenny wants to run it with me on a partnership."

This time, she broke her silence. "The partnerships normally end up in trouble."

"True," he quickly replied as though he was supporting her views. "But Kenny is a nice man. I can trust him." He fumed his cigarette and let the smoke out. "I don't want to work for others anymore."

"The rent will go up when you take over?"

"No," he said firmly. "The current owners renewed the rent for the next five years."

"When are you going to start?"

"Nothing confirmed yet. He can't run it alone. But if I say yes to it, he and I; we go and see the owners. And see what happens."

"Is Lizzy taking any part in it?"

"Lizzy's settled in Cornwall for some long time. And she is a trainee nurse up there."

"Do we have to put any money?"

"Yes. Our savings have to be used."

She didn't speak.

"Are you okay with that?"

"Of course. Where is this restaurant?"

"It's close to the health centre I worked in last year."

"Leonard Street?"

He nodded, then said, "Very close. It's in Tabernacle Street?"

"What's it called?"

"News Café. It's right next to the London News."

"I've seen the London News building. But I don't think I know the café."

"It's situated a little towards the back. But it's nice. A little open area in the front with a couple of tables and chairs under an oak tree. And the back of the shop also has a little courtyard with a few tables and chairs." He waited ambiguously for a moment before asking, "What do you think?"

"I know the area is lovely, busy, and vibrant," she answered with a thrill in her voice. "And we should take this opportunity for good."

The next day, Jeffrey met Kenny in the News Café and discussed the matters with a positive frame of mind. The restaurant didn't need any refurbishment or repairs. The existing kitchen arrangements were fine; the tables and chairs were in good condition; the cooking utensils were fairly new; the cutleries and crockeries were in amazing condition. Only one more item to be settled, and that was the amount of money for the goodwill. But the retiring owners – Barry Taylor and Muriel Jackson – were not in the mood for fudging for a penny on this. To be honest, the goodwill price was very modest. Very well then, Jeffrey and Kenny accepted the full asking price and signed on the contract.

When he came home, it was a real party atmosphere. Debra played her favourite pop songs and danced with him while the other hand carried Daniella in the basket. The music and movements made the little girl smile. She stooped over his strong hands and stared at the girl, telling happily, "You're a lucky baby, aren't you, sweetie?"

The child opened her mouth, seemingly smiling.

"And now you see, your luck's bringing us to success. We're more than a family now. We're starting our own business. Did you know that, sweetie?"

The baby smiled again.

Jeffrey and Kenny planned to open the restaurant in three weeks' time on 10th August and the year, of course, 1972. They registered a new company, where they both had an equal number of shares, which was fifty-fifty, and the accountants were dealing with these regulations. They applied for a business account in Lloyds Bank. There were more paperwork and little issues than they had anticipated in their earlier enthusiasm and inexperience, and by the time they had cleared them all, the time frustratingly went past by the weekend starting on Saturday, 26th August, and the bank holiday on Monday, 28th. Various local strikes and go-slow union policies constituted these disastrous delays. Finally, on the 31st of August, they were absolutely sure they could open the News Café on the next day, which was a Friday and the 1st day of September.

On August 31st, Jeffrey came home quite late in the evening. When he came, Daniella was in the cot bed, and Debra was watching a music show on the telly. She met him in the hall. "How did it go?"

"Everything went well, Debra," he replied pleasantly, giving her a pat on the cheek. "We are opening tomorrow, finally."

"Good. I'm very happy for you. You don't need to run around for jobs."

"Thank God! That's history now. We've something for ourselves to look forward to."

They moved into the lounge, and Jeffery sat down.

"I get you a drink?"

"Please. A glass of whiskey will be fine. Make it a double."

She was standing beside his chair. "Double?" She laughed.

"Why not?" He asked, joining in her laugh.

She poured whisky and slightly diluted it with ginger ale. He drank it rather hurriedly. She stared at him clearly amused. "You want another one?"

"I think we better go to bed now. I've to go early tomorrow."

Part 4: The News Cafe

The 1st of September was a beautiful sunny day. A good number of people, mostly the London News' staff turned up for the opening ceremony at 1 o'clock. The union leader, Jack Bennet, and a few of his close associates were present when they officially opened. Many other local celebrities – mostly from the media industries – attended, but no representatives showed up from the larger paper groups such as the Times, the Telegraphs, the Guardian, and the like.

Jack gave a short speech that highlighted the cooperation between Jeffrey and Kenny, and he added that this cooperation would grow stronger in the years to come. As a good example for our leaders in public lives, they should talk and listen and understand one another for the sake of our country. Everybody cheered his speech and applauded loudly.

It was absolutely a cheerful afternoon for business. The old and new customers turned up happily and had meals or drinks with snacks. Some of them even made the effort to introduce themselves and said they felt very sad when they saw the shop was closed. Jeffrey and Kenny thanked them all and promised them their best service. The café was meant to be closed at about 9 o'clock, but it stayed open until 11 o'clock to meet and greet the customers.

Jeffrey came home at about 12 o'clock, feeling absolutely exhausted. "I was worried," Debra said as he was coming through the doorway. "And nobody was picking up the phone."

Without replying, he kissed her, happy as a child. He struggled to the sitting room and then stumbled to a chair. "Pour whiskey, darling."

Debra asked, clearly surprised and happy, "What's happening today?"

He replied immediately. "Great business. And great customers. And great things should be respected gratefully."

She laughed innocently. "You talk like a poet. New Café turned you to poetry."

Suddenly, he got to his feet. "You sit down. Let me serve you professionally."

She stood, giggling. "Are you drunk?"

"No idea, darling. But we made some money."

He poured whiskey into two glasses. He handed one drink to her and held the other for himself before they chimed the glasses. "Long years of business and lots of money and lots of happiness."

She chuckled, "You're a poet today."

"Call me whatever you want to," he said hilariously, stepping closer to her. "But I'm happy for the first time after a long time. Let me kiss you and kiss the good time that's beginning in our way."

She didn't answer. Instead, she focused on listening to something. And she heard the baby crying upstairs. "Daniella's crying," she said, putting the glass on the coffee table and turning to the staircase. "Let me go."

"That's nothing," he said with a hint of annoyance. "One cry isn't going to kill her."

"We don't want to hear crying while we're enjoying, darling?"

"Enjoying?" He retorted quietly. "When was it we enjoyed?"

She caught his staring eyes gently. "Jeffrey, dear," he whispered nervously. "I'll be here in a minute."

"Don't bother. You stay with your girl, as you always do."

Her crying sound was heard more clearly. "It's our baby. And she's crying."

"Is it? Or is it a bastard?"

Now, Debra started crying. "Jeffrey, love. We love her."

"Alright, go."

She paced to the corridor hesitantly.

He turned back and sat down. The whiskey was still in his hand. He raised it to his mouth and drew a huge sip. He held it in his mouth, seemingly morosely, then swallowed it angrily. He drew another mouthful and swallowed swiftly. She was still there, and he could see her through the corner of his eyes. And the child was crying all the more loudly. "Go," he shouted. "And leave me alone."

"Speak quietly, please. You scare the child."

He moved in his chair and leaned against the back of the chair, then closed his eyes. "Bloody hell. I can't even talk in my own house."

The child was crying badly, so she went upstairs.

In the morning, Jeffrey got up early. "Builders coming."

Debra got down to the kitchen and made a soup and a couple of ham sandwiches.

"Why are they coming?" She asked in a drowsy voice.

"A bit of work in the kitchen," he replied, looking down and drinking the soup.

"Not opening the café today?"

"At 11. And all this week."

She remained silent

"Work should be over by Friday or Saturday."

She continued to be silent.

He chewed a bit of the sandwich quietly, still looking down. A moment or two passed away silently. "Monday on, we start at 8."

The kettle whistled, and she got up and made a cup of coffee for him. He drank it and then raised his face and caught her eyes. "I'm sorry about last night."

She didn't speak. Only a few tears drop down her cheeks as though for an answer.

"I was too tired."

She waited a moment. "I am used to it."

"Yea?"

"But you are upsetting the baby."

"It doesn't concern me."

"No?"

"It's you that concerns me."

She opened her mouth to speak, but she felt confused. And he went out.

The first month, September, went past smoothly, and so did October. Well, no changes were introduced to the routines that were in place. Besides, most of the previous staff decided to continue with the new management. And Barry Taylor, the previous owner, also stayed back for a short while to lend a hand if needed.

The bulk of the business grossed from the staff of the London News. In fact, until 1966, the News division owned the Café', and in that year, the café was subleased as the entire business structure was revalued and reorganized. With this history in the background, the news staff spent their time in the cafe, preparing a few essays and articles while a few others prepared news bulletins and headlines. If absolute secrecy was required, they would hold their meeting in the back room, which was used for storing goods. Now, the stocks were kept strictly to a minimum as fresh ingredients used in the daily cooking, which Jeffrey and Kenny, lately known as the Pair, believed would make the food tastier and, in time, would increase the business nicely.

However, their success was not as rosy as they had visualized because major difficulties sprang up due to their association with London News. To be honest, the Pair weren't aware of any of these in the beginning, but they were in the thick of the crisis now.

The London News publication was owned by a consortium which, in turn, was owned by left-wing politicians and various militant trade unions. As such was the background of existence, the daily and weekend editions and magazines reflected the owners' thoughts on the economy, politics, social issues, and internal affairs, and they fought for a socialist society while condemning capitalist anarchy. Nonetheless, the British men and women didn't queue up in the newspaper stalls to buy the revolutionary papers. In fact, they considered it a national disgrace to have publications of this ethos and substance. The London News perished in bundles in warehouses and retail units.

The financiers finally turned to their overseas counterparts and socialist revolutionary governments and agencies for support and funds. The support and funds did arrive in plentiful, in return for the publications of communist principles across the pages and on the editorial partiality. Accordingly, the papers gave platforms to whistle-blowers exposing numerous war crimes and atrocities of the British military in the Malayan Emergency, the use of biological weapons by the United States during the Korean War, and the mass graves of civilians killed by the South Korean government.

Suddenly, the British government, which had been already embattled with industrial strikes and production line picketing, geared up into action. The paper was brought under frequent censorship, numerous police raids, politically motivated libel suits, and various journalists tried for treason and persecuted.

The News Café also faced their share of the trauma. The police frequently questioned the staff and searched the Café. The worst thing to come was that the café was ordered to close several times, and the customers were told to leave the premises immediately after the police raided the café. With all these activities and the connection to the London News, the gossip circulated that the News Café was the mole of the reactionary forces, and the local people kept well away from the Café. The partners knew what was happening and what needed to be done. They had a good look around before they repainted the interior to a shade of buttermilk and the outside to brilliant white. They put up a new board with the name Family Café. And a new display board was raised on the roadside, 'Under New Management.' And the staff wore a new uniform of sky-blue colour. Overall, the Café looked magnificent. However, the sales struggled to pick up.

Part 5: Problems in Business

One cold Tuesday morning, the café wasn't open even at 8. A notice was hung on the shutters with the handwritten message, 'Closed for the morning, boiler out of work. Sorry.' A few regular customers stood on the pavement as if for loyalty, then they went away.

The doorbell rang, and Jeffrey opened the door. Jack Bennet was outside. "Good morning, Jack."

"I noticed that you're shut?" He asked, somewhat concerned.

"Yes, Jack. The boiler isn't working. Kenny knows an engineer. He went to pick him up."

Jack walked closer to the door. "You have no maintenance cover?"

"We have. But the engineering union is on strike today."

Jack waited as if searching for words. "Everybody is in trouble. The government is putting everyone in trouble."

"You want to come in, Jack? But it is cold inside."

"I better come in. Probably, I can have a look at the boiler." Jack walked into the café floor. "You're right, it's bloody freezing."

"I sent the staff back."

"Good. It's not right to keep them in this cold. Anyway, where is the boiler?"

Jeffrey took him to the back of the kitchen, then into the boiler room at the end. Jack checked the electricity first. It was okay; the water pressure seemed okay. He didn't have any tools to check the gas. Eventually, he turned to Jeffrey on his side. "I was a gas fitter a long time ago and worked with water heaters." He looked at the boiler again before he added less enthusiastically. "This is the modern version and a very powerful one. You better wait for Kenny to come with his friend."

"Anyway, thanks for trying," Jeffrey said. "Shall I get you a hot drink? I can use the kettle."

Jack stared at him, slightly puzzled. "No. Otherwise, you're having as well?"

"Yes, I am. And we can sit in the office. A little electric heater is there."

"Alright, I suppose. Anyway, I wanted to talk with you for some time."

He smiled faintly. "Now is the time, I suppose," he said, switching the kettle on. "At least you can keep me company."

He made two cups of tea and went with Jack to his office, which was by the short corridor before the kitchen. They settled at the small desk and turned on the heater. The Union man took a small sip and tasted it. "Jeffrey, it's a nice tea."

"Only the best. That's all I know."

The union man laughed graciously without adding further.

"What is it you want to talk about?" He asked, sipping on his drink.

"I want to know how you feel about union movements and political policies?"

He swallowed a large sip and stared at him silently for a moment. "I don't think I ever favoured any party or policies."

The hot air started to rise from the heater, and the air around the table was spinning pleasantly. The union man leaned against the back of the chair and looked at him across the desk. I'm sorry to hear that."

He met his eyes, smiling. "Why?"

"You talk politely and sensibly. You should join our union movement."

He laughed courteously. "I don't think it will make any sense."

"Why not? You got a good look. One of the necessities to be a politician or a union leader."

He laughed again. "I put on some ugly makeup."

The union man was silent and stared at him studiously. "It's not a laughing matter," he said in the end. "Because the country needs you and people like you."

He stopped laughing and sipped a mouthful of tea. Slowly, he swallowed it down the throat. "I never imagined anything other than an ordinary man."

"Absolutely right, Jeffrey. About 95 percent of the people think like that."

"What do you think we should do, Jack?"

He didn't answer immediately. He drew a huge sip while he looked at him over the cup. "Who rules the country, you think?"

"The government!"

"Oh, Jeff, you could do better than that."

"The political parties, shall I say? Now, the Tories are in the government."

"Not really."

"Who then? Edward Heath is the prime minister, as you know very well. And he's the Tory party leader."

Jack grinned deviously. "I know. And much more."

Without saying anything, he looked at him patiently.

"Right, Jeffrey," he said, sipping a small amount of the coffee. "The truth of the answer is the super rich. Such as landowners, industrialists, media moguls, and so on. They give large funds for the parties and keep the party under their influence."

Silently, he drank a bit of his coffee.

The union man laughed delightedly. "Alright, you mentioned Edward Heath and the party." He paused vaguely, meeting his stare. "Why are the protests and marches and pickets' line outbreaks of violence now? Heath knows that working-class people are suffering badly from poor wages and soaring inflation. Why can't he increase their wages to an extra couple of pounds rather than pence in their weekly pay packets?"

Jeffrey remained silent.

"Because the rich and powerful won't allow him." He stopped talking as if he was thinking or searching for accurate words to reflect the gravity of the situation the country was facing. "There are other issues, mainly the Israeli Arabs conflicts and the jump in prices for petrol and gas. However, the paramount duty of a government is to help the workingman feed his family. It's as simple as that."

He continued to be silent.

"Don't forget the fact that 99 percent of our population belongs to the working-class group."

Jeffrey broke his silence. "I think I read that somewhere."

Jack searched for a cigarette pack in his overcoat pocket and extended it to him. He picked up one and lit it. "The super-rich are only one percent of the population, who own 95 percent of the wealth of the country," Jack whispered in a depressed tone, lighting his cigarette and puffing on it. "It's murder."

"And the Labour Party?"

"Unions donate millions to their choice of leaders. They are all the same at the end of the day, no difference."

"These practices have been going on for a long time. Isn't it, Jack?"

"I know. But what's the benefit for the ordinary men in the street like you and me? Nothing. Absolutely nothing."

"What can we do about it?"

"We need a revolution, Jeffery. An endless revolution. Until everyone finds his income to feed, to clothe, and to house."

"That will be great as a dream, but will it be achievable?"

Off course. We can achieve it if we can organize a revolution."

"Something that Trotskyists are preaching for?"

He laughed as if he had gone suddenly agitated. "What a marvellous subject you brought over to over discussion. Thank you, Jeffrey. I like it." He laughed again loudly. "Leon Trotsky, what a man he was, full of imagination and ideas and crying out for world salvation."

Visibly anxious, he looked at the man quietly.

"We could have established Trotsky's vision here in our country when we had the 1930s when we had the economic depression. And then we could have helped other countries on every continent. Because we are everywhere, and the sun never sets in our world. But we were blind, and we couldn't see the glorious vision we had received from this great soul, Trotsky. We couldn't implement this magnificent salvation for the suffering people all across the world when we should have. Shamefully, it is too late now." He stopped briefly, seemingly disillusioned. "Now we haven't got the power we had once. Or the influence!"

"I don't think Trotskyism will work in this country or Europe."

"It will," he said in a triumphant enthusiasm. "We all got to work together, Jeffrey. And then it will work."

He sat there, almost immobile, catching his staring eyes. "I'm a married man, Jack. I have a child, too. And I invested everything I had in this business."

The union man laughed easily. "I know."

"And I'm not going to do anything other than manage this business."

"What about your social responsibility, which you ought to possess to support your comrades."

He hesitated as though he was facing a hurricane. "I am only good for cooking and feeding. And I'm happy about it."

"Alright," he said, getting up to his feet. "Just to think. That's all I'm asking."

Jeffrey got up, too. "Thank you, Jack."

He saw off Jack Bennet at the front door. He stood there watching the union secretary going up Tabernacle Square, then returned to the kitchen and poured himself a whisky. He took it to the office and engulfed a large drink.

On that day, they didn't open the café to the public. The boiler needed a new pump. They managed to get the pump and got the boiler working. But it was too late for the business.

The next day, Debra brought Daniella to the Café. It was a dark, freezing day, and the sky was covered with huge bands of grey clouds. Overnight, it snowed lightly but continuously, and by morning, the roofs and streets were partially under a thin layer of snow. However, Daniella wouldn't settle inside the house. She had wanted to go out. In the end, Debra thought about taking her to the café. She got there in a taxi. "What are you doing?" Jeffrey asked, absolutely annoyed.

She looked at him calmly. "I don't want to send her to the garden. It's freezing. And she'll catch a cold in no time."

He turned and looked at Daniella who was playing with Mavis, a temporary cook, at the back of the kitchen. "It's bloody embarrassing," he whispered, suppressing his anger.

"She is dressed for the cold weather. No one can see her body."

"What about the face?"

"What's wrong?"

"I'm white. You're white. And our beloved daughter is mixed race. What does it mean?"

"She's not that dark. Anyway, she is so beautiful, people wouldn't notice anything else."

Mavis moved back to them with Daniella. "She talks very nicely."

Debra tried to raise a smile. "She does, doesn't she? And she got a lovely vocabulary."

"And I like her tan, too," she added pleasantly. "Nice tan. You just came back after a holiday in the sun?"

Jeffrey had a quick irritation in his throat to vomit, but he managed to turn it into a cough.

Debra stared at him, obviously annoyed, before replying, "Yes, Mavis. Just two weeks in Tenerife."

Mavis courteously paced back to the cooker. And Daniella stood behind her mother.

Kenny was behind the cash till. He took a short break and joined the Smiths. "Why don't you go to the office with the princess." Stooping, he looked at the girl. "Ella, princess, what do you like? A glass of vanilla milkshake?"

Daniella shot a glance at her mother first, then nodded her head, smiling.

"And a slice of Cadbury chocolate?"

"Okay," she said this time. "And thank you."

Debra, bending slightly, said, "Say thank you, uncle."

She smiled reluctantly, then said shyly, "Thank you, uncle."

"And you, Debra?"

"A glass of juice, Kenny. And thanks!"

All of them settled in the office. Janet, a kitchen staff, brought their items and two glasses of beer for the men.

Kenny sat down and drank a mouthful of beer. "Looks like our sales are picking up," he said slightly cheerfully. "But we need the spending of London News' staff. Without them, we can't pay our expenses."

"Well, when is the court ruling coming out?" Debra enquired.

"On Monday," Jeffrey replied. "The government against the London News. I don't think this time the News will get an easy exit. And........."

"They will," Kenny cut in gently. "Otherwise, hundreds of jobs will disappear. Everybody knows that."

"What's the government's concerns?" She asked. "Anything new?"

"They don't want a left-wing newspaper in London," Jeffrey answered, looking at his daughter eating the cake slowly with a spoon. He looked back at his wife. "And they think these owners are dealing in money laundering with the communists abroad."

She listened without saying anything.

Kenny added quickly, "Some of the funds go to the striking unions. In other words, our enemies are controlling the unions who are fighting with our government."

Nobody spoke immediately, and an uneasy calm drifted around them.

"Well, we wait and see," she whispered. "Anyway, our business is definitely picking up."

Another silence elapsed.

"The princess loves the cake," Kenny said, glancing at the girl.

"She loves anything if she is in the right mood," Debra replied softly, deliberately not to disturb her eating.

All three of them watched her happily. A minute or so later, Kenny whispered.

"Seems like the princess is having a nice tan," Kenny murmured fondly. "Having a tan in the middle of the winter. Please tell me the secret of it, darling."

Jeffrey and Debra shot a glance at each other. Nonetheless, they didn't say anything.

On Monday, the court verdict was announced. It severely punished the management of the London News with a substantial financial penalty. However, it allowed them to start publishing the newspaper with honesty, decency, and accountability to the public.

Jeffrey and Kenny raised glasses of champagne for the good times to come.

Three days later, the London News appeared in the streets, and this time with more vengeance on the business entrepreneurs, elected national government, and peace-loving general public, but wholeheartedly supported the militant unionists who advocated for severe violence along the picket lines. Another week later, the News serialized articles about the Korean War, furnishing evidence of the use of biological weapons by the British Airforce jointly with the United States. The government acted immediately, as the national security was left open, and dragged the News back into the courtroom. In three days' time, the paper was closed yet again. In three weeks' time, it was banned from publication for three months.

Jeffrey left the café at four o'clock in the evening to get home early. He was absolutely shattered by the news of banning the News. He should be home by five o'clock, he thought absently. Along the way, the bus stopped by flying pickets, and it was 10 o'clock before he arrived home. Debra was putting Daniella to sleep. She came out and met him in the corridor. "Why are you late, dear?"

"Strikes," he said under his suppressed distress. "Bloody strikes." He moved into their room and sat on the edge of the bed. "You can't even travel these days."

She stood at the foot of the bed, staring at him steadily. "Shall I go and serve your supper?" she enquired quietly.

He shook his head before answering rather sullenly, "Whiskey."

She brought his drink and sat next to him. He had a couple of sips hurriedly. For a few minutes, neither of them said anything. "What's the way out of it?" He said as if he was thinking loudly. And before she could say a word, he answered it for himself. "None whatsoever!"

She asked in a reassuring voice, "Any response to our business sale advertisements, dear?"

He waited. "Not a single decent enquiry yet," He sipped his whisky again. The head lease belongs to London News. Will anybody dare to buy it besides all these general strikes and power cuts? And even the government isn't stable at the moment. Who will take the burden of running a restaurant in these chaotic times?"

Another uneasy minute elapsed.

"You think Kenny can buy our share?"

He hesitated. "He put all his money into the business. And we put everything in it."

"Will the bank help?"

He shook his head slowly. "We owe a lot of money to the bank. "

"What are you thinking, dear?"

He finished his drink and put the glass on the bedside cabinet. "Declare bankruptcy and close it down."

"What about the money we invested?"

"Forget it."

She sighed heavily. "All?"

He slumped back heavily against the headboard. "Every penny of it."

She hunched forward and placed her elbows on her thighs, then propped up her face in her hands. They stayed for a long time without any words. It was absolutely still, except for their breaths.

"Christmas holidays are not far off," he muttered in the end. "Sales should pick up."

"And then the January 1st holiday," she joined in slightly cheerfully. "And on the same day, we are going to be part of the European Union."

"True."

"Bound to be some parties and celebrations for it. We should get some extra business."

Christmas holidays came and passed, and January 1st came passed, but the sales didn't show any sign of improvements. On the 31st of January, there was no money at all in the bank account to pay the rent. The overdraft arrangement was also used up. On the first of February, the News Café went into liquidation.

"Can you go back to your old job in Victoria?" She asked, looking at him across the kitchen table.

Without replying, he sat, looking down on the empty beer glass.

"Six weeks has gone since we closed down. And how long more can we go?"

He continued to be quiet.

"The housing benefits alone don't keep us going much longer."

He remained silent.

"The child doesn't know our new situations, does she?"

He raised his face and stared at her. "I'm trying to find a job," he replied, obviously annoyed. "But there aren't any jobs I want to do."

"Try anything you can get. At least for the time being!"

"That's exactly what I am trying to do. But it's the bloody economy in the country. Nobody is taking new staff, unless it's very important to them."

"If you go to Victoria, they will find something for you."

He hesitated. "How can I?"

"Why not? Most of your friends are still working there."

"That's the problem."

She turned her face towards him. "What do you mean?"

This time, he hesitated a longer while. "We told everyone that she's our child."

"Because she's our child!"

"But, Debra, we're white. But the child is a mixed race. What does it explain?"

"They don't need to know that?"

"But they all know it."

With a sigh of tension, she dropped her face back into the hands. "She's a good tan, that's all," she said rather downheartedly. "But she's not a mixed-race child." She went quiet briefly. "And if she is, what does it matter to anyone."

He didn't say anything further. In fact, neither of them said anything before they fell asleep.

In the morning, they were having breakfast. "I know a man in Bristol," he said, chewing his bacon sandwich. "He says a company is looking for a chef. I'm going to make some enquiries today."

A FEW TALES

The enquiries turned out to be fruitful. Hughes Transports employed him in the chef position in their Workers Restaurant, and he would start work there in three weeks' time on the 2nd of April 1973. He and his family arrived in Bristol a week early and rented a two-bedroom terraced house. The back garden was in a neglected, terrible state, but as if to compensate for this drawback, the house overlooked a beautiful park that rolled over in the distance.

Hughes Transports was a large company with about 100 vehicles of various sizes and located fairly close to the junction of motorways M4 and M5. They picked up goods from anywhere in the UK and delivered them anywhere. They stored goods in the warehouses until they had to be delivered and carried to the airports, docks, or factory gates. They had four massive warehouses clustered around at the far back of the compound and a large packing hall in the middle. About 300 people worked for the company in the three shifts known as the early day shift, late dayshift, and the night shift, and this number included the warehouse staff, drivers, and the mechanics, but the office staff were excluded.

The 2nd of April was a Monday, and Jeffrey went in an hour early at 5 am. It would give him a chance to feel the atmosphere in the kitchen before he'd officially take over the work at 6 am. He met some workers, had a pleasant introduction, and talked to them. Their shift was going to finish when his time started. They showed him the dining hall, the kitchen appliances, the storerooms for food and drinks, the crockeries and cutleries, and the washing places. At 6am, when he was starting, he already had a good idea of the kitchen arrangements and what to expect during his shift.

Until 9 o'clock, it was breakfast time. If drivers returned late, they would still be served. The lunch started at about 12 and would finish at 2 pm, and again, special adjustments were in place for drivers who might arrive even later. The shift progressed smoothly, and Jeffrey felt a little proud of himself. But at one o'clock, everything came to a halt as the leaders of the transport and general workers union declared general strikes in solidarity with the striking miners' union. Under the frightful eyes of the management, the workers walked out.

The company hung up a notice on the main gate, which read, 'The Hughes Transport company closed until further notice.'

Chapter 5

Stormy Weather and Rumpling Thunders

Part 1: Meagre Jobs

Debra was in the front bedroom when the door gate reverberated on its hinges. She looked out the window and saw Jeffrey coming in through. He waited momentarily to shut the gate before he turned back to the door.

Debra had been thoroughly cleaning the room. She stopped all of it and stepped out to the corridor. She shot a glance at Daniella through the open doorway. The girl was at her table and adding colours to some sketches of scenes. "Alright, sweetie?"

The girl didn't catch her gaze or reply. Instead, she shook her head for an answer, her eyes staring down at the sketches and mind concentrating on the colours.

The mother smiled as if pleased, then rushed down the stairs. Jeffrey took off the hat and hung it on the hanger. She stood by his side, her eyes on his face. "You okay, darling?"

He didn't answer. Instead, he removed his coat and put it close to the hat. "What a terrible day," he said finally. Absolutely annoyed. He turned his head and met her eyes. "I wasted the whole day for nothing."

She put her hand on his shoulder. "Never mind," she whispered in a calming tone. "Let's go to the kitchen."

She led the way, and he followed down the short corridor. She pulled out a chair from under the table. He sat down on it, sighing quietly. She moved to the cooker, put a bowl of water on it, and then turned on the fire under the neath.

Neither of them spoke until she came back to the table with a coffee. He picked up the drink and looked into it. "Black?"

"No milk, dear," she replied as easily as possible. She didn't want to worry him.

He sipped a small amount and swallowed it hurriedly. Obviously, he didn't like the taste. "Well, it's nice to know how black coffee tastes. You know I never had it before."

She smiled vaguely. "Shall I make something?"

Without speaking, he nodded lightly.

 "What would you like?"

He waited a moment. "A bacon sandwich. Or whatever."

She went back to the cooker.

"I went three places today," he said rather depressed. "And wasted a whole day for nothing."

"What happened?"

"I was with Mr Watson, the actor, and worked over an hour. And then the electricity's gone." He drank a sip of his black coffee. A faint expression of dislike of taste showed up on his face. "I've to go again tomorrow. Two days' travel and work for one day's money."

"Never mind, darling," she chuckled. "These things won't happen every day, do they?"

He was silent for a moment before he spoke again. "I went to see Sidney Barnes, the disabled builder."

Sidney had been a successful property builder and made a fortune. However, one windy afternoon, he lost his balance on the ladder and fell down. He didn't know anything for three days, then he woke up from a coma and started to swear at the medical staff around. It was definitely highly applaudable as it reconfirmed that he had recovered the faculty of his normal conversation. Three days later, they found out the painful fact that he had lost his power completely below the waist. This accident happened in 1971 when he used to drive a range of sports cars to go out. Now, in 1973, he went out in a wheelchair, powered by a man. It had to be a strong man because Sidney weighed about 18 stones. Somehow, two days a week, Jeffrey pushed him in the wheelchair in the city centre for two or three hours, depending on Sidney's mood.

Suddenly, Jeffrey wasn't sure whether Debra had heard him mention Sidney. "I went to see Sidney Barnes," he repeated.

She had wanted to make a couple of bacon sandwiches, which he liked very much. She ran through the whole fridge for bacon. Sadly, it wasn't there. In a small packet, she found a few slices of ham. And she changed the sandwiches to it. She was preparing it when she heard Sydney's name again. "You can't push him every day, dear," she protested, turning to look at him over her shoulder. "You will break your back."

"Three days' wages and a bit of state hand-outs won't get us through a week, will it?"

She turned back to the cooker. "You've to find another little job."

Jeffrey didn't say anything immediately. Instead, he moved in his chair and leaned heavily against the back. "It's not easy to get anything now," he uttered utterly hopelessly. "And don't forget it's a three-day week in the country. Lots of people are there, searching for anything. And prepared to do for any reward."

Another long silence slowly ticked away while they sunk into their own thoughts. In the end, she brought sandwiches on a plate and a new cup of warm coffee. She took back the old cup, which had gone cold. "No bacon," she muttered casually.

He didn't respond to it. He took a bite on one of them and chewed quietly.

She sat down on the opposite side. "I didn't see the headmistress."

He stared at her across the table.

"We didn't go to the nursery. She wouldn't simply come."

He was silent.

"Some kids think that she's a talking dolly. They come and touch her."

He sipped on his drink and put it back on the table.

"But I can understand it," she said, sighing vaguely. "Most of the kids around here grow up on farms, and their knowledge can be limited." She sighed again, clearly in anger. "But calling her names is very bad."

He chewed and swallowed the bit of food he had in his mouth. "What do they call her?" He asked softly.

She shot a glance through the corridor to see the girl anywhere around. No, she wasn't. Her eyes rolled back to him. "Peacock," she whispered, deeply embarrassed. "Or little monkey."

"Where is she now, in the room?" He asked cautiously.

"In her room. Doing colouring!"

He searched for a cigarette in a packet and lit it. "I'm afraid she couldn't escape from it."

Debra looked at him, confused.

He picked up his cigarette packet and pulled out a cigarette. "Kids tease each other. And, in her case, what do you think they pick on her?"

She shook her head mechanically for an answer, though she was sure what he was hinting at.

He puffed heavily on his cigarette and blew out slowly. "In her case, her colour. And…....?"

She interrupted him, clearly annoyed. "What is wrong with her colour?"

He drew on his cigarette and blew out the smoke away. "Nothing wrong at all with her," he replied, absolutely sincerely. "She's the most beautiful girl in her class. So, maybe other kids will get jealous. And they taunt on her colour." He puffed again. "And you have seen the other kids. They all are white English kids, aren't they? And maybe this is the first time they see a mixed-race child in flesh and blood."

Debra moved forward in her chair and propped up her face in her hands and elbows on the table. "Daniella won't like it," she said, almost crying through her fingers. "And I won't like it at all. I can't see her living in misery and shame."

He looked at her. "She will get used to it, Debra."

She raised her face and caught his gaze. "That's cruel."

"What's the solution, you think?"

Hesitantly, she looked out the window. The garden behind the house looked dark and cold. The view to the distance wasn't long, as the low cloud hovered in the atmosphere. Slowly, she turned her face back. "We go back to London."

For a moment, he thought he had gone deaf and breathless. He moved up in his chair and sat straight up, the burning cigarette between his fingers and held close to his face. "What did you say, Debra?" He asked finally.

She could feel tears bubbling up behind her eyelids. "We've no other choice. We've to go back."

A smile grew on his lips with a twinge of sarcasm. "True, we're keeping in touch with our friends. But do they really know what we're going through?"

Without saying anything, she kept staring at him.

"I'm washing others' dirty clothes, cleaning the toilets, tidying up the kitchens, hearing mouthfuls. And……"

She interrupted loudly. "We don't need to say that, do we?"

"No?"

"No," she answered firmly. "It's not our fault. The government and the unions are punching each other. Sadly, we're in the middle, and we've no choice but to take the pain."

Completely annoyed, Jeffrey cast down his eyes to the floor.

"And millions of families are in our position. But they are surviving!"

He didn't say anything. An uneasy calm soared over them. In the end, he asked, "What are we doing with the girl?"

She waited. Her eyes widened as she stared at him. "What do you mean?"

He answered quickly. "It's not our child?"

She stared back at him. "I love the child."

Jeffrey caught her eyes silently.

"She was a white child."

Quietly, he looked out the window.

"None of us knew she would grow into a mixed-race colour."

Without speaking, he got up and stepped nearer to the window.

Debra looked at the back of his head. "To me nothing matters. I love her exactly the same way I loved her when I first saw her." She paused as if to stock up a little more courage. "And I was stubborn to say that she was our daughter. Because I thought you could feel proud........."

"Proud?" He interrupted her, apparently annoyed, turning halfway and meeting her stare. "Why?"

"Well, I didn't tell you then."

"What?"

"I want the whole world to know that you're the father."

"Really?"

"Everybody was laughing behind your back. That.... that you're barren."

He turned back. "Yes, it helps a lot. We've a half-cast in the family."

A deeply frustrated expression clouded her face. In a rush, her mouth opened to speak something, but no voice came out.

He asked, rather angrily, "Do I look like a black American GI?"

She continued to sit there with her stare fixed on his face.

"Or did you go to Africa for a month's holiday?"

That was enough, she had thought. She got up and went upstairs. He came to the hallway, picked up his coat and hat, and went out. And out he was even at eleven o'clock. It was pitch dark and freezing cold. Against the street light, it was clear that it was drizzling on and off, and in between, fluffy snowflakes flashed cascading through the misty air.

Debra sat on the edge of the bed, her face dropped into her hands, and her elbows were put on her legs. Definitely, the Three-Day Week regulations added difficulties in family circles - three days to work to buy food and pay bills and the remaining four days to waste for the government to save fuel. How would one waste the days if there was nothing to do? It needed money to go anywhere, places such as theatres, clubs, pubs, or even cafeterias. Staying home was indisputably risky. One wouldn't have favourite food and drinks, or maybe none whatsoever. Necessary conversation would start that would end up in disputes between the spouses or relatives. These disputes arose always in the past, but much more widely and frequently now under the Three-Day Week. It was okay if Jeffrey wanted to go out, but he had always told her where he was going.

He returned about midnight. He took a quick shower and got into bed beside her. He didn't say anything. She didn't speak either for a few minutes. "Where did you go?" Debra asked calmly. He rolled over to his side, away from her. "This is not the time to talk." He replied equally calmly.

"Why not?"

"I've work in the morning."

She didn't ask anything else.

Suddenly, a stillness engulfed them. Slowly, they fell asleep or pretended to be asleep.

Debra got up before him as usual and went down to the kitchen. She made two fried egg sandwiches, filled a large mug with coffee, and put them on the table. Jeffrey was already downstairs in the hallway and had his coat and hat on. "The breakfast on the table, Jeffrey," she said, pacing near to him.

He was close to the door. He opened it, deliberately avoiding her presence, but whispered over his shoulder, "I'm late." And he went out and shut the door behind before she could say a word. She stood there breathlessly, her eyes staring at the back of the door.

Part 2: Explains

He came back very late in the evening. "I had some work," he replied sullenly.

"Where?" Debra asked pleasantly, obviously to start a conversation.

"At Mr Watson," he said, then rushed for the shower. And when he came out of the bathroom, she asked, "Shall I take the food?"

"Not for me. I already had the meal."

A mixed expression of shock and sadness crossed her face. However, she didn't say anything. She went to Daniella's room. The girl was sleeping. She stood there for a couple of minutes, watching her impassively, then quietly went to the room.

It was uneasily tranquil for a short while. "Where do we go from here?" Debra asked herself finally.

Jeffrey didn't reply straight away. He pulled the quilt over his legs up to his stomach and propped up his head over a pile of two pillows. He reached out his hand and turned off the bedside light. "I'm rather ashamed of the whole situation," he answered rather vexed.

She hesitated. "Because of the little girl?"

"Not strictly in that sense."

"Then?"

"We've to tell the truth."

"That she is not our daughter?"

"Thanks. You said it for me."

Debra didn't speak. A long, unbearable silence sprang up between them. "We must tell her first," she said finally, in a voice almost breaking into crying.

"Of course," he readily agreed. "That's fair. She should know it first."

"And you can tell her."

He waited. "That's difficult."

"She's always in her room."

"Because she's scared of you."

He didn't say anything.

"You don't talk to her."

He was silent

"You don't play with her."

Again, he was silent.

"You don't take her out for a walk. Or shopping."

This time, he spoke rather mutely, "I feel embarrassed."

"Why?"

"When people start staring."

She was quiet.

"Can't you tell her?"

"When?"

"Well, she's always with you."

"Like when she hugs and kisses me, calling me, 'Mama, Mama?'"

He rolled over to the other side. "I need to grab a little sleep," he said with suppressed anger. "I've a job to start at six."

The rain started to patter heavily on the roof, and the water gushed down the gutter and downpipe noisily. Somewhere in the distance, the howls of the wind trembled the calmness of the night as they lashed across the trees. Debra waited nervously while her mind was analysing their current situation. Shortly after, the heavy pouring down slackened, and the wind became less noisy.

"Well, Jeffrey," she said somewhat sympathetically. "I know you're right. We've to be honest with ourselves and honest with Daniella. I was scared to face the fact."

Without speaking, he lay watching the light rain under the street light.

"We'll face some thorny issues, such as school admission or church registration or……. or maybe a hospital appointment. Then we've to inform the authorities the truth," she paused as if words were hard to come out and then said quickly, rather crying, "that Daniella is our adopted child."

He waited a moment. "I hope it will turn up quicker. We can look at other's faces proudly."

And an issue turned up quicker than they had wished. Daniella used to go to ABC Nursery School at the top of Green Park, which was about ten minutes' walking distance. It was a private school, and Vicky Millar hired the building and managed the school with four other teachers and two teachers' assistants. Vicky ran the school efficiently despite all the power cuts and unions' flash strikes and unrest. However, when the Three-Day Week was imposed on the country, Vicky's school started dragging the way. The parents couldn't pay the fees for their children, and reduced days' work sliced down their take-home wages. Feeding the children was inarguably more important than sending them for nursery rhymes. The income from rent dwindled day by day, and all the available resources diminished, and then she came to her senses that she couldn't hold out the school anymore. There was no end in sight for normality to return to the country. She closed down the school. It was very painful for her – her grandmother initiated this idea into operation, her father built up the stability and reputation, and now Vicky had to close it down helplessly.

However, she introduced all the kids to the local schools for places in their kindergarten. Jeffrey and Debra had to go with Daniella to Avon Primary School and meet the headmistress. Their appointment time was at 10.30 on Friday, 22nd of February 1974. Two days earlier, on Wednesday, Debra decided she should talk to her, and the sooner, the better. She didn't want to talk about the whole episode, but just enough to sense out how she would value the human relationship within her innocent mind. She was downstairs in the reception and was about to watch Scooby Doo, the children's program on BBC 2. Unfortunately, there was no electricity at the moment. She sat down on the floor in front of the television, hoping the power would return soon, and started colouring on a page in her book. Debra also sat down next to the girl, then held her close and kissed on her cheek. "You okay, sweetie?"

The girl kissed her back. "Yes, Mama. And you, Mama?"

Debra didn't know to cry or laugh. Instead, she held the girl more tightly. "Yes, my sweetie," she replied, kissing again.

A moment or two later, the girl moved back to her book and started to colour.

"Is it a rose flower?"

"Yes, Mama."

"You like rose?"

"Yes."

"Is it your favourite flower?"

"All flowers are my favourite, Mama."

"Which is your favourite, favourite flower, sweetie?"

"They all are favourite to me, Mama."

Debra paused. "What's your favourite colour, sweetie?"

She answered quickly and cheerfully, "All colours are my favourite, Mama."

"Nothing special about red or blue or pink?"

"No, Mama, they all are colours like any other colours."

"Why is that, Sweetie?"

The girl turned her face to her. "All these are part of our world, Mama. And the world is beautiful." She returned to the page, saying gently, "Because everything in the world is beautiful, Mama."

She stared away immediately to avoid the bubbling tears in her eyes. After a while, she asked softly, "How did you learn this, Sweetie?"

The girl answered slowly, fully concentrating on the drawing along the edges of the rose petals. "Our teacher, Winifred, told us, Mama."

"Well, I hope I can learn from you."

"Oh, Mama!" she exclaimed absently, dropping the pencil and picking up another colour. "Mothers don't learn from daughters."

"No?"

"No, mama," she muttered, while a trace of pink colour followed behind the moving pencil. "It's children who learn from mothers."

She stared back silently at the girl for a moment. "Your teacher taught this?"

The little girl waited, filling the edge of a petal. "No, Mama. I just thought."

She opened her mouth to speak. But no word came out until she forced her strength into the voice.

"Yes, sweetie. I agree with you, darling."

The young girl was too innocent to grasp the thrill of the hidden meaning. But she chuckled happily, "That's fine, mama."

The electricity came back in the evening, just a few minutes before Jeffrey came home about 7.30 in the evening. He was soaking wet in the cascading rain and swirling gusts of wind. The buses stopped running from early afternoon onwards; no explanations were given in the local news yet. He walked as fast as he could, nearly four miles. It was pitch dark under the black clouds that stretched between the horizons. He struggled through the front door into the hallway. Debra took his hat and coat and put them on the hanger. He went upstairs to the bathroom, dried himself with a towel, then changed his clothes in the bedroom before coming to the kitchen. She mixed a whisky and gave it to him. He took a large sip and sat down at the table.

"Why so late, darling?"

He had another sip and put the glass on the table. "Bus strikes," he muttered in an exhausted voice.

"Why?"

"This is the era of strikes. You don't need many reasons for strikes."

She looked at him, confused.

"A black man hit a white conductor. Nobody knows why. Well, Bristol." He paused and sighed heavily. "Always racial issues, coming back from the slavery dates."

She waited and then asked, deliberately shifting the subject. "Did you have a nice day at work?"

"Just the normal," he replied in a trivial tone. "Two cooks had a beat up."

She asked quickly, rather worried, "Did you get involved?"

"No. They didn't let. They were too busy."

"How it finished."

"One got badly hurt. The other is absolutely tired."

She didn't speak quickly. "I hope Hughes Transport operates fully soon." She stopped talking and glanced towards the cooking area for a moment. "Then you don't have to work in these notorious places."

"We've to pay the rent," he whispered as though thinking loudly.

Debra stood there awkwardly as she couldn't find anything to say. He was also quiet but continued to sit in his seat, looking down at his empty glass.

Suddenly, she woke up and moved toward the cooker. She toasted a couple of slices of bread and spread margarine on them. She brought them in a saucer and put them on the table. She filled his empty glass with whiskey and soda. He grabbed a big bite of bread, started chewing, and looked across the table at his wife. "How was the little one?"

"Bored," she answered, meeting his gaze. "No power, no light. No TV. Not even heating." She sighed almost desperately. "The poor girl is very lonely."

He swallowed down the food. "Sleeping?"

She nodded. "She went to bed at seven. Too cold. Too bored."

He sipped on his drink and then took a bite of the bread.

"I hope she'd be fine with the head teacher on Friday and start schooling on Monday."

He nodded for an answer before he swallowed the food in his mouth.

"Did you arrange the day off?" She asked rather nervously.

Jeffrey drank a large sip of whisky. "For what?"

She stared into his eyes, confused. "We're seeing the headteacher on Friday, you forgot?"

216

"Oh! For that?"

"Only one more day left, Jeffrey," she reminded desperately. "And tomorrow is Thursday."

"Did you talk to her?"

"I talked about the school. And about her appointment."

"About the damned birth certificate and her name in it?"

She stared at him sombrely before she shook her head feebly.

"Why didn't you, for goodness's sake?"

"We agreed we would tell her together."

"But I couldn't come early."

continued to stare at him for a moment, completely lost. "I Couldn't talk to her myself. I'll get a panic attack."

The drink was in his hand. He sipped a mouthful and put the glass back on the table. "To be honest with you, I couldn't care less," he said in a twinge of remorse. "We brought this burden on us for nothing."

"What are you talking about?" Debra was feeling mixed emotions of sadness and anger. "She is our daughter. We adopted her."

He grinned silently. "Yes, darling, Debra. I know that." He took another sip, then continued, "But we knew nothing about her parentage, did we?"

"Does it matter now?"

Jeffrey ignored her question deliberately. The grin on his face grew wider. "A man wanted some company, if I may say so."

She suppressed her growing frustration inside her mind. "Yeh?"

"And a woman wanted some cash, if I may say so."

"Yeh?"

"One of the two was black, the other white. That's much we know for sure."

"Yeh?"

"And they had a rendezvous in the back of a lorry, if I may say so."

 didn't say anything at all.

"And nine months later, our Daniella girl was born behind some hedges."

She couldn't take his talking anymore. She retorted furiously. "I'm ashamed of you. You are drunk."

He retorted equally furiously. "She's on our neck now. Somebody who doesn't fit in our life." He reached out for the glass and drained the drink. He put the glass back and got up, then turned to the hallway and walked away. She stared at his back. She couldn't see him, though; her eyes were clouded with the darkness of fear.

Part 3: Dealing with Problems

Jeffrey took the shower and stayed in his bedroom. She waited for him sometime downstairs before she came up, too. She opened Daniella's door and walked in softly. The young girl was having a cosy sleep under the sheets and quilt, her eyes gently closed, and her face partially declined to one side, which was fully visible and so stunning. She gently stooped over and kissed on her cheek, as lightly as possible, not to disturb her at all. Nonetheless, she opened her eyes and saw her mother's face inches away from her own. A trace of a smile sprouted on her lips while she caught her mother's eyes. "Mama," she whispered like a faint breeze, yet distinct and gentle.

"Sweetie, darling," she said, her voice carrying all the love her heart had tendered over the years.

The girl's eyes stayed open for a second or two, watching her mother's face all over, and then softly closed. In another moment or two, she fell asleep while her mother's watchful gaze hovered over her. She kissed the daughter once more before she straightened up herself reluctantly and went out.

Jeffrey was at the edge of the bed, sitting and smoking a cigarette. He didn't say anything when she walked into the room. She walked close to him. "I warm up the food," she said, standing in front of him. "Shall I serve?"

"Okay," he replied. "Something light will do. I'm not that hungry."

"I made sausage casserole, boiled potatoes, and cabbage."

They returned to the kitchen and ate the supper quietly. In the end, he said abruptly, "I'll take the morning off from work. We can talk to Daniella."

"Thank you, Jeffrey."

In the morning, Daniella got up at seven and came down for breakfast at about 8. Jeffrey was already at the table, and she sat on the opposite. Debra made fruit Brute cereal in hot milk, a sausage sandwich for the baby, coffee, toast for Jeffrey, and the same for herself. She took a seat, almost in the middle of them. Nobody talked about anything at all while they were eating. After a few minutes of misery, Jeffrey asked once, apparently to break the silence, "You like your cereal, don't you, Daniella?"

She was just putting a spoonful of it into her mouth at the time. She looked at him, obviously confused. She swallowed it before she replied in her innocence, "Very nice. Mama got it for me."

Surely, Jeffrey didn't like her answer. In fact, it made him furious inside. He finished his breakfast quickly and went to the reception. He turned on the telly and sat on his usual chair. A good few minutes later, Debra came in, followed by the baby. They sat down in the settee close to him. Everybody's eyes were on the telly, but only the baby listened to the show. The other two got their minds tangled in the past and puzzled about the way out.

Abruptly, Jeffrey spoke, "You're going to school soon, Daniella."

She turned her eyes and looked at him, almost confused. "Where? ABC Nursery?"

"No, dear," he replied slowly and enthusiastically. "It's a new school. And I told you about it, didn't I?"

Confused, the girl looked at her mother. "Mamie, which school is this?"

"Ella, it's a new school. And you'll love it."

Still confused, she asked, her eyes staring at her mother's face. "Is it true, Mama?"

She grabbed the baby for a hug. "Yes, Ella darling," she whispered gladly. However, she felt an aching inside her chest. The time had arrived for them to tell the truth to the girl. She grabbed the child again and kissed on her cheeks. "Ella, you're going to Avon Primary School," she said very proudly. She rested her on the lap and put her arms around her. "It's the best school in the county."

The girl turned her face up to look at her mother's face. "Is it the school before the church we go to?" She enquired, her lips half curved up into a smile.

"That's the one, dear," Jeffrey cut in quickly. Obviously, he didn't want to be left out of the conversation. "They teach you to sing and dance. You like singing and dancing, don't you? And you'll love there." He paused, meeting the girl's staring eyes. "Lots of kids there. And you'll have lots of friends."

Somehow, the girl couldn't take his words seriously. She turned to her mother. "Is it true, Mamie?"

"Yes, darling."

"Oh, thank you, Mamie." She raised her hands and punched the air in a celebration gesture. "Can I go today?"

"Not today, Ella," he chuckled. "But tomorrow, you're going?"

"Thank you, Mamie."

The aching inside her mind increased. She coughed for a moment as if to get an extra moment to suppress her feelings. "You enjoy every day while you're there," she said gently, catching the girl's eyes steadily. "And ….and, the head Miss wants to see you."

"That's okay, Mama," she said calmly.

"She will have a talk with you," Jeffrey said.

Her eyes rolled towards him. "That's okay."

"In the school record, you have a different name, dear."

"Why is that, Mamie?" She whispered as if asking herself.

A cold shiver shot up her spine. For a split second, her senses ceased to exist. This was the question she had feared during every breath she inhaled since the day they met. Now, it had arrived in front of them. She shot a glance at Jeffrey helplessly. But his face was devoid of any suggestion. She looked back at the baby, still sitting in her lap and being held in her arms. "Ella, my dearest darling, ...," she stopped talking, obviously unable to continue talking.

He came to his wife's support. "You see, Mamie is very upset."

Silently, she stared at her. "Why you're upset, Mamie?"

She clutched her tighter and kissed on both cheeks. "Nothing makes no changes to us, sweetie. Everything will be just the same between us. Mamie and Dady will always love you."

The girl looked at Jeffrey, then looked back at her – a startled expression displayed in her eyes. "It's the name, Mamie?" she asked, her voice carrying a mixed tone of fear and sadness.

Debra looked at her husband briefly before she looked back at the girl's face. "For us, you...... you're Daniella. And always will be Daniella. I chose that name for you. Because that was my mother's name, the dearest of all names to me."

The girl stretched up her body and threw her arms around her mother's shoulders. "Thank you, Mama. I like my name, Mama. Why, Mama, you're crying?"

Jeffrey intervened immediately. "Your name is not a problem, Daniella. We can make the changes to the birth certificate. But ... but...." He paused, unsure of himself, then said swiftly before his wife could speak. "We'll love you always. But we've to be honest with you. Mama isn't your mother."

The girl took a brief moment to digest what he had said to her. In the end, she stared at her, seemingly her eyes almost immovable on her face. "What did he say that, Mamie?" She managed to ask; her voice virtually frozen.

Seemingly to cheer up the situation, she raised a faint smile. "This means nothing, dear. We always love you." She broke off the talking.

"Daniella," he said quickly. "This Mamie didn't give you birth."

She struggled and turned her face to her mother. At that precise moment, a big drop of tears from her eyes trickled down onto her face. She knew it, and so did her mother, and their gazes collided in an unexplainable question. Unable to resist, her mother nodded for an answer that it was true. Slowly, with fear more than curiosity, she turned to him. He caught her stare gently for a moment before lightly shaking his head. "I'm not your father either, dear."

The girl leaned back heavily against her mother and continued to sit on her lap. And nobody said a word. It was absolutely silent except for the heavy breaths that mainly arose from Debra. They all have their own thoughts. Daniella, with her innocent mind, feels confused or lost. On the other hand, he was relaxing because the battle to be a father was over; sadly, there was no great gain in it now. However, there was no loss either. No one among his friends could say that he was bringing up a child his wife had from an illicit affair. Debra felt completely disillusioned because she used to proudly say that she was her mother. She said it with complete love, which gave her a great belief in life that her dreams circled around Daniella and that her world intertwined with this little girl's dreams that she might nourish as she grew. Regrettably, a crack had cruelly managed to split her belief; it wouldn't be the same again. And the whole family of three sitting in complete silence would surely agree that nothing would be the same.

Abruptly, Daniella broke the silence. "I want to go to my room, Mamie," she whispered softly.

"Okay, Sweetie, I come with you."

"I can go."

"I know. But I'll come, Sweetie."

The girl walked towards the staircase. Debra followed her.

In the morning, Debra and Daniella met the head teacher, Ms Greener, and set the paperwork for enrolment. On Monday, her schooling started at Avon Primary School. Debra took her to the school at 9.20, ten minutes before her class started. In the afternoon, Debra would go again and reach the school gate at about 3.20 to pick her up and bring her home safely. It was about three miles from home to the school; she had to use two buses for the trip. However, buses were so unreliable due to the strikes and riots of early 1974, and even if they were on the bus, there was no guarantee that they would arrive at their destination as flying squads jumped in and disrupted the journey. There were days she and her daughter walked all the way to the other end. One day, Miss Greener had a meeting with Debra to find out why Daniella was late for school and anything the school could do to help. And during the meeting, it came out that Debra had worked as an accounts clerk for a company called Prudential Investment Ltd on Victoria Road, right in front of Victoria Station, London, where the company office occupied all of the large first floor and underneath, the ground floor and the basement, was leased out to a pub called Royal Oak where Jeffrey worked as a barman.

"It's very nice to hear that you've had a clerical experience," Ms Greener said. "We could do with somebody with your experience. Would you take a part-time work in our office?"

Debra opened her mouth to speak, and even her lips stirred as if speaking, but she couldn't find her voice.

Ms Greener noticed the favourable signs of emotions on her face. "Good. You can come with Daniella in the morning and go back in the evening. And the time in between, you could do some work in our office."

She turned her face away deliberately, not letting Ms Greener see her tears trickling down her cheeks. Her eyes went past the office window, then crossed the sandy ground immediately outside and the grass meadow beyond. Again, at a distance, the sun reflected its radiance over the waves of waters cascading down the river Avon.

Ms Greener watched her for a moment, then joked, "It's only a part-time work. It can be regular if you want to. But remember, it's not a lottery to be emotional."

Slowly, she turned her face back. "I haven't heard any good news for a long time," she said, wiping her tears off her cheeks with a tissue. "It was bad luck, one after another and ...."

"Debra, look at the country now," the head teacher interrupted her rather comfortingly. "The government is in trouble. They got their policies wrong. The unions are out in force, but they got their policies wrong, too. And in between them, the nation is crumbling. She stopped talking, inhaled a deep breath, and blew it out quietly. "The question is this. Who should run the country? It should be the elected ministers or the militant unionists. While these questions rage, you and I and people like us will all suffer."

Debra sat quietly and listened to the teacher respectfully.

"Don't think too much about the troubles in life," she continued. "Because one day, good times will move in and take over life." She paused thoughtfully for a moment. "My mother used to say, 'Don't be afraid of the night because the day is right behind it."

After the meeting, she ran to the phone box outside the school gate and phoned her husband. "Jeff, you don't believe it," she said with all the excitement she could muster in her voice.

"What is it?" His voice was guarded from any emotions.

"I got a job," she replied quickly, as if she could not contain it anymore.

"Congratulations, dear. A great news for us."

"I am starting it tomorrow."

"Why in a rush?"

"The paperwork is so much behind due to the general strikes. Anyway, no worries. I've plenty of clothes."

"Good."

"And did you hear?"

"What?"

"Labour is caching up Tories in the gallop poll rating."

"If it's so, it's no good because it will be a hung parliament. Which means the unions will stretch their muscles and ask for even higher wage increases."

"We'll know it on Thursday night after the election results. If the results are good, Hughes Transport will reopen, and you'll be back at your full-time job. And, thank God, that's all we want."

"Hopefully, one party will win the overall majority. And that's what the country needs desperately. Anyway, I have to cut you off, dear. I am in the middle of something urgent."

A FEW TALES

After the election, contrary to the confident expectations, the nation had voted for a hung parliament, which created a crisis at Westminster. Now, the country didn't have a national government, theoretically. All parties sought some form of alliance for a national government and power, unsuccessfully. In the end, on the 4th of March, a minority Labour government was formed under the premiership of Harold Wilson, who had the respect of most unions. He calmed the industrial strikes and managed to get the country back to work. On the 7th, three days later, the three-day work restrictions were removed. Jeffrey resumed his full-time job at Hughes Transport. It was a very happy evening when Jeffrey returned. They were definitely in a celebration mood. Jeffrey had whiskey, Debra wine, and Daniella juice. And they had all the reasons for celebration. Jeffrey regained his job, Debra became part of a school administration, and Daniella studied in a famous school; everyone found their role fine in life. Daniella's position was re-adjusted to the truth that she was adopted and that she was well-loved as a daughter.

A year later, they bought a three-bedroom and two-reception property fairly near the school and on the bank of the river Avon. Mother and daughter walked to the school in less than ten minutes. The property was also close to a junction where Jeffrey picked up a bus that went past Hughes Transport. However, in 1976, he bought a new Cortina car, which helped them to visit family and friends. The boot of this car was spacious, so it was fairly ideal for holidays, too.

In 1978, a miracle happened in the family. Jeffrey and Debra were in the lounge. He was having a drink of whiskey, and she was having a glass of wine. Daniella was in her room, lying awake, or maybe, she was asleep. It was already quite late, but it was Friday night, and he was off for work the next day, and Debra had never worked for the weekends.

She sipped on her long wine glass and held the drink in her mouth for a moment before she swallowed it down. She put the glass back on the low table and turned to him. "I talked to my GP today," she said, looking at his face, her blue eyes twinkling that wasn't there for a long time.

Jeffrey was sipping on his glass precisely at that moment. He swallowed the drink down the throat and, turning, seized her stare. "It's about your vomiting feeling?"

She kept staring at him without speaking, "You're not far from it."

He waited, looking rather thoughtful, the whiskey glass held in front of his face. "They found the reason for?"

The twinkling in her eyes grew and zoomed down into a sweet smile on her lips. "You're not far from it?"

Again, he waited. "You're drunk?"

"Not really?"

"You want me to carry to bed?"

She chuckled in a beaming, happy voice. "In a minute or two?"

"Alright, I give up."

She took the glass away from his hand and put it on the table. She threw her hands around his neck, drew him even closer, and kissed him.

"What is in that wine," he asked teasingly. "Can I have a drop of it?"

Her face was right in front of him, her hands still around his neck. "You're a stud," she said, kissing again. "I'm having our baby."

Part 4: Baby J J

His eyes grew wide, and they stared into her face while the rest of his body was absolutely in a kind of lifeless state. 'Did I hear her?' In a split second, this question rose and fell inside his mind a million times. 'Or the dream of his past echoing at the distance?'

She sensed the thoughts that were haunting him. She smiled, the biggest smile she ever had. "Yes, darling."

He could clearly feel a tremor mounting up. "You sure about it?"

She didn't reply immediately. Instead, she touched his cheek tenderly, her eyes seizing his stare continuously. "Why did you think I went for check-ups regularly?"

He whispered, still his voice shaking. "You said you have back pain?"

 stopped smiling. "I didn't want to tell you until I am sure," she explained earnestly. "I didn't want to hurt you in the end." She paused and kissed him before she continued softly. "They did every check-up and test they could. And every one of them proved positive that I am pregnant."

Absently, Jeffrey held her tight without saying anything. She didn't say a word either but settled into his hold. A refreshing silence drifted over them while several thoughts, memories, happiness, and sadness of the past swayed through their minds, but they were fully aware that their past was behind them and that a new dawn was ascending in their dreams. It was a nice feeling they were having – a feeling they constantly dreamt that they would cherish one day. And now, it dazzled pleasurably at a touching distance. However, the echoes of realties rattled close to their minds that she was forty-one in a fortnight, and wasn't it a dangerous age for pregnancy to nurture?

Jeffrey wasn't sure whether he had got a good sleep during the night. Nonetheless, by dawn, he was absolutely sure that Debra required vital support with her daily routines. Fairly shortly, he started taking her shopping in his Cortina car and cooking for the family. No problem with these issues – cooking was his profession, and he thoroughly enjoyed it and knew her tastes and flavours and favourite food. Another subject was traveling and working. She wasn't happy at all to resign from the school – she had an amiable group of colleagues. She would miss them if she resigned.

In the end, listened to him and reduced her working hours. She didn't have to accompany Daniella anymore. The girl was nine years old, quite big for her age, and she would go with her friends who went past her front gate. Anyway, school was not more than ten minutes' walk. However, a taxi dropped Debra at the school gate and picked her up after work. The same taxi firm took her for the medical check-ups and physical exercises. They went if he could get back home early for a walk in the Avon Riverside Park or a drive down Cardiff Bay. Nonetheless, she always felt tired and sleepy. Worst of all, she hated food and drinks. Even the name of them made her nauseous, and she started to lose weight. Several times, she was admitted to Bristol Maternity Hospital for various complications, mainly due to the scary feeling of having a still baby. One time, it was almost confirmed that the baby had died, and another time, it was that the mother and the baby would die in minutes. However, they both outlived the findings; the errors on both occasions were due to the old machines and equipment.

Three weeks later, Debra was brought into the hospital again. She was critically ill. Her pregnancy was almost seven months old then, and the consultant obstetricians rushed her to the operating ward. A boy was born; it was a caesarean birth, and the mother and the baby were doing fine. Jeffrey was so happy, and he punched the air – at last, he heard his child crying, and he cried as well. He called his son with his own name, Jeffrey, and then gave his father's name, John, for the middle designation. So, all in all, it was Jeffrey John, but they shortened to J J.

Debra and J J spent a further six weeks in the hospital for continuous check-ups, treatment, and supervision before they came home. J J stayed in his parents' room in a cot, which was placed close to his mother's side of the bed, and positioned it in such a way so that she could glance at him immediately and find out why he had cried for attention. And if he needed the help of any sort, even for a touch of love, she could do it right away without struggling herself a lot. She wasn't physically any good either; she suffered from chronic age-related diseases like diabetes and high blood pressure. Jeffrey spent all his spare time with them, mostly sitting on a chair by the cot side, playing with the boy, or talking with his wife. When they fell asleep, he prepared the food for meal times or did not see the other works that remained unfinished. If everything went okay on the day and a few minutes were free in his possession, Jeffrey read a book about catering or the hospitality industry in general. When he had to be away, mainly for his work, Daniella should be close at hand for the baby and the mother in her off-school time. Jeffery insisted on this and said that she should skip the class for emergencies. She was almost ten years old, but she appeared definitely much stronger, bigger, and mature for her age. She rushed to the bedside whenever Debra called "Ella" or to the cot side when J J made any uncomfortable noises, although she moaned every now and then that she had homework to do or sometimes rebelled that she wasn't a slave girl.

Anyway, Debra managed herself alright in most of the difficulties. She would call the doctor or ambulance depending on the gravity of the illness. As soon as Jeffrey received the phone call, he'd take the time off and rush home, and, in most cases, he'd reach before the medical team arrived. All in all, it was a seriously problematic situation, as he went out to work to earn wages to keep the family going while his wife and child needed his continuous love and care simply for their survival.

Nevertheless, towards the end of 1978, the situation turned all around deadly as the political, economic, and social conditions took a severe plunge down to the unknown. The government couldn't give in to the union's demands. The inflation was already flying high, almost 26 percent, and a sensible wage settlement was absolutely paramount to curtail the price rises for the sake of the country. The unions and the other labour moments clamoured for high wages, and some union leaders threatened to ask for wage increases as high as 40 percent. The immediate and inevitable outcome was political unrest, as the powerful unions declared national strikes, or picket line blockades, eventually termed as the winter of discontent. Absolute chaos and anarchy rolled into the towns, cities, and other regions. The orderly way of life was a forlorn memory. During these days, there was no guarantee that the local or national transport would be there in the mornings for anybody or no knowledge that the jobs were safe in the offices and factory floors and that they would have the transport to get home in the evening. Even if it wasn't the day of a national general strike, a local union steward could bring havoc into the area by calling disruptions over a trivial issue.

And against these widespread industrial strikes, Jeffrey depended entirely on the state for his wife and son's treatment, medication, and safety. However, it didn't always work out to his satisfaction; ambulances arrived late, relevant doctors or nurses were not available, wards were not cleaned up, paperwork was missing, and, worst to come, the checking equipment was out of order. Once, the authorities transferred J J to another hospital due to a shortage of staff, and the ambulance crawled behind a huge rally; a fifteen-minute ambulance journey took two hours and twenty-two minutes.

A FEW TALES

On the 12th of December, it was a Tuesday; problems escalated beyond tolerance. Debra was in the hospital for the third day. She suffered severe exhaustion and blood pressure increase, combined with the complications of late pregnancy and childbirth. She had to be in the hospital so that the doctors could closely monitor her changing conditions.

J J, on the other hand, behaved well with his illnesses over the last three to four days, which helped Daniella manage him mostly on her own. Jeffrey had been at home for the weekend, and yesterday, he was supposed to be at home with J J and then at the hospital with his wife. But a call from his boss came that he had to rush to the company and assist the others in the canteen, due to a shortage of staff due to the local bus strikes which had been going on for weeks, on and off. He had to go this morning, as well, and he told Daniella what to do and what not to do if this didn't happen, and she should call the ambulance if J J seemed serious for one reason or another. And these talks were like a compulsory ritual before he'd leave home, and Daniella hated them to bits. She had known and done it all, so why couldn't he trust her?

However, today, J J was very different and challenging for her, especially compared to the last few days. He was continuously crying, and to be honest, there was no end to it. She used all the tricks in her array of love and care. Perhaps he wanted to go to sleep, she had thought and kneeled down by the side of the cot and started to stroke his cheeks, hands, and sides of the body while trying to talk to him, laugh with him, and hum a tune for a good few minutes. No, the baby was still crying. She checked his pantie; it was dry. She had fed him only about half an hour ago, and yet she gave the feeding bottle again. He didn't want it but continued crying. She lifted him up from the cot and carried him around in the room, then, coming down, paced between the lounge and the kitchen, talking, singing, laughing. He still cried, and his

233

breaths became harder and noisier. She rushed to the phone and dialled 999 for an ambulance, followed by a call to Jeffrey.

Jeffrey hadn't got his car today. It was at the garage for repairs on the clutch. He called for a tax, but none was currently available. His boss dropped him at the bus stop on High Road. "I'm sorry, Jeffrey," Alan said. "With the number of staff we've now, I couldn't be away from the office too long."

"This is more than enough, Alan," he replied gratefully. "I appreciate it very much."

"You're alight, Jeffrey," he said. "Buses are running along here."

Part 5: An Emergency

Exactly at that time, a bus appeared in the distance, and Jeffrey could see it heading in his direction. He thanked Alan and stepped out, then crossed the road to the bus stop. As the bus moved closer, he identified the number plate SB46, which was one of the buses he used when he hadn't got his car. He got in and took a seat. The bus was running when the conductor stepped near to him. "Ticket?"

He picked up his purse. "Avon Road Junction."

He marked something on a ticket. "This bus terminates at Clark's Square," he said firmly, holding the ticket in his hand.

Jeffrey paid the fare and took the ticket. "Another bus coming right behind this?" He asked, slightly alarmed.

The conductor stared at him impassively. "Maybe, I don't know. But no service beyond Clark Square."

"Why not?" He asked, with his voice in a mixed voice of increased alarm and anger. "I had the bus two hours ago."

The man leaned against a pole that was close to him on his right, then looked back at him. "You're right on that. But you should also know that our country is in the middle of a general strike."

"But ………. but," he lost his words in his frustration and anger momentarily, then added quickly, "buses were running two hours ago."

"Forgive me for saying so, but two hours is a long time in politics, sir."

As though unable to hold the conductor's stare, he looked across the seats on his right side and then turned to his left. Only a few passengers were there, and most of them were looking out, and the others were reading papers. He turned to the man, "What happened?"

"We've orders, sir, to limit the services."

"It's crazy," he literally screamed. "No wonder the country is in this dire state."

He laughed quietly. "Who are we to talk about the country, if I may ask you so, sir?" He looked out the windows as they bypassed an empty bus stop. "We've the government and the unions. They take the decision, and we follow it. And that's what we call democracy."

Jeffrey was not in the mood for an argument. "I've to get home quickly. My wife is very poorly in the hospital. And my child is very ill at home."

"I sympathize with your concern, honestly. But there are many children hungry right now. Their parents aren't earning decent wages. And there aren't enough beds for all the poor wives right now. The government is not allocating its resources adequately for the public. I'm sorry for speaking my mind, sir." He paused vaguely, reading the annoyed expression on the passenger's face. "Well, in the current situation, it's better for you to get off at Clarke Square. It's more likely to get a taxi from there than the Avon Road Junction."

The bus terminated at Clarke Square as informed. He literally ran to a minicab office for a cab. They didn't have one available. The next door was a café and a driver came out of there and started his lorry. "Are you going to the south, sir?"

The driver gave him a cautious glance but noticed the hopelessness on his face before he nodded his head lightly.

"Go past Avon Road Junction?"

He nodded again. "I'm going through Avon Road."

"My child is severely ill. And he's being looked after by another child." He stopped and drew a heavy breath. "Will you drop me anywhere there, please? I'll pay you anything."

"Where do you want to go?"

"Meadow Fields down the Avon Road."

"Get in. I'll go past it. But…"

"But?"

"I've some goods to deliver at a warehouse," the driver explained quickly. "Just three pallets; it won't take long."

He got in and sat down in the passenger seat. The driver started the engine, and the lorry headed towards the south.

"The buses are suddenly on strikes," Jeffrey said as if to make a conversation. "And I had to get off at the Clarke Square."

"The public services are a joke now," he replied in a serious tone. "Nobody knows where the country is heading into!"

Without speaking, Jeffrey turned his face and stared at the driver.

"The prices are soaring up," he said somewhat bitterly. "And petrol is the core reason, and the Israeli-Arab war is the cause. What can we do about it? We've no control over any of them, and it's a shame we gave them the freedom. We've to kick up at our own backsides. Now, they're crippling our country. High inflation, high unemployment, and nonstop strikes, see what we are facing day after day, month after month, and nobody knows when it will be all over – nobody – no union tyrants or no media barons."

Jeffrey didn't make any comments. Instead, he stared in front as the lorry rushed forward.

"The government's propaganda is that they are for full employment, decent wages, and value for money." The driver stopped talking, picked up a cigarette packet, and offered it to him. He took a cigarette; then the driver threw him into his mouth. They lit them and started to inhale. "The union's argument is that," the driver added slowly, blowing out a mouthful of smoke, "they are for the higher wages, full investment, and full employment. And, to achieve these, they are adopting the strikes."

He was silent.

Slowly, they came around a slip road and ended up in the backyard of a huge building. He turned off the engine and got out, saying, "I won't be long."

In fact, he came back quickly. "Sorry, they can't use the forklift today."

"Why not?"

"Some kind of dispute between the management and unions. The workers have to deliver the boxes from the pallet, piece by piece, and it takes an awfully long time."

"I know," he whispered, coming down from the cabin.

"You know this place, Jeffrey?"

He beckoned his head positively. "We're quite close to the Avon Road Junction."

"Good," he sighed faintly. "What time is it?" he whispered to himself, staring at his wristwatch. "Oh, yes. 4 o'clock. Go to the junction. You should easily get a taxi at this time. Or, to the worst, you can walk as fast as you can. You'd get home in about 20 or so minutes."

Jeffrey literally ran to the junction. But there were no taxis anywhere in the view. He went into a grocery shop. "Where do I get a taxi, please?"

The grocer looked at him. "No taxi today. They are on strikes?"

"Why?"

"It's against the petrol price increases."

He stared at the grocer thoughtfully for a moment. "If I pay extra money, do you know anybody who may give me a lift? It's urgent. My child is very ill."

He shook his head, seemingly helpless. "Where do you want to go?"

"Meadow Fields."

"That's not far. Fifteen minutes if you can walk fast!"

"My track and field days are over. I'm 44."

"Don't be silly," he replied, clearly encouraging him. "No such things as age. If you put your mind to it, you can fly."

Jefferey waited a moment, meeting the grocer's eyes. "Can I use your phone for a quick call? I'll pay."

The man didn't reply. Instead, he moved the phone on the lead closer to him. "Be my guest," he said finally.

Jeffrey dialled quickly and waited on the phone impatiently.

"Who is there beside your child?"

"My daughter, nine years old."

"And this child?"

"Five months old."

At this precise moment, Daniella's voice sounded along the wire. "Hello?"

"How's J J?"

Suddenly, she started to sob. "Very bad, daddy."

"What do you mean?" He asked hurriedly. "He's breathing?"

Apparently unable to contain her emotions, she burst out crying. "Very slightly. And he's crying on and off, but no sound."

"What did the ambulance people say?"

She replied, mingling with her bursts of cry. "They haven't come."

A shot of freeze sprang up his spine. "You called them before you called me, 2 hours ago?"

"Yes. And I called them again four times."

He waited, completely confused. "I won't be long." He hung up the phone and turned to the grocer, taking a pound note from his trouser pocket. "Can I pay you now?"

"No, you won't do that, I'm afraid."

"Thank you."

"My son would've dropped you off. But he's gone to the market. Anyway, you better start moving off."

Jeffrey started to move, staring back at the grocer. "I'm going to run."

"Why not?"

"I'll come and see you one day."

He laughed gently. "You don't need to bother about it unless you're alive."

Jeffrey didn't hear him well or understand. He was already on the Avon Road, racing towards the Meadow Fields. However, he couldn't run for 5 minutes straight, and he was getting out of breath and coughing. He would amble to get back his breathing before he'd run again for another short spell. A few times, he had to hold on to the lamp posts or trees, or whatever would come in handy, along the road in order to support his body to stay on the wobbly legs.

In the end, he reached outside the gate of his house, absolutely shattered and struggling hard to breathe. He stood there, hanging on to the rails and coughing acutely, while his eyes drifted along the kerbside. There was a police car parked close to the gate, an ambulance car next to it, and then an ambulance van further down. He pushed the gate away and then dragged himself to the front door. The door was open, and he went in.

A FEW TALES

At the bottom of the staircase, where the hallway curved to make the way forward, a policeman was standing and facing into the sitting room. Immediately after him was his colleague, a woman police officer! She saw Jeffrey first and asked him professionally, "Good evening, sir," she said professionally, "And you are?"

Jeffrey held to the banister of the staircase and stopped walking. "I'm Jeffrey," he replied, shooting a glance into the sitting room between the bodies of police. Two female medical staff were on the floor, squatting and tidying up their equipment into heavy bags. He said as if replying. He exhaled clearly audibly, then quickly inhaled, seemingly storing up the courage. "How's my son?" He asked in a mixed voice of fear and nervousness.

The police were quiet, obviously letting the medical staff answer him. One who was nearer to the door looked up partially and answered politely, "He is with the doctor upstairs."

As he went upstairs, he heard voices spilling out softly from J J's room. The door was almost fully open, and he entered quickly. There were three medical staff, all in all; a male doctor who was listening to J J's heart beating through a stethoscope and also feeling the pulses at the wrist, a female nurse who was monitoring the oxygen mask on his face, and a female paramedic very gently messaging his little legs. They acknowledged his presence through sheer glances but continued to engage with their tasks. J J was in the cot, but he could see him as the base was fixed in the high position. And it had always been like that, mainly for Debra's convenience. After childbirth, she couldn't bend down much and sometimes hardly at all. Daniella was also there, behind the staff, her hair in a mess and her face completely wet in tears. As he entered, she hurried to him and hugged him, sobbing and crying.

He put his hand on her shoulder. "How is J J?" He whispered.

"I don't know, daddy," she replied frightfully.

The paramedic looked up at him. "You're Jeffrey?"

He nodded lightly for an answer.

"We'll tell you in a minute," The paramedic said calmly.

He stared at the man silently.

The doctor turned to him, but he didn't answer directly. Instead, he said carefully, meeting the eyes of Daniella and then the father. "We've to take him to the hospital. That's absolutely important."

"Then why don't you do that?" Jeffrey asked rather frightfully.

The doctor looked at J J, straightening his body, then looked back at the girl and then Jeffrey. "We're checking whether the boy is well enough to take the travel. And ………"

Jeffrey interrupted quickly. "Oh no. If it's not safe, don't take him."

The doctor silently turned back to the child. He looked more like a doll in the cot and had no movements on the face or on the hands or legs. In fact, there was no sign of life whatsoever. He met the staring eyes of his colleagues, clearly for their endorsement, before he looked back at the father. "If J J stays here, I'm sorry; there is no guarantee that he'll make it through the night."

Suddenly, Jeffrey grew petrified, visibly shaking, and unable to speak. The restrained tears behind the eyelids started to force out, filling the eyes and quickly dripping down the cheeks. Daniella's cry got all the louder and more distressing. Jeffrey pulled her head against him, obviously sharing the emotions. He looked at his son again, all the anxieties mystified in his eyes, and then, slowly, he turned to the doctor. "Please do, doctor," he said in a mixed tone of absolute inability to know what was best for J J and the compelling impulse to do the best instantly, "Whatever is best!"

The doctor stared at Daniella, then looked back at him. "Can we talk outside?" He whispered politely. "Maybe in the next room if it's free."

He nodded his head and went to Daniella's room. The doctor followed him. "It's not as easy as that now, Mr. Smith."

Silently, he stared at him.

"We've progressed greatly over the last twenty, thirty years. But having a baby in the forties is still very much of a risk."

"We didn't plan it, doctor, if I can say so. But my wife became pregnant, and we accepted it."

"Of course, I know. I've seen the records." He paused briefly as if unsure of himself. "But we can't alter nature's way very easily."

He didn't say anything.

"And poor J J is paying a heavy price for it."

"I know. And his mother, too."

"And there is another issue."

"What is that?"

"Well, the police are working on it, and they will let you know in due course."

He was silent. Obviously, he didn't know what to say. But in his shattered state, he wished he wouldn't hear any more painful news.

"I didn't want to say these things there. Because I didn't want your daughter to know!"

While Jeffrey and the doctor were discussing, the paramedic and nurse moved J J into a Moses basket. Daniella pulled out a white blanket from a drawer, and they wrapped him comfortably with it. A deep freeze was reigning outside. Daniella pulled out light socks for his feet, but she suddenly changed her mind. His feet felt very cold. She gave them heavy cotton socks and leather shoes to put on his legs and then gave him a heavily knitted hat for his head. They pulled it down over his ears. The medical staff told her, "Thank you, Daniella. You thought everything rightly."

Jeffrey and the doctor returned.

The doctor whispered, lifting everybody's spirit, "Hello, young man," he said to the child, "you're ready to go to the hospital."

Daniella quickly kneeled down by the Moses basket and kissed the child on his face. Suddenly, as if hurled back, she raised her body to her knees and stared up at her father. "J J is cold, daddy. Icy cold!"

Sadly, they didn't need to take him to hospital. He had already gone to a new world.

Chapter 6

Sailing Against the Hurricane

Part 1: Life after J J

23 days passed by – long 23 days – each day had been painful, problematic, and traumatic, and each day was more unbearable than the day before. This period started with the death of J J on the evening of Monday, the 3rd of December 1979, and his death time was estimated to be 5.30 pm. Doctor Davis prepared the temporary death certificate and arranged the removal of the body to the hospital morgue.

Daniella was on her knees at J J's Moses basket side. She stooped further over the basket and kissed his exposed face, the only part of the body that was exposed of the vestment. Tears trickled down from her eyes and filled his eyeballs, then channelled down to the garment around. "J J, my dearest of all, are you leaving us?" She managed to mutter while weeping woefully and gasping for air. "You haven't seen Mama for days. Nor Mama seen you? How can you go like this?"

Jeffrey gently guided her a little away. Then he took his baby up in his arms from the basket. He held the baby close to his heart and face. "My son," he cried, his voice only audible for his child alone, wherever he might be, "Mum and I, we waited for you with our full love. But……. but you're gone. What a time to go, son? What a way to go, son?" He rubbed his face on his son's body. "But we'll remember you every day of our life."

The removal van had been outside for about 30 minutes. The driver stayed in the vehicle, but the body attendant came out again and saw the doctor outside the room. They discussed about their duties for a couple of minutes before they both turned to Jeffrey in the room. "Sorry, Jeffrey," the doctor spoke very politely and tactfully. "They've to take J J, shall I say, in about five minutes, the most."

Daniella instantly moved closer and rested her face on the basket, continuing to cry louder and kiss more passionately. And it took a minute or two before Jeffrey could bring about himself to the situation. "Are you taking him to the funeral parlour?" He asked, confused, his voice close to crying.

"Not now, Mr Smith," the doctor replied courteously. "Now they are taking him to the hospital."

"You've issued the certificate?"

"I gave you the temporary certificate," he explained quietly. "But I couldn't issue the proper one. I wasn't J J's GP. I work in the emergency department."

"Alright, can I go with them?"

"No, you don't?" He waited as if unsure of himself, but suddenly he resumed taking, "you can contact them in the morning. They'll organise everything for you."

A few more minutes tearfully ticked away. Then the engine started on the ambulance. The van rolled forward into the pitch dark and disappeared shortly. Only the rear lights persisted up the road, seemingly like a pair of eyes staring back at them. They were still on the kerb, standing aloof in a lost world of their own, and watching the rear lights, which all the while diminishing to the distance, but still, an indication for them to know the whereabout of J J. He wasn't coming back, and that much was absolutely sure. And suddenly, on the other end, where the road curved sharp, the van's rear lights also went out.

Absently, they continued to stand there, staring their eyes through the night, wishing to see something that wouldn't be there anymore. The doctor was behind them, and he moved forward into their view. "My sincere condolences, Jeffrey, and you, Daniella," he whispered, stretching out his hand. In the light filtering out through the front room window, he saw his hand, and he took it silently.

He moved further to Daniella, saying, "Your parents will be proud of you. You're a brave girl."

Without speaking, she caught his eyes.

He turned to Jeffrey. "Are you going to see Debra tonight?"

He didn't answer quickly. "I suppose so."

"When did you see her?"

"This morning."

"How is she?"

"Very poor!"

The doctor waited. "Think well before you speak to her about J J."

Without speaking, he looked at him.

The doctor caught his eyes steadily, then, turning back, walked away towards his car. They watched his partially disappearing figure in the dark. He got into his car, and the light came on as he started the engine. Slowly, he drove away and disappeared down the road.

They went back to the house. He moved further forward into the kitchen for a whisky bottle and, removing its cap, drew a mouthful of drink hurriedly. He put the bottle on the table in front of him and stood there, seemingly immobile, staring down at the bottle; the cap still held in between his fingers, and the drink in his mouth still remained there. A few moments ticked away, and suddenly, as if woken up, he swallowed the drink down the throat. Absently, he raised the bottle to his mouth and drank a mouthful of sip rather quickly. He threw the bottle down on to the table as a fierce cough pressurised up his throat. He coughed badly for a couple of minutes, and his whole abdomen shook violently. In the end, he took a couple of quieter breaths and then took the bottle again. However, Daniella was standing behind him. She swiftly leaned forward and held back the bottle, crying, her voice clearly pleading, "Please don't!"

He turned and stared at her angrily. "Why not?"

She hesitated nervously. "Mama always said."

"What?"

"Don't drink too much."

He let the bottle go from his hand.

She put it back in the liquor cupboard.

Jeffrey went upstairs and waited outside J J's room. Somehow, he felt extremely strange up there. It wasn't his son's bedroom anymore. Normally, Debra was always there, doing something for him, like cleaning, washing, changing, feeding, or talking and playing. Now, nobody was there. The room was absolutely empty and alarmingly haunting. However, he entered and walked further in, carefully staring into the cot as if J J was still in it, awake and staring back at him. Everything else was a sheer frightening bad dream. The cot was clearly empty. He kneeled down by its side and stretched his arm gently over the patch on the mattress where J J used to lie down. He dropped his face flat on the edge of the mattress, then he remained motionless, not even a faint swell of breathing. However, the drops of tears filtered down and formed a teeny puddle discreetly on the waterproof sheet under his face.

Minutes elapsed painfully, and then the voice of Daniella rose from the doorway. "Getting late, daddy," she said, her voice was heavily trodden with sadness.

He didn't reply.

She waited for a while. "Are you going to see Mamie?"

This time he waited before he raised his head a little and nodded slightly for an answer.

Another half hour passed when they spoke again downstairs in the reception. "I take you to Christina?" He asked tersely.

She replied quickly. "I'm also coming, Papa."

He caught her eyes. "No buses or taxies. All on strikes."

"I know. Uncle Gareth will give us a lift."

Their immediate neighbour was Mr Willies and his family. They were on the same side of the road, about thirty yards away on the right. They didn't enjoy the presence of Jeffery and his family. Shameful to say, young Daniella had something to do with it. Despite being told the fact, they stubbornly tended to believe that Debra had an illicit affair with a black man, and Daniella was the result. Jeffrey didn't concern himself too much about it, as he was fairly used to it by now. Anyway, he and Debra lived in their own compound, and that was that – as far as they were concerned. The property on the left belonged to Joe Milner's households, about forty yards away on the same side of the road. They didn't associate with anyone outside their family circles. A few more yards away from Milner households, Gareth Miller lived on the opposite side of the road with his wife Joanna, daughter Christina, and sons James and John. Christina and Daniella were in the same age group, went to the same school, and studied in the same class. In fact, they were close friends.

Gareth hadn't come home yet after his afternoon shift. Joanna was home, and she was more than happy to take them to the hospital. Christina also got in with them, obviously to share the pain of her best friend.

"I'm really annoyed with you, Jeffrey," Joanna said in the car. "And also with you, Daniella. You didn't let us know. We're like a family. Sad I couldn't give a kiss to J J."

They didn't reply.

"I'm more than sure Gareth will be very upset when he'll hear it."

This time, Jeffrey replied quietly, "Everything happened in no time, Joanna." He paused and sighed painfully. "And there was no time for thinking. And thank you so much for dropping us."

"No, no," she said rather rebelliously, "we'll wait for you in the car. And if it's okay, we'll come with you."

They exited the dual carriageway and drove down the slip road towards the hospital. The car park was before the hospital building, and as they approached it, they suddenly noticed that the car park was in absolute darkness except for a couple of dimmed tube lights over the direction boards to departments, but lights were very fuzzy through the misty air. Joanna managed to park the car in a bay close to the exit. "What do you think?" She asked softly.

"Alright," he answered, staring into the pitch darkness outside, "you better come."

They headed through the pedestrian pathways. There was a mount of earth partially in front of them, and they had to come around it before they could see the hospital buildings, which were, in fact, a group of single-storey annexes slightly over lower ground. It would take about five minutes in the daylight to reach there. They waded through the dark and bypassed the mount and saw to their alarm that the lights at the windows of the rooms were very poorly lit. Hesitantly, they moved further and arrived at the gate. Two elderly men were there, sitting facing one another, with a small table in between them and two candles burning. It gave them a fair amount of light inside their timber cabin. The men looked at them rather curiously for a moment, then one on the right who, pulling down the cap on his forehead against the cold, asked, "What can we do for you?"

Part 2: Meeting

Jeffrey stepped into the front. "We want to see Debra Smith. She's in the ICU."

"And you're?" He enquired, lifting the hand to his mouth with a burning cigarette stuck between two fingers.

"I'm Jeffrey Smith, her husband."

The man drew on his cigarette and let the smoke out through his nostrils while he spoke. "Have you been here?"

"Yes. Many times!"

"Well, then you should know that the visiting time is already over. But...."

He interrupted, "We're sorry."

"That's okay, but it's not safe to go in. There is no light anywhere in the buildings. It's the generator that keeps the machinery going. And a bit of low lighting!"

Joanna said from the back. "I don't think it's a power cut. Light everywhere except this compound."

"Yes, you're right," the man agreed right away. "Something's faulty in the system here." He took another puff and blew out the smoke speedily. "The electricians were working on it. But the unions ordered to stop the work until further instruction."

"I don't believe it," Jeffrey said impatiently. "They are killing the sick and the helpless. How can they be humane?"

"That's very sad to hear, sir," the man said absolutely annoyed. "The unions always stood for the sick and the poor. And the sick and the poor have gained lots of progress over the two generations, why? Because the unions fought for it, and the labour movements supported it. Don't forget this when you listen to the bourgeois media."

Jeffrey didn't say anything, nor did Joanna. Obviously, they weren't standing in the freezing cold for an argument.

He took another puff on his cigarette hurriedly. "Anyway, the unions kindly took the initiative for a talk with the management. And the talk is going on right now. And, hopefully, by morning, we'll have a satisfactory agreement."

An uneasy silence engulfed for a moment, and then Jeffrey broke the silence. "My son died this evening," he said in a breaking voice of sadness. "At least, can we go to the ICU and see my wife through the glass panel and grieve with her, please?"

A FEW TALES

The man took the last puff on his cigarette and grounded it in an ashtray while the second man said pretty authoritatively, "What my colleague is saying to you is this." He stopped talking and shot a glance at his colleague as if for an understanding. He nodded automatically, and the second man continued. "It's very dangerous for visitors to go in now. The machinery is everywhere, live cables are everywhere, and not enough light anywhere. You might blow up yourself. Or you might blow up the whole building with all the sick and the poor in it. We can't allow that because we are humane." He shot a glance at his colleague again before he continued, "So, please go home now for everyone's sake and give them a call tomorrow on the hospital switch board and they will guide you."

Without speaking, Jeffrey stared momentarily at the men before stepping back into the foot way. Joanna and the girls followed him. When they were at an open path, he stopped walking, stood by the border wall, and gazed towards the hospital divisions, especially the building at the far right. This was the one known as the intensive care unit, ICU for short, where seriously ill people like Debra were treated.

He gestured to it with his hand, saying, "Debra is there. And we're here. What a shame."

None of the others spoke; only the sobbing of the Daniella rose, breaking the silence. Christina was on her side. She turned and hugged her. "Stop it, Daniella. Stop it."

Daniella didn't stop it. Instead, she sobbed more loudly and more rapidly. Heavy drops of tears dripped down onto her friend's winter coat, then soaking it, filtered onto her body. "Mama's here," she wept wretchedly. "And J J's gone."

Christina didn't say anything. Instead, she tapped on her back soothingly.

On the other side of the girls, Joanna was standing, with her one hand holding onto a fence railing, her eyes fixedly looking at the ICU building. She whispered to Jeffery who was next to her, "J J is also here."

He sighed audibly before he answered softly, "No. My son is in the Children's Hospital."

"Is it too late to pay a visit?"

He shook his head. "We can't until they call tomorrow."

"Alright," she said firmly, "we'll go as soon as possible."

His eyes were steadily on the ICU building. "I saw her this morning," he said, exhaling noisily. "She wasn't very well."

Joanna was silent for a short while. "Probably, it's better for her if she doesn't hear about J J. I suppose we all go home rather than stand here in this cold. It's absolutely freezing."

However, they continued to stay there, as if immobile and said nothing. An uncomfortable quietness sprang up around them beyond their ability to understand anything. Finally, Jeffrey spoke. "If I was allowed for a few minutes with her…"

Joanna interrupted him gently. "You'll see her tomorrow. Take Daniella with you as well."

He didn't reply.

Shortly, they returned home.

The following morning, Jeffrey got up very early. In fact, it was very late when he had gone to sleep, and the sleep itself was distressing as he was drifting off through his subconscious mind. He raised his head and, turning on the bedside lamp, looked at the clock on the wall. It was 3.45. He switched off the light and dropped the head back on the pillow, then pulled up the heavy quilt over him, shutting off the torturous gloom that was engulfing him.

Nonetheless, Jeffrey couldn't put his mind a little calmer and ward off the memories to a distant bay. The reality was that he had no control over himself at present. He could hear the voice of the past echoing, faces appearing out of darkness and staring at him. He shut his eyes and ears tightly, freezing his mind and soul and letting nothing in to pierce his existence. Nonetheless, the desired effect wasn't there. The noises echoed louder, and the faces grew larger. He hurriedly got out of bed and then stayed there, completely confused. Slowly, he paced towards the wardrobe and, picking up a nightgown, he slipped into it. He came downstairs in the hallway and then went to the kitchen. He reached out a bottle of whisky from the cupboard and hurriedly swallowed a mouthful of drink. Quickly, he took another mouthful, and the drink went down, warming up his throat.

Jeffrey paced back to the hallway very quietly as if unsure of himself. He drank up another sip and, holding up the bottle close to his mouth, lingered on aimlessly. He couldn't decide whether to remain downstairs or go upstairs. Abruptly, he opened the door to the reception and went in. He slumped to the settee, stripped off the cover from another chair, and pulled it up over the gown. He remained quietly, sipping from the bottle and trying to sleep.

It was about 8 o'clock in the morning on the 4th of December. Outside was very dark under the heavy clouds that extended to the distance far more than the eyes could see. The heating started at 6.30, but the house was still cold. This winter would be one of the worst for a long time; Daniella heard this news on the radio. She'd generally wake up also at 6.30, but this morning wasn't normal. Her brother passed away yesterday. Her mother wasn't told about it; she wasn't well enough to be told. This time, she had been in the hospital for almost a week. In fact, she had been in the hospital on and off since the day she became pregnant with her brother and lately more frequently admitted for longer spells. She put on an extra layer of clothes and came downstairs and saw for her shock that Jeffrey was on the settee, sleeping, his upper part of the body resting between the back and the arm of it and his legs down on the carpet, the large whisky bottle in his hand and held close to his chest.

Daniella rushed to the kitchen and made a strong cup of coffee and returned with it. "Daddy, you're alright?" She asked clearly in a mixed sound of fear and alarm.

He didn't respond.

She called this time more loudly, "Dad, daddy."

He moved his face slowly towards the direction of the sound and then struggled for a moment to open his eyes. "Yes," he muttered, looking at her through his hazy eyes.

"Coffee, Dad."

His eyes opened fully. "I'll make it later."

"I made it, Dad."

He waited a moment. "Take it away. I'll make one in a minute."

"It's good, dad. I made it exactly as Mamie makes."

Jeffrey held her stare steadily for a moment. Her words about his wife opened up a world of its own in his mind. He moved up his body to the back of the chair properly and sat a bit straighter. He was still holding the whisky bottle, but he knew of it now. He leaned forward and put it on the coffee table by the side of the settee. He looked at her and gestured with his hand to the table, saying, "Leave it there."

She put it politely. "What time are you going to the hospital?"

"I've to call the Royal Hospital first before I go."

She hesitated. "I'm coming with you."

He replied quickly, his voice sounding firm, "You go to the school."

"No, not today," she said woefully. "And I've to see J J. How many days am I going to see him – one day, one week?" She paused, trying to inhale a breath of air. "And Mamie. I haven't seen her for three days."

"This is your decision, then?"

Daniella waited, catching his stare gently. "It's not a decision, Dad. It's important for me. I'd grieve for my brother."

Jeffrey leaned towards the coffee table and stretched his hand. Daniella thought for a moment that he had picked up the coffee mug. However, he pulled back himself, without the mug, and leaned heavily against the back of the chair. "You've taken several days off lately."

"Well, J J wasn't well. Mamie has been on and off the hospital."

"I've to speak to your class teacher," he said rather heavily. "Or perhaps to the head teacher."

"No need for that, Dad. Christina will see them today."

"Did you ask her?"

She nodded her. "Yesterday."

"You rushed."

"I thought it'd free us to deal with our urgent duties."

He continued to stare at her, then looked out the window. The region, in his view, was very misty and dark under the cloudy sky. Suddenly, he turned back. "I've to go to two hospitals."

"I know, Dad."

"But it isn't sure whether we'll be able to see them."

She didn't speak anything.

"And they don't like to see children on health grounds."

She was silent.

He waited vaguely for a moment before he said almost stubbornly, "You stay home then. I go alone."

Daniella looked over to the window unconsciously. However, she didn't see anything; her eyes were misty, and tears were swelling up. She stood as if motionless, then turned to him, resisting the mixed feeling of anger and pain that was growing in the bottom of her heart. "I wanted to ask you this several times over the years," she said finally and very calmly, "Now I'm asking you, Dad. Am I giving you any difficulties?"

Silently, he looked at her for a moment. "What gave you that idea?"

A few drops of tears jumped down to her cheeks. She wiped them away with her nervous fingers. "You don't even talk to me, Dad. Why is that?"

He hesitated. "This isn't the right time to talk about anything else."

"You never had the right time to say anything to me."

He waited. "I'm talking, aren't I?"

"Just instructions, as usual!"

His eyes grew wide into a stare. "May be that's what you think."

"You don't take me out for anywhere, do you? Shopping, cinemas, concerts, dramas, anywhere? At least for a little walk?"

He waited again. "I was having a dreadful time. My son wasn't well. And so was Debra! And most of my time was spent between hospitals. And then work, whenever possible."

"Long before J J was born, you were the same. No time for me!"

"Well, we went to churches."

Daniella wiped out more tears. "Mamie kept me beside her," she said uneasily. "When others stared at me, you used to get awkward. I was too embarrassing for you."

"That's what you believe," Jeffrey retorted quickly, "I've nothing to do with it."

"Because you don't like my colour," she said, hurriedly rubbing off the teardrops that fell down on her cheeks. "And my mixed complexion. And......."

He interrupted her. "I'm not having this conversation. You better go back to your room."

She moved to the door way, then turned back. "I didn't choose my colour. Or my mixed complexion. I was born as I am. So, I've to live as I am." She turned back to the door and went upstairs, but her voice retreated the airway, 'Don't blame me for reasons I had no say on them.'

Daniella absently left the door open, and his eyes followed her as she crossed the hall way and then up the stair case. She disappeared at the top into the landing space. However, Jeffrey remained on the sofa with his body heavily sunk against the back of the chair, his arms flung on his sides, and his mind scrutinising her words and imagining the limitless boundaries of its realities. Slowly, he pulled back his face and stared out the window. He wasn't sure he was seeing anything. He turned to look at the coffee that Daniella had put on the coffee table for him. He reluctantly moved in his chair and reached out for it. He picked it up and swung the hand towards the mouth. However, he didn't sip on it. Instead, he got up with it and went into the kitchen. He poured it down into the sink and made another drink in his own preference. He drank it, then went upstairs. "Daniella," he called out, getting near to her room door.

However, her voice strained out from J J's door, "I'm here."

Jeffrey moved over and gently pushed it to open. His eyes swiftly dashed to the cot, even though he knew very well that J J wasn't there. He caught her stare from the cot side. He went in and stayed there, leaning against the wall. He didn't speak anything, but his breathing grew faster and louder. He said between the sobbing and crying voice, "It would have been less painful if we didn't have him."

"He's in heaven now," she said mournfully. "He's watching over us."

He didn't say anything.

An uneasy silence engulfed them.

"You can go," she said. "I'll stay here."

He continued to stay there, however. "Joanna will come to keep you company after her children have gone to school."

"I know."

Quietly, Jeffrey came out of the room and then went to his room. And after a few minutes, he left for the Royal Children's Hospital.

Part 3: Meeting Dr Jenkins

He went to the receptionist, and a female staff member guided him to one of the inner rooms. "I've an appointment to see Dr Jenkins."

A woman behind the desk looked at him intently. "You're?"

"Jeffrey Smith! I made the appointment this morning."

She picked up a file from one of the drawers and put it on the desk in front of her.

"I am a bit late," he spoke quietly. "No buses running. "Another strike day, I suppose. Luckily, I got a taxi?"

She didn't say anything. Instead, she gestured him to take a seat on the opposite side. He sat down. She opened the file and looked down on a sheet. "One of the other staff made your appointment," she said, looking back at him. "Normally, Dr Jenkins comes on time. Regrettably, this morning, she is late."

He didn't say anything.

"She normally drives. But today, the railways are on strike. And every passenger took to the road, as you can imagine. Which, in turn, created endless traffic deadlocks. And she got delayed. Anyway, she is here now."

"Can I see her now?"

"Not right away, Mr Smith. Dr Jenkins is in a meeting."

"In a meeting? That's crazy. I need to organise the burial of my son."

261

She looked into his distraught face. "This meeting is important for you as well. Because one item in her agenda is about your son."

"What about my son?" He asked impatiently. "It's all your fault. I'm going to sue you."

"I don't know, Mr Smith. I've no further information. I'm afraid you've to wait until Dr Jenkins is available."

He looked down on the desk, absolutely frustrated.

"We're very sorry, please understand."

He looked up. "If I've to wait a much longer, I think I better go to the General Hospital. At least let me stay by the side of my wife."

"Your wife is admitted there?"

Jeffrey didn't speak as he tried to fight back the emotions. "Yes, my wife is there, very poorly," he said quietly.

"I feel sad for you. And you better go. I don't think Dr Jenkins is going to be free soon. As you know, General Hospital is only ten minutes away. You better go and see your wife. And come back an hour or so. Dr Jenkins will be waiting for you, I promise."

Quite obediently, he got up. "Thank you."

"If you can get access to a phone, give us a call."

He was at the door. He turned half towards her and looked at her. "I'll do that."

Jeffrey rushed out to the wide hallway, headed towards the main front door, and walked out to Central Road. The central Road bypassed Central Park, about two hundred yards away. On the other side of the park was the

Bristol General Hospital, and its main entrance hall overlooked the gardens. He hurried through the park, half-walking and half-running, and through the garden zones and reached the hospital fairly quick.

He started walking down the main hallway, and halfway down the way, he bounced into one of the nurses who worked in the ICU ward. "Hello, Angela."

She met his eyes courteously. "Can you wait here? I'll be back in a minute."

Jeffrey nodded his head for an answer, and she went ahead quickly and passed through a door. He moved to the side of the wall and waited. And she came back very soon. "It's my breaktime. Let's go to the café. I'm sure you could do with a coffee?"

They went further on, then came up through a corridor. The cafeteria was situated in a corner with a clear view of the park. She ordered a coffee for Jeffrey and a tea for herself. They collected them shortly, then moved to a corner and sat down. "Debra didn't sleep much last night," she said. "The nurse put it in the night sheet."

Without asking, he looked at her.

"The good news is that she's starting to breathe herself. And this morning, we took her off the ventilator." She absently touched her cup of tea and sensed that it was still too hot to drink. "I think the Glasnostina is beginning to work on her, you know, the new American medicine my consultant told you about."

He nodded lightly.

She stared at him for a moment before she asked rather confidentially, "Are you alright, Jeffery?"

263

He was quite for a moment, fighting hard to keep the emotions off his face. "No," he whispered in the end.

This time, she waited for him to continue.

"J J died."

She held her breath, staring at him. "When?"

"Yesterday evening."

She stretched her hand across the table and held his hand for a moment. "I'm so sorry, Jeffrey."

Without speaking, he looked out the window to the road and beyond to the Central Park. Lots of people were mingling there, most of them either coming to the hospital or going away, and others were wandering around the bushes and plants. He wasn't seeing anything at all. His mind was tangled on issues he had wished he didn't have to face. Suddenly, Angela's voice interrupted him, "What happened?"

"I don't know," he said, his eyes still gazing out. "I suppose his conditions got suddenly worse."

Silently, she listened to him.

"The ambulance staff took over two hours to arrive." He coughed quietly as if clearing the tension of his chest. "If they had arrived on time, he would've been alive now."

"Are you going to tell this to Debra?" She asked in a concerned tone.

He turned back to her. "She should know it, I feel," he said firmly.

She hesitated. "But the time isn't right, Jeffrey. She isn't fit to hear such painful news. You've to wait until she recovers her health a lot more."

"When's that going to be?"

"Nobody knows the answer to it, Jeffrey."

Silently, they drank their drinks. Another minute or two slipped away before he said, glancing at his watch. "I got thirty minutes. I better go and see Debra now. I don't want to miss Dr Jenkins's appointment."

"I know Dr Jenkins," she said. "We're one hospital in two campuses. Sometimes, Susan Jenkins practises here. Don't worry. If you're late, I will let her know you're on the way."

"Do you know what it's about you're talking?"

"About the funeral of J J!"

"Why – any issues about his death?"

"Yes, the appalling delays of the ambulance."

She hesitated. "Any faults from your side?"

"None whatsoever. I'm going to sue the hospital."

She shot a glance into the park pensively, then continued sincerely, "Listen to Dr Jenkins first and understand their reasons for the meeting." She paused thoughtfully, seizing his sombre eyes, then added, "Don't tell your intentions until necessary. Suing a hospital could be risky. You could lose everything."

Jeffrey nodded lightly. "Shall I go now?"

"I'll take you to her room. You know it's not visiting hours."

"I know. Thank you."

The ICU ward was located at the back of the building, and a corridor connected it to the main hallway. It was a spacious ward with few small rooms built along the walls. Debra was in one of the back rooms. Inside the doorway, there was a small office on one side, and a nurse, Jayne, was sitting inside, filling notes on the worksheets. Angela waved a friendly gesture as they walked in. As a reply, the nurse told back, "Eileen is inside. May be Rosy also."

"Thanks, Jayne!"

They moved further in and saw Rosy coming out of a room. She looked at Jeffrey and then at Angela. "Debra woke up," she said softly. "And I gave the medicine. I also checked the pressure. It was like morning, 180 over 95. Now she's back to sleep."

"We won't disturb her," Angela replied considerately. They moved to Debra's room and, standing outside, watched her through the door panel. "Well, you're here, Jeffrey. You can go in when you want to."

He turned his face and looked at her.

She caught his eyes briefly. "You've to keep the emotions down."

Jeffrey opened his mouth to speak; however, he didn't try. For an answer, he nodded his head, then tear drops shattered from his eyes. She continued to stand beside him as if confused. Abruptly, she walked away, saying quietly, "I'm in the office."

He watched her go to the office, then turned back to the glass panel. Jeffrey closed his eyes briefly before he looked at his wife. Suddenly, he lost his composure as he got into the grip of crying, his breathing getting fast and slow, and his body hysterically shaking. Definitely, he didn't want to go to her in this condition. He stayed there seemingly motionless while memories flashed across the tear-drenched, misty views. In their school days, they used to run after the buses to jump in, walk up the school compound fighting playfully, and the sand crushing under their feet. Debra would giggle about anything and everything, and Jeffrey watched her cheerfully. Then they would become quite as they departed to different campuses since he was two years her senior.

Years passed through the seasons while the flowers bloomed, fruits changed colours, howling wind lashed the wings of nights of autumn, and the meadows shrouded with crispy snowflakes of the winter. And through these seasons, their lives also picked up colourful dreams, exciting desires, and a glowing future. The day before Debra's sixteenth birthday, her close friend Salome gave them a huge party. Salome's father, Paster Samuel Laurence, lived in a rented house, and he half-heartedly consented to his daughter to hold the party. As the party progressed, they moved into the centre of the floor and started to dance. Other boys and girls joined in dancing. The music was loud, and so was the hum of talking and giggling and shrieking. They sneaked out into the rear garden. It was a very bright night under the full moon, which shone down from below the zenith of the sky. They went further back and stopped behind some shrubs. "Yes?" he said, zooming with a jubilant expression on his face.

"Are you enjoying?" She said, equally jubilant.

He stepped close. "Of course. And you?"

"Very much so?" she giggled. "We never had anything like this."

"Well, these things are becoming quite normal these days, I suppose."

She stepped close to him. "Well, your birthday is coming soon. An occasion for another party."

He held her and kissed.

Her arms went around him. "I love you."

"I hope so."

She laughed and pulled him very close to her, then kissed him. The kiss lingered for a couple of minutes or might have been longer. And then Salome's voice came through the shrubs. "Are you alright?"

Abruptly they stopped kissing and stared into the direction of the voice. "You're watching us?" Debra asked, slightly embarrassed.

"I was searching for you. You're the stars of the show."

They laughed, then Debra chuckled, "How did you know we are here?"

"I see stars only in the night."

Without saying anything, Debra and Jeffrey laughed again. "What do you want?" Debra asked finally.

"Why're you having all this trouble? Please take the comfort of my bedroom. I've already left the door open for you."

"Thank you, Salome," she chuckled. "We're fine. Anyway, Jeffrey and I'll be going back soon. Uncle Samuel insisted that all should be over by nine. I'm sure it's already over nine now."

Salome sniggered loudly. "My mum and dad are in Manchester for a big convention. They won't get here until tomorrow. The house is ours for the night. And we're going to enjoy it."

A girl shouted from the garden door. "Debra, we're going."

In about ten minutes, everybody left in singles and groups. In the end, Debra, Jeffrey, and Salome were left alone in the lounge. As if it were the last drink, Salome gave a glass of wine to Debra and then whiskey to Jeffrey, and then she took a whiskey for herself. They sipped their drinks in between telling jokes and laughing. Suddenly, Debra felt a light squeeze in her stomach, and thinking that it was the reaction of the drink, she ignored it out of mind. However, in minutes, the squeeze turned to pain and then started to spread upwards, especially into her head. "Only the headache," Salome said trivially. "Lie down for a few minutes. And you'll be alright soon."

Jeffrey looked confused. "Lie back to the chair," he said, holding and helping her to move in her seat.

"I want to go home," she whispered, feeling fearful.

"It's nothing," Salome said convincingly. "Let her rest. We take her to the guest room."

To be honest, she preferred to go home. But she wasn't well enough to do it. They helped her to the guest room behind the lounge. As soon as she got into the bed, she closed her eyes and slipped into a sleep. Salome put her hand on his shoulder and, making a gesture with her eyes that they could go outside the room, said courteously, "Don't worry, darling. It was a strong wine for her, I think. She will be alright in a few minutes."

They came back to the lounge. "You're alright?" Salome asked looking at his face.

"I am worried about Debra."

Silently, she smiled curiously. "You can't disturb her," she said rapturously.

"Oh no. I only want her to be okay."

She hesitated. "You don't look well either. Let me take you to another room. You need to rest a bit as well."

She took him upstairs and into a room. He sat down on the edge of the bed, saying, "Sorry, I'm feeling a little dizzy."

269

"That's fine, darling," she answered, standing right in front of him. "This is my room. Lie and rest for a while." She gently pushed him to a lying position on his back and kissed him.

Part 4: Doctor's Appointment

Almost two hours went by, and then Debra managed to find him sleeping with her best friend. "You dirty bastard," she shrieked, slapping him on his face. He woke up and stared at her, "What are you doing?"

Debra caught his eyes for a moment, obviously unable to reply with feelings of anger, humiliation, and disbelief. She managed to make a gesture with her hand. He turned his eyes to her direction and found Salome lying on his side, absolutely naked. Frantically, he looked at himself and noticed that he was stark naked, too. "Oh my God," Jeffrey screamed frightfully. And he did scream again now in unison with the incidents as the memories flashed through his mind. However, he awakened to the present immediately and heard Debra's frail voice, "Jeffrey, is it you?"

He opened the door quietly and entered into her room. "Yes, dear," he replied softly, trying to be brave not to burst out crying.

Debra struggled again to raise her voice. "I thought I was dreaming."

"No darling," he whispered, moving further in. Holding her palm gently, he kissed her hand and then whispered obviously emotionally. "I'm right here, darling."

Without saying anything, she closed her eyes. Watching her, he stood almost still, his hand still holding on to her palm. One end of a plastic tube nurtured drips into this hand, and the other end joined to a half-filled bottle on a stand. A couple of tubes connected to her legs from other free-standing machines. Slowly, she opened her eyes and muttered, "How's J J?"

He struggled to restrain a powerful sobbing that surged up immediately. He turned backwards and coughed tactfully before he answered as calmly as possible, "He's …. He's fine."

"He's with Joanna?"

"Yes, darling."

She closed her eyes again. "And Daniella?"

"She's also with Joanna."

She moved her face slightly to her side so that she could see him more easily. However, her eyes remained closed. "She's okay?"

"Yes, darling."

"Tell her. I've asked for her."

"Of course, I will!"

Without saying anything, Debra continued to lie down restfully. Jeffrey sat down in a chair, his hand still holding her palm. She audibly wheezed as she breathed and kept her eyes shut. She might be falling into sleep, he thought to himself. However, tears sprouted between the eyelids and then trickled down on her cheek. He leaned over and gently wiped it out with his finger.

A few minutes ticked away, and the nurse, Angela, appeared through the door panel and signalled that she wanted to talk to him. He let his wife's hand go off free and came out quietly.

"Dr Jenkins will you see you at one," Angela whispered quickly. "You've twenty minutes to get there. I suggest, you get a taxi."

"I can walk through the Central Park. I don't have much money on me."

"Don't be silly. I'll pay."

"That's not right."

"You can give me later. Don't miss the appointment."

The taximan dropped him outside the main front door of the Royal Children Hospital. The receptionist then guided him to Dr Jenkins' office. "Good afternoon, Doctor," he said as he entered.

"Good afternoon, Mr. Smith," she said, pointing to a chair across her desk. "Please sit down."

Jeffrey sat down. "Thank you."

She had an open file on her desk. "I'll be with you in a moment," she said politely while her eyes ran through the page she had been studying. Then she flipped a couple of pages and ran through them quickly. Abruptly, she leaned back in her chair and looked at him across the chair. "Can I get you tea? Or coffee?"

"I'm okay, doctor. Thank you."

Dr Jenkins shot a glance at the file before she asked. "I'm sad to know that your son died yesterday. I knew him very well. I've myself examined the little child a few times."

Jeffrey didn't say anything.

"I also come to know that your wife is in the General Hospital. And that Debra isn't told about her son's death."

Silently, he shook his head for an answer.

She said immediately. "She'll get better, I hope. Because they are treating her with a new medicine, which is very successful in America."

He cleared his throat before he replied. "I hope so, too."

She didn't speak straightaway. "Sunday at 1 o'clock, nurse Marcia visited your home. And your neighbour was there."

"Joanna?"

"Well, her name is not on the work sheet. Anyway, Marcia checked J J, and J J was okay, not brilliant, but okay." She stopped talking and waited for him to add anything. He remained quiet, and she continued, "Yesterday, nurse Janet visited you. And you were also there?"

He nodded to confirm her findings.

"Again, J J was just the same. Nonetheless, in the evening, very sadly, he died."

He turned his head away to hide the emotions flocking on his face.

"Anything else you want to add on to my findings?"

Jeffrey tried to regain his composure. "JJ's breathing got slower and noisier," he replied in the end. "And he started to cry. And the crying made him worse. His breathing got heavy. Immediately, she called for an ambulance. And she called seven times for the ambulance. And ...."

She interrupted him gently. "We've records of all these incidents. What I want to know," she stopped talking and thought for a moment. "I understand you are thinking of suing the hospital?"

He waited. "I need to discuss it with my solicitor."

Meeting his gaze, she waited.

"I feel very strongly that your neglect killed….," he broke off momentarily as his emotions overwhelmed him. "Your neglect killed my son. And you've to face the consequences for it."

She turned to the file and entered his statement. "You're charging very serious allegations," she said politely, looking back at his face and her pen in between her fingers above the page she was recording into. "Have you got evidence to back up these allegations, Mr Smith?"

Silently, Jeffrey caught her stare for a moment. He moved in his chair and leaned against the back of the chair. He wasn't sure whether he should lay out his reasons now. Nonetheless, he decided to do so. "J J had these breathing difficulties several times. Paramedics used to arrive in minutes and help him."

"Yes?"

"This time, they took over two hours. And he died."

She looked down in the file and filled in his concerns. And then she raised her face. "You have anything else to say?"

"At the moment, no."

"Anything else to ask?"

"Can I organise my son's funeral?"

The doctor watched his face intently. "The nurse Angela of the General asked me the same question about an hour ago. You know her?"

"I do."

"Relation of you? She was talking about you very caringly."

"She is a kind lady, but no relation. We know her through her sister, Joanna. Joanna and her family live two doors away from us."

Wordlessly, Dr Jenkins tossed the pages of the file carefully. "I'm not a member of the legal department," she said professionally. "At times, they ask me to find facts about certain cases, which I've to present to the legal department. However, I'm not supposed to advise anybody on the choices they should adopt."

He stared at her, bewildered. "I'm afraid I've to see my solicitor."

She watched the time on the clock on the wall and announced in a business-like voice. "The meeting is over at 1.30 on the 4th of December."

Jeffrey got up, apparently annoyed.

Dr Jenkins reached over to the end of the desk and switched off the recording machine. "Please sit down," she said somewhat sympathetically. "Now the machine is off. We can talk off the record."

Without saying anything, Jeffrey sat down.

"Our responsibilities drive us to one way," she said attentively, scrutinising his face steadily. "But our hearts occasionally take us different routes. What's the outcome of it?"

He moved in his chair and leaned back, but he kept silent.

"I've to ask you this." She paused momentarily, her eyes rolling away fleetingly and then rolling back. "You left a 9-year-old child to look after a six months old sick child?"

Jeffrey couldn't find any words for the answer. He looked away, absently rubbing his cheek. Slowly, he turned back and caught her yes steadily. "I'm not a proud man. I feel ashamed of myself."

Dr Jenkins waited for a moment before she asked calmly. "You could do better than that. Please answer me."

He spoke in a mixed voice of guilt and helplessness, "I'm a one-man band. No friends either!"

She hesitated. "I understand that. But there are millions in this group."

"I know. And I have commitments. I've to earn to pay my bills, lots of them – gas, electricity, water, government taxes, clothes, travels. And then the big one, the mortgages! I've to go to work. I've to go to work. It's as simple as that."

She nodded for an answer and then said, "I know."

"And the food isn't cheap anymore. Inflation is going around about 26 percent. And children's food and clothes are more expensive. I've to earn money."

Without replying, she stared at him.

"When I go to work, I let Joanna know. And she pops into my house and keeps an eye on the children. Yesterday, she got stuck in her job. Anyway, the fault is mine. And I paid the heaviest price of my life."

"I understand," Dr Jenkins said respectfully. "Yesterday was one of those days. We had nothing but havoc all day." She stopped talking and looked at him helplessly. "The snowfall was appalling yesterday morning and the night before. On most of the roads, conditions were atrocious. They couldn't clear the roads, not even the major roads. And the weather was freezing cold, minus 5 degrees – I heard. And in the snow and the cold, people couldn't get work. Vehicles skidding or engines freezing! There were multiple car accidents and the usual long delays."

"I know," Jeffrey said. "But how can they ignore the cry for a sick child?"

Dr Jenkins was quiet for a moment. "We've 67 ambulances in our operation. Even if all vehicles are fit and running, and forget for a moment about the strikes, and bad weather and petrol shortages and picketing and who knows what else, how can they cope with the turmoil across the county."

"A child should get priority."

"I couldn't agree with you anymore, Jeffrey. And as soon as they were able to provide priority, five paramedics and a doctor arrived at your home to treat your child. And that two police officers were there, too."

"They couldn't save him."

"No?"

"No. Debra was too old to have a baby when J J was born. The medical authorities had warned you about it and the medical consequences of it for both the child and the mother. But you and Debra ignored the medical advises."

"We've our reasons, I'm sorry."

"But if you're thinking of suing the hospital, you're bound to lose."

Jeffrey waited quietly.

"They used all the modern technology and medicines. And they kept him alive on a daily basis. But he wasn't making any progress at all."

Again, he waited.

They've legal departments with the best solicitors and barristers in the country. What have you got? And when you lose, they sue for all their cost.

How are you going to finance? That means you lose your home. Why do you want to take these risks? Nothing is going to bring back J J?"

Without replying, he leaned back in his chair and looked at her face.

"Before you decide on anything, I would suggest that you better talk to your friends, such as Angela or Joanna or your solicitor. And if you could let me have your decision in a week or as soon as possible, we could move on."

"I have made the decision."

"Yes?"

"Not suing the hospital!"

"Don't you want to think it over, at least for the night?"

"No. I want to bury my son as soon as possible."

She waited. "To find the whole truth, they want to do a post-mortem."

"My God, you want to cut his tiny body into pieces?"

Part 5: Suing Medical Staff

"We also want to know exactly what had happened. If it shows medical failures were the reason for his death, you're entitled to compensation."

"Alright, you can organise the funeral arrangements any day after this Monday. That will also give us time for a post-mortem."

The post-mortem was done on the 7th of December, and J J was buried on the 13th. Friday afternoon, on the 14th, Debra came home in an ambulance. Two paramedics helped her come up the staircase and go to the bed. She took a few minutes to get to know her whereabouts. And then she said happily, "Where are my children?"

Jeffrey gave the easier answer first. "Daniella is in the school, darling."

"Alright. Where is my son?"

Jeffrey coughed to clear his throat. "Yesterday, he wasn't too well."

"Is he okay?"

"Of course. He had a little temperature. They took him to the hospital."

"And?"

"Well......well, they are monitoring him today, as usual. Nothing to worry."

"When is he coming back?"

"Tomorrow, darling."

"Did you see him today?"

"Of course. And you know I will go and see him."

"How's Ella?"

"Daniella is fine. She is the best student in the class."

"She is. I know that."

"She is good for singing, dancing, and studying. Everybody loves her."

"I miss her."

"Well, she'll be home soon."

As he said, Daniella arrived. She ran up the staircase and ran into her mother's room. Swiftly, the girl fell down to her knees and, lying over the edge, dropped her face lightly on her mother's chest. "Mamie, I missed you."

Debra didn't say anything. The intensity of emotions inside her frail body was overpowering her, and she wasn't fit enough to say anything. Her view was limited, too. As her head was on her chest, her massive strands of hair amassed onto the mother's face. Somehow, she managed to draw her hands up and hold her daughter closely to her as her strength tolerated. The girl spoke nothing more. Without realising, they were engulfed in the depth of silence and listening to the beats of hearts.

"I miss you," the girl said finally.

"I miss you, too."

"You're okay, Mamie?"

"Getting better, darling."

"Good. I was very lonely."

"J J was here. And daddy."

Daniella didn't reply.

"How was J J?"

"Okay."

"Did he scratch you?"

She didn't answer. Somehow, she couldn't answer directly. "I can't remember."

"Good. He didn't do it, then. He does it only when he is desperate for your attention."

She was quiet.

"Are you crying, darling?"

This time, she spoke. "No."

"I could feel your tears falling into my chest."

Daniella knew she had to be careful here. "Because I'm happy, Mamie."

Another long silence slowly ticked away. "Did you go to see J J today?"

"No. I went to school."

"He's coming back tomorrow."

"Did daddy say?"

"Yes."

Daniella didn't say anything.

"I saw him every day. He's a big boy." She paused as if for a moment to remember. "He runs towards me and hugs me. Talks to me. Laughs with me. Then runs away, looking back playfully at me."

She kept quiet.

"But he always said loudly, 'I love you, Mamie.'"

"He's a good boy."

"If he doesn't come back tomorrow, we'll go and see him."

She waited. "You won't be able to travel, Mamie."

"Hopefully, I'll be."

The next day, Debra got up early. "What time is J J coming?"

Jeffrey was awake but was still lying on his side with his back towards her. And, conveniently, he pretended to be in deep sleep. After half an hour or so passed, she asked again and fairly loudly, "Jeffrey?"

He tossed about sleepily for a moment, then muttered, "What is it, Debra?"

She asked rather vigorously, "What time is J J coming home?"

He waited. "Late afternoon, I think."

"Why can't we go," she asked, clearly impatiently. "And we can bring him back, as well."

"We've to wait until they tell us. We can't put pressure on them."

"Alright, we just go and see him," she insisted angrily.

"We can't go in our car, darling," he told calmly. "You're not steady on your leg. Please wait."

Saturday passed, and Sunday came and then went. On Monday morning, Jeffrey helped her to get downstairs and then to the lounge. She sat down on the settee, and he turned on the telly for her. "Shall I get a tea for you, dear?"

She agreed.

He made a cup of tea for her and a cup of coffee for him and brought them over to the lounge. "Aren't you watching the TV, darling?" he asked, putting down her tea in front of her on a table. Without replying, she stayed obviously immobile, her eyes glued to a picture of Daniella holding J J in their garden.

"I'll phone the hospital today," he said. "Maybe they will pick you up in an ambulance."

She turned and caught his eyes. "Can we talk, Jeff?"

"Of course, darling," he whispered readily. "What's it, my darling?"

Her eyes grew wide while she tried to restrain her surging feeling from the pit of her stomach. "Our son is waiting for us?"

He moved in his chair and sat facing her directly. He opened his mouth to answer and his mouth stayed open but no voice came out. "Why…. why did you ask …. ask this?"

She was sitting close to him. She leaned further and rested her face on his chest. "I see him………"

"Where?" he asked, his voice audible enough to hear. His arms fell around her body, and held her close to him. "Where?"

"On the mount of his cemetery."

"Yea?"

"He's alone there." She stopped as the constrained emotions chocked her. "And looking at me crying!"

Jeffrey cried silently.

"If he died, I wouldn't be sad at all because……." She couldn't finish her sentence, though, as the pain froze her willpower to stay alive. In the end, she somehow completed her sentence, "Because I just……. Just don't want to see him suffering forever."

Jeffrey didn't speak, and she didn't continue talking. An intolerable, intensive silence shrouded them cruelly for a brief period. "I was waiting for a right time to tell you. But …but when will I find the right time to tell you that our son died."

Debra didn't say anything.

"And I was so scared about you. How would you face the news that our child died? How would you attend his funeral? You were not in the best of health either. I couldn't face one more death."

This time, she replied in a breaking voice, "I understand, darling."

Jeffrey wanted to say something, but he couldn't get the words out of his mouth as painful memories of his son numbed his mind.

Debra was silent for a short while before she said, "Jeff, I want to go up."

"Why darling?" He managed to ask. "Take your medicine."

"That can wait, Jeff. I must go up and lie down. Please help me."

Jeff held her arm to steady her balance as they went up the stairs. She went to bed immediately. He hung idly in the room for a couple of minutes. "What can I get you for breakfast, dear?"

"Give me anything," she replied, wheezing audibly. "Get my inhaler."

He picked it up from the little box kept on the beside unit. She drew a deep puff and let the air out quietly. She repeated the exercise one more time.

"You're okay?"

"Yes, dear," she replied, holding her eyes closed.

"You don't look okay to me?"

"Well, Jeff," she whispered, opening her eyes. The tears that filled them seeped down to the sides. "I've to grieve and find my own peace."

Before he could speak, she closed her eyes. He continued to stay there, watching her face and thinking what he could do for her. And then, deciding better not to disturb her, he left the room.

Jeffrey came down to make something for breakfast. Well, it was too late to say breakfast. Nothing seemed to have any order at the moment. And when he walked into the kitchen, he wasn't happy at all. The place wasn't very tide. The kitchen sink had plates and cups and bowls and food bits. And the worktop wasn't very tidy. He used to tell his staff off whenever the kitchen wasn't clean. He was a proud chef, and the cooking areas should be spotless. However, homes couldn't be put under this norm. Daniella got up late, prepared something to eat, and ran to the school for an exam. Again, everything that was happening at home was affecting her as well.

Jeffrey washed everything that lay in the sink and put it away on the tray, cleaned the worktop, and then started to make the breakfast. Debra was happy with cold milk and cereal – nothing more. He would fancy a couple of ham and tomato sandwiches and a cup of tea. He was about to pour the milk into the bowl, but he had a strange urge to go up and check on Debra. He turned off the cooker and the kettle and went upstairs.

He got petrified as he came nearer to the bed. Debra was gasping for air, and her face was wet with perspiration. He ran down. He grabbed the phone, dialled 999 for ambulance, and ran back to his wife. He picked up the inhaler from the medicine box and helped her to draw on it. Hopefully, it should help her breathe easier. He lifted her body and pulled in his pillows behind her back. Now, she could lean back rather than lie down, and this position should help her breath more comfortably. Whatever he could do, he was doing, but her inhaling was getting harder and louder.

Luckily, the ambulance siren was sounded at the bottom of the road. He rushed to the front door.

Chapter 7

Dreams and Realities

Part 1: Paramedics Arrive

An ambulance van with two paramedics arrived first. They quickly started providing her with oxygen from a cylinder. They put her on high-tech machinery and checked the rhythms of her heart moments and normalised. They put her intravenous drips and administered drugs. In about twenty minutes, she appeared coming back to her senses. "It's better if we take her back to the hospital," the senior paramedics said in a reassuring voice.

Jeffrey immediately agreed to it. A few minutes later, they were on their way to the hospital. Jeffrey was also in the ambulance, sitting next to her, holding her hand, and whispering along the route, "You're doing fine, darling."

When she was in the hospital for two hours or so, she started to show signs of improvement. The emergency doctor who had been with her since her arrival met Jeffrey and said, "She's in a much more comfortable stage now."

"Thank you, doctor."

"And I think we need to monitor for a couple of days."

Without saying anything, he met the doctor's eyes steadily.

"She's going back to her previous ward."

"Thank you!"

She stayed in the hospital until the 23rd of December, and that was Sunday. In the afternoon, she was sent back home in the ambulance van. "If you need us," one of the paramedics said to Jeffrey, "please phone."

And they returned.

Debra settled in the lounge. Daniella was on her side, hugging and kissing her. "How nice to be home."

Jeffrey smiled. "Of course. Party time. What can I get you, Debra? A glass of wine?"

"Tea, dear. Wine may not be good with my medication."

"Alright'. And You, Daniella – a glass of Juice?"

She looked at him from the other side of Debra. "Okay."

"Alright," he said as if they were in a restaurant. "A tea for you, Debra. A glass of juice for you, Daniella. And for myself, alright, I'll kindly serve a whiskey."

Debra laughed lightly, then added, "I can't remember when I laughed."

In the evening, Joanna turned up with Christina. "Merry Christmas and a happy new year," they shouted when Jeffrey opened the door.

Jeffrey smiled. "Merry Christmas. Please come in. The lady is waiting inside."

They came into the lounge. "Merry Christmas!"

"Merry Christmas," Debra wished them back, struggling to get up.

"No, no, don't bother to get up, Debra dear," Joanna said. "We're very happy that you're back and back for Christmas."

For half an hour or so, they spent together, Joking, laughing and talking. They talked about the price increases on food, clothes, toys, and gifts. Another subject was who was coming to the city for entertainment and where they would appear. Of course, they talked about new movies and the actors in them. In the end, Joanna got up. "Sorry, we've to go. We haven't sorted anything yet. Everything stays in the bags and boxes."

"I don't think I could be any help to you either," Debra chuckled.

"Any help or not," Joanna invited them, "you're celebrating Christmas in our house. Because last year, we were here, remember?"

"See how I feel," Debra replied courteously.

"You'll be alright. Anyway, we'll be popping in all the time."

"Thank you," Jeffrey said. "I'm starting full-time from tomorrow."

"Can't you wait until after the Christmas?" Joanna asked. "In case Debra needs help."

"Oh! I wish – severe shortage of staff. And I can't say no. I took several days off. Luckily, Christmas day, I'm off."

Johanna mentioned suddenly. "Don't forget. You've the meeting in the hospital tomorrow."

Jeffrey said tersely, "I know."

Debra looked at him. "What meeting?"

He shot a knowing glance at their guest before he replied cautiously. "To discuss about the overall treatment of J J."

However, the meeting was convened to talk about the post-mortem on J J and the verdict it had concluded with.

A committee of two women and one man represented the hospital. They sat on one side of the desk in the meeting room, and the man sat in the middle of the women. "Any solicitor attending the meeting for you, Mr Smith?" the male officer asked respectfully.

"No, sir," he replied.

"Can you conduct the meeting yourself?" The female on the right side asked courteously.

"I can tell the truth."

Quietly, they looked at one another as if for some sort of agreement. They nodded silently before they turned to him.

"Shall we introduce ourselves?" The male officer said professionally. "I'm Steven Norris, deputy coordinator of legal operations."

The female officer on his right introduced herself, "My name is Mavis Brady. I'm a lead social worker."

The other female officer said, "I'm Annette Parker. A social worker on child abuses."

He caught their eyes alternatively.

Steven looked into the file in front of him on the desk, then turned to Jeffrey. "We understand you had a meeting with Dr Jenkins?" Steven enquired, checking on the writing sheet.

"Yes, Mr Norris," he admitted.

"How did you find the meeting with Dr Jenkins?"

Without replying, he caught their gazes one by one for a moment. "Quite painful conversations. We lost our son."

Mavis said, sounding sympathetic, "We know how you're taking it. And
......."

He interrupted her. "No, you wouldn't know that. Because you couldn't
until it happens to you."

Annette glanced at her quickly, then looked at Jeffrey. "Dr Jenkins told
you all the troubles we had on the day your son sadly died."

"Yes. I suppose. But you have treated him several times before. And you
had known how fragile his conditions were."

Annette shot a fleeting glance at her colleagues before she added gently.
"But Dr Jenkins didn't tell you about one important subject."

"Why?"

"She didn't have the proof."

"Proof. What proof. And for what."

"We're aware of his illness. We've been treating him. But he didn't die
of his illness."

Bewildered, he started at them.

"We're sorry we've to tell you this."

He waited for them to continue.

"He died of an accident."

"Accident?"

"Of course, it was an accident," Mr Norris said politely and tactfully. "But
Daniella sadly dropped the child."

"What?"

"The child fell on his head. And his neck got severely injured."

"I don't believe it."

"The paramedics found out the neck injury. They asked Daniella about it."

"What did she say?"

"J J was crying violently. She got frightened and ran down to call the ambulance."

"What's wrong with it."

All three of the officers waited. In the end, Mavis replied, "This is where the accident happened."

"What accident?"

"The child was hysterical now. I mean, crying badly. And somehow, his fingers hit her eyes. She got terrified, and the baby slipped off her hands."

He waited, struggling to find his voice to speak. "She told this?"

"Yes, she told this to the paramedics. And to the police who came to your house on that day."

"Did she say that?"

"The police had a meeting with her. And she confirmed it."

Jeffrey shut his eyes to contain the tears that were bubbling up behind his eye lids. And a moment later, he slowly opened his eyes. "She didn't tell me this?" He said in a voice that was trembling with pain.

They waited silently for a moment. "Well, Daniella is a child, too. Poor girl, she must be having a traumatic time ever since."

Without speaking, he just stared at them.

"And the post-mortem confirmed whatever Daniella told us is true."

A silence engulfed them. In the end, Norris broke the silence. "It's an accident, and Daniella is a minor. And we have no desire to take this matter any further."

Jeffrey paused while he was restraining the crippling pain soaring inside him. "It's been always bothering my mind. What happened to my son?" He paused again, fighting to regain his composure. "And when I hear this, it's more painful and disturbing than the worst I ever feared."

They didn't speak immediately.

"I don't think I could tell this to my wife. It will kill her immediately."

They shot a glance at each other. "There is no need you've to inform Mrs Smith," Mavis said courteously, "at least now as she is very poor."

Another silence drifted as they scrutinised their open files in front of them.

He asked quietly, "I take it that this is the end of it?"

Mr Norris looked at the women on his sides before he answered.

"Yes and no!"

He waited silently.

"As far as the hospital is concerned, it's the end. But we're asked to provide a copy of our report to the police."

"What for?"

Steven looked at him silently while the former was contemplating the whole issue. "We have a child here who died while he was in the care of another child. Maybe police might see it as a serious charge." He stopped talking and continued to look at him briefly. "Well, I don't know. You've to wait for their report."

"Daniella was an orphan," he said ruefully. "Now, I am paying a heavy price for my compassion."

They hurriedly searched their files thoroughly, then shot glances at each other, clearly concerned. "Did I hear you correctly that Daniella was an orphan?"

He nodded quietly. "She is adopted. But we never told anybody about it because we brought her up as our own child. Our own blood and flesh!"

"If I may ask you," Annette asked politely, "Why did you tell us that now?"

He looked at them one by one, completely confused. "I've been always vexed about this situation. But my wife never allowed me to tell anyone. To her, Daniella was her daughter and daughter alone."

"Thanks for telling us," Annette told. "None of us have this information in our files."

"This is a separate issue," Steven said quickly. "And we've to deal with it in a separate meeting."

Jeffrey sat quietly as he started to feel unsure of himself. Perhaps it would have been better for him if he hadn't disclosed Daniella's identity. "I need to contact the police?"

"I don't think it's necessary," Steven answered. "They will contact you if they need to. Or they will get in touch with us." He stared at his colleagues, saying, "I think we've covered all the points. Or anything else you think we omitted?"

They both replied almost in unison, "No."

Steven turned to Jeffrey. "You've anything to ask?"

He needed a couple of moments to have a mental view of all the problems in front of him. He coughed quietly, pretending to be clearing his throat. "Is there anything I need to be afraid of with the police?"

They passed glances at each other solicitously before they looked at him silently. A moment later, Steven said in a business-like voice. "I would suggest to seek legal advice on this. We're not at liberty to discuss anything outside our mission."

"I understand that. But I'm literally penniless at the moment. I haven't done a full week's work for a year now, ever since my wife became pregnant with J J. She has been very ill even before the birth of J J."

Silently, they sat there.

"We're living with high inflation, high interests, and high mortgages. Having a home is like a crime and punishment. Because people are forced to pay the penalties for the mistakes the politicians are creating."

They continued to remain silent.

"I've to pay the bills – electricity, gas, water, and the rest. And buy the food and clothes and medicines and whatever else are there."

Steven opened his mouth to speak but didn't speak.

"This is why I go to work whenever I get a few hours part-time. Just pay the bills and keep the family together."

"We understand that," Mavis said sympathetically.

"On the day, I wasn't meant to go to work. But my boss pleaded for just four hours due to a severe shortage of staff. And I found it hard to refuse it. They could have sacked me a long time ago for my absences. They haven't done that because they cared about me."

They didn't speak.

"My son was in my hand, and I looked at him. He smiled back. I gently put him in the cot. He moved his hands and legs happily and gave me a big smile. Looking back, that was the very last smile he gave me." He broke off talking as waves of memories surged inside, and tremors of emotions overpowered him. For a few minutes, he couldn't speak up. They didn't speak either. A heavy, uneasy silence drifted around them.

In the end, Steven asked, "Shall we finish the meeting?"

They nodded, looking at each other and at him. They got up and shook hands with him, saying, "Our sincere apologies for the loss of your son."

However, Annette stayed back. "You don't mind if I talk to you for a couple of minutes in confidence, Mr Smith?"

He stared at her. "Not at all, Ms Parker."

She hesitated a moment. "It's an accident. Please don't punish Daniella for it."

He watched her face studiously. "Of course not!"

"You've to be very careful these days, Mr Smith. Child abusers are dealt with very seriously."

"What's the point of this talk, Ms Parker?"

"My information is that you don't treat Daniella very well."

"Goodness gracious! What did you hear?"

"You were using the girl to look after your child."

"Who told you that?"

"In my profession, I talk to all sorts of people. But the materials are strictly confidential."

"Daniella said this?"

She protested it. "Don't be silly. She's a clever girl."

"Who else could do this?"

"It could be anybody. Maybe her teachers. Or school children and their parents. How many days off has she had lately? You simply don't know who's watching. And they could reap bundles of tales. She's a mixed girl, and this is Bristol, not paradise."

"What do you mean?"

"Keep it close to your chest. Lots of rumours are circling around the city and neighbouring area about racial abuses."

"Yes?"

"Plenty of people are here who don't like foreigners. And they don't like their offspring either, even if they are mixed races."

"Yes?"

"So, love your girl whether she's your daughter or not."

"I do!"

"Not enough. Love her like the way you loved your son."

"You're talking to her?"

"So, it's true?"

"I take care of her."

"Not good enough. It's love that the children need."

"I'm completely depressed."

"I'm glad we understand each other."

"I've no more love in my heart."

"Try and create it. It will spring up like a fountain."

He stared at her silently for a moment before he started to walk. At the doorway, he stopped, turning halfway towards her. "I wish you a Merry Christmas and Happy New Year."

Annette was collecting her papers from the desk. She turned her face and caught his gaze. "Thanks. And the same to you as well."

Jeffrey turned back and walked to the car park behind the hospital. It took about 10 minutes to get there. He got in and started the car. Nevertheless, he didn't drive off immediately. He continued to sit there as though he was blind or frozen. The fact was that he felt dejected and demoralised by the situations that surrounded him. After years of waiting and dreaming, J J came along. Unfortunately, he was born as a very sick child and died, leaving the painful memories in the depth of his life. This late conception of pregnancy destroyed Debra's health severely, too. And the suffering she had to go through on a day-to-day basis was beyond tolerance. Unless some new medicine was invented and made available, the chances of her recovery appeared bleak, and, to make matters worse, she knew it as well. And now, as if to add up difficulties, Daniella's face was staring up at him. Angrily, he put the gear into motion and moved down to the exit of the car park.

Jeffrey took the road towards his home. Suddenly, he changed direction and changed his mind to go to Hughes Transport instead.

Part 2: Christmas Party

There, they were having a Christmas party. In their company's calendar, the Christmas party was a major event. Brian Hughes, the managing director of Hughes Hauliers (International) Ltd, would personally invite various dignitaries, such as the Gloucestershire Steel Manufactures (PLC), Somerset Coal Mines (PVC), and Somerset Quarry Foundation (Groups) Ltd, and the party usually held about a week before the Christmas day and, if possible, held on a Friday.

All the staff and their spouses turned up in their best suits or dresses. The drivers were under strict orders not to bring their roadside pickup girls, though it was challenging to implement. There was good food, plenty of choices, quality wine, and classical music to dance. Also, Brian Hughes would meet the dignitaries privately in his office and give them an envelope, and nobody would ever know what else would be in it besides the Christmas card. May be large sums of cash or vouchers for free holidays in the Caribbean Islands or countries of their choice. In return, they would provide him with huge contracts for storing their products in his warehouses or transporting goods and raw materials to various destinations.

In 1978, nothing worked as it had traditionally done. There were various turbulences of one thing or another.

A FEW TALES

Just about midnight, Jeffrey reached home. Debra was in bed and was half-sleepy and half-awake, still subconsciously waiting for him to come home. The lights were on downstairs when he reached. He stayed in the living room briefly, watching the Christmas tree by the side of the window and the decorations on the walls and ceiling. Plenty of decorations were there in the hallway, kitchens, and up the stairways. He came up to the room and sat on the edge of the bed. "You alright?"

She didn't answer straight. "Did you drive? After all those drinks?"

He was silent for a moment. "The decorations look nice."

"Daniella did them."

"How's she?"

"She was here a few minutes ago to check on me."

"Did you eat anything?"

"Yes. We didn't have to make anything. Johanna and Christina brought food."

"Well, I have a long day. I better sleep in the guest room."

"Why?"

"When drink and I toss about a lot."

"I know."

"I might hurt you."

"It doesn't matter anymore. I'm used to all kinds of pains."

"But Christmas Eve, tonight. You remember how we were on Christmas Eve?"

"I don't hold memories. It's more depressing."

"We would go to concerts or dancing. Or just go for drinks and talks. Or go to visit friends. And those talks and laughs."

"And lots of giggles!"

"We had lots of friends."

"Lots of them were good friends."

"Yes, yes. We had good friends. We had the health and time. And also the money."

"And above all else, we were very happy."

"Because we had dreams!"

"Yes, we had dreams. But dreams died first when you......."

"Oh, no. Please don't go into it. We grew up through the sixties. Sweet sixties, people wanted fun and joy in their life after the disasters of the war."

"I also grew up through the sixties. I also had fun and joy. But I kept the values and moralities and traditions of our way of life." She stopped talking and drew a breath of air. "Let's sleep, Jeff. I want to get up early. Christmas day, for memory's sake."

However, Christmas Day started with a bang. Debra got up early and fought her way to the bathroom. Since she wasn't safe on her foot, Jeffrey put his arm behind her back and held her closely as she struggled to the bathroom. Daniella heard the sounds of movements, hurried to her mother's room, and bumped into them outside her door. "You okay, Mamie?" she asked anxiously.

"I'm fine, darling," she replied kindly. "You can go to bed."

"Okay."

He helped his wife further along the corridor, then down the step to the landing. On the side of the landing was a short corridor that led to the bathroom. He helped her into it. "Can you manage?"

"Yes, dear!"

He shut the door behind her. "Don't lock the door."

"I won't."

"I'm here."

"Thanks!"

All this while, Daniella stood outside her doorway, rather awkwardly, because she wasn't sure of herself. A few moments ticked away silently, and he was fully aware of her presence. Nonetheless, he stood on his side of the corridor, leaning against the wall with his back towards her, and avoided any possible eye contact. In the end, she bypassed him, going to downstairs and then into the kitchen. She filled some water in the kettle and turned on the switch. She picked up a small aluminium bowl, poured some milk into it, and then put it on the hob. She had to get it right exactly as her mother would make it.

So, Daniella chose the bigger mug with the picture of coffee beans on its sides and filled it with a spoonful of coffee powder and two spoons of sugar. The mother usually measured the amount of milk that went into the drink. So, she searched for the same large spoon and scooped the hot milk twice into the mug, then poured the hot boiling water and stirred it properly. In the end, she carried the drink upstairs and into the landing.

This time, Debra was outside the bathroom, and Jeffrey had her safely in his arms and was about to help her back into the bedroom. The girl passed them and waited at her doorway. They moved further and into the landing. Suddenly, she saw the girl standing at her doorway with a cup in her hand. "Didn't you go to bed, darling?"

"No, mama?" She replied courteously.

Debra climbed up to the corridor. "What's in your hand?"

"I made dad's coffee."

"I don't want it."

Debra stopped walking and, freeing herself from his arm, stood alone, holding on to the banister. She breathed in heavily and then let it out, wheezing loudly. "You want coffee in the morning, don't you?"

"I'll go down and mix my whisky."

She managed a couple of steps forward. "You had too much of it last night. You were stinking."

"It's Christmas morning. I need my whisky drink. I'll go down in a minute."

Daniella put away the coffee on her desk and stepped back into the doorway.

"You could have thanked her. At least she took the trouble and made it for you."

"Thank her? For what – rubbishing our names in public?"

Debra shot a glance at her before she questioned him, "What are you talking about, Jeff? Rubbishing our names?"

"You ask her."

"Ask what?"

"What she is taking?"

Wordlessly, Debra looked at her with her eyes wide open.

The girl didn't say anything.

"We keep her here for shopping and housework?"

She helplessly looked at them erratically.

"And looking after our child?"

She looked at her sympathetically. "Did you say these to anybody, darling?"

"Yes, mama, but not in that manner, mama."

"Who did you tell?"

"Control yourself, Jeff. Yesterday's drinks are still powering you." She moved carefully to close her. "Why did you tell, darling?"

"To teachers, mama. They ask why I miss classes."

"Who told you these ghastly stories, Jeff?"

"Yesterday in the meeting!"

"They misunderstood. Or you heard it wrong."

"So, it's their mistakes? Or it's mine? But your daughter is perfect. She doesn't tell lies."

"When did my daughter lie?" She asked, moving back to the door, obviously sheltering her from his shouting.

"My daughter. My daughter. Always my daughter. But is she your daughter?"

"Yes, to me, she is my daughter," she retorted, turning her face and passing a glance at the girl, and then she stared back. "Why you're bringing her into it?"

"Then ask her what she did to your son."

With a terrified expression, she moved a bit and held her mama's gown apparently trying to steady herself from falling.

"She loved him; that's what she did," Debra replied. "And looked after him like her real brother. And that's what she did."

"Who killed him? Did she tell you yet?"

"Killed?"

Daniella opened her mouth and was about to cry in absolute fear. No sound was heard. The only sound that rumbled was his. "Yes. She dropped our son over the stairs."

Unable to say anything, she raised her hand and held on to the door frame.

"No. J J fell on his head and broke his neck. Did she tell you that?"

Bewildered, Debra turned to her left side to look at Daniella. She couldn't turn her body as the girl was clinging onto her gown on the other side. She swung back and tried to see her through the right side. However, a freeze shot up through her body, which destroyed her balance. She fell down to the floor and took Daniella also with her as the girl's hand caught stuck in the gown's belt. And all happened almost like a horrible hallucination and right in front of Jeffrey, who was only two yards away. He couldn't move himself for a moment; he had gone frozen.

Suddenly, Daniella's voice rose. "Mama, mama," she cried hysterically.

Jeffrey also came back to life. He fell down to his knees and, doubling, got to her face. She didn't show any sign of physical movement other than a shallow breath. "Debra darling, Debra."

"Mama? Mama?"

Debra didn't respond to their cry. She was in a coma.

Jeffrey looked at the girl. "Call 999."

Daniella ran down and rang for an ambulance. She also called at Joanna's house.

Joanna's daughter Christina got the message first. They had a few visitors already in the house. They all left in a group to Jeffrey's house, and Joanna and Christina rushed in front. Some other neighbours saw this group going, and the others also joined them. A little boy died only three weeks or so ago, and now the mother had a fall and was lying in a coma. 'What a Christmas the poor family was having, God?' a few of the people in the crowd thought to themselves.

This time, the ambulance arrived fast, and two paramedics came into the house. "Happy Christmas. "

The people replied, "Happy Christmas."

"It's a freezing cold Christmas."

"It's terrible today. We haven't had this weather for a long time."

They went up. "Please go downstairs, except for the family."

They disappeared quickly.

Debra was still on the floor and lying across the door. Her body below the waist was out into the hallway, and the upper part was in the room. Jeffrey was next to her, sitting and stroking her face with one hand and the other hand staying crossways on her stomach. Daniella was on her side, in a kneeling position, her face full of dripping tears. They moved back as the paramedics stopped at the doorway.

"You're?" the female asked.

"Jeffrey. This is my wife, Debra."

The other paramedic had a good look at her and said to her. "I think I better get the stretcher."

She nodded for an answer. And he went.

"What happened?" she asked, holding her wrist and listening to the beats.

"She fell."

"Anybody was with her."

"We were both. I was bringing her from the bathroom."

She checked her beats. And also listened to her shallow breath. And then she looked at her once again. She looked at the girl, then looked back at him. "We've to take Debra away."

"I'm coming."

"That's good."

"I'm coming, too."

"It's Christmas day. Don't you want to celebrate it with your family?"

"Yes. My mama and papa are my family."

A FEW TALES

The male paramedic brought the stretcher. And in minutes, Debra was on her way to Bristol General Hospital. The sooner they reached the front gate, they transferred her to a mobile bed and rolled her into the ICU Ward. Jeffrey and Daniella stayed in the downstairs waiting room on the side of the main hallway. The hallway was very busy with staff rushing around on their duties or families and friends visiting the patients for Christmas. Three Christmas trees were lit up along the way, and four Christmas star lights were hung from the ceiling, obviously, all in small numbers and sizes to save the maximum amount of electricity. Even though Jeffrey was seeing all these, he wasn't aware of any of them. He and Daniella were close to the glass window, standing for a while and then back to sitting. Their eyes were struck on the hall, and they saw anybody coming for them with a word about Debra, anxiously hoping it would be good. Unfortunately, nurse Angela wasn't on shift, but she was told that she was on the timesheet for the afternoon shift. It wasn't helpful now. Seemingly more distressing was that he would see a nurse mingling down the hall towards the waiting room and then keep going further on. He and Daniella had been at the reception of the ICU ward twice, and sadly, the nurse didn't have any updates.

Suddenly, Daniella saw Angela coming up the hallway. "Papa, Papa?"

His eyes were staring out. He turned and looked at her.

"Aunty Angela is there," she said nervously. "Coming this way."

Quickly, Jeffrey rubbed his eyes with his hands and then stared in the girl's direction. 'In the uniform, they all look the same,' he first thought to himself in desperation. "Yes, that's Angela," he whispered, clearly nervously. "What she got for us?"

"Let's go to her."

Jeffrey puffed a heavy breath, almost storing courage. Silently, he started walking, and the girl was by his side. They met Angela halfway up the hallway. "Aunty Angela," the girl asked as she was in the front and still running. "How's mama?"

Angela opened her arms and caught her. "Hello, young lady," she said, hugging her. "I didn't know you're here."

Jeffrey reached by their side. "How's Debra," he asked in a mixed voice of hope and fear.

She met his gaze. "Debra is better than when she came."

"What do you mean?"

Angela looked around and found a quiet place, and they moved over to them. "What do you mean, Angela?" He asked again in panic.

"She's breathing a little easier now. But she is still on the ventilator." She paused momentarily. "Her pulse rate is poor. Blood pressure is low. The doctors are working on it." She again paused. "The fear is, at some stage, she had …. well, it's not confirmed yet, but they believe that she had a heart attack."

As if too hard to bear it, Jeffrey turned away his face.

Daniella cast down her eyes and started sobbing. Angela's arm was around her body. She held her closer. "Be brave. Debra will make a full recovery."

"You sure about the heart attack?" he asked, turning back.

"Well, the tests all are proving she suffered an attack. The question is this. Did she fall due to a heart attack? Or she had a heart attack due to a fall?"

"The answer to it makes a difference?" He whispered, discreetly trying to restrain the shiver rising from his legs.

Angela looked around. There was no privacy as other medical staff were passing by them, and Jefferey appeared to be tired. She shot a glance down the hallway before she said, "Let's go back to the waiting room. We might get seats."

Slowly, they went to the waiting room. A few people were in the front, and mostly in small groups. They went past them and went to a quiet corner. Jeffrey sank to a chair immediately as if his legs caved in. Angela took a seat next to him and sat facing him. "If the heart attack happened first, it means she is seriously ill. And if the fall occurred first, what triggered it? If there is an answer to it, it might help the doctors."

Jeffrey didn't reply. Instead, he continued to sit there with his head down. Daniella was sitting on the other side of Angela and was silent. A brief period passed while an uneasy stillness engulfed them, and their heads searched for the realities in multiple ways. In the end, the girl dropped her face on the shoulder of the nurse and started sobbing. "Mama knew how J J died."

The nurse moved in her chair and looked at her anxiously. "What?"

"I dropped J J."

"Good lord. How?"

The girl hesitated. "Papa told."

The nurse turned her face and stared at him. "Why, Jeff?"

He didn't answer.

She turned back to the girl. "Why?"

"They were talking."

309

"Yeh?"

"It turned into an argument."

The nurse waited.

"Mama always gives me lots of love. And Papa detests it."

Angela stared at him, but he didn't meet her eyes. She turned back to her.

"And papa proved that I'm the killer."

Jeffrey raised his head. "This is not the right place and time to talk about these matters," she whispered quietly, but his face reflected the expression of revulsion.

"When Mama heard it, she fell down. And…."

Angela interrupted her. "Alright, alright," she said firmly. "Like he said, we'll talk later if necessary. But now." She paused briefly. "Debra is in a critical condition. And that's where our thoughts and prayers should be."

Another uneasy, long silence sprang up.

"I thought your shift starts at 2," Jeffrey said, obviously changing the subject.

"That's right, my rota is 2 to 6. But Joanna phoned. And my children were very disappointed when I left."

"I am sorry."

"Anyway, Debra is in safe hands. Two doctors and two nurses are constantly monitoring her." She paused, trying to recapture her medical conditions. "She's a little progress in breathing. However, don't forget that she is still on the ventilator."

Jeffrey was silent.

"She needs to improve a lot on her pulse reading and heart beating. And the blood pressure is very low. But I'm sure they will get right by the evening."

"Will they allow us to see her sometime today?"

"I doubt it," Angela replied flatly. "They want to come here as they think necessary. They don't like any obstacles."

"I'm worried about her."

"You know she is in good hands now. And you know I'm here," she said supportively. "I'll be in touch with you regularly."

"When you finish at six?"

"Jayne is taking over. And you know her. She's a very good."

"Thanks."

"You go home," she insisted. "And spend the Christmas Joanna and the family, as you've done over the years."

"It was different then. Debra was in the driving seat." He sighed heavily before he continued evidently devastated, "I'll go and see them. And wish them merry Christmas."

Angela turned to Daniella and watched her sadly for a moment. "Will you go and enjoy the Christmas with your friend, Christina?" she persisted forcefully.

The girl waited to catch a heavy breath. "Today is not a good day for me. It's definitely not my Christmas day. I wait until my mama comes home. And on that day, I will celebrate Christmas."

She held her close to her in a hug and kissed on both her cheeks, saying, "A very Merry Christmas and Happy New Year."

"Thank you, Aunty Angela.," she said in a restrained sad voice. "I also wish you a very Merry Christmas and Happy New Year."

Angela turned and hugged Jeffrey. "A merry Christmas and a very happy year for you and…"

"I hope ……………………………………"

"I will be at Joanna's house for a couple of hours this evening. Can I pop in to see you?"

"My dear friend, you are always welcome."

A moment passed.

"I know you came in the ambulance. How are you going to get home."

"That's too expensive. It's Christmas night. Why don't you take my car? It's in the car park."

Jeffrey shook his head. "It's not a nice idea, dear. I couldn't concentrate on the road. My mind is everywhere."

"Don't then. Especially Daniella is with you!"

"Very true. When Debra comes home, it's Daniella she wants to see first."

However, Debra didn't come home after all. She died on the night of 31st December 1978.

Chapter 8

Ashes to Ashes, Dust to Dust

Part 1: Good Old Days

In the late afternoon of that day, Jeffrey went to visit her as he used to do these days after work. Debra was wide awake when he entered her room. He bent over the bed and kissed her on the forehead before he sat down on a chair next to her. "You alright, Jeff?"

Jeffrey was literally terrified in his chair. Her voice was so clear and powerful he had to stare at her as though to convince himself that it was Debra who was talking. In his bewildered, excited condition, he couldn't make up his mind whether to cry or laugh. Definitely, he was so happy he was about to scream without realising it. He didn't scream, though. Only the bubbles of tears burst out in his eyes, and he couldn't stop it either. "I'm alright, darling," he replied, his voice shivered as himself. "Thank you for asking. And....and you, my darling?"

Debra smiled as broadly as the thin skin around her mouth allowed her, and it was beautiful. "I'm fine, Jeff. I never felt like this for a long time."

"You're sure?" He asked in a voice he couldn't get to believe.

"Have I ever lied to you?"

That was it, he kneeled down and moved forward then bent over the bed and hugged her as tightly as he could have. "I love you, my beauty."

"I know. I know."

"How is Daniella, my baby?"

"She's fine."

"Happy?"

"Yes, happy as can be."

"What does it mean?"

"You're here."

"She can come here."

"She has been here every day."

"I might have been sleeping."

"Yes."

Slowly, Jeffrey moved back to his chair.

"I see Salome and her daughter."

"Do you?"

"They come to visit me frequently."

He didn't speak.

"Salome's daughter is very beautiful. In fact, she looks like Daniella. Exactly like Daniella!"

"Darling, we grew up through the sixties."

"Oh no, I didn't mean those things."

"I made mistakes, my darling."

"And I know, Jeff."

"And Salome killed the child."

"Very sad. But I don't think it was your child."

He was quiet.

"The child I see is not a mixed race."

"No?"

"It's purely a black child. The father is also definitely black. I mean ethically."

"At least I didn't put Salome into all her problems. Or Uncle Sam into his predicament."

"I know. Jeff."

"We couldn't do anything. It happened in a different continent, Debra."

"And killed herself too."

"Very depressing."

"She was my best friend. We had lots of giggles."

"I know, darling."

"Now, they keep company with me in my sleep."

He was slow to speak. "It's in your mind, darling."

"We went so many places to adopt. And we could have adopted any child. Even Salome's child!"

He was silent.

"But we adopted Daniella. Stunningly, a beautiful child. We proudly said she is our child."

"And we said."

"And I gave her my mother's name, Daniella."

"True. Very true!"

"When I was myself little, I used to hear in the early morning……"

"I hear what, darling?"

"My dad is calling."

"What?"

"Daniella? Daniella? Where is my shirt? Or trouser? I'm getting late, Daniella."

"I know."

"A moment later, I will hear, Daniella, Daniella? Where are my shoes."

"I know."

"I hear every morning twenty times, 'Daniella, Daniella' before I get out of my bed."

"I know. Aunty Daniella used to tell these stories to my mum over the fence."

She waited. "And then our luck went away. Her complexion started changing. And she turned into a mixed-race baby. And not our child!"

"Very painful. Please forget these, Debra."

"I can't. I'll always love her. To me, she is our child."

"I know. But stop thinking of it. Until you get better!"

"Any killing is evil."

"Darling, please forget it."

"And Salome killed herself when she killed her own child."

He didn't speak. "Killing an unborn child is beyond understanding and beyond forgiveness."

None of them spoke. An uneasy silence engulfed them.

In the end, she continued audibly, "J J has left us. Only God alone knows whether tomorrow is mine or not. We're sowing the seeds of weeds. So, we can only reap the harvest of weeds."

"We didn't do any mistakes, Debra darling. But mistakes followed us."

This time she didn't speak quickly. "I only know one thing. I loved you more than I could ever say."

Jeffrey moved forward and kissed on her forehead. And then, very slowly, he raised his face away and moved back.

Debra continued to remain silent. Slowly, her wheezing began to get louder. And he sensed that she was slipping into her sleep.

Jeffrey continued to sit there, on her side and all alone. However, he couldn't contain his mind. It was flashing back and forward, the forgotten days of life and the simple actions scattered around their lives. In the picture of his mind, he could've been four or four plus, and he was in the rear garden, playing alone with a little ball. She was on the other side of the fence, seemed to be about one year old, hardly able to stand steadily, and was trying to crawl through the broken railings. "You want to play?"

She got in to his garden and, managing raise herself on to her feet, she smiled sweetly for an answer, then falling back on the grass.

Her mother came running. "Oh here, you are," she said sighing of a relief. "I wondered where you've gone?" She came further and picked her through the hole on the fence.

The girl rebelled, crying and tossing her hands and legs. The boy watched them silently. "You can leave her with me," he said in the end. "She will be alright."

"Be careful, please."

"Don't worry. I will be, Aunty Daniella."

Aunty Daniella left her back through the hole and placed her on the grass. As soon as she was off her mother's hold, she stopped crying and, catching his eyes, started smiling.

"She likes you, Jeff, more than me."

Without replying, he smiled.

'That was the time before the beginning of daydream,' Jeffrey whispered and then rose to his feet. And standing almost immobile, he kept looking at her face. Her eyes were closed, and mouth shut. Her breathing was very shallow, but clearly wheezy. And yet, he had a convincing hope that she was on her way to recovery. Abruptly, he stooped over the bed and kissed her on her forehead. He didn't straighten up quickly. Instead, he remained with his face on her forehead, and his hands holding her arms. He cleared his mind off on all his memories and thoughts. Nothing at all should take him away from her. He wasn't even aware that his tears were dripping on to her eyes. A couple of minutes elapsed slowly, and he moved back. Suddenly, he noticed the tears on her face. He picked up a clean tissue from his coat pocket and dried it gently. And he kissed her once more before he went out reluctantly.

Part 2: The New Year

Jeffrey went to the car park, got into his car, and drove off to the side street, then to the main road. The roads were busy; lots of people were on the move to celebrate the new year with their families and friends. The general belief was that this new year, celebrations would be very dismal because of the unruly general strikes, shortages of energy supplies, and high prices of goods. Whatever might be the facts and figures, people would always spend money on occasions such as this.

When he was back home, Joanna and her children brought back Daniella with them. "Oh, Jeff, why didn't you come over there?"

He didn't answer directly. Instead, he said quietly, "A happy new year to you, Joanna, and your children and Gary."

"How's Debra this evening?"

"At one time, she was almost her old self. And then she went to her sleep."

"When we went this morning," she said looking at Daniella, "she was like that, wasn't she?"

The girl nodded gently.

"And then she went to sleep quickly. But I'm sure she's slowly getting better."

"I hope she could come home now," Daniella said obviously in despair.

Joanna hugged her. "Come, let's all have a party there. Please come."

"Not today, Aunty," Daniella said quickly." It's not the right time. Thank you."

"And we need to keep in touch with the hospital," Jeff said, "Thanks anyway."

"Shall we bring some meal for you?"

"No need, Joanna. We've everything here."

They left shortly.

Daniella went up to her room and he stayed downstair in the lounge. A little later, he also went upstairs. "What do you like for the supper?"

"I'm not hungry, dad."

"Why is that?"

"I don't know. Maybe later!"

Without replying, Jeffrey came back to the lounge. The telly was on. He didn't bother to listen to anything or turn it off. He tumbled to the chair and closed his eyes.

Another hour passed.

"I make a chicken soup and toast on butter and tomatoes. Can you eat?"

"I'm honest, dad. I'm not hungry. Make them for yourself."

Jeff met her gaze for a moment. "Whatever happened," he said, his voice cracking with sadness, "we've to live."

Daniella didn't answer.

In the end, he said firmly, "I make fish and chips. I know you like it."

She nodded half-heartedly. "Shall I help you, please?"

"You can watch Telly. And listen if the phone rings."

She nodded lightly.

And he went to the kitchen.

Daniella remained there, but she wasn't watching the telly. It was more like she was staring out the window to see her Mamie coming back as she came from school after work, or the market after shopping, or Aunty Joanna's house after a little talk. 'Just a waiting, like trusting a dream,' she thought in despair. 'And then what are dreams made of? Are they just the sights and sounds of aching hearts?' Until today, she wasn't told who was her biological father or mother. Are they alive still – at least one of them, just to tell her why they abandoned her? Did they love her and hold her warmly in their arms and kiss her for a moment? No, no, this wasn't the right time at all to peel into the layers of lives and fate. Her Mamie was in the hospital and critically fighting for her life. Slowly, she turned back to the telly.

Jeffrey came to the lounge door. "Let's eat."

They sat at the table. In front of them were soups in bowls and fish and chips in plates, and glass of pineapple juice for Daniella, and glass of wine for himself. Silently, time ticked away, and nobody scarcely touched their food. "Alright," he said tenderly, "go to the lounge."

"I help you with washing."

"I'm okay."

She came back to the lounge.

Jeffrey finished washing and tidied up the kitchen. He took a glass of whiskey and returned.

"Anything interesting on?" Jeff asked casually.

"I wasn't watching, dad."

He sat down and put the drink on the table.

"It's ten now," he said, glancing on his wrist watch. "Why don't you go and sleep?"

"What time you're going to?"

"I stay up until 12." He took a sip of whisky. "May be a bit more."

"Why?"

"New Year's Eve. We used to stay up until the bell rings for the new year and the shows. Well, your mama likes these sorts of traditional features."

"If you're staying here, I stay with you."

Jeffrey nodded positively, then finished the drink. He moved in his chair and leaned against the back. He got up very early this morning and had gone to work. The fatigue was finally overwhelming him. He closed his eyes for little nap. When he got up, the comedy show 'Good Old Days' was on the screen and was moving towards the end of it. Debra loved this show, especially the way the host introduced the characters into the audience. He looked at Daniella and she was asleep, too.

The next show was called the countdown which would take the nation to the new year. The Good Old Days finished and the countdown was about to begin, when the phone started to ring. Jeff clearly felt startled as the ringing tone unexpectedly alerted the atmosphere as late as midnight. Daniella woke up suddenly with a frightful expression on her face.

He leaned forward and reached for the phone. "Hello," he whispered carefully.

However, a female voice came along the wire. "Hello," she said softly. "Is it Mr Smith – Jeffrey Smith?"

He replied cautiously. "Yes."

322

A FEW TALES

Daniella was staring at him and listening to the conversation.

The female on the phone coughed for a moment. "My name is Brenda," she said finally. "And you know me. I work in the IQC."

Daniella suddenly felt an anxious tension beginning to grip her.

"Yes, Brenda? I know you."

She waited. "You're okay?"

"Thank you, Brenda. I'm okay."

"Can I talk to you?"

"Of course, Brenda."

"You signed out at 7.10 in the visitors' book."

"Yes, that's right."

"She didn't wake up after you've gone."

Without speaking, he nervously waited for her to continue.

"She was alright at 10.30 when we checked her."

He was silent cautiously.

"When we went for the next check-up at 11.30, I am sorry, Jeff...."

"Yes?"

"But Debra was dead."

The worst of the tension got the grip on Daniella, and she burst out to weeping and crying.

Jeffrey opened his mouth to speak, but he couldn't find his voice.

"You're alright, Mr Smith?"

He managed a little sound, and then he managed to say, "Yea."

"Nurse Alice was with me. She got the Doctor in quickly."

He waited a long time. "Can I come now?"

"It's up to you, Mr Smith. But no need, if you ask me. Anyway, we'll do whatever is required. Again, are you mentally fit to drive tonight?

"I suppose so?"

I hear A&E is receiving lots of casualties tonight. Most of the cases are alcohol-related. Be careful!"

"Can you manage?"

"Of course, we do it all the time."

Daniella couldn't restrain the agony of sadness quietly any more. She had to cry out loudly, but Jeffrey was on the phone. She went upstairs to her room.

Jeffrey's face was wet with tears. He used the sleeve of his pullover and wiped the face. "What are you doing now?"

"We're taking her to the morgue shortly. Doctor Shelley and Alice are here. And the others. If you come late, it will disturb their work. Better come in the morning."

"What time? About 9?"

"Later, please. Maybe at 10. Being the New Year's Day, they would be late."

He agreed to it.

324

Part 3: Dealing with Grief

Jeffrey moved in his seat and fell against the back of the chair. He closed his eyes and continued to sit there, physically still and mentally frozen. Every now and then, drips of tears forced out through the shut eyelids. Abruptly, he got up and went to the kitchen. He picked up a whisky bottle and drank directly from it. He drank again and again continuously until the bottle was completely empty. He left it on the table and came upstairs. The light was on in Daniella's room as he passed her door. He stopped walking and looked in. She was sitting on the edge of the bed, her face down in her hands and the elbow on her thighs. She raised her face and looked at him.

"Aren't you sleeping?" Jeffrey asked, noticing her face fully wet with tears.

Daniella didn't reply instantly. "What time we're going to the hospital?" She asked in a crying voice.

"9.30," he replied tersely.

"Did you tell anybody?"

"In the morning," he answered unhurriedly. "I don't like to disturb them this time of the night." He paused vaguely, then added, walking to his room, "Especially when they're enjoying."

"Dad?"

Jeffrey half-turned back.

"You want to say nothing to me?" Daniella asked. Her voice was breaking with mixed emotions of love and gratitude and memories of her late Mamie and the emptiness and the fear that was engulfing her due to her untimely death.

"What's there to say? You know everything I know."

"I don't know. Maybe you could say that Mama was a good wife. Or a good mother? Or something?"

He stared at her silently. "Any point in it? Will she come back to us?"

Without replying, she stared back into his eyes.

"You're ten years old, Daniella. I'm forty-five." He stopped talking and searched for a cigarette packet in his trouser pocket. He stuck a cigarette between his lips and lit. He drew a deep puff and blew out. "That means I'm a lot older than you. And I've had lots of experiences and failures than you can imagine. And they bring thousands of memories." He paused and puffed again and blew out quietly. "The troubles with memories are that they also bring heartaches when you least expect them." He puffed again, turning back to his room, and saying, "Go to sleep."

However, she didn't go to sleep. Her mind was violently jostling with the anxieties of life and the uncertainties of the future, nor did she have an impressive past to pacify her tensions. Her biological parents never existed in her life. The truth was that she had never known who they were or why they discarded her. Had they ever held her in their arms? Or even talked to her or kissed her? No point thinking about these painful realities, everybody had come to this world without their knowledge or consent, then dragged down along the groove which were carved for them by fate. She leaned against the headboard and gazed out the window. There was nothing to see, anyway. The night was thick black, and nothing existed at all in the night like the aches of love that went past through yesterdays.

On the other side of her bedroom wall, Jeffrey was wide awake and casually thinking about his wife's funeral functions. He had gotten some knowledge of funerals because he had buried his son very recently. Debra didn't play any part in it. As a matter of fact, she didn't know about it at all until she suffered her fateful heart attack when she knew her son had died and gone away. And again, he had to do all alone. Usually, they discussed everything beforehand and was carried out accordingly. Now, could he ask her how she would have desired her own final journey? However, they knew each other over forty years, going back all the way to childhood. And her spirit was not ready yet to abandon him. He moved over to Debra's side and kissed her pillow distraught.

Jeffrey didn't have a wink of sleep during the rest of the night. He got out of the bed and the room at about 6 o'clock. Inside the house, it was freezing cold, though the heater had started half an hour ago. He came down into the kitchen and checked the boiler first. It was working fine. He picked up the kettle, filled the water, and switched it on. From where he was standing, he could make out the southern sky through the dark atmosphere above the rear garden. Huge bands of rain clouds hung low and stretched towards the distance. The sky seemed low, the horizon closer, and the world shrunk smaller.

He made a coffee, went to the lounge, and turned on the telly. On BBC 1, it was a children's show. On 2, no programmes had started. On ITV, it was a noisy cartoon. He chose the cartoon and sat down. At least, let it make some noise in the house.

Jeffrey finished the coffee slowly and then went upstairs. "Daniella," he called out quietly, standing outside her door. "Are you sleeping?"

"No," she replied. Her voice was unrecognisable with sadness.

Jeffrey pushed the door open and then moved into the doorway. She was lying on her back with the duvet pulled up to her neck. He stared at her face for a moment. "You didn't sleep, did you?"

She caught his eyes silently.

He waited, struggling to know what to say. "What do you want for breakfast?"

"Nothing," she whispered. "I will make something later."

He hesitated. "We're going to see your Mama, very soon. And I know you want to come as well."

"Yes."

"Well, Daniella. I'm going to make breakfast for you."

"Please don't."

"Sure, you're not coming to see your Mamie if you're not having breakfast."

She started crying. "Okay, I will try."

Jeffrey made a cereal with crispy wheats and raisins and a toasted cheese sandwich on jam. She didn't touch the toast at all, but had a bit of cereal.

At 9.30, they were at the doorway of the ICU ward.

A male nurse was sitting in the office. He was picking up night sheets from a tray and filing them in the patients' folder. He swung in his chair towards them and looked up at them. "Happy New Year."

"And the same to you," Jeff replied. "We came to see Debra Smith."

"Could you wait a bit until a nurse comes," he said politely. "I'm a temp and started only twenty minutes ago. To be honest, I'm not told anything yet."

Jeffrey was already tired. "Do you know the name of this nurse?"

"Not really, I'm sorry. Three were here when I came. In a minute or two, a phone call came, and two of them rushed to the A&E, and the other just gone to see a doctor." He paused a little, looking at Daniella, "Please wait a little."

Just then, a female nurse walked in, and seeing them, she said rather cheerfully, "Happy New Year and to you, young lady. What's your name?"

The girl hesitated briefly. "Daniella," she replied listlessly.

"Oh! That's a beautiful name, young lady. And I'm Becky. And ......"

Jeffrey cut in quickly. "Sorry to ask this. Do you work here?"

She stared at him. "No. I work in cardiology. And today should have been my day off."

He silently stared back at her.

"It'd have been a nice New Year's Day. But staff shortage. Many staff are off due to strikes and protests."

"Why?" The male nurse asked curiously. "Any special reason?"

"No special reason," Becky replied. "Any reason will do for disturbances." She stopped talking while she pulled the tray on the desk to a side. "But I heard a grave digger in Liverpool fell in the grave he was digging.
"

"Poor chap," Andy said jokingly. "Definitely, he was in a hurry to go."

"It was an accident," she told, obviously annoyed with her colleague's jokes. "The mud wall caved in on him." She turned back to Jeffrey. "What can I do for you, sir?"

"I'm Jeffrey Smith. And we came to see the body of Debra Smith, my wife."

Becky looked at her colleague. "Andy, could you take them to Debra's room."

Before Andy could speak, Jeffrey retorted as if he was assisting them in their duties. "My wife died last night."

The nurses said quickly, "Oh, I'm sorry. I'm very sorry to hear that."

"They phoned me last night and said that they were taking her to the mortuary."

"That's right," she said sympathetically. "That's where we are supposed to go. Andy, please take them to the mortuary."

"Can we go, for God's sake," Jeffrey asked impatiently.

"We'll, sir," Andy answered politely, picking up the phone quickly. "Let me find out where the mortuary is." His phone came alive just then, and he whispered on the mouthpiece. "Where is the mortuary?"

He listened to the phone briefly and then hung the phone on the hook. "I'm sorry we won't be able to take you there today."

"Why not?" Jeffrey asked rather angrily.

"Today we've no access to the mortuary," he replied respectfully. "It's always closed on New Year Day. Or any other public holidays."

"Anybody else can help us?"

"I am afraid nobody can help you here, sir."

"Alright," he retorted, looking rather frustrated. "We come tomorrow."

Becky hesitated momentarily. "Better you check with the office tomorrow before you come."

"Why is that?"

"Well, they've to give her a wash. And give her some new clothes……."

He interrupted her. "It doesn't matter, for God's sake. She's my wife."

"But these are regulations, Mr Smith," the nurse advised. "We've to follow through."

"Good lord, what's this – prison?" He stopped talking as if he was out of breath.

"Mr Smith, I know what you're going through. But please try to listen to me."

Jeff stared at her without saying anything

"Please give us a call tomorrow. Everything will be alright by then."

He waited a moment before he replied. "We'll come tomorrow. And I hope we'll be able to see her. And if we won't, we'll come again on Wednesday."

"Okay, Mr Smith," Becky replied calmly.

Part 4: Seeing Debra

With mixed feelings of frustration, distress, and agony, they left the ward. In fact, Daniella was inaudibly crying when they were walking out of the hospital front and then into the car. For a long time, they didn't exchange a single word. In the end, Jeffrey spoke as if to break the unbearable silence. "This early morning, Angela went to Gloucester."

Daniella didn't respond.

"I phoned her last night."

Without saying anything, she looked at him.

"She's spending the Christmas with her mother."

Quietly, she turned and stared out the car.

"Gary and Joanna went to the railway station to pick up his parents. Christina told me this morning when I phoned."

This time, she asked, "Did you tell her Mamie passed away?"

"I didn't. This is not what people want to hear on a New Year's Day when they are celebrating."

"You want to stay with Christina for the rest of the New Year's Day?"

"No," she retorted suddenly.

The rest of the day slipped away slowly, and it was soon night. He woke up early as usual on Tuesday morning. Nonetheless, he continued to slumber under the heavy quilt. It was freezing inside the room, anyway. When one comes to think of it, what was there for him to do? Nothing! Unexpectedly, there was a gentle knock on the door. "Yes?"

The door swung open. And Daniella appeared with a cup of coffee in her hand. She came further and placed it on the bedside drawer.

"Thanks. I'll be up shortly. What do you fancy for the breakfast."

"Anything," she replied as she came out.

Jeffrey made cheese on toast and a bowl of cereals with warm milk. But she didn't touch any of them, neither did he eat anything either. They left for the hospital.

"Jeff," Angela called out as he and Daniella were walking closer to the office window. She came out and hugged him with one hand and held the girl with the other. "I'm so sorry to hear about Debra's death," she said sadly, kissing his cheek.

He was silent.

"And I couldn't be with you when you needed help."

"Can we see Debra today, please?"

She didn't reply immediately. Instead, she stooped a little and kissed Danielle on her cheek. "How are you feeling, sweetie?"

Silently, the girl searched her face. "Can we see Mamie, please?"

"The mortuary is an independent company. Here it operates with the hospital license. However, they've their own terms and conditions."

"What does it mean?"

"On January 1st, like everybody else, they are on holiday."

"Yes. But today is the 2nd?"

"I know. But they are on strike every Tuesday. It's been going on nearly a month now."

"So, we can't see her today then?"

"No, I'm sorry. But it'll be fine tomorrow. I've checked with their union leader."

"Alright. We'll come tomorrow."

"Please, in the afternoon."

"Why?"

333

"They've to wash her. And dress her properly."

"what's this? We are only her husband and daughter."

"Sorry, Jeff. These are regulations for the safety of the staff and the visitors. Some diseases are easily infectious. That's how unions see it." She momentarily paused as though searching for reasons to calm him down. "Again, it's a matter of human dignity. People, whether dead or alive, must be decently dressed for meetings."

"Oh, God! I give up."

"I'll give you a call this evening, Jeff. Please wait."

He was literally tearful when he left, having been unable to see his wife for the second day. Daniella was more distressed than him. They drove back home.

Jeffrey went to the kitchen straight. The girl hadn't had a decent meal for days. He made mashed potatoes and beef steaks and chopped parsley and served them on two plates. He filled a glass of juice and a can of beer, then called her down. "You've to eat, Daniella. Life must go on."

Daniella sat down on the opposite side and started to eat slowly. He drank half of the beer before he pulled his plate nearer to him and began to have his food. He had thought Daniella wouldn't eat at all. However, she ate more than half of the stuff that was on her plate. He felt a little pleased about it.

"Don't go and stay in the room. Watch the telly for a while."

She nodded lightly for an answer. "Let me tidy up the kitchen first."

"Don't worry about that."

"No," she insisted, "I must do it, dad."

334

"Okay."

Jeffrey picked up another can of beer and went to the lounge. He lit a cigarette and switched on the telly. BBC 1 was showing some cowboy movie. A cartoon was on BBC2. And he checked ITV, which was showing some documentary about African wildlife. He left the show on the ITV and sat down.

Jeffrey swallowed a couple of mouthfuls of bear and put the can back on the coffee table. He leaned against the back, drew a puff on his cigarette, and slowly let out the smoke through the nostrils. The phone rang, and he picked it up. "Hello?"

"How're you, Jeff?"

He recognised the voice immediately. It was George, his colleague at Hughes Transport. "Bearing it, I suppose." He stopped talking momentarily. "Anyway, Happy Christmas."

"I called you yesterday."

"I was in and out. Sorry, I missed your call."

"You don't deserve all these disasters. I can bet my life on that."

He didn't say anything.

After a brief period, George asked, "Any thoughts on the funeral, Jeff?"

"Nothing yet. They haven't issued a death certificate yet."

"They are doing an autopsy?"

"I don't know. Hopefully, tomorrow, I'll see the funeral director. And then I will have some idea about all these and the time schedule. At least, I hope, I will see her body tomorrow."

"I hear some voices, I hear. You've somebody with you?"

"It's the telly. I let it on for noises. The house is dead."

"Shall I come for a short while?"

"Not now. I like to stay with her memories. Thanks for asking, George."

"I'll call you in the evening, just to see how you're."

"Please do so. "

They ended the conversation shortly, and he put down the phone on the receiver. He picked up the bear can. It was almost empty. However, he drank whatever he had in it before he put it back on the table. And then the phone rang again. "Hello?"

"I'm very sorry for the loss of your loved one, Jeff."

"It's Bernard Hughes?"

"Yes, I am! And my father told me about Debra's tragic death. And I called immediately to convey my condolences."

"Sorry, I missed your call."

"Can you see me tomorrow?"

"I've to go to the hospital.

"After the hospital."

"I don't know how long I've to be there."

"As you know, the company will be open the day after tomorrow.".

"I didn't know, Berney. My situation is like that. Is it urgent?"

"Very urgent!"

"Can I see you today? It will do a lot of good for you if you come out and get the pressure from your chest. After all, we all go one day."

Jeffrey was silent, more confused.

And Bernard moved quickly to take full advantage of his confusion. "And I know Debra was a happy girl. And she will be laughing with you if you come out and share a laugh with me."

In the end, he said reluctantly, "Alright, Berney. What time?"

"About an hour?"

"A little early for me."

"Martin Lawson is on his way. What about at 3? In 2 hours' time?"

"That's fine."

"I'm in my office. And bye for now!"

The gate was open when he approached the entrance door for the staff car park. He got in and was driving up the driveway when Martin Lawson's metallic silver Capri car was heading down on the opposite side. Martin was the warehouse manager, and had been with the company long before Jeffrey joined. Jeffrey flashed his headlights as a signal, and Martin flashed back in reply. They stopped their cars when they came closer and wound down their windows. "I'm sorry to hear about Debra," Martin said sincerely. "A genuine loss for you!"

"I'll cherish her memories. Sadly, that's all I could do."

A moment passed silently.

"You had a meeting with Bernard?"

He nodded gently. "You're going for it, Jeff?"

"Yes."

"Good luck, Jeff."

"What's it all about?"

"I'm not supposed to disclose, Jeff. Wait, he will tell you." He drove off before he could ask anything further.

*****

Exactly at 3 pm, he showed up at Bernard's office door.

"Thank you very much for coming to see me, Jeff," Bernard said considerately, taking him towards a chair across his desk. "And coming right now, especially when you're having the difficult time of your life."

"Thank you, Berney."

Abruptly, he stretched his hand. Jeffrey took it in a handshake. "Jeff, will you please sit down."

He sat down.

Bernard came round his oval desk and sat down in his massive leather chair. "First of all, Jeff. As I said on the phone, Debra was a great lady, and her death is a great loss for you. My sincere commiseration to you."

Jeffrey nodded his head in acknowledgement.

"You think we'd raise two glasses to toast Debra."

Confused, Jeff stared at his boss.

Jeffrey rolled his eyes towards an expensive oakwood showcase cabinet unit stretching from wall to wall. "You know we've everything there."

"Berney, we've a dot on Thursday. Even if I can't make the whole day, I'll stay for a while."

"That's fine, Jeff," he agreed pleasantly. "We are opening on Thursday after the Christmas holiday. And we will definitely have a drink then. But why can't we have one now?"

He didn't reply immediately. However, Berney opened his cabinet hurriedly, picked up two glasses, and then turned back. "What do you like?" He asked pleasantly. "Johnnie Walker, Black Label? I know that's your favourite."

He met his eyes impassively. "A small dot will do."

"Anything you say, Jeff. And I will have the same, too."

Bernard took a small sip and put the glass on the desk. Abruptly, he fell silent for a moment as if he was pondering on something.

Jeffrey waited and drank a drop of his drink.

"And I'm glad you mentioned the subject," the host spoke suddenly, gazing at him steadily. "We're here to talk about the new year's business plans."

He was silent.

"Well, Jeff, as you know, Hughes Transport has four divisions. Let's pick them one by one. And to start with, let's pick the Warehouse division."

Jeff nodded vaguely.

"To be honest, the Warehouse belongs to Bevan, my grandfather's younger brother." He paused as though he was recalling the man. "I knew him well. He was a very proud man from Cardiff. At the break of the Second World War, he wanted to join the Army and fight the Germans. But the Army refused to recruit him. He was a small man. And he had a weak leg. In the end, in 1940, they recruited him to be a storekeeper in the battle zone in France. And he was in charge of an ammunition depot."

"Very interesting," Jeff whispered.

"His depot was bombed twice. Nine of his colleagues were burned alive to death. But a lot more people got injured seriously. But he survived and came back in 1946 and started to work with my grandfather, Floyd. Uncle Bevan didn't drive, but he was a good storekeeper. In 1948, he built a warehouse. A small building, it was then. Gradually, as the business grew bigger, he added on several extensions. Anyway, it became very handy for my grandfather. He desperately needed lots of spaces at the time."

"What kind of business your gran was engaged in?"

"In the early days, he was a poor farmer. And to be honest, he was known as the Scrappy Metal among the locals."

"Why?" he asked curiously.

"Definitely, we weren't the royals. My gran had a tatty battered truck; that was all his fortune. He went around with it to house to house. If they had any old or unwanted metal items to throw out, he would pick them up and take them to the local ironmonger for something. Something as little as a farthing. And hence this nickname got stuck with him."

Jeffrey didn't say anything.

"In 1939, when the war broke out, he delivered farm produce to the garrisons, such as meat, eggs, or milk, and all sorts of vegetables. Quite soon, his business expanded, and acquired a cleaner lorry. His elder brother, Daniel, joined in and took around the truck while Floyd supplied new items, such as bread, butter, jam, and sugar, and half-cooked items like chicken, bacon, sausages, and ham. His business grew steadily, and in 1945, when the war finished in Europe, he had ten lorries and seven trucks bought on credits. They remained idle in various yards. He had 18 drivers in his wage's books, but not a shilling was earning to pay their wages."

"Very difficult situation, I suppose," he said, enjoying a drop of whiskey.

"You're absolutely right, a very difficult situation," Bernard repeated rather enthusiastically. "Because gran wasn't contemplating his position in the current situation. But he was more concerned about the 18 staff who were in his care. He didn't want to dismiss them, he couldn't even if he had wanted to. They were happy to work for him in the thick of bombings. Gran used to remind them that military wouldn't march on an empty stomach. Luckily, he used to know a Brigadier called Howard Jones, and he ran to him. "Please don't make my drivers starve and their families, I beg you."

Brigadier Jones had a cousin called Steven Jones in Cardiff. Steven was a young politician, trying to raise his sphere of influence in Cardiff and across the Severn River to Bristol. Anyway, a week later, Floyd Hughes had a telephone call. "Is it the head office of Hughes Transport?" A female voice came through the wire.

Grandpa was gasping for air. He had never given a proper title to his transport services until then. "Yes, yes," he coughed helplessly. "We are Hughes Transport."

"Well," she explained softly. We are going to authorise you as one of our companies' major distributors for food items."

"Thank you."

"You will distribute in Bristol and the rest of the County of Avon."

"Thank you. Thank you."

"You'll receive written acknowledgements and further details very soon."

"Thank you."

Floyd was breathless and couldn't ask or say anything all through that phone conversation. We still talked about it and made fun of grandpa."

"Who was that company?"

Bernard finished his drink and put the glass on the table. "British Farmers Association," he replied. Jeff remained silent, finishing his drink.

"The Hughes Transport grew bigger and bigger. At the peak of our business, we had 135 heavy trucks, 69 lorries, and 29 container lorries. And four hundred and fifty staff and plus, of course, the agency workers." Our garage was busy repairing and serving our vehicles and our business friends. Uncle Daniel was in charge of it. We also opened up a restaurant for our staff and for others where you're managing it now."

"Brilliant set up for staff."

"Yes, Jeff! It was a period when people respected each other, aired their views politely, and acted on them discreetly. No union threatening, no political interference, no backstabbing!"

Bernard pulled out a cigarette packet and, opening it, handed it to Jeffrey. He thankfully took one and Bernard also threw one to his mouth. The host picked up a lighter and lit his guest's cigarette first and then his. "Now Jeff," he said, blowing out a mouthful of smoke, "those trust and care all disappeared over the last ten or fifteen years. The deliveries are falling behind the deadlines, and goods are missing or getting damaged or items missing. The owners can't ask what's happening because many unions and party leaders are there with extreme views and ideas. They all want to be leaders

342

and outshine their opponents. They twist the issues and make workers despise the bosses."

Silently, Jeffrey drew a puff on the cigarette and slowly blew out smoke.

"Now Uncle Bevan's son Aeron is adamant he is shutting down the warehouse. Daniel's son David doesn't want the business for another single day. Hughes Transport is losing heavily every day."

"I'm sorry to hear these."

"I'm sorry, too. But yesterday, we partners had a meeting."

Without saying, he listened to the boss.

"We decided that under the current political situations and union strikes, we decided to close down our operations."

"Oh, I'm sad to hear that."

"I hoped the Hughes Transport will stand forever. But I am sorry I have to say this. Hughes Transport is an history now."

Without knowing what to say, he whispered again, "I'm sad to hear this."

Bernard drew a heavy puff on his cigarette and blew out quickly. "You'll get all your compensation very soon."

Jeffrey puffed on this cigarette wordlessly.

"We are closing down all businesses on the 13th of this month. That's a week on this Friday."

Jeffrey felt a freeze rising up his spine. He waited a moment for a breath before he said, "I'll have a dot of that whiskey, please."

Bernard served quickly. "I'm really sorry that we've to close the company."

Without saying anything, Jeffrey stared at this boss.

"In the Severn Yard, we had 31 lorries. We gave them back to the hire purchasing company." He stopped talking and stared at him, bewildered. "Well not really. They confiscated. We didn't pay their instalment fees for some time."

Jeffrey emptied his glass and put it down on the table.

"Here in our yard, we've 43 vehicles. And twenty-seven of them are going back to the leasing companies. No new contracts are coming to us. British rail is widening its operations and absorbing a lot of jobs. Royal Mail is another big competitor. And several other nationwide operators." He paused vaguely, sipping on his whiskey. "Okay, we can compete against the big companies. But there are numerous individual drivers who work for tuppence. We can't compete against them because we have overheads to pay."

Jeffrey silently sipped on his drink.

"When a war breaks out between the Israelis and the Arabs, as it is now, petrol prices zoom up at the pumps. And so are the gases and electricity. That brings in inflation. Inflation brings in high interest rates. In the end, these factors cry out for higher wage settlements. Did you hear that transport unions settled for a 40 percent increase? Our country can't accept this increase. This is heinous. The pundits predict the unemployment figure will shoot up to 5 million – who knows? Maybe more!"

Absently, Jeffrey finished the drink in his glass and put it back on the desk.

"Unless the elected government starts running the country, the Trotskyists and socialists and communists and union Barons will burn our country into ashes."

Jeffrey waited silently for a moment. "My daughter is alone," he said courteously. "I'll come in on Thursday, anyway, for a short while. "Hopefully I will start organising the funeral functions tomorrow onwards."

"I'm sorry to call you in now. But I've to organise the closing down on the 13th."

"That's okay. "

"I hope the funeral will go smoothly."

"Thank you."

"And, whatever the political situations we're going to face, I hope – genuinely hope – you'll get a good job. Because you're a good man!"

He held out his hand, and Jeffrey took it. "Thank you. And I did enjoy my work here. And I also know that you allowed me to go home several times when my son wasn't well or my wife, or both. I will remember that kindness."

"Goodbye, Jeffrey," Bernard said, letting off his hand. "And all the best."

"Thanks, Berney," he said. "And goodbye."

For a moment, neither of them said a word but stood still, meeting each other's gaze. Then, abruptly, he turned back to the corridor, walked away to the hallway, and walked out of the building.

Part 5: Emptiness All Around

The car park was further down on the right-hand side. He started to walk to the car. However, he was feeling absolutely distressed. He had a good family and a good work. They all had gone one by one, leaving him behind in emptiness.

He came out of the building and went to the car park. The weather was freezing cold, and the beating air numbed his windpipe. He took a cigarette and lit it before he got into the car. He took a deep puff and blew out the smoke slowly as he rolled down towards the driveway to the exit gate.

The traffic on the road was fairly quieter than he had anticipated, and he came home rather quickly. "We had few calls," Daniella said. "One was Uncle Jeremy. He said he would call again tomorrow."

He looked at her thoughtfully. Jeremey was his brother and had been living in New York with his wife and two children for the last ten years. "Did he say anything else?"

"He said they are very sad to hear about Mama's death. And that they will be coming for the funeral."

He waited. "Who else you know?"

"Aunty Sarah called. She said she would call again."

Sarah was his sister.

He waited silently.

She said, "I've taken the other's name and numbers."

Silently, he turned to go to the bathroom.

"Aunties Joanna and Angela were here."

He stopped walking, and half turned back.

"They said they would come again later."

Without saying anything, he went up to the bathroom.

A few minutes later, he came downstairs and then to the kitchen.

Daniella was in the kitchen and had made a cup of coffee for him. "I've put the coffee in the lounge."

Jeffrey hesitated a moment. "I'll have a whiskey."

She looked disappointed. "Shall I get it for you?"

"I will take it."

Daniella walked away silently to the lounge. He picked up a bottle of whiskey and a small cup, then joined her in the lounge.

"Why did you go for the meeting?"

"Just talk about their business plans," he replied uninterestingly.

She got up. "I'm a bit tired. I'm going to my room."

He didn't say anything.

She waited. "When are we going to the hospital?"

"I'm going at 9," he replied, pouring drinks into the cup. "Why?"

"Am I not coming with you?"

"Better if you don't." He raised the cup to his mouth and took a sip. "Tomorrow, I'm going to be very busy. I've a few places to go to organise the funeral. If I can, I don't want to drag you along."

The muscles on her face twitched uncontrollably, and she was about to cry out loud. Nonetheless, she managed to suppress the emotions. "Aunty Joanna is going in the evening," she said, walking upstairs. "I'll go with Aunty."

Jeffrey didn't speak. Instead, he poured more whiskey and continued sipping. He didn't feel the urge to return the calls of the people on the list. However, it would have been helpful if he had got Jeremy on the phone. But it seldom happened, as he was a travelling salesman and spent most of his time on the road. And whenever he called lately, Jeffrey was out. Anyway, there was nothing much to talk about until the date and place were confirmed for the burial. And as the political structure erupted violently and shackled everyday lives, who could name the date or place for it?

He got up and went upstairs.

"Dad?" Daniella called as he passed her doorway.

Jeffrey stopped and pushed open the door. "Yes?" He asked quietly, meeting her eyes.

She took a long pause. "What happened to Salome?" she asked in the end in a mixed tone of trepidation and guilt.

Obviously, it was a shockwave to him. He stood still for a while, his eyes staring at her face. "Salome?"

"Yes, Salome. Salome Lawrence."

"What do you know about her?"

"Everything."

"Everything?"

"Yes. Everything. Mamie told me?"

"I see."

"But she didn't tell me anything about the baby. I mean Salome's baby."

"What about it?"

She waited nervously. "How the baby died?"

"Why didn't mama tell you?"

"I don't know."

"Did you ask her?"

"No. I waited for her to tell me in her own time."

"Have you heard the word 'Abortion'?"

"Yes. And in the classroom. Teachers have explained to us."

"An abortion went wrong. And Salome and her baby died......in a foreign country."

"How did it go wrong?"

"I've nothing more to say," he said, turning back to his room. "Because I know nothing more."

"Dad?" She called him back.

Without replying, he stopped.

"Am I safe here with you?"

The bedroom door in front of him was open. Jeffrey looked up through the room space to the window. Outside, it was full of low-lying clouds above the pitch darkness. But there was no sky above. In the end, he found his words with difficulty, of course. "We found you when you were two weeks old. You were a cute, jolly little baby. We loved you instantly. And that was ten years ago. And we still love you."

"But Mama isn't here with us."

"I know. And I'm going to organise her funeral in the morning."

About 2 o'clock the next day– Wednesday the 3rd – Jeffrey turned up at the parish church's reception room, three hours after the appointment arranged with the Vicar George Miller. "Sorry, Father," he apologised immediately and sincerely as the priest opened the front door and their eyes met.

"Oh Jeffrey, I'm glad you came," Fr George replied graciously, extending his sympathetic hand. "And I've no idea how you're keeping with all these misfortunes."

He waited. "I phoned to Fr Cyril. I hope he ………."

The priest interrupted him gently. "Yes, he told me. Please come in."

They sat down in the reception room. "Would you like a cup of tea? Or coffee. It's very cold. We're having some of the worst weather for years."

"I just had tea from a café down the road."

The priest looked at him quietly for a moment. "Did you manage to see Debra in the end?"

"Yes, Father." He paused, drew a deep breath, and let it out quietly. "Some uproar broke out in the funeral wing. Some local disputes started involving two or more unions. Police were called in. But they don't want to get in the middle of unions. In the end, mortuary opened, somehow, for few minutes."

"Thanks, God, for that," Father said, sighing. "Anyway, you saw Debra?"

Jeffrey sighed off noisily. "I saw her. And I sat by her side, seeing all our lives in my mind, good and bad. And happy and sad." He stopped and drew another breath.

The priest opened his mouth, but he didn't speak as he noticed the tears bubbling up in his eyes.

A moment later, Jeffrey said in a heavy, sad voice, "After our lives together, what I have is a few memories and tears." He paused as if for searching words. "If this is all I can have, is life worth living?"

The priest held his shoulder. "You and I'll have a talk about it when you're in a calmer frame of mind, definitely not now."

Jeffrey didn't say anything.

"Did they say anything about Debra?"

"They need to have an autopsy."

Silently, the priest stared at him.

"They want to know the exact cause of death."

"How long that will take?"

"In 2 to 3 days."

The priest shrugged. "That's a fair decision, I suppose."

"What hurts me is the fact that they haven't changed her clothes."

"What do you mean?"

"She is wearing the same clothes she was wearing when she died."

The priest didn't speak hurriedly. "Maybe they are waiting for the autopsy before they do anything."

"Father, how free are you? If they are ready for early next week?"

"Don't worry about it. We've three priests here. You want to arrange the funeral soon?"

"Well, properly and as soon as possible."

"You've to be careful, Jefferey. Don't rush. Take as it comes because we're passing through very volatile situations in our country."

Jeffrey stared at him, confused.

"Let me tell you one incident that just happened. I was supposed to marry off a couple tomorrow. The bride is in fact my nephew. The bridegroom flew to Lungola to see his bedbound father and his blessings. They arranged everything for this big occasion. Now, they've to cancel the wedding. They boy can't fly back due to airline strikes. And they lost thousands of pounds for food and booking fees and the rest."

"That's very sad. Anyway, Father, I keep in touch with you."

"Please do so," the priest encouraged him. "They can choose any day. And we'll work along with it. You've my word on it."

Jeffrey thanked the vicar and left the church.

Part 6: The Post-Mortem

The post-mortem was arranged for Friday, the 5th of January. However, on that day, the coroner's union went on strike. It was rearranged for Monday the 8th in a rush and failed to function because it was the day of the national general strike. In the end, it was conducted on the 10th on Wednesday and concluded in the death certificate that death was due to the failure of major organs such as heart and lungs. And the funeral director chose the date for the burial on 23rd January and St Michaels Cemetery on the bank of River Avon. Jeffrey agreed to it, as this cemetery was about a mile away from his house, and this was exactly where his son Jeffrey John – J J in short at home – was laid to rest. It was also confirmed that Debra's grave would be next to that of J J.

On the following morning, at about 9.30, Nurse Angela and Joanna arrived. "What you're planning about the burial?" Angela enquired.

Before Jeffrey could answer, Daniella came back to the lounge carrying a tray with three cups of tea. She carefully put it down on the table. "Thank you, sweetie," Joanna said warmly. "This is the best medicine for this bleak winter."

"4 to 5 inches of snow already on the ground," Angela complained, looking dejected. "And -3 degrees at the moment. What's this? I had never experienced anything like this."

Joanna picked up a cup. "I heard on the radio that another heavy snowfall's coming down all this afternoon. And that it may continue until midnight."

Angela sipped her drink. "Very good tea, Daniella."

"She always makes nice tea," Joanna said.

Angela took another sip and then turned to look at the girl. "What sort of send-off you like for your 'Mamie?'"

She looked at Jeffrey hesitantly before she looked back at the nurse. "Dad will decide on that."

"Good girl."

"I love to give her a good farewell. But I'm broke. And as you know, funerals are expensive." Jeffrey picked up his cup of tea and drank a large sip. "Anyway, I'm going to the bank and see what the manager is going to say."

"Bank will take a long time to make a decision. We don't have that much time."

"I can re-mortgage on the house. The deed of the house is with them. So, it should make it easy and fast, I think."

"It will still take time," Joanna said reluctantly.

"I can help you," Angela assured. "I've the funds. You can pay back when you can."

Jeffrey agreed to it half-heartedly.

Shortly, they started to discuss the funeral functions. How many relatives and guests would be invited? Who would be invited to the church, and who would be to the house or cemetery? How many cars should be hired? What kind of dresses would be suitable for Debra in her final journey? What could be the price for a decent coffin, the cemetery cost, church expenses, and the reception after the funeral? Definitely, some guests and relatives ought to stay in outside accommodations. In a day or two, he would know everything: the items he had counted and the items he hadn't calculated yet. Anyway, it wouldn't be anything like J J's funeral – it was strictly limited to a close family affair due to difficult circumstances, such as Debra being in the hospital.

On the 13th, the funeral director suggested that his company would administer the funeral matters brilliantly from beginning to end if Jeffrey was happy to give them consent. Their company had performed burials and cremations since 1905, and every client over the years and decades felt absolutely happy with their overall commitment, responsibility, and performance. For a small fee, it was absolutely worth to let them take all charge. Angela had known them personally, and she also suggested that he accept their reputation and authorise them for the occasion. On the 14th, Jeffrey signed on their contract that they were the sole agent for organising the funeral.

On the 15th, they gave her a wash, put on a new blue dress, and brushed the hair with a little parting on the left temple. She was lying on a white sheet spread over a mattress in a rectangular box. She looked amazingly beautiful and appeared to be having a quiet sleep. He kneeled down and kissed her forehead; warm tears trickled down from his eyes and blotted on her head.

On the 16th, general strikes were declared across the country, involving various unions of railway, coal mines, lorry drivers, ford workers, and the Royal College of Nurses. There was picketing at the hospital gate, and it wasn't safe to visit Debra.

On the 17th, the national strikes continued on to the 2nd day.

On the 18th, he saw Debra in the morning and received a phone call from Jeremy that he and his wife couldn't come for the funeral. The political situation was dire in the UK, and he wasn't sure they could fly back on the return, and that was on the 25th.

On the 19th, Debra's sister, Elena, sent a telex from Sydney in Australia that she and her partner had decided that they were not coming as the political situation was very unpredictable in England, and they were not sure they would be able to fly as per their schedule.

On the 20th, general strikes spread across the country like wildfire.

On the 21st, the strikes continued to the second day.

On the 22nd, Jeffrey visited his wife for the final time. On the evening, her body was taken to St Michael's Church. Some of the relatives and friends gathered around the body and prayed for an hour or more.

On the 23rd, they had the requiem mass at 11, one hour later than usual, for the convenience of the people who were trying to reach the church in this atrocious weather. At 12.30, the funeral cottage started to head up the Avon Road and then moved up the Central Road towards the Bristol Cemetery after the Discovery Square. The new Bristol Railway station was about half a mile before the Square and crowds of people congested out of the station, overfilling the ground and deterring the traffic flow.

They were union activists or ordinary members, and some were holding up union flags, shouting slogans, and moving up to the Square for yet another protest and meeting. The funeral vehicles were budging up in a line inside the mass crowd, and moving up extremely cautiously to avoid possible accidents and worrying at the same time helplessly that they were getting late for the burial. The bus and coach terminals were about a hundred yards in front on the right side, and crowds started to squeeze into the road heavily. For a while, nothing appeared to be moving in the vicinity ahead. Jeffrey wound down the window and asked a man who was standing very close to him. "What choice we've here, sir? We're getting terribly late for the funeral."

The man looked at him through the open window. "I completely sympathise with your predicament," he replied rather helplessly. Nonetheless, the diction of his voice and wordings suggested that he was a man of education and hierarchy in some union. "But I'm afraid you chose the wrong day."

Jeffrey met his eyes steadily for a moment. "Who knows the right day for dying and burying, sir?"

"Very true!"

"If the people had walked on the payment, it would have been easy for everyone to go for their business."

The man didn't reply. Instead, he stared ahead to the distance. "The payments are full of snow and black eyes," he replied politely, looking back into the car. "The Council hasn't salted over there. And we can't walk on there." He paused vaguely and looked ahead again. "And if we walk over, we choose our own deaths and burials. And that's why we are walking up on the road."

"Anything you could do to help us get to the cemetery, please."

"That's exactly what I'm thinking. But the problem is that there are thousands of people in front. They are so hopelessly lost in their burdens. Burdens such as feeding their families and housing their kids! And several heart-burning issues."

"They think these negative activities solve those problems?"

"Looking at your cartages, I get the feeling that you're very rich."

"Not at all. I'm just like any other poor man. But the difference is that I work, they talk."

A group of people bypassed them, shouting slogans on top of their voices.

After they had gone further up, the man said, "Sorry. I didn't hear your reply properly. Did you say you work?"

"Something like that?"

"Good, that's precisely what they are asking. Chance to work. And pay for their work."

"And this kind of negative activities will change the situation any better?"

"Of course. Behind every progress the poor man has gained, it's the union that made it possible. And don't forget that!"

As they were speaking, a slow wave of people moved forward. The cottage vehicles also started to move. Th man stayed on the side of the car, saying, "I'll be around your car. If any delays, I get a microphone from my friend and shout to the people to move sides and let the funeral cottage go."

"Thank you!"

"Anyway, we're out of your way another four hundred yards. We're not going to the square. We're having our meeting in the central park."

It took another fifteen minutes to go through that four hundred yards and then another fifteen minutes to get to the cemetery gate. They drove in through the open gate and waited in the large courtyard in front of the reception office.

The warden, Barry Wilkes, came out from the office and gave a sheet of paper to the front driver. The location of Debra's grave was on it, as well as the drawing of the route to there. The location was no. 14, Graceland Road, off St Michaels Avenue.

"I know the St Michaels Avenue," the driver said.

"Good," the warden said. "Go into the St Michaels Avenue. And as you go up, you will see the Graceland. It's the fourth road on the left."

The driver nodded his head in acknowledgement and started the engine. Slowly, they moved into St Mary's Road, which took them to St Joseph's Road. The second road on the right was St Michaels's Avenue. As they went forward, they saw the Graceland Road on the left. The limousine in the front slowed down and parked first. The other cars were parked behind the limousine and along the roadside. Jeffery, Daniella, and Jeremy came out first and walked along the row to Grave no 14. Others were getting out of their seats, almost about 40 in all, and they moved closer to the limousine where the priest was getting ready for his prayers. Jeremey went all the way down the row of no 14, but he couldn't find any new grave. He turned back and gazed at Jeremy. "Where's it?" he asked, his voice trembling.

Jeremy was already gazing far and wide, as far as his eyes could let him see. He wasn't brave enough to look at Jeffrey. "It's a mistake," he replied, his eyes rolling everywhere in the massive cemetery. "We will go to the reception and find the right location."

They run back to the others. "Some mistakes," Daniella said, crying. "Mamie's grave isn't here."

Nobody said a word as they stood startled. The brothers jumped into a car, and then the driver rushed in. They took a U-turn and speeded to the reception. Warden and Barry were in the bathroom. They got him out in seconds. "They gave us the wrong location," Jeremy screamed.

The warden apologised genuinely. "I'm new. This is my third day."

Jeffrey grabbed the appointment file. He searched for the Debra Smith page. Yes, the grave number was 14 at Graceland Road.

Barry pleaded helplessly, "Please let me call the foreman of the gravediggers."

He found the number and dialled. After a couple of seconds, a male voice came through the wire, "Hello, Keith Fear is speaking."

He handed the phone to Jeffery.

"I'm Jeffery Smith. Where is my wife's grave you've dug up?"

Keith hesitated. "We didn't dig it up."

"Why?"

"We're on strike, sir."

"What a savage man you are! You don't bury the dead?"

"Sorry, sir. We're gravediggers. I mean, we're cheap manual labourers. We've no power to make decisions."

Chapter 9

Bad School Experience

Part 1: Finding Mark

The hallways ran between the wards and were left reasonably bright all the time. Eleven wards were there all in all, with six of them downstairs and five on the first floor. The second floor was sarcastically known as the Upstairs, which meant the hierarchy occupied it, such as senior officers, managers, staff rooms, meeting halls, pharmacy, and medical care workers. All wards were numbered and also allocated with a female name, such as Margaret Ward. It was the sixth ward on the ground floor and was mostly used for solitary confinement. Each ward had its own corridor, going all the way back and then returning, giving access to 20 to 30 cells and finally merging into the hallway at another point. The corridors weren't lit very brightly, especially after the dinner at 6.30. The relevant officers in the Upstairs asserted that darkness around would help a lot to sleep well. However, the inmates claimed that it was the penny-pinching ideas of retardant minds. Anyway, it was an hour and a half after dinner time when Mark knocked on the door of the cell no. 17. There was no response from inside. He waited a moment patiently before he called quietly, "Daniella?"

Again, there was no reply.

He removed the cover over the view hole. Behind it, a strip of strong metal mesh was fixed over it for security reasons. He looked through it, and a large part of the room space fell in his sight. Daniella was sitting at the edge of her bed, with her elbows on her knees and her face in her hands, and sat down absolutely motionless. "Are you praying, Daniella?"

She didn't reply.

"This is Mark Windrush."

This time, she spoke. "I know."

"You recognise my voice, I think. It's very musical, isn't it?"

"No."

"No? Lots of people said so."

She didn't speak.

"Then how did you know? I'm using very low-odour perfumes tonight?"

She screamed out through her fingers. "Who else is there as stupid as you are?"

He chuckled quietly. "That's great. Thank you, Ms Daniella."

She hesitated. "Why are you disturbing me?"

"Sorry, did I disturb your sleep?"

She kept quiet.

"But I heard you didn't eat your supper."

She whispered slowly, "I wasn't hungry."

"Sorry, I didn't hear you."

"Wasn't hungry!"

"And dinner?"

Rather annoyed, she refused to answer.

"Not hungry, I take it."

She retorted, "Yes."

"And breakfast?"

"What's your problem?"

He chortled easily. "I'm the night watchman tonight in this ward." He paused briefly. "I'm starting my shift. And I heard you didn't eat anything at all today."

She didn't say anything.

"I thought you're not well."

She didn't reply.

"I don't like somebody starving in my care."

"Please go away."

"Is it that easy?"

She raised her face from her hands and said rather angrily. "Go away, man. Otherwise, I scream."

"Okay," he said, moving away from the view hole. A couple of minutes ticked away silently, and then he moved back. "You alright, Daniella?" He asked, staring at her and speaking in a concerned tone.

"You came back?"

"I didn't go. I was waiting for your scream. That's all, dear."

Suddenly, the expression on her face changed to dejection as the restrained emotions surged up. Obviously, she didn't want to cry in front of him. She had to maintain her reputation as a strong girl. She turned her face to the other way. However, before her face completely turned away, he saw glimpses of tears sparkling down onto her cheeks. "Let it come out, dear. And free yourself."

She didn't speak. Instead, she discharged her tension through sobbing, which vibrated the silence in the cell. "Freeing for what?"

"For your life, dear."

"What's my life? Held up in confinement?"

"Only for the time being, Daniella. But, as my father used to say, everything will change."

"For the worst?"

"Possible, Daniella! But again, everything will change."

"What have I got? No father, no mother."

"Like my father used to say, everything changes. But then again, he used to say lots of stupid things."

She waited. "I wish I had known my parents. And I hope they're alive."

He spoke quickly obviously to calm her feelings, "Of course, Daniella, they're alive." He stopped talking suddenly and thought for a while." You're fifteen, aren't you?"

She nodded lightly.

"That means they could be in their mid-thirties. Or late thirties."

She looked down, then looked back at him quickly. "I don't know who they are. Or what their names are. I won't recognise them even if I bump into them."

"Really and truly, yes. Because your life appears to be in the middle of a big forest, and you can't see the sky. Or don't know the direction. But don't worry, dear. One morning, you'll find yourself at the edge of the forest. And

364

you'll see the bright, beautiful sky right in front of you. And you'll see your directions clearly up there."

Daniella hesitated. "This is also your father's saying?"

He nodded for an answer before he added quietly. "My mother also had a saying, which she used frequently."

"What's that?"

"He says lots of stupid things."

"Well, your mother knew him well."

"Thank you!"

"Even I don't know my real name. I'm living with a name my adopted mother gave me. She and her husband adopted me to cover the failures in their marriage. I'm just a screen."

"That's better. I like it."

"Do you?"

"Yes. Because being a screen is better than a shadow."

Silently, she caught his gaze.

"My dad used to say, 'No screen, no shadow."

She looked at him. "It's another of his saying."

"I'm afraid so." He laughed quietly for a moment. "He had several of them. He should have written a book of it. Luckily, he didn't. He knew, 'Garbage heap stinks.'"

Daniella felt slightly easier as he talked. However, she kept silent.

"Let's talk about you, Daniella. What can I get you?"

"Nothing," she said adamantly. "I'm okay."

"Quite late," he whispered disappointedly. "But I can get you a bowl of soup and a couple of sandwiches."

"Thank you. But I don't need anything."

"A glass of juice and a few biscuits?"

"No."

"Water?"

She waited. "Why are you so concerned about me."

He grinned helplessly. "I like to help the inmates."

"Thank you. I've been here for almost two years. And I've been in these confinements several times. To be honest, I'm quite used to it."

He stood quietly, staring at her. After a brief while, he spoke in a resigned voice. "I've some paperwork to do. I'm going to the office. And my shift finishes at six. And tomorrow is my day off. Which means I may not see you for two days."

Daniella didn't say anything.

"Please stay out of trouble. And …" he broke off his talking as the tannoy started to sound earsplittingly first, and then the clear sound of a man was heard. "Hello, guards. Whoever is free, please go to Ward 8, also called Bernadette Ward, on the first floor. And go to Cell 16."

"Bye," he whispered as he turned around, then rushed to the hallway.

Daniella moved back in her bed and continued to sit, leaning her shoulder against the wall. She fixed her eyes across the dim light in the limited cell space. Nonetheless, she wasn't seeing anything there nor beyond it, as there

366

was no window allocated, except the narrow ventilation on the wall just under the ceiling level. Yet, she continued to stay there, as if immobile, while several incidents of the recent past flooded into her memories.

For a start, she was brought over here, the Marina Girls' Prison, on the 15th of September 1983, and put in a cell, numbered 11, of Bernadette Ward for one night. However, she was sharing the cell with an incumbent, Samantha Parkinson, for three months, as other suitable places weren't available. She had been very worried and tired by the time police brought her to the prison. They had several questions for her, different sessions for the interrogations, and new officers always attended the meetings. She didn't reply to most of the questions. Frankly speaking, she was about to faint. In the end, they took her to this prison at about 8.30 in the evening. Mr. Paul Davis, the housing officer, met her in the foyer. "I've a lovely chamber for you, Daniella."

She struggled to get her voice out of her mouth. "Thank you."

The housing officer turned to a man who was standing beside him. "Take her to Parkyie's room."

The man sounded anxious when he asked, "Parkyie's?"

"What's wrong with you today, Brian? You've no appetite for work today."

Brian moved closer and whispered. "Can we go to the office for a moment?"

Apparently annoyed, he took Brian to the next room. "Don't put her with Samantha Parkinson," Brian whispered. "She is evil."

The boss retorted quietly, gesturing at Daniella, "And what about this one? An angel?"

"Sammy will kill this girl in no time."

"That's not a bad outcome," the housing officer said cynically. "At least we can manage with one bed less." He had a faint suspicion that Daniella was hearing their conversation. He turned to her and smiled, saying, "Only for today, young lady. Tomorrow, we'll get you a new room."

Brian, carrying some of her luggage, climbed up in the front. Daniella followed him, bringing the rest of her goods. They walked down the hallway to the Bernadette Ward and then turned into the corridor that led the way to cell number 11.

"Welcome, Daniella," Samantha said, apparently looking happy.

"Thank you," she replied politely.

"You're late."

She remained quiet.

The guard placed her goods in the storage stand at the foot of her bed. A small semi-circled enclosure was attached to the stand for a matter of privacy. "This half of the space is yours," Brian said politely. "Please keep it clean and tidy."

She stooped and sank down onto the edge of the bed. She drew a deep breath and said, obviously struggling, "Thank you. I'll do that."

"I heard you had supper?"

She nodded lightly. "Thank you for asking."

"You need anything to drink?"

"I've water in the bag."

"Good," he said, shooting a glance at the other girl. "Samantha will guide you if you need help. Anyway, see that switch," he said, gesturing to a switch close to the door. "You can ring that if there is any emergency. We'll hear it in the guards' office. Somebody'll respond quickly."

Daniella thanked him again, and he stepped outside. He locked the door and walked away. Above the door, there was a tiny tube light that cast only a shadowy light in the room. She entered the enclosure and changed into a night dress. She came out with a sleeping bag, spread it on the small bed, and then slipped herself into it.

Samantha sat on her bed in a lying position and smoked. Suddenly, she dropped the bud of the cigarette to the floor and looked at her companion. "Are you alright, babe," she asked definitely concerned. "For you and me, we're the only two in this world right now. And always remember that."

Part 2: Samantha

Without replying, she caught her eyes impassively.

"I'm twenty-one. I think you're seventeen. I'll consider you like a young sister. And love you."

She whispered. "Thank you!"

"How old are you, exactly?"

She answered reluctantly. "Fifteen."

"Oh my God! You're a baby." She continued to stare at her with an amazing expression. "I can see you've so much in your mind. Talk to me and take them all out. It will definitely help you."

"I am very tired."

"Oh darling, I've something for it," she said enthusiastically, almost getting out of her bed. "You don't pay me anything. We're sisters, remember. And it'll give your strength back." She hesitated for a brief moment. "Shall I get it?"

"No. I'm fine."

"You're sure?"

"Yes," she retorted quietly. "I just want to sleep. That's all."

"That's good, Daniella. I'm so happy to hear it." She quickly sat up on the edge of the bed. "Believe me, I was a bit worried when I heard somebody was moving in. You never know who is who these days."

"I'm here only for tonight. They will give me another room tomorrow."

She laughed hilariously. "They told me the same 18 months ago. I am still here." She stopped laughing abruptly and said kindly. "But you don't need to worry. Though I only met you now, I feel like you're my real sister."

Confused and with a deep frustration, the girl caught her gaze steadily. "I need to sleep, please."

"Of course, darling. But one more moment, please. I'm dying to say this."

"Yes?"

She waited. "You're the most beautiful girl on earth," she said finally, her voice thrilled with excitement.

"Please, I need to sleep."

"Sleep. But, for anything, give a shout."

"Okay."

370

Obediently, Samantha leaned back to her bed.

Daniella closed her eyes, though she was restless inside her mind. She was shuttered away from the broader world into a hole with another girl who was clearly giving her a shiver of fear. Nonetheless, she concentrated on her mind to do a complete shutdown – away from all realities that surrounded her to a mesmerising scene that was inviting her. Quicker than she had imagined, she fell asleep. And when she slept about two hours - or three, she wasn't sure about the time - she began to sense sounds of movements or voices. Absently, she turned onto her side and tried to block off the thoughts of her tired mind as she had assumed.

However, the sounds got more audible, and she woke up into a semi-conscious mind. Abruptly, she opened her eyes and looked up into the pitch dark that hung heavily on her. The tiny tube light was off, and the disturbances were rising from the room itself. Now she got completely woken up and stared into the darkness. The sounds were a mixture of restrained heavy breaths and shaking beds. She turned her head and looked into Samantha's side. She suddenly realized that there was a man in her bed. The immediate question that rushed into her mind was how he had entered and whether her own life was safe in a cell. She didn't wait for her answers. Instead, she shut her eyes and ears and stayed calm as if she were asleep.

After about fifteen minutes, the noises of movements stopped, and the man sat up in the bed and started to dress. "What's the rush?" Samantha whispered in a suppressed voice. "Tomorrow's your day off, isn't it? And Saturday"

"I know," he replied very quietly. "But I'm leaving early for Bristol. Tomorrow is also my son's birthday. His mother is having a party."

She was quiet.

"And next week, I'm off for my training."

"You're lying."

"No, I swear."

"But you haven't seen the new girl."

"I'll see her first. And then I'll tell you."

He kissed her and then got off the bed. "You'll look after her for me, won't you until I come."

"Shut up and get off. She's mine."

"Thank you, sweetie," he chuckled. "With your experience, you could train her for me."

He walked away to the door, opened it quietly, and went. He closed the door and then heard the sound of the lock.

It took a moment or two before Daniella inhaled a shallow breath of air. She was scared to death. Slowly, she exhaled, holding her whole body still. It wasn't fear alone that was petrifying her whole being, but the combined feeling of past experiences and failures eroded her desire to be alive. She never had someone she could depend on and cry with and trust them for safety, protection, and affection. At the depth of the agony, she stared across the emptiness in front of her and wondered what was the meaning of her life in this world. Anyway, her mind was absolutely numbed now, and there wasn't any movement for thoughts and reasoning. She wasn't even crying. She absently lay on her side. The warm tears trickled down over the nose, then merged with that of the other eye and dripped to the bed sheet while her heart ached for life.

A FEW TALES

It was about two o'clock in the night. Nonetheless, she didn't even try to get some sleep. She knew she wouldn't get it.

The night ticked away very sluggishly, and a faint light dimmed outside the window vent. Saturday was dawning.

Saturdays and Sundays, generally known as the happy days among the inmates, had been the days everyone looked forward. For a start, they don't need to get up early, wash themselves, and get ready for the breakfast. The simple reason was that there were no schools and studies, such as languages and science, and the most boring of them all, the mathematics. A large number of girls hated physical training and exercises, and other most disliked subjects were arts and crafts.

On normal weekdays, girls were required to get up at 6 o'clock in the morning, but on weekends, they stayed under the blankets until 7.30. At least by 8, they should queue up in the canteen hall. Two canteen halls were there, one for each floor, and girls were ordered to stand separately on a ward basis. Some inmates, who were elders and had been in the prison for longer than others, volunteered with the cooks and waitresses and served the food at all meal times. It helped the prison management to cut the cost of the services down, and the managers were at liberty to know whether all the inmates turned up for the meals. After breakfast, the girls could return to their cells and clean up their cells, do some homework, or go out for a little walk under supervision within the enclosed ground. After lunch, it was time to meet the visitors in the meeting hall. Visitors such as parents, siblings, guardians, or friends would turn up if they wish and at their convenience and have a private talk under the watchful eyes of the guards. On Monday, the circle of routines would start spinning all over again with either learnings in the class rooms or having trainings on the campus.

On Saturday, the morning after she was locked up here, she refused the breakfast. She stubbornly stayed in her cell, and so she did for lunch. At about 2'clock, a young man came to visit her in the cell. "Good afternoon, Daniella," he wished her pleasantly.

Daniella sat up in the bed. Streaks of her messy, long hair cascaded over her face and blocked her view. She raised her hand, brushed them off her eyes, and tucked them behind the ears. She wasn't entirely successful as some of the streaks sprung back disobediently and oscillated down on her cheeks. She gave up as if defeated by her hair and shot a quick glance at him, saying gently, "Good after.... afternoon," she said, her voice breaking off, as she saw him and her eyes caught his gaze steadily. He was a mixed-race man, just as she was.

He glanced at Samantha's empty bed and then turned to Daniella. "Samantha is doing some cleaning work in the kitchen. And that makes it easy to talk with some privacy."

She looked at him rather nervously.

"My name is Mark Windrush. I'm one of the deputy managers."

Her face slightly changed to a startled look.

He realised it, too. He smiled gently. "The name doesn't mean much. I do just the guards' work."

She didn't say anything.

"You didn't have your breakfast or lunch, I heard," he said politely.

Without answering, she looked away to the far corner by the side of the door.

"Why didn't you eat, Daniella?"

She rolled her eyes back and cast down somewhere near where he was standing. "I don't know," she replied finally.

"You know that isn't true."

This time, she looked up and caught his gaze silently.

He moved a step or two closer to her bedside. "If you don't cooperate with the authorities, they tend to think you're here for trouble."

She asked slowly, "What sort of trouble?"

This time he was also slow to speak. "I'm sorry, I'm not going to name them. But they put you in a mental case."

Her eyes grew wide into a faint expression of shock. "What for?"

Mark stared away briefly. "If you do something, shall I say, something wrong – whatever it may be – they've to protect themselves."

The expression of shock grew visibly clear on her face. "I don't have any mental problems."

He completely ignored her answer. "Once you're classified as a mental case, doctors who practise on mental patients will start checking you on every day. Or maybe twice a day, or more times, who knows."

She didn't say anything, but her mouth hung open partly in fear.

"This prison is an institution, like any other organisations. There are rules and regulations attached to it for the sake of everybody who lives here and works here." He stopped talking vaguely for a moment. "Please follow the orders and try to get out of here as early as possible."

"Thank you, sir," she said, her voice breaking in fear.

"I know you're new, and you don't wish to sit with strangers while having your food. And that you've to get used to the way of life here."

Now she started to sob.

"I have organised some food, and one of us will bring it to you here on a food trolley in about twenty minutes or so. I also make a note that you're not well so that they bring your food here for today and tomorrow. You don't need to go to the canteen and stand up in the queue."

"Thank you, sir."

He waited silently while his eyes looked at searchingly. "Is anybody coming to visit you today or tomorrow?"

She shook her head. "I don't have anybody."

"No father, mother?"

She shook her head again while a few tears scattered out of her eyes.

"Any other siblings?"

She was silent for a moment before she replied, "No, sir."

"We've social visitors who come here and talk with you. And religious groups who work for different churches. And some elderly people who have no children or relations. Would you like them to visit you?"

"Of course, sir."

"Good. And get up. Wash your face."

Silently, she stared at him.

"And perhaps I bring your food myself."

She didn't say anything but stared at him kindly.

Quietly, he walked away.

He didn't bring the food for her, though. It was a young female guard called Janice. The guard said Mark had prepared the food. Then he ran to a cell where two girls were fighting. She also said that fighting over the weekends was more common than on weekdays. Over the weekdays, they'd pick up disputes, and weekends would square up the difference. As a matter of fact, there were more staff working at the weekends than on any other days due to these excessive fights, Janice said.

Part 3: Growing Reputation

Sunday afternoon, she had two visitors: a nun from a local convent and then, half an hour later, an elderly couple from the Salvation Army. She enjoyed the time with them despite everything that was torturing her life. On Monday, she went to her classroom as advised. It was English in the morning. She had always been very good in English. However, all her classmates wanted to be with her. They all started talking to her at the same time – what was her name, where did she come from, what happened to be in the jail? Some of them wanted to touch her, hug her, or kiss her cheeks. Again, some of them stood away deliberately and watched jealously the commotion she was making. What could they do about it? Nothing! They knew it well because this girl was the most beautiful piece in the prison.

Her growing reputation amongst everyone made Samantha very upset, although she didn't show it in front of her. Three to four weeks passed fairly peacefully, and one evening, these two girls were in the cell. Samantha had a shower and, wearing a gown, walked out of the bathroom, and came up by the bedside of the other, humming softly a music of Beatles, called All You

Need Is Love. Obviously, Daniella didn't give any attention to it. Samantha moved up across the space in between their beds in a gentle dance motion and, suddenly, she stopped moving and looked back. "Daniella, darling, do you sing?"

Daniella was in the bed, with her body raised against the headboard. She had a bedside lamp on the wall side, and it was on, shedding enough light around her face. She was reading Shakespeare's Macbeth. Without taking the eyes from the book, she whispered, "No, Samantha."

"Shame, darling. You should do. You've a fantastic voice."

"Thanks."

What does it mean – you'll sing, Daniella?"

"No!"

She waited, her eyes still staring at her. "Do you dance, babe?" Samantha asked in the end.

"No!"

"You're tall and slim."

 "Just as any other ordinary people."

"I'm tall, but fat. I never liked my body."

"To me, you look alright."

"Thanks, babe," she said rather happily. She stepped closer to her bed. "You're the first person who said that, besides Brian. Then Brian, isn't it? He'd say anything to please me." She got into the bed and pulled the sheet over her naked thighs and up to the waist. "Don't take me wrong. Brian is only a friend. And nothing more!"

Daniella was quiet for a moment, then turned her face to the book. "I don't know him, Samantha. I haven't even seen him."

"Maybe not; he's a night guard. Very handsome. Girls love him."

Daniella didn't say anything.

"And when he is here, he's mostly with some girls in their cell." She stopped talking and lit a cigarette. Daniella continued to stay silent.

"Oh, shame," she said quickly. "He was here with me last night. You were sleeping. He was drooling all over you. "

She turned her face and stared at her without speaking.

The elder girl met her eyes. "He came nearer your bed and saw you in the dim light." She suddenly started laughing and then chuckled, "One moment, I thought he was going to kiss you. I pushed him back and whispered into his face angrily. Don't touch her, you filthy bastard."

"How did he get in?" Daniella asked, her voice sharp and angry.

"Daniella, darling. He's a guard. He's master keys to go into any cells."

"Master keys? Why?"

"My sweetheart, you sound very ignorant. Forgive me for saying so!"

"I'm ignorant, as you say. But don't believe I'm hearing this."

"Darling, baby, this is not a paradise. This is a prison. And the life goes on here just as it's outside this big building."

She continued to stare at her, silently, as she couldn't get the words.

"Here is a world of its own, my baby. Here, somebody needs medicine. Or hardcore drugs. Another one is so lonely that she needs a boy for company. You understand this, my honeypie?"

379

She was holding the play Macbeth between her fingers. She dropped it on the bed by her side and sat up. Her lips started to shiver as the agony of helplessness began to grip her senses. She started to cry mutely. Then the noise engulfed the cell.

Samantha watched her for a moment before she said in a kind voice, "Why are you torturing yourself, darling? Childish, very childish you're. Nobody appreciates this. This is a prison. There are different kinds of ethics here."

She continued to cry loudly for another few minutes. Then she restrained it to sobbing and sighing.

"I used to cry a lot," Samantha said. "I was punished for nothing."

Daniella didn't speak. Instead, she put her face in her hands and her elbows on her thighs. She wasn't crying as such, but tears seeped out between the fingers and then trickled down on her hands.

However, Samantha continued rather angrily, "I was a clerk in a bank, and this was my first job. And some days, the bank can't balance the book. Short of cash in the box. And they're big amounts. Police checked all staff but never found cash with anyone – boys or girls." She paused, took a deep breath, and inhaled slowly. "One day, police found two bundles of notes in my jacket pocket. Nine hundred pounds of new banknotes."

Samantha wasn't sure the other girl had heard a word of it. Nevertheless, she added more angrily this time, "All staff suspected the manager for one reason or another. In the end, this evil man set me up. I was the little ignorant person. And the court ordered me to pay back eight thousand pounds they lost and two years behind bars as punishment." She stared at the girl, completely annoyed as she wasn't paying a bit of attention, not even looking at her. "Daniella, my soulmate," she shouted angrily, "you're a damned bitch. You don't listen to a word I say. Not even looking at me!"

This time, the girl raised her face and met her staring eyes. "I've been here almost a month now," she replied politely. "Every day, you tell one thing or another. I've my own life to worry about."

"But you're doing nothing about it, are you? Brian is back now, and I said I'll introduce you to him."

"No. Thank you. I've some decency still left in me."

"Having a guard in your pocket is not a bad idea."

"But I am not selling myself to anyone."

"But you're not in heaven, darling. You're in the prison. Having a guard as your friend is great. You can get free drinks, or drugs, dirty books."

"You don't listen, do you?"

"Brian got pictures of various boys. And you can pick any one of them. Or all of them you want to."

"I don't think I'm hearing all these."

"Including Brian!"

"You're deaf."

"Kind of what I would say!"

"I heard enough."

"You're new, darling baby. Only one month, you've survived. But if you survive one more month, then, baby, you'll be falling on my feet and begging for my help."

"Okay, help me. How do I get out?"

"What the hell is that for?"

"I want to die."

She laughed hysterically. "Why do you want to get out? Kill yourself here."

"Can you show me?"

"I could. But then I won't see you dying."

"That's fine with me."

At that time, a scrubbing sound was heard on the door lock. In a moment, the door opened, and a young man, aged about 25 years and with a good build, stepped into the room. As if naturally, his eyes turned towards Samantha.

Samantha giggled with her arms wide open. "Brian, my darling, come and hug your sweetheart."

"Of course, my sweetheart," he replied excitedly as he walked in a dancing motion towards her. Suddenly, he saw the girl through the corner of his eyes. He stood for a moment as if alarmed with her stunning look. "Oh, my word," he screamed happily. He deviated from Samantha's direction and moved over to the girl. He stood quietly by her bedside, utterly roused by the elegance of her face and the figure of her body. "Darling, believe you me, you're simply the best," he broke off for a moment as if words were very much harder to search out, and then added sweetly as he could do within the circumstance, "The best beautiful girl there ever been."

Daniella caught his gaze briefly before he looked away to the corner by the side of the door. "Please don't embarrass me," she said rather pleadingly.

He kissed her on her cheek and then, playfully, whispered into her ear. "Anything you say, baby. Anything you say."

Samantha shouted at him from her bed. "Kiss her, you stupid."

"No," she retorted under her breath. "I'll scream if you do that."

"Nothing, darling. Nothing at all now, darling, that you don't like." He glanced back at Samantha in the other bed. "She needs training."

"Well, darling, you're here. You've to start somehow."

"In good time, darling, in good time."

"Very disobedient bastard, that one."

He stepped back to his friend's bed. He sat down on the edge of it and by her side, facing the girl.

"You're a very lucky girl today," he spoke politely. "Because I'm in a very good mood. So, you better listen to me carefully."

She didn't reply. Instead, she looked at them through the corner of her eyes.

"Two kinds of people come to serve their times. Some of these are utter fools. They worry and cry all their period. In the end, they become mentally sick and commit suicide or get out of here as homeless or beggars." He laughed vaguely for a moment before he asked her jokingly, "You don't want to be one of them, do you?"

Daniella didn't bother to answer.

"Good girl," Samantha chuckled. "She's quiet. That means she's thinking."

"Good, darling Daniella," Brian chortled proudly. "You can have a smashing time here. And earn plenty of money. And go home at the end of your time as a rich girl. What about that?"

She wasn't answering for anything.

Samantha hugged him happily because the girl had nothing to say against their advice.

"I can see you're coming down to your good senses." He paused, waiting again for the girl to reply. However, she refused to speak up. He thought she was confused to take full advantage of her confusion, he hurriedly explained in a convincing tone, "Daniella darling, your clients will be rich and powerful like ministers, like union barons, film actors, football players, media giants." He paused again as if searching for words. "Darling, sweetheart, you will be the most powerful lady in the entire United Kingdom and mega-rich."

This time, she spoke politely, "What do I do to achieve all these honours, sir?"

Brian turned and met his friend's steady gaze. There were excitement and expectations in those four eyes. They discreetly smiled before they stared back at the girl. "Just listen to your clients and be nice to them."

"What does it mean?"

"Execute their desires. That's all."

"That means I need to do prostitution?"

"Oh no, dear, we don't call it that."

"What do you call it?"

"Having a good time."

"That means prostitution?"

The frustration started to build inside Samantha as the girl talked negatively to their advises.

She looked angrily at her. "It's up to you. You can call it prostitution if you prefer."

"Prostitution? Inside this prison?"

"What difference it makes whether it's inside the prison or outside," he snapped rather rudely. "Whatever happens inside the prison also happens outside in the wider world."

Samantha was getting agitated with the girl. They did not have control over the girl's way of thinking. She stood up for a moment, then paced aimlessly in front of her bed. Suddenly, she stopped moving around and stared at the girl furiously. "And whatever happens outside the prison will happen inside as well. Because it's the same society. And the same world. Everything's interconnected. You bloody fool, you better understand that."

Daniella was beginning to feel enraged and disturbed due to her tolerance. She moved over to the other side of the bed and sat down on the edge. The back of her body was against them. The fact of the matter was that they were revolting, and she couldn't face them. "I'm fifteen years old. And you want me to sell my body in the prison?"

Samantha was boiling with frustration. "Yes, it's prison, not paradise, but who cares?" She shouted. "And you're fifteen or fifty? Who cares as long as you could catch punters." She punched the air in seething anger. "And if they know you're only fifteen, they double your money. What more you want?"

Daniella didn't want to lead the situation into physical violence. For a start, she wasn't a violent person. However, she couldn't let them bully her into accepting their dirty deals. She was a young girl in the prison on an alleged murder charge. There wasn't a single person to shed a tear for her in the whole world. So wisely, a confrontation in the prison would do untold trouble to her murder case trial. Instead, she should act fast to calm the tension and violence. Nonetheless, the words came out of her mouth even before she realised the full meaning of it, "How do you know this? Your mother used to do prostituting here?"

Completely socked, Samantha stared at Brian. "The bitch needs hard beatings. Otherwise, she won't show some respect."

Brian opened his mouth to speak, but she was on the other side of the bed towards the girl.

"Don't come near to me," Daniella warned, getting up to her feet.

Brain got up but stood there confused. "This is not the right time to beat her," he said quickly in the end. "We'll do it later."

It wasn't sure Sammy heard it. She hurried to her with her full force and the full weight of her body. Daniella panicked first, then abruptly, she sprang up into the air, and her body bent to the left while her right foot landed on the woman's neck. She staggered on her legs before she collapsed onto the floor.

Brain rushed to the scene. "What have you done, you bitch of a filthy animal?"

Daniella rose again, and this time, her left foot crushed on his face. He fell on top of the woman's body; his body slipped down.

She ran to the door and pressed the alarm bell.

Part 4: Daniella Smokes Samantha

It took a couple of minutes before the guards arrived running. Hurriedly, they pushed themselves through the door, and their eyes had a quick look in the cell. Confused, one of the female guards asked, "What's your problem?"

Daniella was standing by the side of her bed. With nervously trembling fingers, she made a gesture to the bodies of Brian and Samantha lying on the floor on the other side of her bed. They moved closer to the bodies and listened to their heartbeats. "Okay, they're breathing," one of them said, "We need two stretchers."

Shortly, they were taken up to the clinics and put on oxygen. Another thirty minutes passed before the ambulances arrived and transferred them to suitable hospitals. The next morning, at about 8'clock, two police officers from the local station and two prison guards visited Daniella in her cell. She was crying all night and morning until then. One of the officers asked, "You want some water?"

She waited. "No," she said.

The other police officer, who was a female, said seriously, "We're not questioning you now. We believe we've information already."

She raised her face and looked at the officer briefly.

"Brian Oldfield and Samantha Parkinson are admitted to two hospitals," the female officer said. "And they will be there for ten days. Maybe more!"

The male officer interrupted her. "Brian Oldfield is on suspension for the time being. And I don't think he's coming back. Ms Samantha Parkinson will be referred to a women's prison whenever she is fit to leave the hospital."

One of the prison guards explained professionally, "And you'll be shifted to Katherine's Ward, which is a single cell. And where you'll be alone."

Daniella didn't speak.

The other prison guard said, "You won't be attending any classes from now on or no contact with any other inmates. Every day, you'll be allowed 30 minutes of running exercise alone and under the strict observation of the guards. You understand all these."

She nodded slowly for an answer.

At about 3.30 in the afternoon, Daniella was transferred to St Kathrine's Ward. Her cell number was 17, and the space behind the door was very small and, in fact, much reduced than the other single cells. The ceiling was slopping, and a broken toilet pan was right under the lowest height. One had to crawl to get access to it access to it. Next to it was a badly battered metal bathtub in the shape of a short canoe for washing. A narrow, wrecked bed and a tiny drawer for clothes were squeezed up in the rest of the space. The top of the drawer was also used as a table for eating. Above the drawer was a small squarish hole with a metal mesh shutter, and only the guards opened it from the corridor when they handed in food, medicine, or memos. However, she tried to settle in with tears in her eyes.

Another three weeks passed by very slowly. And one evening, the shutter opened. She was sitting in the bed, hunched forward with her face in her hands and her elbows on the thighs, as there wasn't enough headroom to sit properly. She turned her face sideways and looked up. Mark was behind the hole and looking at her face. Their eyes met steadily and silently as neither of them knew how to start a conversation. She was terribly embarrassed, and he was quite saddened to see her struggling in a box with everything else around her rather than living in a room. In the end, he started talking. "I've your supper."

She whispered just under her breath. "Thanks."

Nevertheless, he didn't bring up the food from the trolley and place it on the top board of the drawer. Instead, he stood still as if immobile.

A couple of moments ticked away, and then she asked, "How was your trip?"

"The flight was alright?" Mark replied languidly. "And that was it."

"What do you mean?"

"I sent the money for the headstone," he replied actively. "It was convenient for me if they had fixed it on my dad's grave. And there was some money to modernise the family home."

She opened her mouth to say something, but she restrained her words.

"It was his tenth anniversary. And that's why I took this trip."

Without speaking, she steadily looked at him.

"I sent the money to my uncle. And he took the money and ran away to Canada."

She remained silent.

"Daniella," he said, changing the subject. "You've chicken soup, tomato sandwich, sausage casserole, and boiled potatoes." He put them on the drawer top through the hole. "Enjoy it."

"I'll in a bit. I'm not very hungry now."

"Eat them now, Daniella. Food tastes better when it's warm."

"I don't mind, Mark, whether cold or warm."

He was intently looking at her without saying a word. Nevertheless, he wasn't seeing her at all. Absently, he stared at the food and then looked back at her face. "I was thinking."

"Is that right?"

Mark was staring at her as if his eyes were frozen and immobile. However, he looked aloof, and his mind was caressing against something that wasn't visible. He whispered almost to himself, "The BA aircraft was flying over the midway zone of the great Atlantic Ocean and flying over forty-thousand feet high. And suddenly, this thought crossed my mind."

"You're going to crash into the ocean?"

"No, dear."

"Somebody is about to rob you about forty-thousand feet high?"

"Shut up, will you?"

"What was it, then?"

Mark waited, seemingly connecting himself to the current location. "You know why I picked up a job in a prison?"

She took a moment before she answered, "To find out what happened to your father!"

"Clever girl. You lost your freedom. But your mind is still fresh."

"Thanks!"

"I thought I could find out one or two things about his death. But I couldn't find anything."

Wordlessly, she waited for him to continue.

"My dad died ten years ago. And there weren't any papers. The staff are all new in there, and not a single one had heard of his name or death. In the end, I left that prison job for my own sake."

"I'm very sorry to hear all this, Mark. I'm genuinely sorry!"

"Aren't you eating, Daniella?"

"Later. I'm not hungry at all."

He was silent for a moment thoughtfully. "But your case is different."

Daniella didn't speak. Instead, she waited anxiously.

"You're fifteen now."

She nodded her head gently.

"Alright, your mother gave birth to you 15 years ago. The next question is how old she was then. 16 years old? Or 17? Or in her early 20s? Or mid-20s?"

She remained silent.

"Your mother could be anybody from 30 years onwards to 40 at the most, I bet."

She was anxiously quiet.

"And the same goes with your father."

She was silent.

"They are out there, maybe living separately or together – we don't know."

She continued to sit there, tears dripping down on her hands.

"And in normal circumstances, I don't think any of them is dead. They are young people and too young to die."

The tension was bubbling up inside her heart, but she managed to restrain her feelings.

"Some tragedy happened beyond their control. And they had to give up on it. And you were passed on for adoption."

The aches and pains of emotions circled inside her heart, and she was struggling to get out despite her desire to restrain them.

He fell silent briefly as her sobbing rose into the small space around her. "Maybe they lost you somehow. And, now, they may be frantically searching to find you, and at any cost." He paused, unsure of himself, and asked gently, "Do you miss them badly?"

This time, she cried loudly. The resonates of her crying thundered across the little space in the cell. "At every breath I take."

"Good, have your meal," he said, glancing along the corridor. "While I go and have a look around the ward." He turned his face towards her. "The food must be cold. I can warm it up."

She shook her head. "That's fine."

"Alright, I won't be long," he said, putting back the shutter and then left.

Daniella took a deep breath and blew out slowly as the waves of memories upsurged towards her. She dearly hoped all along that her adopted parents would tell her how they had come to know about her, why they had adopted her, and whether they had known her parents. However, they never discussed any of the above questions. For Debra, her Mama, discussing about adoption was strictly a forbidden commandment, and she successfully upheld it until the end of her life. For Jeffrey, Daniella was an eyesore due to her mixed race, colour, and appearance, and he routinely kept a practical distance from her. She was pretty sure Benjamin Cooper, the foster father, and his family hardly knew nothing at all about her past. In this situation, whom could she trust for help in getting to know her biological parents?

About an hour later, Mark returned to the window. "Bit of niggling between two inmates," he said as he removed the shutter. "Anyway, all sorted." He looked inside and noticed her food was there, untouched. He said, rather annoyed, "This is a prison. And if you fall ill, there is no one to help you. Please eat your meal."

"I'll eat it later."

"Promise?"

"Definitely."

"Good. And stop worrying. Worrying can only put you really ill. You will even lose your mind. What will you do then?"

Without saying anything, Daniella looked at him.

"I'm only a deputy manager as per title. But as per work, I am only a prison guard. And I know nothing, to be honest." He fell silent momentarily. Obviously, his mind was juggling with the logic of his thought. "I tried to find out how my father died." He stood quietly, looked up the corridor, and then looked back at her. "But I didn't find anything. I was against various powerful organisations."

She raised her head and met his gaze.

"But your case is different. You were born not that long ago. Only fifteen years ago, and the chances are that somebody will remember you."

Daniella started sobbing again.

"I think it might take time. But you'll win. I can't see any institutionalised organisations standing against you, which I had to face when I was searching for my dad's death in prison."

"I hope so," she said, her voice tangled with the tone of crying. "But you know I won't be able to help. I'm locked up here."

He waited silently for a moment. "You can go back in time and tell me about people starting from Ben Cooper and ......"

She interrupted him. "Ben Cooper died. And that's why I'm in prison, you know."

"I know. And your adopted parents, Jeffrey Smith and his wife Debra."

"Mamie died."

"I know."

"And Dad is settled in the States. But I don't know where."

"I know. He's in California, near to his brother."

She stared at him anxiously. "How did you know?"

"I had a peek through your personal profile in the office. I should say that people like me are not supposed to search for it. It's illegal."

"God bless you," she said, crying.

"Tomorrow is my day off. And I'm going to Bristol."

"Why?"

"To see your old neighbours, especially Angela and Joanna. They might know something...."

Daniella spoke quickly. "I doubt it. Because, for Mamie, I was her daughter. For Dad, I was a kind of embarrassment. And neither of them wished to talk about me to anyone."

"Well, I've to start from somewhere, Daniella. And I'm used to failures, especially when I was trying to find my father's death." He looked down along the corridor before he said quickly, "Night manager is out for checking. I've to go. Make sure you have your food and leave the plates on the drawer top. I'll pick them up in my next round. I won't disturb you then. And go to sleep, please."

And before she could speak, he locked the window and went away rushing. She sighed a little, hopefully. If Mark had said he would do something, at least he would try his best for it regardless of the outcome. He did it about his father and tried the best for him. He told Daniella about it from the beginning to the end, as a picture. And the pictures ran through her mind as exactly as he had narrated.

The social system in Jamaica started to change as the strikes began to spread across the island nation. The unions of sugar cane workers, banana farmers, and street cleaners participated in the mass movements for better working conditions and decent wages. Mark's grandfather, Delroy Sweaty, hired plots of ground on fixed prices and ran banana plantations. Through the lucky years when there were no storms and hurricanes, the price of bananas was good in the international market, and he made good profits and saw his family growing happy. Nonetheless, these lucky years wouldn't go continuously because, always around the corner, adverse forces were all in motion.

The landowners watched the situation very carefully and terrifyingly. When the climate and conditions were good and the banana prices buoyant in the market, they would demand higher rent for their lands. Against unexpected storms or bad weather, there was no protection for growing stem plants or heavy fruits.

However, he survived in his business for a long time, just as his father had before him. And these bananas came out to the market after various quality check-ups, packed in presentable cardboard boxes with the brand name 'Sweaty Bananas'. Delroy loved the business and continued until the political climate changed from bad to worse, which brought in the cost of production more than the proceeds. There was no system in place to pay for the workers when they were sick or on holiday. Eventually, he was forced to close down the business. But he couldn't stay home doing nothing. He had two children from one woman dancer, called Ruby, and Leroy from Jacinta. When the money was coming alright, all relationships survived fine. A month after he had declared bankruptcy, Ruby screamed at Debroy, "You bring me money for food. Otherwise, we finish!"

Debroy turned to her, suppressing the bursting anger inside, and stared at her. She was still very attractive. Suddenly, he calmed down and replied as gently as possible. "I'm giving what I have. You've to wait until I get big."

She couldn't wait much longer. She took her two children and ran away one night with her dancing partner, and if the rumours were any reliable, they ran away to New York. Delroy was very sad for weeks and months, especially for his children that he had lost. Slowly, he settled down completely with Jacinta and continued his business on a very small scale. He used to buy the banana bunches from the local households and sell them to the wholesalers in the markets, mostly in Kingston. One late afternoon, he sold his goods to a wholesaler in Kingston and was walking back to his lorry a few yards down the road. Two youths suddenly appeared from behind the bushes and started fighting with him for his money. He fought back vigorously and almost managed to get into his lorry. But one of the men had a knife, and he pushed it down on his throat.

That was the end of Debroy's life. And Leroy was fourteen years old then. Normally, both father and son used to go together when they took the goods to the market. On that fatal day, Leroy was down with flu, and it took a long time before he managed to forgive himself for it. His mother's brother, Uncle John, had a river bamboo rafting business for tourists, and Leroy started to work with him for anything the uncle gave. 3 to 4 years gone by, and one evening, Jacinta had a talk with her son. "How do you find working with Uncle John?"

"What do you mean, Mum?"

"You got anything? You been working with him for four years."

"True, mum. But I've no money."

Without speaking, she looked at him.

"He isn't making any money either, Mum." He looked away as if searching for words or facts. "When the season comes, more tourists come and more rafters at the river, which is not good for business. When it's not the season, less rafters but less tourists. Again, not good for business, mum."

"But son, Leroy, you've a life to lead on. And you can't lead your life on nothing."

He didn't reply.

"Now, I clean others' kitchens and wash their clothes. And when you come in the evening, you have something to eat and somewhere to sleep. When I go, what will happen to you, son?"

He was clearly in an annoyed mood. "Why you've to go? You have the shed here."

She retorted helplessly. "You look stupid and talk stupid."

"What else do you expect me to be? I am your son, you say?"

She didn't say anything. She had known well that arguing with him wouldn't make any sense. "You got to find a proper job, Leroy."

"Where, mum? Thousands of people chasing a few jobs?"

"When I clean and sweep these rich people's houses, I see advertisements for workers in their papers."

"Yeh? Where?"

"In England. In our mother country, England."

"I never heard of it."

"No. These are rich, clever people's subjects. You're not clever, are you?"

"There is a sea up there, mum. Can I fly across it holding up a towel above my head?"

"You don't fly with a towel. You go in a ship."

"Why they need cleaners?"

"You travel in the ship to your mother country."

"You got plenty money?"

"Don't bite my head. I am putting sense into your empty head."

He waited as if he was getting his temper under restraint. "It takes real money. What we got, pence?"

"I know it, stupid. And I'll raise the money."

"How?"

"This little land where our little tin shed stands is ours. Your great-granddad lived here. Your granddad lived here. Your dad lived here. It's ours. We can raise money on it from English banks here in Kingston."

He listened to his mother silently.

"And when you come back from our mother country with bags and barrels full of English pounds, you finish their loans. And then remove this shed and build a big house for your children in this land where your ancestors lived."

"Is that so?"

She didn't answer. Instead, she continued talking enthusiastically. "I live on the top floor. I want to see you coming and going in those beautiful ships of our mother country."

He didn't reply. Instead, as if tired of everything his mother was saying, he continued to sit on the veranda and stared across the sandy ground in front of them and beyond to the sparkling waters of the Caribbean Sea in the distance. His eyes curiously wandered over the mighty waves in the distance to see whether there was any sign of ships. No, none was visible in his view.

"You start looking for a suitcase. And start packing your stuffs. And ………"

He interrupted her. "Are you going mad? And I do all these before I get some work?"

"You'll get the work, son. The man whose house I wash and clean is a big man in the embassy. He said he will get the papers for you to go to England."

VALUKALAM ANTHONY THOMAS

As his mother said, her boss arranged the papers, and they came to the harbour to say the final goodbye. It was in the early hours of 24th May 1948 when they stood on the fringe of the large crowds and had highly charged emotions. All of them had something to say to their loved ones who were about to sail to England. The suppressed voices of crying and talking persisted amongst the groups. Leroy and Jacinta were in a hug, and the trickles of tears tied them together. She sobbed as silently as she could have managed against the pains in her heart, "You must write to me every week."

He whispered into her ears. "I'll mum. I'll!"

"Write to me. And say where you stay. What you do. And what you eat."

"I'm not a toddler, mum. I'm a big boy. I'm okay."

"Be careful when you choose a friend. I mean a girl. They are like snakes. Strangle your neck."

"Why did you teach them your skills?"

"Shut up and listen, you fool."

"Okay, mum."

"Always remember you're my only child, my first and my last."

"I know, mum."

"Remember to write to me, please."

"I'll mum. I promise you, Mum."

"If you're free, write to me twice a week, at least, if it's not expensive."

The crowd started to separate, and those about to enter the departure hall and then board the ship continued to stay outside the huge glass panes of the security hall and watch their loved ones moving towards the ship.

"Don't forget mummy. I'm always here praying for you."

He opened his mouth to reply, but the emotions inside him choked his voice. He nodded, meeting her tearful eyes. Suddenly, he kissed her cheeks and managed to mutter, "I love you, Mummy."

"And don't go for fighting."

He shook his head.

"When you see troubles, walk away quickly. Remember?"

Suddenly, she closed her eyes as if she couldn't bear to see anything anymore. Her only child was going away to a faraway part of the world through the never-ending waters of the Atlantic Ocean. For a while, she wanted to shut out the world all in all. When she was finally able to open her eyes, he was already in the departure hall.

On Sunday, 27th of June 1948, the ship - HMT Emperor Windrush - arrived at Tilbury Dock, and the next day, Monday, the passengers checked out to the country. Leroy's destination was London and the address was No. 22, Trinity Road, Notting Hill, West London. He travelled in a coach from Tilbury to London and then a local ride on a bus to Notting Hill and a 10 minutes' walk to his new address. The No. 22 Trinity Road was a huge house with 11 rooms, and each room managed two adults. Besides the officially registered bedrooms, there were reception rooms, dining rooms, storage rooms, and corridors, and all in all, on a busy day, there could be as many as forty tenants living legally or illegally. However, the facilities, such as bathrooms and kitchens, were less than the minimum, which resulted in violence. Ambulances were arrived frequently to treat the cuts, bruises, and wounds of the injured, or to take them to the hospital. Hence, this building earned the nickname, 'Meat Palace.'

VALUKALAM ANTHONY THOMAS

In the evening, Leroy wrote to his mother that 'England is not the country we see in the movies and magazines. It's as poor as any other place, and I am living in a slum. I need to queue to go to the toilets or kitchen in the house. Every hour, people fight here for one thing or another. And this is not the mother country, Mum. Because I'm a foreigner." He stopped writing and stared into the wall of his side. 'No, I couldn't send this to Mum," he thought to himself. "It will kill her." He picked up the letter from the table and tore it. 'I'll stay here until I get a better room.' He didn't cook any meals there. And he ate outside and used the public toilets.

After a week, he found a job at the Devonshire Cleaners Ltd, ten minutes walking distance from where he was lodging. They needed a cleaner in their laundry department. In a way, it was a lucky job that he could have a wash after the shift and that he could eat meals free from their canteen. However, there was also a hitch or two. His wages were very low and lower than his white teammates, the difficult jobs were constantly allocated to him, and he never received a word of credit for the good work he did day after day.

Six months later, he got a studio flat about a mile down the road in Shepherds Bush. In fact, his teammate, Lucille Johnson, in Devonshire Cleaners, told him secretly about it. She was living on the second floor of the same property, and this studio flat was on the third floor. It was very small in size, but he had all the facilities he needed. He could cook whenever he wanted to and prepare anything he fancied, and above all, he had privacy and freedom when he was at home.

Lucille used to come up discretely and spend some time with him. It was forbidden at the time in the public eye if a white woman shared the privacy of a black man. In July 1956, she was found with a black man in the small park known as the Shepherds Bush Common at about one o'clock in the night. It was a warm night, and Lucille was having a night out. Unfortunately, a few Teddy Boys, the rebellious youth group, happened to be going up the pedestrian footpath and spotted Lucille and her black partner behind the bush. "You're humiliating the white race, you bitch," one of the Teddys snarled at her and caught her by the neck while the others had a punch-up with the man. Somehow, she made herself free and fled across the Common and then across the Uxbridge Road and escaped through the tunnels of the underground station. Her partner, named later as George Winston, suffered badly in the brawl and spent a week in the hospital.

Around this time, racially motivated acts of violence erupted across West London very frequently. This situation was exploited and inflamed by groups, such as Oswald Mosley's union movement, and far-right groups, such as the White Defence League and the Teddy Boys damn. Slowly but steadily, the violence turned to riot on 29th August 1958, when Elsa Karlsson, a Swedish woman, was verbally and physically abused by a gang of white youths. Leroy intervened immediately with a machete and rescued her to safety. However, the acts of violence spread around the neighbourhood. Groups of white youths attacked properties that black families occupied. The black people stayed indoors in fear of racial attacks first, then came out in self-defence. Various arrests were made during the night by the police, who contained the riot by morning.

On the evening of the 30th, Elsa was out at the Notting Hill Gates underground station – a nearby area to Shepherds Bush. A few locals, who had been in the previous night's riot, recognised her by her long, wavy blonde hair and tall body. She was a known person locally for the wrong reasons. She worked as a pole dancer for a London hotel in the Park Lane area and became very friendly with rich businessmen. She travelled with them as an escort to foreign cities and island resorts and stayed with them for longer breaks. She also kept Leroy as her bodyguard whenever she travelled alone, which led to the rumours that there was a concealed relationship between the two, and lots of her beauty worshippers watched it with jealous eyes. And while the radio, television, and newspapers were covering the destruction of the properties and local reputations caused by the riot, she was out again with her bodyguard. A few white youths surrounded them hurriedly, and a fight broke out. And that was the beginning of another night of riot, this time more widespread and destructive than the previous night. Elsa and Leroy suffered severe bodily injuries and were taken to the hospital immediately. The riot went on until the 5th of September, and then an uneasy calm was returned as numerous criminals were arrested and put behind bars with long-term jail sentences.

On the 9th of September, Leroy was discharged from the hospital, and on the 11th, Elsa returned home. And on the 14th, they met at her flat. For a long time, they didn't speak about the outbreaks of violence or any of their personal problems. In the silence, they hugged tightly and kissed. "Thank you for saving me, my darling," she whispered finally into his ear.

He didn't say anything.

"Lucky, we're here. Alive and together!" She kissed him hurriedly and madly. "It's more than a dream."

He stared into her eyes which were close to his face. "I had only one dream."

"What was it?"

"To see you safe until the moment I die!"

"Oh darling, I'm safe," she muttered kissing him passionately.

Without saying anything, he held his hands around her.

After a brief silence, she moved back. She put out two glasses and poured wine. He took a drink and sipped on it thoughtfully. "We've to think now," he whispered as if to break the silence.

She drank a mouthful of wine and looked at him wordlessly.

"You're not safe here. Everyone knows you."

She drank another sip and emptied the glass. She picked up the bottle, refilled it, and then poured into his glass. "What are you thinking?"

"You've to move. And I come with you?"

"Thank you. But where can I go, darling?"

He hesitated. "I know a family in Bristol. Aunty Mavis, a distant relation of mine lives there."

"Will Aunty Mavis let me stay with them?"

"They will."

"And you?"

"I'll stay with you."

"Oh, darling. You know I love my independence."

"For a while, darling. And you can't go on the way you are. You've to change."

"Alright, we'll go. And see what happens."

They went to Bristol and stayed with Aunty Mavis. A week later, Aunty Mavis had a private talk with Leroy – well, it was a row. "What's this woman doing in my house?"

"What's it, Aunty Mavis?"

"I heard her talking on my phone. And some men were calling her, too."

"Yeh?"

"I can't let her mix with my children. That woman is a tart. She must be out in two days' time. You heard?"

The next day, they moved out to a one-bedroom flat in Avon Villa, which was fairly close to the city centre. They took it mainly due to job prospects in the area and travel convenience. However, it was expensive, and the space inside was small. They left their belongings in the hallway and corridor and slept in the sitting room. "I don't want to move again," she said. "It's very tiring."

"We've to be careful here, Elsa. You've got to cut out your contacts, please."

"Sorry, it'll never happen again."

"We've to respect each other. Nothing behind my back."

"Nothing, I promise!"

They lived in that flat for one year. Elsa had never been happy there. She had kept complaining that the flat was too small, dirty or smelly. He felt sick of hearing them and shifted to another flat in Cromwell Street. It was a new building, and the flat was on the first floor with a spacious lounge and a large bedroom. She changed her job to a receptionist at St Georges Hotel on the riverfront Severn. He had vague suspicions about her new post and her past behaviours. Well, he kept to himself, "I couldn't care a damn."

In September 1962, she whispered excitedly, "I'm having a baby, darling."

They were watching a movie at that time. He quickly turned his face and caught her eyes steadily. He opened his mouth, but no voice came out as a vague despair bubbled up inside him, pondering who could be the father. However, he said, apparently cheerful, "That's great, darling. I love you."

She gave birth to a boy in May 1963. Leroy looked at him intently for a while before he picked up in his hand.

"Hold him properly," she giggled quietly. "It's your son."

"I hope so."

"Beautiful, just like you!"

"Thank you."

"Have you chosen a name?"

"Not really." He paused briefly. "What about you?"

She waited cautiously for a moment. "I like Mark. That was my father's name."

"Okay then. We name him Mark."

Time went by fast and slowly. To be honest, summertime rolled like a full-speed racing car, and winter just crawled like a slug. Elsa worked at St George's Hotel while Leroy looked after Mark and managed the housework. Whenever he had free time, he worked for a building company as a builders' assistant for cash in hand.

In July 1968, she didn't return at six o'clock as usual. He and Mark waited for Elsa to come. By then, it was seven o'clock, and there was no sign of Elsa. He waited another half an hour before he called the St Georges Hotel where she worked. The lady on the switchboard informed him that Elsa Karlsson hadn't reported to work today and that today was her day off, anyway. He phoned the local police station and gave them her description. About two o'clock in the night, the phone rang, and he picked it up quickly. "Hello?"

The line appeared to be dead for a moment, then Elsa's voice came through. "I'm with my friend in London," she said in a drowsy, tired, and drunken voice.

He suppressed his surging anger. "Thanks for letting me know."

She hesitated a moment. "Thank you for the memories. But family life curtails my life. I want my freedom back."

He was about to say something, but the line went dead.

Part 5: Mark is Back

Suddenly, the noise on the trap window rattled, and Daniella awoke from her deep thoughts. She rolled over in her bed. It was Mark on the other side of the opening. She sat up and stared at him. "Where have you been hiding?"

He chuckled, putting her food on the drawer top through the hole, "Only three days. One day was my day off, which I told you about."

"And the other two days?"

"I was in London."

She looked at the food, then turned to him. "Why?"

"To do some searches?"

"About what?"

He laughed happily. "About you."

"About me?" suddenly she asked thankfully. "What did you find?"

He paused momentarily as if pulling together all the bits and pieces he had heard in the last couple of days while in London. "You know Jeffrey and Debra come from London?"

She waited thoughtfully. "Yes. Or that they had relatives up there."

"Jeffrey had a restaurant called News Cafe in London?"

She shook her head gently. "Not in my memory!"

"It was a partnership. The other partner was Kenneth Logan."

"I can't help you. Sorry!"

"Kenny for short. Kenny and Jeffrey got along well."

She didn't speak. "But that wasn't the reason for it."

"Kenny had a sister. Well, a half-sister, to be honest. Called Lizzy Logan."

Daniella continued to be silent, but the expression on her face changed slightly as an unknown fear started to cross over there.

"You may not like this news, but Lizzy was Jeffrey's girlfriend."

"I don't believe it."

"I know, Daniella, you can't believe it until you know the full truth."

"Anyway, what's Lizzy got to do with me?"

"Lizzy used to work for the adoption agency right here in Plymouth. And she also worked for the hospital as a trainee nurse when you were born."

Every tissue in her entire physique stood still as a freezing shock shot up her spine.

"That means you're born here in Plymouth. Or close to Plymouth!"

Her breath even ceased.

"The chances are that your biological parents are living somewhere here."

Chapter 10

On the Case

Part 1: The Social Worker

Three police officers turned up at 11 am – two females and one male – they were already half an hour late for the meeting. A guard guided them to the meeting room. Daniella was there, sitting behind the desk with a young man from her solicitor's office and a middle-aged woman from the social department. The police walked further into the large rectangle room, and as they walked, the female officers whispered to each other, flicking through the papers in their hands. The policeman listened to his colleagues quietly and kept his eyes casually on the people behind the desk. When they were at the deskside, the policeman looked at the woman and asked politely, "You're the solicitor, I assume?"

She shook her head gently. "I'm Carol Walker. A social worker!"

The policeman looked at Daniella impassively for a moment as he rolled his eyes at the man who was sitting after her.

"I am a trainee solicitor, sir. My name is Peter Murphy. And we're waiting for Alex Bennett, the solicitor. He should've been here about half an hour ago."

A female officer, who was almost as tall as her male colleague, said softly, "My name is Vivian. Do you know why he is late?"

"Alex is in the court," Peter replied. "I think he's held up in his case."

Vivian asked, turning slightly frustrated, "Can you call your office?"

Peter nodded firmly. "I've already phoned twice. But nobody picked up."

411

She shot a glance at her female colleague, Kimberly, and then at the male colleague, Braden. "What do you think?" She asked. "Can we clarify a couple of points with Daniella Smith while we wait for Alex Bennett?"

Peter said quickly, "Thank you if you can wait for him. But...." he paused as if searching for words before he added gently, "but Alex won't be pleased if you question Daniella without his presence."

Kimberly turned to her partners with a knowing glance, then turned to the social worker. "Is it alright if we ask Daniella a few simple questions?"

"Well......," Carol broke off, obviously pondering.

"We don't go into the depth of any issues," Kimberly continued politely. "We haven't got much time."

Before Carol could answer, Peter cut in quickly. "I don't think Alex will appreciate that."

"Peter is right," Carol said finally. "Daniella is a minor. And if you ask Daniella anything at all, anything whatsoever, without her solicitor, that's immoral and inhumane."

Without saying anything, Kimberly looked at the social worker rather blankly.

"Daniella is a minor," Carol explained softly. "She hasn't got any parents or relatives. Nor any legal guardians! And you shouldn't be putting her under any pressure."

"Not for a moment, Ms Walker," the policeman said rather firmly. "We won't do that. You can be rest assured."

"Thank you," she said. "I'm worried about Daniella."

Suddenly, he and his colleagues moved away a few steps and stood together, whispering. And a little later, they moved back to the desk. "Alright," the tall policewoman said, looking at the trainee solicitor. "Arrange another meeting and let us know, please."

"Okay. I will do that."

"And do it as soon as possible," Branden insisted. "We want to clear the cases as quickly as possible."

"Of course, we'll do that."

"Alright," the policeman said while they all turned back to the door. "Have a good afternoon."

"And you, too," Peter said.

And they went. At the door, the security guard opened the door. They went out and disappeared into the corridor.

Peter looked at Carol. "Do we've anything else to discuss?"

"I need a few minutes with her," she said casually. "I want to update her file. That's all."

"Alright, them," he whispered. "I better go back to the office."

"Please keep in touch."

"Of course." And he left the meeting room.

Carol moved around in her chair and looked at Daniella. "You are born on 23rd January 1970," she said, staring down at a sheet in her file on the desk. "But you don't have your birth certificate?"

"No," she replied somewhat embarrassed.

413

"Sorry, we had a leak in our office. And some files are damaged beyond recovery. Sadly, one was yours."

The girl was quiet.

"And I didn't think I've seen a proper file for your cases." She stopped and breathed in quietly. "Emilie is charging you with murder for Ben Coogan's death."

Without knowing what to say, she glanced at the window on her side and the sky beyond. The sky was cloudy; the air was misty. She turned back limply. "I know," she said uneasily. "Aunty Emilie's affidavit was read out to me."

"Emili went further with the allegation that you killed J J."

Tears rolled over to the back of her lids. She tried to keep them off her face in vain. "I know."

"And you held Debra improperly that led her to fall. And in the end, she died."

"I know."

"Now, Brian."

She nodded for an answer.

"And Samantha."

She managed a nod again.

She hesitated to ask further questions. She leaned forward and wrote a few notes on the sheet in her file. After a brief period, she turned to look at her. "How are you?"

"I'm fine."

"You want to drink some water?"

"I'm fine."

She hesitated. "Can I ask you a few more questions, please?"

"Of course!"

"I know you've no knowledge of your parents?"

"No," she shook her head lightly.

"Do you think Jeffrey and Debra might have known them?"

"I don't know," she said tersely.

Carol waited for a moment, staring at the girl's face. "Didn't you ever talk about them?"

Silently, she shook her head.

"If you can say, tell me why you didn't talk about it?"

"For Dad, it was an uncomfortable situation."

"Yes, I can understand that."

"And for Mamie, she couldn't simply accept that I was somebody else's daughter."

"Was she very possessive?"

She looked along the room and saw the two guardsmen at the doorway. Slowly, she turned to the social worker. "I know my Mamie loved me very much. And I loved her, too. And that's all I know."

"Any other reasons?"

The girl's eyes grew larger as the pressure of intensity increased. Of course, there were other reasons – some were very personal to Jeffrey and

Debra, and some very heartbreaking to them and Daniella. If she let out one piece out of its place, the whole structure would collapse. In the end, she whispered nervously. "That's all I know."

The social worker gazed at her calmly before she asked, "You've to be honest with me?"

"You have known me for more than three years. Have I lied to you?"

She waited. "You've serious cases coming up. And I want to rescue your life."

"What's my life?" Daniella asked, her emotions filtering out of her restrictions. "I'm shuttered in a hole-like cell twenty-four hours a day. Isn't it better for me if I can finish my wretched life? And sooner the better."

Carol waited for the girl to calm down. In the meantime, she entered some notes into her file. "Sometimes a little cry is good. It washes away the pain in your heart." She waited again, watching the girl removing the tears with her fingers off her cheeks. "But your life isn't wretched. You're with me, and I've been a social worker for twenty-four years. And I've saved a few lives. And, also, in your case, you've got a brilliant solicitor, Alex Bennett. It's not normal for him to lose any cases."

Without saying anything, the girl stared at her.

Carol caught her eyes. "You go to your room. And forget everything."

"Is it that easy?"

"Why not? Everything will work your way."

The girl didn't say anything.

Carol went over to the guards at the door. "Please keep an eye on her frequently," she advised them discreetly. "She's very depressed now."

The guards took her to her cell and locked the door from outside. Suddenly, one of them opened the window shutter and looked at her kindly, saying, "If you need us, please ring the bell. Anyway, we're around here all the time." And then the shutter slipped down on the window frame, and the face of Daniella disappeared from their view.

Part 2: Daniella Faces Charges

She sat down on the edge of her bed and slumped against the headboard. Slowly, she closed her eyes, more fearfully than sadly. Nothing was there she could stare at and take her mind off from the terrors which were traumatising her to bits. The crimes brought against her were severe, as she was blamed for the death of her stepbrother J J, her adopted mother Debra, and her foster carer Ben Coogan. She was also blamed for the attacks on her roommate, Samantha Parkinson, and the guard, Brian Bricks. There were no ways out of all these endless tortures other than committing suicide – an idea she had never had before but was now constantly on her mind. Precisely on that moment, a knock was sounded on the trap hole before it was opened. One of the guards had brought the lunch, she casually thought and paid no attention. However, even before she had realised, a tumult shot up as she heard Mark's voice. "Lovely lady, how are you?"

She turned her face negligently and looked out through the hole. "You still here?"

He chuckled happily. "Well, you see me. Don't you?"

Without answering, she continued to look at him.

"I brought your dinner."

This time, she spoke. "You can leave it there."

Mark left them inside on the drawer board, then moved them to a side of it so that he could see her directly. "Boiled potatoes, chicken casserole, cabbage and a bowl of soupe. You will love it!"

Silent, she turned her eyes away.

"Well, come on Daniella. What's bothering you today."

She rolled her eyes back to him. "Nothing really. Three murder charges one me. Aren't they bothering me? And two charges of physical assaults. Anything is there to bother me?"

Quietly, he continued to stare at her.

"I'm locked in a cell which is smaller than dogs kennel."

Mark laughed silently at first, but then his voice crept into it. "Anything new?" He asked calmly. "Your solicitor knows it. Your social worker knows it. And the court knows it."

"I'm the one burning my heart – day and night."

"I know that," he replied quickly. "That's why I took days off in the past couple of days."

"You always come and tell some weird stories. What are you going to say today?"

"I'm sorry if that's how you feel." He stopped talking and looked along the corridor. A moment later, he turned back to her. "I've some news for you."

She looked back at him. "Ya?"

"I know your mother's name."

A bewildered expression crossed her face. Nonetheless, she remained calm. "You've to promise me that you won't tell this anybody."

Again, she didn't speak. Instead, she waited eagerly for him to answer.

"Her name is Abigale. A lady from Atlantica!"

She stared at his face while tears trickled down on her cheeks.

"You've to be very careful. You don't say a word of Abigale to anybody."

"Where is my mum now?" She asked amongst the bottled-up sobbing. However, the word mum came out easily and smoothly through her mouth as if she had been practising all her life.

"That's what I'm asking. Where is Abigale?"

"How did you know this, Mark?" Daniella asked, getting up and sitting on the bed, her voice trembling, the trickling tears on her cheeks gleamed on the light overhead.

He looked up the corridor and confirmed himself that nobody wasn't hearing it. "Whatever happens," he whispered under his breath, "You won't tell this to anybody. Until such time comes when you and I, we both are safe."

She nodded her head as if unable to find her voice for an answer.

"Jeffrey had a restaurant in London, with Kenny Logan?"

She whispered cautiously, "Yes?"

"Kenny has sister, Lizzy Logan?"

"I've heard. They grew up together and studied in the same school."

"Of course. And they were great friends."

"Yes. Mamie used to talk about her."

He chuckled amusingly. "Dad didn't talk about her?"

She hesitated. "No?"

He continued to laugh for a moment. "Let's cut short the subjects that don't concern you at the moment."

She remained silent, with a confused expression on her face.

"Lizzy used to meet a journalist, Craig, in the News Café' in London. They became close friends in a short time. He eventually returned to his hometown, Ashburton, which is 10 minutes' drive from here and …………"

Daniella interrupted gently. "I know Ashburton. Ben Coogan had taught karate lessons up there. I used to go there with him."

He chuckled in a mock fearful voice. "I used to wonder where did you get your karate kicks."

Without saying anything, she steadily caught his stare.

"Anyway, you hold on to your karate skills until I finish."

"Okay," she replied, smiling faintly.

Mark smiled back happily before he added quietly, "He got an editor's post up here in Plymouth for a national newspaper. Shortly, Lizzy followed him and picked up a job as a trainee nurse in the maternity hospital."

"Mamie had talked about Lizzy and Mamie's other friends. But I didn't know much about Lizzy or anybody else."

He ignored her politely. "And this was the time, Abigale gave birth to you."

She sprang up to her feet and crossed the little space of a step or two to the window shutter. "Lizzy was there? Please tell me. Lizzy was there?"

As if confused, he stood calmly, watched the changing emotions interacting on her face. Suddenly, he realised that he couldn't hold her out for any more. "Yes, dear. Lizzy was right there."

"You're sure?"

"She was helping the midwife."

"She remembers all this." She sighed off heavily. "Can I talk to her? I've several questions to ask her."

"I don't think it's possible right away."

"I want to know whether she loved me. She was happy with me. Why she gave me away for adoption?" She sighed again. "Why can't I talk to Lizzy? I want to know where is my mum. And who she is! I still love her, my mum."

"Because I haven't talked to Lizzy yet."

"No?"

"No. And I haven't even seen her yet."

"Who told you all this?"

"Kenny."

She looked bewildered. "How do you know this is true?"

Mark lightly nodded before he said quietly. "I'm going to talk to Lizzy on Sunday."

"My god! On this Sunday?"

"Yes."

"Where?"

"I don't know where. But I'm meeting Kenny at the Exeter railway station. And then he will take me to Lizzy."

"Why so much secrecy? Is it anything to do with my mum?"

Mark waited uneasily. "Wait until Sunday! I'm working on the night shift."

"I'm really anxious now."

"Don't be! Everything will be fine."

Daniella didn't speak.

"I work my shifts until Friday. I'm off on Saturday. I need it. I'm going to the maternity hospital just to see the working practise in the hospital. Just to know, that's all!"

"Will they let you in?"

"True. But I applied for a part-time job. And they've offered it to me."

"Why? Are you going to leave this job?"

"Not at all! How can I even if I want to?

"Why?"

"You're here."

Daniella couldn't hold his stare. She cast her eyes down.

"I think Abigail's papers are still there. Somewhere in the basements!"

"Thank you."

Mark smiled. "Seeing you, I think your parents are somebody really great. If I can find them, your problems are over."

She raised her face and looked at him through her misty eyes. "I hope so. And thank you."

He glanced at her food. "It's must be cold now. Shall I warm it up and bring it back."

"It's fine. I'm used to it."

"It's no bother to me."

"It's okay, I swear."

Mark waited impassively for a moment. "Did you prepare for your meeting?"

"What meeting?"

"Ben Coogan's murder case? What time is it?"

"Oh, thank you. It completely slipped off my mind. Anyway, it's tomorrow at two-thirty. Thanks for reminding me."

"Have you prepared for it?"

"Not really! Every day, one thing or another. How can I prepare for all this? I'll tell you as it happened. And that's it!"

"Anyway, have your meal. We'll talk later."

And he went.

Daniella ate a bit of the lunch and threw the bulk into the bin. A minute or two later, she moved up on the bed and slumped back against the head board as memories flashed across her mind. She tried to suppress them hopelessly or then struggled to minimise the varieties. However, they crowded more forcefully and crystallised in her view as though they were just occurring right now. She could imagine it clear as day.

VALUKALAM ANTHONY THOMAS

It was a Thursday, she remembered it clearly. Daniella was in the living room and waiting for her dad rather uneasily. He didn't come home as he had told her. After mum's death about three weeks ago, he had always been punctual on his time and, if not, he would inform her on the phone. But today, he was late for over two hours and she hadn't received any phone call.

He was late for further one hour and arrived about seven o'clock. She went near to him. "What happened, dad?"

"I had to meet somebody. And then the bus strikes. And the vandalised phone boxes." He took off his coat and hung it on the hook in the hallway. He turned to look at her. "Why the house cold? Heater not working?"

Daniella met his eyes. "I didn't turn it on," she said politely. "I am alone. And warming up the whole house?"

"You feel cold. And may get sick."

She shrugged her shoulder. "I got an extra jumper."

He moved over to the thermostat which was fixed at the end of the hallway. He turned on the heating system. "Keep it going when you need it. I'll pay it."

She kept quiet.

He went upstairs, changed to home wearing clothes and came down. "What do you fancy for the supper?" He asked, entering the lounge. "I'm going to cook."

Daniella was standing at the front window. She turned and looked at him. "No need to cook. We've enough sausage casserole in the fridge."

"I kept it for your lunch. Didn't you eat anything for your lunch?"

She casually shook her head. "I wasn't hungry."

"You ate nothing, then?"

"I had a couple of sandwiches. That was enough, I thought."

"That's not enough," he whispered, walking into the kitchen. "I know we've problems with money. But we've to eat."

He boiled potatoes, and made a fried cabbage bacon dripping. They ate them with sausage casserole, the remainder of last night. She went back to the lounge. He continued to sit at the dining table, drinking a beer. After a short period, he joined her and turned the telly on. Another short period ticked away silently except the sounds on the telly. In the end, he turned to her. "I told you I had to meet somebody."

Daniella met his eyes across the floor and nodded her head for an answer.

"It was the manager of the building society that I meant to meet initially."

She didn't say anything.

"And then another meeting with two other people and the manager."

"What's this meeting for?"

Without replying, he went to the kitchen and came back with a glass of whiskey. He sat down and sipped on it. "You have heard, I'm sure."

She interrupted gently. "What's it, dad?"

"Debra and I – we used to talk about mortgage arrears."

"I suppose so. Normally, you talked about these kinds of things very quietly."

"True. Very true! But we always had problems."

She didn't speak.

Jeffrey didn't speak, either. The subject was more complicated for a ten-year-old girl, he had thought. However, the facts of failures reeled up in front of his mind. The arrears accumulated to large amounts as he was unable to pay the monthly instalments in full, or even a part of it at all as they fell due. However, the building society knew that he was going through a rough time, and he needed sympathetic support as much as they could offer. They were also familiar with the sad state of the national economy because of the political instability, such as the industrial strikes, unbearable inflation, and numerous redundancies. In the end, the bankers allowed him longer time to pay back the arrears while he was asked to keep up the monthly mortgages on time. That was an amazing deal, Jeffrey had felt.

Nonetheless, his personal situation led to unexpected difficulties when Debra became pregnant with their son J J. It was meant to be a dream come true, and it was a dream! But Debra was quite old to be a mother, and various maternity complications arose out of it, and he had to be away from work frequently and face a salary reduction. After J J was born, she continued to be sick of one issue or another and to make matters worse, J J wasn't in the best of health either. Sadly, J J died, and it cost a fortune for the funeral. Then Debra passed away, and the cost was even bigger this time, much bigger. Helplessly, he neglected the payment commitments.

"What's the problem now, dad?" Daniella asked as if to break the silence, because the silence was painful.

Jeffrey didn't reply. Instead, he raised the glass to his mouth. He didn't drink though. The rim of the glass remained between his lips, and his eyes cast down on the carpet. He was quiet, and still. He must have been thinking, or looking through the days and years that passed by. Abruptly, he woke up and drank a mouthful of whiskey and swallowed. The spirit of the alcohol passed down his throat, warming his chest. He whispered as though he was drained off his energy completely, "The building society is repossessing our house."

She stared at him with wide eyes. Though she heard it clearly, she didn't want to believe it that she heard it. "Sorry, dad. What do you say?"

He thought she hadn't heard the word, 'repossess,' before. He rephrased his sentence. "I've to pay all the arrears in 28 days' time. If I don't, they'll take the house away from me."

She waited. "Will they pay back our deposit?"

"I don't think so," he replied, more like to himself. The housing market was stagnant, and the prices dropped seriously over the last two or three years. Nobody dared to buy the houses or would be able to obtain the mortgages for them. The economy of the country was in such shambles that any jobs of the time were not reliable for long term contracts, as the general strikes and political chaos continued endlessly.

An uneasy silence engulfed them heavily. Daniella continued to sit there with her face in her hands and the elbows on her thighs and her face displayed a mixed expression of sadness and disappointment. She hadn't fully understood the consequences of their house being repossessed. Even if the building society managed to dispose of the house, say, through an auction, it must fetch enough money to pay back the mortgage balance and, if not, he ought to pay off the difference. He reached out the glass and drained his drink.

"What do we do?" She asked, clearly anxious. Are we going to rent a house?"

"I'm also thinking the same," he said with downcast eyes. "I'm proud of being an Englishman. And I love this country. But I don't want to spend the rest of my life here. My country has been taken over by militants, criminals, and opportunists."

Without saying anything, she waited for him to continue talking.

Jeffrey continued clearly tired, "There are no decent jobs. Part-times or temporaries, and I'm tired of all these." He pulled out a cigarette and lit it then took a deep puff. Slowly he blew out through his nostrils. "I know a hotel in Cornwall. I've worked there." He puffed on his cigarette and blew the smoke out. "But I'm not happy in this country, at least at the moment."

She remained silent.

"I'm going to America."

Daniella spoke gently. "To Uncle Jeremy?"

"May be for a week. Then I move on."

She hesitated to speak as vague but uneasy emotions started to startle her.

"Angela will take care of you. Until such time that you can manage yourself. And you like her, don't you?"

She didn't speak immediately.

"I'm going away. To America."

"To uncle Jeremey?"

"Maybe for a few days. And then I move on."

"That's fine. I come with you."

Jeffrey took a puff before he answered. "No, you're not!"

The vague emotions that were startling her started to form clearer in her view. He was going away alone. "You adopted me 10 years ago?"

"True. And true that it was Debra's idea."

Daniella didn't reply directly. "You loved me and cared me. And I looked upon you as my own parents." She tried to stop the tears dripping from her eyes. "Is it easy to forget as simple as this?"

"Well, you know it didn't work out. J J went away. Debra went away." He stretched his free hand and picked up the drink and swallowed a mouth of whiskey. "You start a new life. You like Angela, don't you? She can foster care for you."

"I don't think so. She's a like friend now. If she isn't good as a foster carer, how do I tell her? It's better for me to go to social services."

Silently, he stared at her face.

"Maybe it's better I get a new family that I know about nothing at all."

This time he spoke uneasily, "I think you're right. I'll talk to the social workers' department tomorrow."

"I know a social worker. Rebecca Spencer. She's told me I can call her anytime. And I'll do it in the morning."

Jeffrey stared at her silently for a moment. "If that's what you want to."

Daniella nodded gently at first for an answer, then said rather nervously, "I take the decision now on. Because I'm going to be alone."

Next day, Daniella phoned at the social workers' department. "This is Daniella Smith. Can I speak with my social worker, Rebecca Spencer, please?"

"Hold on, dear," the lady on the other end said attentively. "Let me get Rebecca for you. And what's your name again?"

"Daniella Smith."

"Okay, Daniella. Please wait a moment." Suddenly the line went silent. And it remained silent for two to three minutes before the sound came alive. "Daniella, alright?" Rebecca asked cautiously.

"Yes, Ms Spencer. But I've to see you."

"Of course. Can you speak? Anybody with you now?"

"Nobody with me."

"What is the problem, dear?"

"I've to find a new home."

"Where is Jeffrey?

"He's going to America."

"He isn't taking you with him?"

Daniella started crying. "No."

"Don't cry. I'll see you tomorrow."

They met in the next day and discussed about the girl's changing predicaments. Rebecca introduced three foster parents to Daniella, and she chose Dinah Ashdown out of those three. Dinah had looked after two boys and one girl in her foster care responsibility and was currently free of any commitments. On the 5th of April 1980, Daniella moved out to Dinah's house, and Jeffrey flew out to America the next day on the 6th.

Part 3: Daniella is Happy

Fairly quickly, Daniella settled down well with Dinah, as if a kind of dynamism was there that favourably kindled the fuse to merge the lives of two people in one direction. One didn't stay in the kitchen, and the other in the bedroom or somewhere else, but they were always together. They never had enough time to talk because they had so much to talk. In the morning, they went out together, side by side, talking about movies, music, singers, actors, and writers. At the school gate, they would hug and kiss, and then Daniella would head towards the front door, running over the sandy grounds and throwing back flying kisses while Dinah went ahead towards her part-time work in the tax office. In the evening, Daniella would rush out of the classroom to the four court, running across the grounds fast and overtaking every other student, with one hand held high, waving at Dinah at the gate among other waiting relatives. She would run into her foster mother's open arms. "Careful girl," she would criticize her, clearly happy and proud. "You'll fall and hurt yourself."

The girl would laugh giving a peck on her cheek. "This is nothing, Dinah."

"You're alright?"

"Yes, Dinah!"

They would start walking home, and talking about her lessons on the day and anything she couldn't understand thoroughly. "Not to worry, darling. I'll go through it again tonight until you understand it well."

"Okay, Dinah," she would reply, with a smile gently sprouting on her lips. "It's not difficult really. But the teacher wasn't sure. That's all."

"Oh, I forgot to tell you the concert."

"Which concert?"

"Spandau Ballet."

"Oh, I love them."

"Alright, I get two tickets."

Thus, their lives moved on, talking, giggling, going to movies or shows, and mainly, staying together. Every now and then social workers visited for finding out how Daniella was getting on with her life under the new arrangement. "I'm absolutely happy," she would reply with a sparkling smile on her lips. Obviously, there were no problems such as personal differences, frictions, or disagreements in the house. The house was rented. Dinah would pay a part of the rent from her wages, and the social workers would pay the balance. They also paid a fixed amount to Dinah for caring for the girl, and therefore, there was no financial problem. There were no outsiders or outside influences. Only Daniella and Dinah were there! They liked each other, and cared and loved and trusted. Sometime during the autumn, Daniella asked humorously, "What's the problem?"

They were in the sitting room, watching Tom Jones' show on the telly.

Dinah turned her eyes from the telly and looked at her who was sitting on her side. "What?"

Without answering, she giggled.

"What? Tom's wriggling is giving you any problem?"

The girl giggled again. "No."

"What's then?"

She continued giggling. "I want to ask, 'Haven't you got a boyfriend?'"

432

She waited a moment, meeting the girl's eyes pleasantly. "Boys are good. But they'll give you lots of problems."

However, one day before the Christmas of 1984, Daniella saw Dinah kissing a man outside, under the cherry tree. Her eyes remained tangled on them curiously. Dinah's arms were holding his waist, and his hands round her shoulders. They were whispering one minute, then continued kissing. Half an hour later, they came in and came straight to her. "My darling, this is Benjamin Coogan," Dinah said, smiling broadly, and her eyes on his face as if stuck. "Ben for short. At least easy to remember," she said laughing joyously. Gently, she withdrew her eyes from his face and turned to the girl. "This is my best friend, Daniella." She moved further and hugged her. "I love her to bits."

"Hello Daniella," he greeted her affectionately. "I've heard so much about you."

The girl laughed, looking at Dinah. "Are they all good?"

Ben shot a glance at his friend before he replied. "Every word, I must emphasise. Except one thing!"

"What's that?" Daniella asked, meeting Dinah's steady gaze.

Ben laughed as though embarrassed to answer. Slowly, he looked at Dinah, then looked back at her. "She never said you're so stunning, and may be…." The girls both laughed loudly, and he said over their laughter, "Maybe Dinah couldn't find the right words to contain your glorious beauty."

The girls laughed louder this time. Dinah joined in laughing. "I know him for a long time. We worked a couple of doors apart."

"That means she forgot one thing," he chuckled, looking at the girl. "Old age, it's quite natural to forget."

"Speak for yourself," Dinah retorted amusingly. "We're same age. You forgot that?" She turned to look at the girl. "We were together in the primary."

"Shame about that," he laughed.

"But I didn't like him, Daniella. He was a bully boy. And to be honest, nobody liked him."

He pulled a funny face. "But you rushed to me when you found me outside the company I worked?"

"Yes, yes. A big mistake, I should say. But you made a habit of hanging around outside my office, hoping you'd see me."

"I apologise." He burst out laughing. "What can I say? The weakness of a loving heart."

"And you are still coming?"

"True. The weakness of a loving heart."

All of them laughed in unison.

Ben stayed with Dinah for the night and left in the morning after the breakfast. The girls continued to stay at the table. It was a Saturday, and there was no need for any rushing. Daniella drank a mouthful of orange juice and put the glass down on the table. "You're a real cat," the girl said, looking at her across the table. "You never said a word about him."

"It wasn't as easy as it sounds now, darling?"

"No?"

"I moved in with him when I was 18."

"Yeh?"

434

"A week later, he walked out." She paused and drank a bit of coffee. "We get back together for one week, then split for one year. That's our lives for ten or twelve years. What can I say?"

Silently, the girl stared at her.

"In last February, he was here for a few days. And then not a word, until a month ago." She drank a mouthful of coffee before she continued quietly. "Since then, he's calling me every day. And he came to see me a few times in my office."

"What's he talking about?"

She laughed quietly. "Promising me everything, as usual. And now he starts talking about marriage."

"Wow. That's great. How do you feel?"

"Very excited. But I also have my own fears."

"Like what?"

"I don't know."

"Looks like a genuine guy. The way he talks and laughs, he's amazing."

"I know him from childhood. But somehow, we haven't tied the knot."

"Do you love him?"

"Very much."

"What does he do?"

"He's a karate instructor."

"Karate instructor?"

"Yeh. He trains boys and girls."

"Where?"

"At 'Your Life, Your Defence' club. You heard of them?"

"I've seen their posters."

"He mostly teaches in Bristol. But he goes to Plymouth or Exeter when they have a shortage of trainers."

"I don't mind studying. I am always excited with it."

"You look good for it."

"What you mean?"

"You're tall and slim and strong. Fit for karate manoeuvring."

"Thank you!"

A week later, Ben Coogan moved back with Dinah, and this time, he had moved in to stay permanently. Dinah was very happy because of his unexpected change in behaviour. So was Daniella, that she hung up a few balloons around the sitting room. "We decorate rooms, one by one," she said teasingly.

"What for?" Dinah asked smiling confused.

The girl smiled back. "Your wedding's coming up soon, isn't it."

The elder girl stared at her angrily and then looked away, smiling discreetly.

In April 1982, they married in the local parish church. Dinah's relatives didn't turn up for the function. They didn't like the choice of her man. He was literally notorious for violence, womanising, and dealings in the black market with drugs. He was behind bars a few times. Not a lot of guests liked Daniella as a flower girl, it wasn't very traditional they accused. However, Dinah took the decision to marry him because she loved him. She chose Daniella as her flower girl because she loved her as if she was her own sister. 'That's all that matters,' she whispered. Anyway, it was a good day, and they all enjoyed it. Daniella was very happy with the changes in the living conditions. They were no longer three individuals in one property. Instead, they were three members of a family.

However, the Falkland War brought in difficulties. In March, Daniella was promoted to the yellow belt for karate learning, and she was delighted, though yellow was only one rank above the white belt, which was the lowest. She had been attending the lessons since January and attended Saturdays and Sundays regularly and one or two evenings on weekdays as long as they didn't disturb her school studies. In May, she earned the ranking of the orange belt, and then in July, the green. She was excellent with karate manoeuvrings, turning, reversing, stretching, and kicking.

The Falkland War erupted unpredictably on the 2nd of April. The navy officers who were stationed in Plymouth sailed to the South Atlantic to reorganise the British forces and defeat the Argentinian invasion. Few of these marine commandos used to instruct the students of 'Your Life, Your Defence,' in the Plymouth unit, and suddenly, there was a shortage of instructors. Therefore, three of them from the Bristol unit and two from the Exeter – a city quite close to Plymouth – were asked to go over there. Luckily, Ben Coogan was listed in that category. Ben always liked Plymouth, especially the coastal areas towards Salcombe to the east and Falmouth to the west.

More than that, the company was offering free accommodation, and his accommodation was in Derriford, a prestigious, sought-after area in Plymouth. In his contract, it was also stated that whenever he was requested to cover any staff at Exeter, he must be quickly available there and take on the task due to someone being ill or whatever might be. With this in mind, he was allocated a brand-new car. Without a second thought, he grabbed the opportunity and drove to Derriford with his wife and foster daughter. Dinah had already obtained a receptionist job in one of the Marina hotels, and Daniella was admitted to St Peters school in Barbican, which was about 5 minutes' walk from 'Your Life, Your Defence,' karate club.

Daniella kept her school studies at the top of her priorities. Equally, it was true that she didn't overlook the values of karate second to none, and she really enjoyed the physical training and mental concentration that made this art extremely joyful. She obtained another two-coloured belts, raising her status. This was the time the marine commando unit, which was normally based in Portsmouth, visited Plymouth while they were on their way to the Falkland Islands. Nonetheless, they didn't need to sail any further to the southern hemisphere as the Argentinian military surrendered unexpectedly as the war was declared over, and they were asked to stay in Plymouth for the time being.

A number of officers regularly visited the karate club mostly to exercise, and two or three of them offered their services to train the students with their excellent experiences. Daniella volunteered immediately, and her instructor was a Chinese descendant named Kim Teo Leung. His father, Captain Hua Teo, came from a warrior race in China. There was a legend that Captain Hua held a Japanese platoon single-handedly from entering a narrow Timber bridge over the Kowloon River on the northern side of Kuala Lumpur in Malaysia and saved 7 British army men who were severely wounded and waiting for the escort to reach in the morning. Kim Teo 'never belonged to that calibre' – in his own words – but was still good enough to battle to keep the enemy at a distance. He was very famous for his sky kicks – as they say –

a sort of manoeuvring he did enviously beautifully in which he would rise like a bouncing ball while one of his feet would land with the awesome power of body and mind on the enemy's chest, preferably below the neck. He taught Daniella this ancient craft absolutely in a masterly style, and she responded to his imagination and instructions magnificently. "My father taught me this," he said. They were sitting on the training floor, facing each other. He took a small sip on his beer can. "And his father taught him before he taught me. And likewise, it goes back in our ancestry. Sadly, I didn't have a child to love and care and teach."

Without speaking, she looked at him intently.

"The great Confucius, you heard of him, Daniella?"

"Yes, teacher."

"He said. One should sow the seed in the spring and watch it grow through the summer. You understand me?"

"Yes, teacher."

He took a large sip. "Reap the harvest in the autumn and enjoy it through the winter."

She waited for him to continue.

"I've been a mariner and always in the sea. There are no seasons as such in the sea. The sun is always there. And I enjoyed it too much, without realising about the seasons in life." He drank a little before he continued softly. "Surely, I enjoyed my life, also sure committed so many mistakes, now I face the pain of failures. My worst failure is that I didn't have a child to teach my family ancestry." He paused, staring at her. "Now I feel different. I'm happy I met you. You're like a grandchild to me."

Daniella moved on the floor towards him, then hugged him, saying. "You make me so happy."

"Me too," he added gently. "And I see the skills and precision in your movement. I am sure your father or mother or, maybe, both must have come from warrior castes."

"Whoever they are, I am very proud of them. And I love them."

Part 4: Dealing with Ben

It was almost the end of the day, and Ben Coogan came down to pick up Daniella. He trained the students in their twenties or over, and they trained on the first floor. "What's happening between you and Teo?"

She turned and looked at him rather curiously. "What do you mean, Ben?"

Ben smiled, looking ahead on the road, obviously to avoid her eyes. "I know you are a grown-up girl despite your younger age. I know some nice boys. I can introduce them to you if you need."

Daniella laughed cynically. "I'm ashamed of you, Ben. How can you say such ridiculous rubbish?"

"Alright. Forget what I said."

That was a Tuesday. The next day, Ben was taking his class in Exeter. And on Thursday, they were going home. "Did you have a good day, Ben?"

He didn't answer straight away. "I suppose so," he answered sullenly. "What's the problem?"

She laughed unintentionally. "What's the problem? You tell me?"

He waited again. "Why is that Josh coming to see you?"

She stared at his face. "Why can't I see him?"

"He's crippled."

"He's crippled by birth. So what? Is it a barrier?"

He didn't reply.

She continued to stare at him, expecting him to speak. In the end, turning her face, she looked ahead on the road.

A short silence erupted before he said tactfully. "Definitely, you can do better than him."

She laughed innocently. "What do you know of him, Ben? He's just somebody I know. And that's all."

The rest of the way, they remained quietly.

In the next ten days or so, Daniella didn't see Jos. Normally, she saw him outside the fruit shop two buildings away from the school gate or around the old oak tree on the way to the school. One day, she met him at the bus before the Oak Tree. "Are you okay? I didn't see you for a few days."

Without replying, he stood there, a couple of yards away and seemingly frightened.

"Have you been in the hospital?"

He shook his head before he replied, "Ben threatened me."

"Threatened you? For what?"

"He said I shouldn't come to see you."

She looked at him bewildered.

"He said he would break my other leg, too," Jos added quietly.

"And I don't................."

Daniella interrupted gently. "Don't worry about him. I'll talk to him."

In the evening, after work, Ben showed up on her floor. "Come on, lady," he said cheerfully as usual. "Let's go home."

She moved over to him. "I want to talk to you," she said impassively.

"We do it in the car," he responded quickly.

"No, we talk now."

"What's the urgency."

Without replying, Daniella looked around. Students were hanging around, but nobody was in the office. She gestured him towards the office and walked without waiting to see his reactions. He followed her, pulling a sarcastic face. When they were both inside, she shut the door and turned to him. "What's your problem with Jos?" She asked angrily. "Why do you want to break his leg?"

He made a gesture of pettiness with his hand. "Is that it?"

"I want to know it. It's important to me."

"Important?" Ben asked sarcastically. "You want to go out with a cripple?"

"Yes, he's cripple. But he's human."

"But you're elegant, classy, and stunning. Do you want a boy like him?"

"That's your flashy talk. I don't consider myself anything at all."

"You will tarnish your image. Keep up with what you have." He laughed in a mocking manner. "I'll choose somebody for you, for goodness' sake."

"What do you know about him before you make all these judgements?"

"I know he has no father."

"No. And why? His father died in the Falkland Wars."

"And mother?"

"She died in the explosion at the Flamborough chemical plant."

"So, he's in the care?"

"No. He is with his grandmother."

"Well, I can sympathise with his situation. But you need a good boy. Leave it to me. I'll find out for you."

"You make me sick. And I don't wish to talk anymore."

"Alright. Let's go home."

"No. You go."

"You're going to Jose?"

"Oh, you're sick in your head."

"What do you mean?"

"I'll take the bus."

"Why the bus?"

"I don't trust you. The bus is safer."

Ben angrily went out to the car.

Daniella stayed back for a while, apparently to regain her composure. Or more aptly, she was visualising the situation that evening at home. It wouldn't be pleasant because Ben would reach home before her, and Dinah would immediately ask why he didn't bring back Daniella with him. With it, arguments would start.

Over the last year or so – maybe two years – they would disagree a lot and argue loudly. The reasons could be anything, such as why Ben wasn't bringing home money to keep them all going as a family. Practically, they lived on the income from Dinah's part-time work in the tax office or social workers' payment for Daniella's welfare fee. The rent for the flat was quite expensive, especially for their income. But Ben never wanted to move out to a cheaper flat or house in a cheaper area. He preferred to brag that he stayed in Derriford. The flat they had was spacious and modern, and it was on the second floor of a three-story building. The view from the front balcony was breath-taking, with the tree canopy cover over the slopping hill and the green fields beyond in the distance. And then, on certain days, more frequently during spring, a dazzling mist would drift up along the valley with the sparkling colours of the rainbow, shutting out the earth totally. The women stayed hours on the balcony, if they were home, and would watch these nature's wonders.

However, 'the money dictates the world.' Ben never contributed a reasonable amount of funds for his share of rent, food, utility bills, or anything else. But he would expect the best food and drinks when he was at the table. Another issue was that he was always out for one thing or another, and whenever he would return, he'd be absolutely drunk. And when he was angry, he'd swear and shout at the top of his mouth. The neighbours, crowding into their balconies, would listen and watch everything in detail. Somehow, he seemed to be enjoying these occasions of violence in the house.

Dinah, feeling ashamed, would stand up for her rights and give him back the way she gets. One couldn't predict his actions or reactions when he would kick about anything as long as he enjoyed it. Two quarrels burst up lately with the accusations that Dinah would always take Daniella's side whenever he tried to discipline her, although he couldn't remember what he was shouting about. And on both occasions, Daniella was right there. How many times these kinds of quarrels might have occurred when she was away!

She entered the communal forecourt with all her mixed feelings of fears and worries, also attempting to restrain it, then climbed up the steps. She searched for the front door key and found it in her denim jacket. Holding it nervously, she inserted it into the keyhole. She first listened to whether she was hearing any sounds from inside, 'nothing,' she thought to herself, and then turned it to open the door. "Hello," she called out, more nervously than happily. No reply was heard, although. She got into her room and dropped the school bag on to the bed, then turned back as she sensed a movement at her door. "Oh, it's you, Dinah!" she shrieked, gasping for breaths.

Dinah didn't react to it directly. "Where were you?" She asked, obviously relieved.

"I meant to take a bus, Dinah," she said, breathing out noisily. "No bus. Strikes! I had to get a taxi."

"Why didn't you come with him?"

Daniella didn't reply. Instead, she steadily caught the other woman's gazing eyes. "He told Jos he would break his legs. And when Jos told me this, he was literally shattering. Ben might have frightened him badly."

"Well, that's Ben, isn't it."

"What he said to you, Dinah?"

"Don't want to hear it. His words are not repeatable."

445

"If you rephrase?"

Dinah waited tactfully. "You went to sleep with Jos."

"You don't believe that, do you?"

"Not for a moment, Ella."

An uneasy silence ticked away.

"Jos' days are numbered, Dinah."

"What is it?"

"Jos doesn't want any sympathy from anyone."

"I won't tell a soul, Ella."

Daniella struggled to contain the pressures building up from inside her without speaking.

"What's it, Ella? Tell me."

"He has cancer, Dinah," she replied hurriedly, this time as if she wanted to get it out of her mind quickly.

"Oh, poor soul. I feel sorry for him."

"The doctors told him that Jos got another 3 to 4 weeks to live."

Dinah paused and sighed heavily.

"What a life he's having? He lived his life as a crippled. And now he knows he's about to die soon. How cruel his life can be?"

Dinah remained silent.

"His father died in the Falkland War. His mother died in the fire at the Flamborough chemical plant." She stopped talking as mixed emotions of sadness and helplessness started to grip. Slowly, she managed to regain her composure. "He didn't expect anything from me. When he dies, he wants to believe he had loved me."

Without saying anything, Dinah put her hand on her shoulder.

"And wants to see my face in his mind before he fades away."

Dinah pulled her closer and hugged her.

Outside, Ben's car came and stopped.

"You stay here," Dinah said, obviously fearfully. "Don't worry. I'll go to the living room."

Shortly, Ben was outside the front door. He opened it, got inside the porch, and slammed the door shut. He came into the hallway and slammed the door behind him. Slamming the door was a signal that he was angry and nobody should mess with him. He entered the living room, his eyes rolled over to the telly vision, and then he turned to the sofa seat where his wife was sitting and watching the show. Her eyes or head didn't move at all, as if she didn't know he was there. "Any news about the bastard?" He growled, standing in front of her on his unsteady legs and staring at her fiercely.

She turned her face and caught his eyes. "She has a name."

"I didn't ask for the name. The bastard in?"

She rose to her feet, still meeting his eyes. "Anyway, I'm her guardian. What's your problem?"

"I don't want a cheap tart living in my house. It's shameful for me. I'm a respectable, gentleman."

"Is that right?"

"No point telling you. Cheap tart like you won't understand."

"You understand?"

"Yes, of course."

"Understand then. You're dying to sleep with her."

"Does it matter to you?"

"Yes. I am her guardian."

"Who taught you this? Your mother?"

"What about my mother?"

Daniella was listening to all the conversations in the other room. But she had refused to come out and endanger the arguments worse than what it already was. But the situation seemed to be getting out of hand in all proportions. May be, this was the time she should make her presence so that it might, perhaps, calm the situation down. She came out and said politely, "Please keep your voices down."

He swung around swiftly to stare at her, and as he moved, he lost his balance and staggered forward by a couple of feet. The girl and his wife watched him breathlessly, fearing that he was about to strike the girl. Nonetheless, he managed to regain the balance quickly and told her, "The cripple finished his business. And you're back. And I'll talk to you in a minute. And stay quiet." He swung back to his wife. "Yes, my dearest darling wife. Why did you mention my mother?"

"I can't remember," she said tactfully, "while all these uproars are going on."

"I heard it well."

Without replying, she stared at him with a fuming expression in her eyes.

Daniella said, as if expecting unnecessary arguments, "That's all over. Let's talk something else."

Ben ignored it completely. "If you ever mention my mum, you are a carcass, and I promise."

"Don't you frighten me? I know you got a black belt."

"I earned it."

"You also earned the reputation. That you are born out of a whore."

He jumped towards her and smacked on her face. She appeared to drift on her feet momentarily, then tumbled down to the floor while her head banged on the arm of the wooden chair. Daniella ran to her and put a cushion under her head.

"You leave her," Ben screamed.

However, blood started to pour out through the strands of her hair. She rose to her feet and ran to the phone near the balcony door.

"Don't touch the phone," he told furiously.

"Her head's bleeding."

"It's none of your business."

She ignored him and picked up the phone.

He accelerated to her, shouting, "I'll kill you."

She dropped the phone and, getting out to the balcony, locked the door behind her. Now, she could scream for help, and he couldn't do anything. "Call the ambulance and police, please."

He moved to the door and ordered. "Stop it, you girl of a gun. If you don't, I'll kill you."

She didn't listen to him at all. Instead, she cried out all the more loudly. Please call the police. And ambulance. "

"Stop it, you stupid bitch."

However, she cried as loudly as she could. "Please help. Please, call the ambulance and the police."

The family on the flat above looked down over their balcony rails. "Ambulance and police are on the way, Daniella," the elder man of the family replied. "They will be here in no time."

"Stay there, darling," the mother shouted down. "You'll be safe there."

Behind the door, Ben was almost frantic. He pulled the phone cord out of its socket and damaged the connection. He could say Dinah slipped and hurt herself. The phone wasn't working. Daniella, therefore, cried out for neighbours' help. Everything fitted well, he had thought in his head. But he had to get the girl inside before she would tell the truth. He moved back from the door, frightfully shot a glance at Dinah – she was lying motionless, might be died – he dashed to the door and kicked on it. The door came off the hinges with a loud bursting noise and flew over the rail and then down to the forecourt. He hurried out to the balcony and turned to the girl with a feverish look in his eyes. She was trapped at the other end. There was no way there to run anywhere. Her mind assessed her situation quickly, and she couldn't jump two floors down, as it was too deep. And Ben was racing toward her.

The vision of Kim Teo, her teacher, flashed in her mind. He had advised that when her life was threatened, and there was no way around to escape, she should draw the Sky Jump. Before she had realised, she rose to the air. Her body whirled like the trails of smoke, then descended, and her right foot landed on his chest with all the power of her body, mind, and soul. He was flung backward and then slithered over the rails and dived down through the air, upside down, and landed on his head in the forecourt, then the rest of his body shrank down. Almost at the same time, two vans arrived on the roadside, and numerous policemen and women jumped out of them. Daniella remained on the balcony, absolutely frozen. Her eyes stared fearfully at the forces who were moving into the forecourt and the body of Ben lying on the ground, completely immobile. She didn't cry, although she couldn't control the horrors or the perils that would spring up in her life.

Part 5: Remembering Dinah

However, now as she memorised the incidents, Daniella started to cry. She had always cried for Dinah. On that fatal night, Dinah died in the hospital. Daniella was already in the police cell by then. She couldn't give even a goodbye kiss, whispering, 'My dearest friend, thank you for looking after me. I will always love you.'

As Mark had told her, he was on duty on Sunday night. "Hello, dear," he said pleasantly through the trap window. "How are you?"

She was sitting on the edge of the bed, half sleepy and half awake. Perhaps she couldn't decide what to do at one o'clock in the night. Her body was so tired and literally dead, but her mind was erratically active. She heard him, though. She lifted her face from her hands and looked at him.

The light was off. However, a faint light was filtering through the ventilation window 2ft above her head level, and he just about made out Daniella was looking at him. "Turn on the light?"

She didn't move or say anything.

"I couldn't get here any earlier," he said apologetically. "Few troubles broke out in the wards. Anyway, how are you?"

"I thought you'd tell me that?" She replied somewhat annoyed.

Mark laughed quietly, clearly to cheer her up. "I've some good news. But not so good news."

"Yeh?"

"I met Lizzy."

Breathlessly, she waited for him to continue.

"A doctor and three nurses were with your mother when she gave birth." He stopped talking for a moment as if recollecting the scene properly. "Lizzy was a trainee nurse, a kind of assistant. The second nurse and the doctor attended on and off, as your mother was having some kind of difficulties. The third person, a midwife, was with Abigale literally all the time, like a good friend. Her name was Margery Wilcots." He paused momentarily before he added thoughtfully, "If anybody knows anything about Abigale, it's only Margery and nobody else."

"Where is Margery?" Daniella asked suddenly, with all the energy and enthusiasm she could muster.

Without replying, he searched for a cigarette and lit it. He drew deeply on it and blew out through the nostrils. "She is dead."

She stared at him silently as if unable to speak.

"She was found hanging from a tree."

"My God! Why am I hearing all this?"

"Don't give up hope completely because she had a confession with a priest. Lizzy thinks Margery had said everything to this priest."

"Do you know him?"

"No, but I know his name."

"What is it?"

He hesitated. "I'll tell you later."

"Is he alive?"

"Yes. And I know where he is."

"Anybody else knows?"

"Only Lizzy. And me!"

"Why can't you tell me?"

"I don't want any harm happening to his life."

"All because of mum?"

"I hope not!"

"If Margery said anything in the confession………."

He interrupted her. "That's what Lizzy says. And she is very positive about it."

"What priests listen in the confessions, they can't reveal to anyone."

"I know it, Daniella. I'm a Christian. But I'm off tomorrow. I'll sleep two or three hours in the morning. And then I'll go."

"Long way off?"

"No. And I'll be back for the night shift."

The next day, at about 2 pm, he came off the A30 Dual Carriageway and headed up the winding road towards the coastal hills. Wheat fields stretching to the distance run along on his right while plots of woodlands cascaded over the mounts and valleys on the left. As he headed further down over the fresh country neighbourhood, the spire of St Magdalene Church appeared at the horizon on a ridge. It took another twenty minutes before he reached the church. He left the car at the back of the churchyard and climbed up to the priest house. It was a detached property on a lower slope on the right side of the church. An elderly woman opened the door and looked at him clearly puzzled.

He spoke quickly as if to ease the introduction, "Good afternoon," he said politely. "Can I see Father Michael Hollings?"

She waited. "You're Mister?"

"I am Mark. Mark Windrush!"

She hesitated vaguely. "You haven't got an appointment?"

"I don't have. And I'm so sorry to turn up like this."

"He's in his study. I don't know if he will see you now or not. Anyway, I will go and tell him. But what will I tell him why you're here?"

He stared at her without finding an answer. "It's a very personal matter, I'm sorry. And this is why I didn't phone you for an appointment."

She looked at him rather confused. "Okay, let me see him." She turned back, closing the door behind her.

After about five minutes, the door opened, and a man about 60 years old appeared. "I'm Father Michael Hollings," he said respectfully. "I understand you want to talk to me?"

"Yes, father. And thank you."

"I'm preparing for a sermon for the Sunday mass." He stopped abruptly and looked at him kindly. "Is it something very important?"

Clearly, an expression of despair moved over to his face. "Hopefully, you can save somebody's life, father."

Without speaking, the father looked at him steadily. Obviously, he was waiting for him to continue.

"I won't take too much of your time, father. Please allow me to talk to you."

Fr Michael glanced the time at his wristwatch. "I suppose I could do a little break away from my preparations. You better come in."

He came in and followed the priest to the reception room.

It was a bigger room and, at the centre, was a rectangle table with chairs. Mark was asked to sit down, and Fr. Michael took a seat on the opposite end. "What's it you want to talk about, Mark?"

He moved back in his chair and met the priest's gaze steadily. "Father, do you remember Margery Wilcots?"

He didn't say 'yes or no.' Instead, he whispered to himself, 'Margery Wilcots,' as if he was jogging his own memories. "She was a midwife nurse in a Plymouth hospital."

He was silent briefly before he spoke. "I was in St Thomas Church in Plympton, which is a suburb of the city of Plymouth. But I went to the Cathedral church to celebrate Masses when they had shortages of priests. And I met Margery in the Cathedral church."

455

"I'm from Bristol. But now, I work in Plymouth for the last ten months or so. And I am slowly getting the hang of places in Plymouth."

"I see. Are you a relative of Margery?"

"No."

"What's your interest in Margery?"

"Abigale, an African lady, was in the care of Margery when she was having her baby."

The father waited. "I knew Abigale very well. She was from Atlantica. She was staying – shall I say – in the wrong place at the time. Well, in those days, not everyone in this area knew how to treat foreigners respectfully. And I helped her to shift to another hotel."

"She was pregnant when you met her?"

"She was. And she was four or five months old with her pregnancy at the time." He paused. "A fine, intelligent lady – she was. And I liked her."

"Did she ever mention who the father was?"

"No at all! I don't think this subject ever popped up in our conversation."

"Did Margery say anything?"

"About Abigale?"

He nodded silently.

The priest waited as though he was memorising. "I met her twice, first time in the Cathedral church and then in my own church in Plympton. On both occasions, she was shaking badly. She was terribly confused and scared because she knew a lot about Abigale." He waited more cautiously this time before he added quietly, "She wasn't sure whether she could tell me what she had in her mind. In the end, she asked for a confession."

Mark moved back in his seat and stared out the window on the side wall into the church garden. Obviously, he wasn't sure of himself. A moment or two later, he looked back at the priest. "Did she take the confession?"

"Yes, she did," father Michael replied calmly. "I gave a secluded time for her alone because she was scared to mingle with others at the normal hours."

"Why was she scared?"

"She had certain fears that somebody was up there to kill her."

"The fears are related to Abigale?"

"Yes. Two weeks later, the police found her body hanging from a tree behind her house. And it made it look like she committed a suicide."

Deeply distressed, he looked out the window again.

An uneasy silence elapsed.

"Father, if I may ask, did Margery tell anything about Abigale's boyfriend?"

"You mean in the confession?"

"Yes, father."

"Mark, the confession is a sacrament between the confessor and the God. The priest is only an instrument between them. He has no part to play in it, and as such, no memories exist when he leaves the confession box."

"But…. but father…." He broke off, seemingly unsure of himself.

"Yes, Mark?"

"Forgive me if I clear my mind." He waited vaguely at first before he struggled himself to continue, "You've good memories of Abigale. And Margery. And then, how can you forget what Margery told you?"

"Oh, Mark. How pitiful it is that you came to this conclusion?"

"Father Michael, a life is in total peril. I'm trying to save her. Nothing is more important to me than this. Please help me."

"I'm sorry to hear it. Mark, you have a great name, the name of one of the four apostles who wrote the gospels. How can you talk so feebly?"

"I know, father. These are church teachings. But ………."

Fr Michael interrupted him gently. "You're right. They are church teachings. But church teachings are founded on the Holy Bible. And Holy Bible are the words and actions and teaching of God." He halted talking briefly, apparently thoughtfully. "Surely, you should talk better."

"My dad was a catholic."

"But are you a catholic, Mark."

"I suppose so, father."

"Mark, my young man, you know that's not an answer. Either you are a catholic or not at all!"

"Yes, father. I am a catholic. And my dad used to tell me lots of stories from the Bible."

"Did you believe them?"

"I don't know. Maybe I believed some."

"So, you pick and choose what to believe and what not to."

"I'm sorry, father."

"Oh, Mark, my dear friend, you believed some. Have you ever read the bible?"

"No."

"Well, there you are. Never read the bible! Your dad told you stories from the bible, and you believed some, but not all of them, which meant you picked and chose the messages from the bible. And yet, you claim that you are a catholic."

"I'm sorry. I don't think I'm doing all right."

"Not at all! Because you sound like a modern critic of the bible. Or an atheist. Or the enemy of Jesus Christ." Fr Michael leaned back in his chair and looked at him silently for a moment. "That's easily understandable. Jesus never harmed a single person in his life, and he also told his followers to love their enemies. Therefore, all these egoists attack the Christians without any fear of consequences."

Mark caught his eyes rather uneasily. "Sorry, father. I don't think I'm saying the right points." He stopped talking and drew a deep breath. "But I'm desperate to save the life of this girl."

"I'm a priest, and saving the life is paramount to me. Tell me who is this girl?"

"Abigale's daughter."

"Abigale's daughter?" The priest asked rather eagerly.

"Yes, father."

"I was told she died during birth."

"She is alive and well. But she is held in a prison."

"That's not very good. What happened?"

"Long, long story, father. We'll talk later."

"Where is Abigale?"

"My information is that she was sent back to Africa."

"And the girl's father?"

"I don't know. But I've a strange feeling that he is someone from this area. Because I think that's why she came to Plymouth for the delivery of her child."

"Possible. As I am talking to you, my memory flashed to an artefact she left with me for safeguarding."

"What's it?" Mark asked almost breathlessly.

"It's a carving on a piece of wood – say 8 inches by 6 inches. It's fairly heavy for its size. Some kind of precious wood! And I think it's a gift given to Abigale on a very special occasion."

"Anything on it, father? Or any picture?"

"Yes – as I said – it's a carving. And if I remember properly, an African mud hut on it over a sandy slope towards a beach and a black girl on the water's edge. She's standing on the water's edge and staring back at the house. And near her feet, there were three words. 'Love you always!'"

"Anything else, father?"

The priest waited, staring at him absently as his mind focused on the article, which wasn't in sight. "Oh, yes," he replied as if he woke up. "Atkinson. M. Atkinson, more precisely, I remember now. That name is etched on it." He paused intently. "Perhaps the name doesn't mean anything because it can belong to the artist. Or, may be, with a bit of luck, the name belongs to the man who gave this gift. Do you know anyone with this name?"

He thought for a moment. "Not really, Father. But an Atkinson family owns the Great Atlantic Hotel in Cornwall."

"Do you know them?"

"No. But two friends of mine – Ian and Craig – work in the hotel as cleaners. They are ex-prisoners and were in my ward before they were released."

"They know the owners?"

"I shouldn't think so. The owners are very rich and powerful. Not all people can get access to them."

Fr Michael looked confused. "Anyway, you have somewhere to make a start."

Equally confused, Mark stared back at the priest. "Please give me the artefact. It will help me to convince somebody if it's necessary."

The priest was silent briefly. "I saw it last in my study when I was transferred to this parish four years ago. I was storing my belongings." He got up slowly. "And I hope it's still somewhere there."

"You need any help," he responded kindly, "please give me a shout."

"I will," the priest replied, moving over to the doorway. He stopped walking and turned to his visitor. "You want a drink – tea? Coffee?"

"No. Thanks anyway. I'm fine."

"A glass of Juice? Or water?"

He smiled. "I'm fine, father."

"Okay. Hopefully, I won't be long." Without expecting a response, he returned to the doorway and headed towards the storm room. And he returned fairly shortly with a plastic bag. "It was in my personal drawer," he said, getting the artefact out of the bag and showing Mark.

Mark took it gratefully and looked at it quickly. The artwork on the board was exactly as the priest described it except for one aspect. The girl was not standing on the water's edge, but she was in the water and sunk down up to her waist. He looked at the priest, saying, "Thank you for this carving."

"I kept it safely over the years. I've been very sure that it's a sentimental piece to somebody. And that it can be a priceless object to someone."

"Hopefully, it could be found true very soon."

They moved over to the front door. They looked down over the slope absently towards his car.

"Very careful who you talk to," Michael advised him quietly. "You might come across very dodgy characters."

"Thank you."

"Keep me informed, Mark."

"I will, father," he replied gratefully. "I will come and see you."

"Please do. And bring me a lot of good news about Abigale. And if you see her, tell her I've asked for her."

"I will, father."

"Tell her to come and see me."

"Definitely!"

He walked down towards his car.

Mark headed down along the A 30 towards the Atlantic Hotel. It was a fair way away, about sixty miles. A cool breeze from the English Channel lashed onto the car. At Falmouth, after the river, he swung to the right and reached the Bawcock junction. Craig was waiting there, in front of the Cornish café. "Thank you," Mark said through the car window. "The phone line was terrible. I couldn't hear anything. And I couldn't find another booth."

"Anyway, we met."

"Ian is at work?"

"Yes, until six. Why? He got in the car and looked at Mark intensely. "You're expecting troubles?"

"No. And then again, I don't know what to expect."

"And again, you don't know which M Atkinson you're looking for?"

"True. Very true. But I've to start from somewhere."

Craig waited. "The one you're going to see now is Mathew Atkinson. We come here every week to clean up the ground around the house. We haven't seen him yet, but the other staff say that he is a very pleasant man."

"You know the way from here?"

"I do. Go straight up here."

They went straight up almost a mile before they came across a roundabout where they turned right into a dual carriageway. In another half a mile or so, they came off to a rural highway and then into a winding road that climbed erratically as the land level changed up and down. The sea appeared on and off on their right through the clear patches. Wherever the sea appeared, there stood the sun as well, growing in size and gathering a faint spectrum of colours on the lazily drifting bands of clouds. The night was still away, at least for another hour.

Shortly, they stopped outside a metal gate on the Hill Side. "Well, we're here," Craig said quietly. "The gate is electrically wired. And CCTV cameras are everywhere. We can't do any stunt here, you understand?"

Without speaking, Mark stared at him rather nervously.

"Inside the gate, it's a private road leading to the mansion on the slope on the seaside. It used to be known as the Atkinson Mansion. Now, they changed the name to Abigale House."

"Thank you for all the information, Craig. But you're not telling how we're going to get in?"

Craig caught his eyes before he got out of the car. He moved further and pressed on the bell switch fixed beside the huge gates and waited for a reply. This time, Mark came nearer to him. "The car is okay up there?"

Craig looked at the car in the bay, then turned back. "It's okay. It's not blocking anybody."

Shortly, a light beamed up on the switch, and he spoke to it, "I'm Craig Colins. I'm one of your cleaners. Can I come in with my friend?"

Another moment later, a narrow gate swung open a few feet away. They entered, and the gate shut itself behind them. They started walking to the house. A young girl was at the window of the reception room, watching them. They came to her. "I've this article," Mark said politely. "And I believe this belongs to Mr Mathew Atkinson."

The girl looked at it idly. "I know nothing about these things," she said politely. "But Janice is in the art gallery. She's in charge of it. I go and call her."

In the end, Janice came and looked at the craving. As she looked, her eyes grew wide with excitement. "This is absolutely amazing," she whispered to herself. She paused as if she was lost for words and continued to stare at it. And then, she raised her face and looked at Mark. "Mr Atkinson has a few of these in the gallery. But I haven't seen one like this. This is a classic piece of artwork."

"Mr. Atkinson owned it in the past?" Mark asked nervously.

"Only Mr. Atkinson can answer that I'm afraid," she answered, smiling helplessly. "Anyway, he's in the lounge. And I'm sure he'll be more than happy to see an artwork of this magnitude." She stopped talking as she looked at them gently. "Can I take this to Mr Atkinson, if it's okay with you?"

"No problem at all, Janice!"

She turned to the girl behind the window. "Ask them to come in. And let them sit in the foyer. I won't be long." She took the artefact and stepped out into the foyer. About twenty people could afford to crowd easily within its walls. A wide corridor stretched from there into the inner rooms. She walked up along the corridor before she disappeared through a door. After five minutes or so, she returned to the corridor. A tall man was right behind her, this time the carving in his hand. They reached for the foyer and crossed towards the men who were standing in a corner. Looking at Mark, she said respectfully, "The carving belongs to him, I think." She glanced at the other man, "Craig works here in our yard."

The tall man glanced calmly at Craig, then told Mark, "I'd like a private talk with you."

"Yes, sir."

The tall man walked in front of him, and Mark followed him. They entered a room behind the foyer. "What's your name?"

"Mark. Mark Windrush is my full name."

"I'm Mathew Atkinson. I haven't seen this property for years, at least for fifteen years."

He didn't speak.

"The background is a bit of the Colonial District in Atlantica city. And the girl is Abigale, the love of my life. And I gave this to her on her eighteenth birthday."

He continued to be silent.

"I should admit that this gives me the biggest surprise since I lost her. How did you get this?"

"I borrowed it, to be honest."

"Borrowed it."

"Yes, sir."

"From Father Michael Hollings."

"How did he get it?"

"Abigale gave him for safekeeping."

"Father Michael Hollings knew Abigale?"

"Yes, sir. For about four months or so."

"The girl in the carving is Abigale."

"I know. Lizzy told me. But the name is there, M Atkinson. I thought it could be the artist's name."

"It's my name. I sponsored the work."

"Thank you. I need your kindness."

He sat down on a chair and stared at him silently.

"Somebody is in deadly trouble. I may not be able to save her."

"What do you mean?"

"It will take a long time even if I get the right verdict. And then I am not sure she will be alive by then?"

"Alive by then?"

"She is approaching the end of her tether."

He stared at him without speaking for a moment. "Where is she?"

"In the prison!"

"In the prison? And you didn't tell me who she is?"

"You want to hear it now, sir?"

"Of course. You want to save her, don't you?"

He waited bewildered for a moment, then said uneasily, "It's Abigale's daughter."

He sprang up to his feet. "That means I'm the father?"

"Of course, sir."

"Then what are we doing here? Let's go."

It was ten minutes past ten o'clock when they reached outside the trapped window. Mark knocked on it. No response was heard from inside. Mark knocked hard on it this time. And yet no response was reached. And he knocked much harder this time. And this time, clearly, a tired, sleepy voice was heard. "Who is this?"

"Mark."

Daniella yawned slowly before she said, "See you in the morning. I want to sleep."

"We are coming in."

"Wait, you stupid. Let me put something on properly."

A few minutes ticked away uneasily before Mark opened the door. "Can I turn the light on?"

"Yes," she replied, obviously sounding angry.

The dim light turned on. Mathew stepped in first and caught her staring eyes. Mark also entered and squeezed into the little space left by the side of Mathew. None of the three said a word for a couple of moments. In the end, she said, "What's it?" She asked awkwardly.

"Daniella," Mark told, gesturing at the other man, "This is Mr Mathew Atkinson." And then he turned to him. "This is Daniella Smith."

Mathew told her, clearly uneasily. "You are not Daniella. You're Gemma. Gemma Atkinson!"

She stared at him bewildered. "Who are you?"

"I am your father."

She sprang to her feet and threw herself to him. His open arms held her tightly to his body, their faces met, and tears from their eyes merged and trickled down over their bodies.

Chapter 11

Father and Daughter Together

Part 1: Back to Mathew

Mathew stretched his hand to his barrister, James Cunningham, who was standing in the front row. James turned half back and took his hand while he shot a glance at the judge's chair. The judge had already retired from his chair, and the jury section was dwindling down in numbers. His eyes rolled further to the prosecution bench, and he noticed that everyone up there looked utterly disarray and angry. He turned back completely and met the stares of Mathew and Gemma who was on her father's side. The men shook the hands triumphantly this time.

"Congratulations, Mathew," he said, his face glowing with the verdicts. "I don't think you had enough faith in me."

"Congratulations to you too, James," Mathew replied, apparently delighted with the verdict. "Yes, there were times I thought we would lose to the fabrications of lies from the prosecution benches."

"James managed a triumphant smile. "You know what I say to my opposing teams?"

Mathew shook his head before he whispered jokingly, "I wouldn't even bother."

James' smile grew broader. "The darkness cannot hide the sun."

"Thank you. I'm learning."

"Good." And then, James released his hand off his clasp and held Gemma on her shoulder. "Thank You, Gemma," he said, pretending to be grateful, "you saved my reputation."

She met his eyes, somewhat confused. "What did I do for you?"

He smiled gently. "Keep it a secret from your papa. He will refuse to pay my fees."

Gemma chuckled, glancing at her, "Alright, it's a deal."

"Judge Healey is very shrewd. He takes no nonsense from defendants, or prosecutors, or witnesses. He makes them all come clean in the dispatch box."

"I was clean in my replies."

"And the judge knew it. And he accepted your explanations and your honesty!"

"I'm very pleased about that."

"And that made my task of contesting easier." He paused briefly. "And in theory, I won yet another difficult case and I get the huge credit for it."

"That's all you're getting," Mathew chuckled quietly. "Don't send me bills for your fees."

"Definitely not! If Gemma joins our firm and practices to become a barrister!"

By then, the trainee barrister Joe McGovern, solicitor Barry Bell, legal secretary Amanda Collins and office clerk Julie Wills of the defence team stepped further down the court room and stood waiting in the corridor. James glanced at his wrist watch, saying, "Shall we move on. The staff are waiting for us."

They crossed the court room and went over to the staff. Suddenly, they started celebrating – thanking, congratulating, and huging each other. This merrily party went on for five minutes before Joe McGovern reminded pleasantly, "We've a case beginning in forty minutes in Court 7 and in the Family Division."

"Alright, Joe," James said pleasantly. "You probably have to lead the case. I've to be with Mathew and Gemma for another half an hour. But I'm pretty sure, I will meet you before the proceedings commence."

"Okay, James," Joe said easily. "And we'll see you later." He and the others turned to the clients, especially to Gemma. "We wish you all the best. And if any problem, you know we are here."

Gemma nodded her head for an answer before she added with a twinge of sadness in her voice, "You have been great, and I miss you always."

They waved at her, while walking ahead, and disappeared through the door at the other end of the long hall way. James turned to the Atkinsons. "If we go ahead," he said gesturing through another corridor, "we might find a consultation room and get some privacy."

They went ahead and found an empty room.

"Did you notice the prosecution bunch today?" James asked carefully, looking at his clients across the desk. "Or the other days?"

The father and the daughter shot a glance at each other before Mathew answered. "They were very clever."

"Clever? They are the best in London, Mr and Ms Atkinson. And the most expensive."

William retorted humorously. "After you with fees!"

Gemma laughed quietly.

James didn't notice the humour. "The judiciary wasn't prepared for this long trial of three days. They had known this mindless thug, Ben Coogan. And the crazy Samantha Perkins. And the prison guard, Brian."

She stopped laughing and stared at her papa, and then looked back at him. "I always said in the court that I was defending myself."

"Thank you, Gemma. You did the right thing. Samantha or Brian won't attack anybody again. They are both paralysed for life."

The father and daughter didn't speak.

"Government wouldn't finance it. Anyway, they are bankrupt after the general strikes and the coal miner's violence and Falkland wars."

"Anyway, their legal team did a brilliant performance," Mathew said pensively. "So, somebody has to pay."

James moved back in his chair and looked at Gemma for a moment then looked at him. "The question is, 'who is it?'"

Mathew held his eyes steadily but didn't speak.

James spoke again as if to himself, "And why?"

Mathew turned to Gemma and met her stare momentarily before he turned back to the barrister. "I always had this fear," he said slowly.

"Fear?" The barrister whispered. "What fear?"

He didn't reply directly. "When I go to Atlantica, I take Gemma with me. Or I take Gemma to France and leave her with my sister Isabella in Paris. I never leave her alone in Abigale House."

James stared away thoughtfully before he asked reluctantly, "Is it because of your fear?"

"Yes, I admit."

"Then tell me what is this that's bothering you?"

Mathew looked at his daughter silently for a moment. "I fear my ex-wife Isabella will harm my daughter."

Gemma stretched her hand quietly and held her father's hand that was rested on the desk.

"How?" James asked curiously. "Have you got any evidence?"

"Why we look outside, James? See the execution bench! Who is financing them?"

"Your wife, you think."

"Of course! Isabella wants to lock Gemma behind the bars for life." He looked at his daughter calmly, as if studying the expressions on her face. "My ex-wife never had much respect for black race. And she doesn't want to see Gemma taking part in the business."

James stroked his cheek impassively. "So, you knew it."

Mathew looked at him silently.

"I had this conviction all the time. Now, I'm glad you're on the same wavelength."

"Also, I've increased the security around the Abigale House, James. With high walls around and electric barbed wire above the walls. And a few good loyal guards are on duty round the clock monitoring the premises!"

"Good, Mathew!"

"My daughter also has female attendants. Tanya – same age as Gemma – is one of them and she never keeps Gemma out of her sight when Gemma is in the Abigale House."

"Oh, Tanya! She's an angel! I really like her."

"I'm pleased to hear that."

"The other girls, Pamela and Brenda, are very good, too. But I share my secrets only with Tanya."

"But even Tanya doesn't know where my daughter lives in Paris. Or in Atlantica!"

James kept silent, looking at him and then at her. "In Paris, you live with aunty?"

She shook her head.

"In Atlantica, you live in your own house in the Colonial District."

She shook her head again.

"Where are you then?"

"In my own addresses, which are not known to anybody else. And there, I'm not known as Gemma Atkinson."

"What they call you, then?"

"Daniella Smith!"

"Good. Much better than I could have advised!"

"Isabella knows Elenor and her Paris home. And she also knows our home in Atlantica City. So, there is no absolute safety for Gemma."

"I know, but we will have a meeting about it soon. And now, let me safely get you out of London. All your enemies know where you are now."

They followed down the hallway and came out of the Law courts of London to the forecourt. And they crossed it and continued walking to the car park where their driver had been waiting. He opened the back doors, and Gemma and Mathew entered.

"Pleasant journey back to Cornwall, "James said. "And I'll be in touch with you."

"Thank you," Mathew said.

James came around the car to Gemma's side. He stooped slightly and said to her through the partly open door. "My offer stands for you to be a barrister." He laughed amusingly. "You don't need to be under Papa's care all your life."

They laughed, including the driver, before she said, "Thanks. Now Papa knows he has to be careful with me."

They laughed again while the car rolled forward out of the parking bay.

Part 2: Playing Games

The beach garden was on the west side of the house. It spread over the small peninsula, stretching into the sea, and was protected by cliffs on its three sides. Various flowering plants, bushes, and fruit trees grew there. Finely cut-out paths rolled down towards the cliffs, with green turf shielding the floor and coloured stones bordering the flanks. At the other end, safely away from the cliff, boasted a tennis court where Gemma played singles, mostly against Tanya, and, when playing doubles, she'd pair with Tanya. Either end of the court was furnished with comfortable seats under cover.

Further back, the cliffs parted right down to the ground about six feet apart, which allowed a suitable entrance to the seafront, although the sea water embraced the narrow beach about thirty feet below. However, the end of the land still continued in a slopping formation to the water, and rocks covered the surface. A couple of centuries ago, one of the Atkinson's ancestors cut out steps on the rocks and facilitated a passage, teasingly known as the Atkinson Gate, to the waterfront and built bathing and swimming facilities and jetties for yachts at the beach. Three to four yards away on the right side of this gate, a brilliant view was granted to the beach below and beyond as the cliffs were low and reedy. Mathew's grandfather, William, placed a dozen chairs there – special chairs carved out of colourful rocks brought from Atlantica City and coated with marbles on the interior.

Today, there was no game on the tennis court. Tanya was away in the Grand Atlantic Hotel. She had been training there to be a secretary. It was Gemma who suggested it, and Mathew employed her. Today, she was working in the office of Lloyd Jones, who was also Eleanor's nephew. She had been there on and off for nearly a year now. Other times, she got training in Eleanor's department, which dealt mostly with finance affairs. It also helped Mathew to roughly know what went on in those two departments. 'Tanya is a good spy,' he had thought humorously.

Father and daughter walked around the garden, checking the flowers and fruits and talking about the plants and bushes, as well as trees that grew in an orderly distance and harmonised. Some of these were planted over two hundred years ago by his ancestors when they first brought these seeds or young plants into this country. They came round and sat down on the rocking chair.

"Gemma, darling," he said in his gentle tone, "you asked me several times. But I haven't given an answer yet."

She was staring out over the rough waves of the Atlantic Ocean. At the distance, she saw a passenger ship shuttle away. "What's Papa?" She asked, her eyes still on the ship far away.

He waited rather uncomfortably, "About the slave trade."

Gemma turned back and caught his eyes. "I like to learn, papa. That's all."

"I thought about it several times. But I am not sure of how to start this complicated subject or what to say about it." He paused as if unsure of himself. His eyes absently rolled away from her and watched the ship in the distance. "The slave trade sprouted as the first light of civilization dawned. And it strengthened through all nationalities and races." He turned to her and smiled. "I don't think I'm making any sense to you?"

She smiled back. "Not really!"

"Alright, let me put it in a hypothetical way. The first man was born in the African jungle. Evolutionary scholars are on this theme. God's man, Adam, is also in a jungle called Eden Garden, which is, in fact, next door to Africa. So let us say safely that our man was born in a jungle in Africa?"

She replied happily. "I like your narration."

"In a cave?"

"Again, you're right."

"By the side of a river for water? And shall we call the river the Nile River? Or the Congo River?"

"Yes, Papa. Water is important. And forest got an abundance of fresh air – two essentials to support life."

"Thank you, Gemma. And shall we name him 'cave-man'?"

"I'd name him simply, 'the first caveman."

He smiled agreeably. "If he's the first caveman, who are his parents?"

She laughed this time. "That's a hypothetical question. We ignore it."

"Alright, I agree to that!"

"However, he can take one woman to keep him company."

"Only one? Can't he take two? Or three? May be another Eve is still hanging around, and the snake. Anyway, he is the first man. He can set the rules, can't he?"

Without replying, she continued to laugh.

"Anyway, this time, he couldn't stay on in the cave. The caveman and his woman, their children, his parents and her parents and possibly other relatives – they all couldn't live in a cave."

"Too many for a cave!"

"Our Caveman put up a house. Maybe it's a mud house or timber shed. And in due course, their children grow up, and they need to live somewhere and then grandchildren when they grow." He stopped talking and thought briefly. "Houses after houses, they sprang up gradually. And the river banks changed into clusters of dwellings. You know what they call it?"

"No, Papa."

"Human settlements."

She remained quiet.

"Here, we see brothers work together and hunt the animals for food, or daughters feed the feeble relatives. Everyone is getting engaged in the running of the family."

"Delightful sceneries, I like it, Papa."

"As you see, there is harmony in these settlements. No abuse or slavery of any kind. And everyone lived peacefully."

Gemma didn't say anything.

He turned his face to look at her. "But you see, there are several other cavemen, too, moving out with their bigger families and building bigger dwellings and settling along the riverfront or across the open land between the forests. Centuries after, this is not simply a human settlement, this is more like a state. And they call it Chiefdom because their ruler is known as Chief."

"How does he become the Chief?"

"Obviously, he ought to be the best fighter and the quickest killer. Well, I didn't mean as I sounded. There are very good Chiefs as well."

She smiled.

"And he should take advises from a body called, 'The Council of Elders.' However, he is the supreme power and the rightful owner of the Chiefdom."

"What do the elders do?"

"The elders' duty is to agree with the Chief, and they, in return, get lands and gallant titles."

"In effect, a kind of democracy?"

"Not yet! Now we're talking about the birth of tribes, which means people in a territory with a language budding for communication – having similarities in food, clothes, and worshipping. A unified people, shall I say, with unified thoughts and views. And they are, therefore, the same people and known as the members of a tribe."

"Good. And we don't hear a word of any abuses or maltreatment from anyone, even from the ordinary people who work all day in the farm or fields to feed the family."

"Well, sadly, it's coming up now."

"How?"

"And there are numerous other tribes, too – living totally independent and different and secluded by mountains or forests or deserts." He paused and drew a deep puff. "The trouble is all these tribes don't necessarily respect one another. Each tribe believes they are the superior race. And each chief dreams to be the greatest among the neighbours or beyond."

"Why?"

"The answer lies in greed and wealth. They all want to be wealthy but wealthier than anyone else." He puffed his cigar again. "One chief and with advising body called 'the council of elders' is planning for attacks while the neighbouring chiefs are preparing to defend. In the middle, ordinary men and women who are legally barred from their free will but ordered into the battlefields."

"Very evil!"

"A mayhem for killings and burnings."

"Evil!"

"And this is about the time the civilization emerged."

Silently, Gemma sat there, looking at the ship in the distance. Its hull was completely disappeared behind the waves.

"Around this time, people's number doubled or trebled. Slowly, they spread across the rest of Africa and then started moving out to Asia and Europe through Arabia for better opportunities and faster progress. But they also took with them their practises of exploitation."

"As you see, Gemma, there were not enough jobs to go around for everyone. And not enough food for everyone. People, therefore, travelled to all parts of the world. Some went on their own free will, while others were lured or forced. It was not fair to everybody, but a rude system was established in the world, which legitimated people to trade on people. And it went on for millenniums in the old world, which meant three continents – Asia, Europe, and Africa."

"Very interesting, Papa," she said enthusiastically. "I am thoroughly enjoying it."

"What about the American continents and Australia?"

"Thank you. I was coming into them."

She was quiet.

"Europe was poor, then. Besides this fact, the local fighters in Persia stopped the vital supply of spices and herbs from India. We'd to find another safe route to India because India was then the centre of attention."

"Did we find?"

Without replying, he smoked. "Yes, we found through the sea. Around Africa, then round Arabia to India."

"Was this route okay?"

"Not really. Arabs pirates waiting along the routes to capture the goods and, worst, to kill us brutally."

"That's a shame!"

"Well, necessities bring other options. People started to think that if the earth is round, why can't we keep going to the west?"

"And then?"

"And then we come from the east and to India."

"Amazing, I didn't see that. Did anybody try to go?"

"Lots of sailors tried from Italy, Spain, and Portugal. And as they crossed the mighty sea, most of them died, especially in the early days. And whoever was alive threw away the dead bodies into the sea."

"Why?"

"Well. It's the open sea of thousands of miles. And nobody knew the way or what to expect along. And where were they going to bury the dead?"

"Very sad!"

Part 3: The New World

"However, some Spanish and Portuguese made the journey. They ended up in Caribbean islands and in the two unknown continents."

"Great."

"The Spanish and Portuguese settlements grew in the New World."

She was quiet.

"This created large-scale problems. They needed manpower for farming, agriculture, house building, road construction, and transporting."

"What did they do?"

"They went straight to Africa. There were about 15 countries who specialised in the enslavement of fellow human beings and selling them in the street."

"How do they get them?"

"Conquer the neighbouring countries and capture the people as prisoners. And there are cases they captured their own countrymen who opposed the regime."

"What was the blame against the Europeans?"

"Well, they bought the slaves."

"What did the Europeans say?"

"They freed them and gave them a better life in the new world."

"Was it absolutely true?"

"The discovery of the new world offered a wonderful hope to everyone. Whether you're the president of a country, the chairman of a company, or simply the breadwinner of a family, this new world offered them all a great opportunity in life. But these opportunities came with lots of risks and dangers and deaths."

Gemma waited for him to continue.

"This new world is far away, on the other side of a mighty ocean. And we didn't have the right vessels to cross it, neither the equipment to foresee the dangers ahead. And, tragically, millions perished in the big ocean from all nationalities and races."

"Were these sacrifices worth it?"

"I would certainly say yes. You see, now the richest country on Earth is in this new world. And the descendants of all nationalities and races are living there as equals. It's truly the greatest achievement of modern times."

Just then, Tanya appeared on the top of the garden, literally running down the grass lawn over the lane. Her white dress dazzled in between the bushes. "Tanya is earlier than she promised on the phone," Mathew said.

Gemma smiled amiably. "She knows I miss the games."

Tanya hurried down the lawn and then cut across the court. Finally, she reached by their side. She slightly stooped and kissed on his cheek.

"How are you, love?" He asked cordially.

"Thank you, Mathew," she replied, moving over to Gemma. "I'm okay." She stopped looking back to him. "But today wasn't a good day.

"Why?"

"The computer was down. Some important work got delayed. Jacob is frustrated, as usual. And Isabella is absolutely mad!"

"I hope they have contacted the maintenance company."

"Yes, Mathew. Anyway, I was producing a report on VIP rooms and facilities. I suppose I've made a good start."

"You like it?"

"I do," she said enthusiastically. "I do like it so much. Meeting the clients and talking with them. That's the job I like."

"Good. I put you in Victoria Wing."

"Oh! Victoria Wing? I love it. Thank you." She turned back to Gemma. She bent down towards her chair and held her warmheartedly. "Sorry for the delay, Gemma. But if you want to, we can start playing now."

"Not today," she said caringly. "You look exhausted."

"I'm tired. But, if you're free, what about going for a yachting?"

"Excellent!"

"You're not going out to sea?"

"Well, we can stay close to the shore."

"Where you are going? Falmouth?"

"That's nice. I wasn't thinking that. We could have their fish and chips on the dock."

"You're coming, papa?"

"No, darling. You girls have a day out. And sail carefully."

The girls rushed back to the house to tell the other girls, Pamela and Brenda! Another half an hour or so, they went out for the yachting trip. Mathew stayed in his office and ran through the tax papers that the auditors had prepared. His secretary Kathrine stepped in and sat on the opposite side. "You had a few calls when you were in the garden."

"Yeh?"

"I handled the majority of them. But there was a call from Atlantica."

He waited for her to continue.

"I don't think I got his name clearly. But he said he's the state secretary of APP."

"Was it Nelliken Johnson?"

"That's it. How do you know him?"

"He is Abigale's cousin. And once, he was our gardener."

"He's saying that his party is preparing to launch a severe complaint with the British Foreign Office. He's saying Abigale held here in Britain."

"This is nothing new. The oppositions always bring up fabrications about Abigale's disappearance when they have nothing good to say about the country. The opposition's leader is Kuthenco Adai, and he's an expert in fabricating promises."

"Do you know him?"

"Of Course, I know him. He was my car cleaner."

The secretary smiled cynically. "Now he is cleaning up the party?"

"No, more than that. If he gets a chance, he will clean up every penny they have in the country."

She laughed gently. "Good for him!"

"Of course. Now, he's promising heaven and earth to everyone in the country. But why didn't he do that when he was in power three years ago? For them, one policy when they're in power and the opposite policy when they're outside power. To be honest, just like here."

She continued laughing, "I disagree. Not as bad as here!"

He joined in her laughing but said, "Now he wants to talk about Abigale. And he wants to blame the British Government for her disappearance. Why didn't he do it when he was in power? Now he's blaming the British police. British systems are racist. It wins votes."

She continued to look at him quietly.

"The records show that Abigale took the baby and ran away. All departments – hospital, social workers, police – they all tried to find the mother and the baby. But they failed. And, finally, they concluded that they ferried to France and then went to Atlantica."

"Why do you think she ran away?"

"Abigale might have been fearful of the social workers at that time."

Confused, she stared at him.

"The social workers removed tens of thousands of newly born babies from their mothers."

"Good God! Why?"

"It's estimated that they removed forcefully over 500,000 babies for their grieving mothers. And they did it from the single mothers who couldn't afford to look after the babies."

"Really evil, how did they do this to those babies and their crying mothers!"

"One of the darkest eras in our long history. My philosophy is that we grin and bear it."

He waited sadly for a moment before he continued, "I did vast searches for Abigale in Atlantica for a long time. To be honest, it's still going on even though we found Gemma. And I dearly hope that Abigale will turn up one day."

Part 4: Meeting in Abigale House

He had a call after three weeks. He was in his office at the Hotel. And the call came on his personal phone. He stared at the phone for a moment, pondering who could be on the other end. "Hello," he whispered on to the mouthpiece.

A familiar male voice reached out on the wire. "Hello, Mathew."

He paused, wondering who it could be. "Stuart Campbell, the one and only CID of Cornwall?"

The man on the phone chuckled. "I always enjoy lavish introductions."

"I wasn't very sure. Just took a chance."

"I wouldn't blame you. We haven't spoken for a long time."

"You don't tell me where you're hiding."

He laughed quietly. "Are you in a meeting as usual?"

"No, for a change!"

"Anybody with you?"

"No, for a change."

"Where can we meet?"

"Why not in my office?"

"I don't know who is watching."

"Alrright. In the wine bar."

"I need privacy."

"Alright, in my house."

"I like your garden; it's a hot day. I don't mind the breeze from the shore."

"Alright, agreed. You bring the wine."

"I don't buy anything, Mathew. My fingers shiver when I touch money."

"As if I don't know that you're a stingy bugger!"

"That's fine, my friend. It's not as bad as what my wife calls me."

"What she calls you?"

"All sorts. But I don't hear. I go deaf."

Without speaking, Mathew laughed.

Stuart waited. "When can you arrive?"

"I've a meeting in half an hour."

"Cancel the damn thing. This is important."

"Very important, I guess?"

"Yes, very important for you."

"One hour?"

"Fine."

In one hour, they met at the Abigale House. They sat down on the stone chairs by the sea wall. The butler rolled a food trolley over the turf towards them. He left the trolley between them, then picked up some glasses from the trolley and placed them on the stone table. "Thank you, Barry," Mathew said good-naturedly. "We will manage."

Barry smiled. "Thank you, sir."

"I'm a giant, too, to walk away from responsibilities."

They laughed, and Barry joined in laughing. In the end, he started walking back to the house.

Mathew looked at the bottles neatly arranged on both shelves of the trolley. As he ran through the brands, he said proudly, "We've whisky, brandy, and wine. What would you like?"

"We'll have it in a minute," the CID whispered quietly while his eyes followed the butler, who was still crossing the garden but safely away not to hear their conversations. He looked back at Mathew. "We'll have it in a minute," he replied, obviously concerned. "Let's start on the subject."

"Okay."

The CID waited thoughtfully. "Do you know Cyril Baker?"

He searched his memory for a moment. "Not off hand, Stuart."

"You've heard of Margery Wilcots, haven't you?"

"Very well!"

"She was the midwife when Gemma was born."

He nodded silently.

"She was Cyril Baker's wife. He was also a hospital employee – a porter, in fact. They met each other there and got married. She was a widow and a good few years older than him. Her late husband was a farmer and left her with a small fortune. As soon as he heard about the fortune, he pleaded with her to marry him."

Mathew remained silent.

"However, he was also dating a girl - discreetly off course. Her name was Aliesha Browning – a much younger and audacious girl, much more of a darling to him. And Aliesha continued to stay in the background. Well, she was getting whatever she wanted. And yet, problems were there."

"I suppose Margery found out he was cheating on her?"

"No, Margery wants him to go to the police."

"Why?"

He stared at him curiously.

"And suddenly, Margery run away."

"What happened?"

"Nobody had a clue. In fact, it was a great shock to her colleagues in the hospital. And her dear friends in her parish church or in her neighbourhood. But they all said she was acting a little strange lately. Only Cyril Baker suspected she had some mental illness. For months on end, she suffered the pangs of agony and emotional depression – poor soul! And all this happened until last night."

"What about last night?"

"Last night, Cyril went out to see somebody. And Aliesha came to the police station."

"Ya?"

"She is so frightened?"

"Why?"

"She wants a new life. And with a new man?"

"Nothing wrong with that."

"But she's scared. She thinks he will kill her."

"Kill her?"

Yeh. Kill her like he killed Margery."

"Killed Margery?"

"Yes. Last night, she took us to the Devon Forest. And showed us where he buried her in the woods."

"Goodness gracious! How did Aliesha know it?"

"She was with him when he did this murder and covering the body."

"Why did she kill Margery?"

"I think I need a drink now."

"Wine?"

"No. Whisky. I need something very strong."

"Johnny Walker, Black Label?"

"I can manage with that."

Mathew picked up two whiskey glasses from the bottom shelf of the trolley and put them on the marble table. He opened the bottle and poured the drink for the officer first. The latter took his drink and drank a large sip while his eyes drifted over the rolling waves in the sea. Slowly, he started describing the events as they happened.

Part 5: Margery

It was January 9th of 1970, and the day was Friday – a terrible day in many ways. The weather was freezing to begin with. The icy gusts of wind lashed from the north all through the previous night, mingled with snowflakes and howling in the distance. The morning wasn't any exceptional either until around ten o'clock when the wind steadily calmed down, and the snow turned heavy, shutting out the outside and the sky above. The world shrank into a little bubble. She looked back, slightly alarmed, as she heard a knock on her door.

The door softly opened inward, and a woman appeared into the view. She stood there, her one hand holding on the handle and smiling; her eyes went past the room to the window. "Abigale, how are you, love?"

Abigale's face suddenly changed to a mixed expression of calm and blissful and happy. "Come in, Margery. I didn't see you at all today?"

Margery entered and closed the door behind her. She came further into the room. "Busy day today," she replied politely, smiling gently and meeting her eyes continuously. "Three deliveries this morning. And one was a difficult caesarean. Thank God we saved the mother and the baby." She paused and stood still for a moment. "And I saw your day sheet. And noticed that the nurses are checking you promptly."

Without saying anything, Abigale looked out the window. The snow was coming down heavily and swayed violently by the erratic wind. The view to the distance was seriously limited, and also by the faint frog formed by the breaking flakes of snow. She turned back to the midwife and looked at her face. The latter was viewing the scenery outside, and she whispered disappointedly, "I can't take you for a walk, Abie."

"In this weather? Even the duck will freeze to die."

Margery chuckled pleasantly, "I didn't mean into this blizzard, love. I meant the long corridor on the ground floor."

Abigale didn't speak immediately. Instead, she stared out again.

"The lift doesn't work. And, in your condition, I wouldn't dare taking you down the staircase."

She turned and stared at the midwife's face. "Whose fault is it that I'm here? I had a nice room on the ground floor, and the room window opened to a flower garden. Now I'm trapped on the fourth floor, trapped away from humans and voices." She paused, rather emotionally, and then continued somewhat angrily, "Your friend didn't like me being there. He disconnected the heating pipe in the empty room above me and destroyed my room."

Margery caught her eyes silently for a moment before she pulled a chair nearer and sat down next to her. "Abie, I've said to you about this. Cyril is a maintenance engineer. And he was laying a new pipe. But didn't tighten the joins enough. It's an unfortunate mistake."

Abigale didn't reply.

"Well, you like the sea, don't you? And you can see the sea rolling in the distance."

"I'm worried about you, too. I don't think you know him."

"Yes, love! That's true. As you know, we don't live together. He has his place. I've mine. And to be honest, we meet here. And that he visits me every now and then. And that's it."

A gust of wind lashed against the window and left plenty of snow on the panes, literally preventing the light from entering the room. Abigale watched it momentarily, then turned to her halfway. "Is it enough for a successful life with him, Margery?"

"I don't know, Abie. But I can say this much. At the outset, he's rough and violent. And when you know him, he's different. He's kind, loving, and caring."

She met her eyes this time. "I hope so, my friend. I dearly hope so."

Without saying anything, Margery laughed quietly.

The gusts of wind continued to blow, and each time, they dumped further flakes of snow on the window pane and on the ledge. The warm room temperature loosened the flakes on the pane, and slowly, they started to sketch their own diagrams as they slipped down. Quietly, they watched them casually, then Margery whispered, "Have you told everything about you and Mathew, Abie?"

She caught her eyes silently.

The midwife chuckled, "I wondered whether anything I could learn from you?"

She turned to the window, but nothing much she could see other than the cascading snow by the gales. The view of the sea was beyond her reach right now. Perhaps her mind recalled the past like the waves of the ocean, the same water surface but the waves different in sizes and shapes, and telling different tales. She turned to her and caught her glance. "My life was very simple. I was his servant. I washed his clothes, cleaned his room, and made his food. And then I saw him as he was. A super rich man, but very lonely and waiting for me to love him. I fell on his feet and worshipped him."

"Very lucky girl, you, Abie."

"No, dear, let me correct you. I was not the lucky girl. But the luckiest girl on earth. And everything between us was magic. But then, the military Junta took the power through a coup."

Without speaking, Margery continued to listen to her.

"Suddenly, the country changed. The militiamen spread the evil theories. The foreigners are abusing the kindness of the people and exploiting the economy. And they must quit the country. And I took my husband out of the city, and we fled to another province."

"Oh, I know it. You've told me that. And I still can't believe how you managed it. Running through the back street and through the country lane and then through the forest in the fading daylight."

"I had no choice. I've to take my husband to safety."

"I couldn't have managed it. And then crossing the ferry."

"In the ferry, my half-brother turned violent. I had to kill him in the end. When my husband's life is threatened, I've no country or brother."

Tanya was silent.

"But the police knew that I killed him. Immediately, Mathew sent me away in an English merchant ship."

"Why didn't Mathew leave with you?"

"He had thought he would be safe where he was. And that the Junta would've seized all our properties and other business assets."

"Where is he now?"

"The militiamen caught him in the end and put him in the prison."

"Have you spoken to him?"

"Impossible at the moment. Phone connections are cut off. No letters are permitted. The funniest thing is that people can't even send money into the country. And if anyone dares to send money abroad, alas, they will be executed in public places."

A few moments passed uneasily.

"How you are managing?"

"The original plan was to draw the money as and when I need it from our bank. Sadly, the junta closed down the foreign Branches. I had money that finished some time ago. And then Father Michael Hollings gave me some loans that's what's keeping me going for now."

Just then, a loud knock was heard on the door. The girls shot a glance at each other, then turned to the doorway. By then, the door swung open, and the figure of Cyril Baker stood behind it.

"Hi Cyril," Margery said politely, "you're okay."

He didn't answer directly. Instead, he said, rather unpleasantly, "I'll be in the café in 30 minutes."

Margery asked tactfully, "Come in. Say 'hi' to my friend."

"I've better things to do," he replied loudly while he pulled the door back to him and disappeared behind it.

Margery stared at her friend, clearly embarrassed. "Quite shy."

"How can he be? He was a union leader at the port."

"I'm sorry, Abie."

"What for? Aren't you, my friend?"

Margery smiled cheekily, "I try."

"This is the fourth time he opened the door like that since I came here three days ago."

"I'll have a word with him. Anyway, I'm sorry."

"Maybe he wants to know what I am doing inside. Or maybe he wants to see the layout in the room."

"What for?" she chuckled. "There is no floor above to cut the pipe from there."

"Well, the roof is there. He could remove the tiles."

She laughed. "He's not that bad."

Again, a knock was heard on the door. It was comparatively soft, though. The girls stared at the door immediately before they looked at each other. "Come in," Abigale answered.

The door opened softly, and Barbara Gilbert, the maternity ward matron, was there, holding a file in her hand. "I'm glad that nurse Margery is also here," she said courteously while walking towards them. "I have a few questions to clarify with Abigale."

"I'm sorry, Barbara. It's my lunch time. It's almost finished. I must get back quickly to my theatre."

"Alright, dear. I'm sure I can manage with Abigale."

Margery smiled. "I'm sure you will do." And then she crossed the room to the door and went out.

"You're okay? Can we have a little talk?"

"Of course, Matron."

"Thanks." She sat down on the chair Margery was sitting on. She opened the file she was holding and ran through a sheet full of scribbling. "The doctors are slightly concerned, dear," she said, looking back at the patient.

"I know. And I am also worried. Dr Alex had a talk with me yesterday. He said that the baby is overdue. And he estimates it's a week by now."

"That's correct," the nurse agreed quietly. "Any delay now can be dangerous for the baby, and it can be dangerous for you, too."

Without replying, she stared into her eyes anxiously.

She waited. "They have taken the decision unanimously that they've to stimulate the labour by induction."

She opened her mouth to ask something, but she chose to be silent. Obviously, she was more fearful about the answer than the question.

Suddenly, the nurse said as if she had realised her fear. "Nothing to worry about! We do this literally every day here."

Now, she found her courage and asked carefully, "If it fails?"

"I've seen your records. And I'm sure an induction should assist you for normal delivery."

"Please understand. I want my baby safe. My husband is so crazy about this child, whether it's a boy or a girl. Or whether it's black or white!"

Silently, the matron met her pleading eyes for a moment. "Your child is kicking and moving and healthy," she said respectfully. "And you've no reasons for any concerns. If induction fails, we'll consider a safe caesarean birth."

"Thank you!"

"We'll monitor you closely this afternoon and tonight. And then, in the morning, we'll decide what to do next."

"That's fine!"

"You have any other questions?"

"Please make sure our baby will be fine."

"We'll do our best all the time."

"Thank you."

A moment ticked away quietly while the matron ran through her file and then closed it. "Can I ask you a couple of questions?"

"Of course, matron. Please ask."

The matron looked out the window for a moment as if unsure of herself. Anyway, it was still snowing, though the density had lessened. She turned back and asked as if she remembered, "The police are investigating two cases?"

"Yes!"

"One was an incident in which you smashed the window of Tamar River Hotel!"

"I entered this country through Plymouth Dock. My husband sent a telex to a relative and asked him to meet me. But he didn't turn up. Or he didn't get the telex."

"That's bad."

"I asked around and found this hotel."

"That's a nice hotel."

"But I think the telex went to the wrong people."

"In his family?"

"Or maybe to his first family. I am his second wife. But I see a man always stalking me where I go. And one night, I saw a man standing outside my bedroom."."

"He was the hotel's night watchman."

"Maybe so. But I couldn't see him. He was wearing a hood. And when I saw him, he was behind the window."

"Maybe he was repairing something."

"Two o'clock in the night?"

Without speaking, the matron moved back in her chair.

"And he wasn't repairing. He was trying to enter into my room from the backyard."

The matron remained silent.

"I got frightened. The stalking man's face flashed through my mind. I grabbed my chair and smashed it on the window. The glasses burst to shatter on his face."

The matron spoke this time. "He lost one eye. And spent three months in the hospital."

"Well, I did it to protect my child."

A brief silence broke out again.

"What happened to the car accident?"

"Well, I used to see this car frequently, and I thought it's a crazy driver."

"Why?"

"He had almost knocked me twice before."

"Didn't report to the police?"

"No. But I had the weird thought that this man may be the stalker. Or a new stalker."

She waited for her to continue.

"On that day, I was going for my usual walk. And suddenly, his car appeared from round the bend and zoomed towards me. Luckily, a huge oak tree was on the roadside, and I threw myself to the back of it. But the man swirled too fast and lost control of the car."

"But you escaped?"

"Yes, thanks to God. But the car crashed into the oak tree and rotated back violently. It finally stopped into the low-lying field beside the road. The car was a complete ruin. And the man also was seriously hurt."

"But you hurt him too?"

"I went to see him to help. But he was swearing at me, calling me names, and then he got out of the car. And when he was up on his feet, he swayed towards me. He wanted to kill me. I've to be careful. My child is inside me. I kicked him hard where it hurts him the most."

Another silence erupted briefly.

"I suppose it's a matter for the police and the court to decide. And as I know, no verdict has been made on either of these cases."

"Not yet."

She hesitated. "If the judge finds you guilty, you've to go to prison."

"That's a long time away. I'm not thinking about it now."

"I'm afraid. You've to! Your baby is on the way in any minute."

"I said I'm not thinking about it."

"Alright, we assume you'll come out as the winner from the court."

"I strongly believe so."

"Good. Please tell me. Are you financially safe?"

"Not really!"

"You broke?"

"Yes, I admit I'm rather broke."

"Okay. Tell me, where are you going to stay? How are you going to feed, especially the baby?"

"I've to find a work."

"Going to work? Who is going to look after the baby? Child minder, I suppose?"

"I haven't looked into these things yet?"

"And the child's father is still in jail?"

"I've no news about him. The military government cut off all communications with the outside world."

The matron caught her eyes silently for a moment, then absently looked out the window. She couldn't see anything, though. The window panes were clouded with moisture or the snowflakes stuck on the outside. Slowly, she turned back and caught her eyes. "You're in a difficult situation, aren't you?"

She didn't reply.

"The baby's father is not with you. You've no other relatives with you. You have no home and no money."

"I know that!"

"And two serious court cases are there against you."

"I know."

"Isn't it worth giving your baby for adoption?"

"Madness," she retorted angrily. "I love my baby. My husband loves our baby. And I look after my baby until my husband and I meet again. And then we'll look after our child as parents."

"But the question is when?"

"I'm sorry I can't answer that."

"Please understand me. I am a nurse, and I look after them with their medical needs. But this is what the social workers will ask you."

"They have met me three times already."

"I know. But don't get me wrong. They have helped 350,000 mothers from 1945 to up until now."

"Yes. they told me. But I'm keeping my baby."

Part 6: Gemma Arrives

"Alright, Abigale. I hope you understand everything. Anyway, I see you tomorrow.

The next day that was Saturday, 10th of January 1970, they induced Abigale at about 10.30 in the morning. In half an hour or so, the pain of her contractions started on and off. About 2.30 onwards, the frequency of her contractions increased, and also the pain grew unbearable. In the evening, at 7:41, the baby was born. It was a girl, contrary to everyone's predictions of a lazy boy. And that she was bigger than a normal baby. Margery and Lizzy, the trainee nurse, cleaned her and then gave her a wash and dressed her in the clothes her mother had treasured for her. Margery put a tag on her hand with the name 'Gemma' – the name her mother had chosen for her if the child was a girl. She looked adoringly beautiful, and the nurses carried her one after the other in their arms and kissed her fondly. Abigale took another half an hour to wake up from her trauma. She grabbed her daughter and kissed her, crying hysterically, 'We love you, Gemma darling. We love you. Your mum and dad, we love you."

The mother and the baby moved back into room 39 at about 10 o'clock. Gemma slept on her side, her right hand gently passing across the baby's body protectively, and she kissed all the while on her crown. She also worried, as usual, about her husband. 'Where is he now?' she would ask herself. 'And what condition is he in? How will I let him know we have a beautiful daughter?'

On Sunday, the 11th, Margery was supposed to have her day off, but she volunteered herself for overtime because of Abigale, who was there with her baby. She took charge at about 9 am and went to see her friend. "How are you, love?"

Without answering, she met her eyes and raised a tired smile.

"You didn't sleep well? You look exhausted."

She smiled again. "I'm okay."

"Did you have your breakfast?"

"Yes?"

"The nurses keep popping up and checking up on you."

"They are good."

"Gemma is fine."

"No troubles, thank God. She sleeps like a doll." She paused, staring at her. "You think the social workers will come today?"

"They don't come on Sundays, Abie. Are you worried about them?"

She nodded gently. "They had already snatched "350,000 kids from their mothers.""

"It's not as bad as it sounds, Abie."

"What's it then?"

She hesitated. "Some girls have them without thoughts or love or preparation."

"Yeah?"

"They discard them at the doors of other people. Or worst, kill them."

"Yeah?"

"So, the government has to ensure these things won't happen again. And they made laws to safeguard the little babies."

"But I want to raise my child. I will adore her."

"I know."

"They will come on Monday?"

"Probably. And they will come again and again until they are sure that Gemma is safe with you."

"Only my heart will ache for her. Because she is my daughter."

"Please have a little sleep."

"How long are you here?"

"Until 9 in the evening! So, I will see you a lot today."

She smiled, this time pleasantly.

On Monday, the 12th, the social worker Jaison Milford and his colleague Joe Brown returned in the afternoon and met the matron Barbara Gilbert in her office. "The situation is very grave," Jaison asserted convincingly, looking at Barbara across the desk. "Abigale is a murderer in her own country, Atlantica. They could extradite her anytime, though the country is run by a junta. Here, two cases are closing on her. Her husband is in jail and in a foreign country run by a military junta. And, to my knowledge, she is penniless in this country."

"Very difficult situation! The child is in severe danger."

"Without a shred of doubt."

"What's your plan, Jaison?"

He picked up a cigarette, then got up and moved away, walking slowly. He lit a cigarette and drew a heavy puff on it, still walking. He stopped at the window behind the desk and blew out the smoke through the nostrils. He took another puff while he turned back to look at Barbara. "Abigale having further check-ups and treatment?"

"Yes!"

He returned to his chair hurriedly. "Is she having any further check-up or treatment?"

"Yes. On Thursday, we're removing the stitches."

"And she will be in the operation theatre?"

"Yes. About 2.30 to 3.00, I reckon."

"That's fine. Tomorrow and Wednesday, we're busy in other places with similar issues. And Thursday is fine. I can come with my colleagues, Dana Thompson and Francine Robson."

Barbara was silent.

"While Abigale in the operation theatre, we can take the baby to safety without any troubles."

She continued to be silent for another moment, uneasily. "I'm glad Thursday is my day off. I have no part in it?"

Catching her eyes, he sat down on the same seat he was before. "Barbara, see how many babies were found dead in their own homes. How many babies were discarded by their own mothers on others' doorsteps? Or garbage bins? Or buses?"

"Those were very cruel, too."

"What we are doing isn't a clear-cut solution either. In fact, this is no solution at all. But until we come to know something better, we've to protect the babies and mothers, and, in the end, we are saving our pride as a people, as a culture, and as a nation."

She didn't speak.

"A childless couple will adopt the baby and give her a happy world. And … and... Abigale could start a new life, whether or not she is inside the prison or outside."

"Don't forget that Abigale is very violent."

"I know. But once the baby is safely taken away, her violence won't make any difference." He paused thoughtfully. "We call the police if necessary. Or better yet, we can keep Cyril Baker there as if he's doing some maintenance on the radiator. Or lights. Margery also stays. Margery and Abigale are good friends."

"No, don't tell Margery. She will tell the secret to Abigale."

On Thursday, Margery was meant to cover the afternoon shift. However, they changed her rota on Wednesday evening and added her name for the morning shift, which would end at 2.30 pm. On Thursday, Margery couldn't finish her duties at 2 pm, though. She was very busy on her shift and couldn't complete the daily incident sheet on time. In the end, she stayed back to fill up the records. And the sooner she finished, the sooner she could go up and visit Abigale and then go home for the day's rest.

About this time, two nurses brought Abigale to her room in a trolley bed and assisted her to her bed. She lay on her back and hurriedly drew a couple of breaths before she turned to her side and looked into the cot. A terrified expression instantly crossed on her face. "Where is my baby?" she cried loudly, staring back at the door. She saw Cyril Baker first, sitting on the floor and mending the radiator, and the nurses had already gone out. "Where is my daughter?" She screamed at him, hastily raising her body and sitting up. "A nurse was meant to be here?"

"Are you crazy," Cyril retorted furiously. "I'm a bleeding nurse?"

She swiftly got up and held onto the headboard to steady herself on her trembling legs while the hand reached out to the alarm string and pulled it to convey the emergency to the nurses' office. But the string was broken, and the message didn't go any further. She fought her way towards the door behind him. However, he stood up straight and put his broad body in front of her. "Where the hell are you going?"

She didn't answer. Instead, she struggled near to him and threw her head ferociously onto his face. He swung on his feet, but he managed to deliver a heavy punch below her belly while he was tumbling to the floor. In the blinding pain that pitched from her head, he lost all his senses and, rolling over the floor frantically, ended on the door with his body pressed against it.

Abigale jolted back and leaned against the wall behind her. Bending on her knees, she stooped her body. She wasn't ready to go down to the carpet as she probably wouldn't get up. The excruciating aching on her head and stomach virtually froze her, as the agonising worry about where her daughter was taken to. She couldn't get out, as the huge body of Cyril lay against her body, and she wasn't fit at all to pull him away.

She sank down to the floor and crawled laboriously to the window. Probably, she could have opened the window and screamed as loudly as she could, and luckily staff on the floor below or people outside on the street might hear a cry. She reached by the window and, holding on to the sill, painfully raised herself up. Catching on the handle, she pulled up the window latch. But the window didn't move up at all. It's absolutely stuck in the freezing cold and falling snow, which have been a regular feature for the last few days. She stood calmly, then took a heavy breath of air before she turned back to the window. She hit hard on the frame a few times and, took another heavy breath of air, then pushed it up with all her strength. And the latched window slowly rose and rose enough to stick her head out, and she cried as loudly as she could, "Help, help, please somebody."

There was no reply. Or anyone asked who she was and what the problem was. In the falling snow, which was very dense at the moment, the road was deserted completely, and the windows below were shut tightly against the cold and the wind. Again, the gales were frequently lashing all day against the buildings and the wind howling at the distance fearfully as they advanced.

Abigale managed to make the gap under the pane a little bigger and pushed out her body up to her abdomen. Her hands were on her sides, and she clutched the frames firmly. She stared straight down the floors below and the road beyond, "Please help. Help."

No sound of response arrived.

"Help. Somebody help, please."

No response arrived.

By this time, she was absolutely showered with the falling snow, and the cold started stiffening her body. "And yet she cried out even louder than before. "Please help. My baby is missing. Please help."

This time, she felt somebody behind her. She became petrified and stared back inside while the snowflakes fell into her face and eyes. She gasped for air as she saw who it was. It was Cyril Baker. "Go away, you evil."

He didn't reply. Instead, he bent down and held her legs. However, she bent one leg onto the wall below the inside sill to balance herself and then kept kicking him hard with the other leg, and, in the meantime, she struggled to slip back into the room.

Just then, Margery's voice came from the doorway. "What are you doing, Cyril?" She asked in a petrified voice, running further into the room.

Abigale replied hurriedly, "He's throwing me out the window."

Margery couldn't do anything, though. In a split second, Cyril pushed her out the window.

As Abigale descended through snow and gale, she cried miserably, "Gemma darling, wait, mama is coming with you."

The gale lashed against her body. She swung in the air and her head on the sill of one of the windows on the ground floor rooms. She bounced off from where she hit, then stumbled down into the snow on the ground. She lay there on her side, her face downwards, though. Both her hands remained above her head as if she had tried to protect her during her fall. Her body had sunk into the heavy fall of snow, and nothing in her made any further motion of life except the blood from her head, which tickled down into the white snow. Slowly, the white snow around her head changed into a pink colour. More blood trickled slowly, and the colour changed again to red. Gradually, the red area grew into the shape of a circle.

And at the centre of the circle was Abigale's face.

Chapter 12

Abigale's Legacy

Part 1: Father Michael

It was a bright afternoon, and the time was close to 2.30. From the southwest direction, a steady breeze blew over the fields at the distance and caressed along the slope towards the top. Mathew drove to the car park, which was on the side of a small church on the lower part of the hill. He came out and locked the car door, then turned to glance at the presbytery, which was halfway up the hill on the east face, before he started walking up the stoney steps towards there. Bushes and plants with beautiful foliage spread over the sides of the steps and all the way up.

The presbytery was a small building, and its white walls gleamed down between the greenery. It stood on a straight plot with a spacious forecourt. He walked over to the entrance and rang the bell. A couple of minutes later, the door opened partially, and an elderly woman appeared. "Good afternoon, sir," she said, looking at him studiously.

"Good afternoon," he said politely. "I'm Mathew Atkinson. I've an appointment with Father Michael Hollings. But I'm sorry I arrived a few minutes early."

Fr. Michael Hollings was passing through the inner room and heard the conversation on the porch. "Arriving earlier is always better, Mathew," he said quickly and said it rather loudly to reach his voice at the front. "Janet, please let him in."

"Okay, Father," she replied, removing the chain lock and then opening the door fully.

He entered into the hallway. "Thank you."

"Janet, Take Mathew to my study, please," the priest's voice reached through an inner door. "I won't be long, Mathew."

Janet took him to his study room and, gesturing him to a couple of chairs in front of a desk, said, "Please take a seat, sir." He went further into the room and sat down on a chair.

And the priest turned up. "Janet, I've heard of Mathew about seventeen years ago," he chuckled. "But we never met."

Mathew smiled faintly. "I've heard about Father Michael two years ago. But we never had the chance to meet."

Janet looked slightly confused. "How did you hear about it?"

"His wife told," the priest answered quickly. "She attended the parish I served."

"In my case, it was sheer luck. Mark Windrush, a prison guard, managed to find Fr. Michael."

She hesitated. "Definitely, you've a lot to talk about." She paused briefly. "Can I offer a hot drink? Or something cold."

"A glass of water is nice. And thank you."

"And you, Father?"

"Water, please, Janet."

She went to the kitchen.

Michael sat down in his chair. "Did you find the way alright?" He asked, looking across the table at him.

"It was fine. Your instruction on the phone was spot on."

"Good."

Janet brought two glasses of water on a tray. She put the glasses in front of them. "Father, if you need me," she said, holding the tray in her hand, "I'm in the office."

"Thank you, Janet."

She left.

"Have you got time, Mathew? Or do you need to rush back?"

"I've all the time in the world, Father."

Michael waited vaguely for a moment. "You want to talk about Abigale."

"Yes, Father. The more I hear, the more I feel at peace. As if I'm close to her."

"I answered your question, whatever I've known. And we talked a few times. But I think we didn't cover the beginning."

"Anything will help, father. You're the last person who has seen her."

The priest moved forward in his chair and, picking up his glass, had a mouthful of water quietly. He put the glass back on the table. "I belong to a small congregation of missionaries. And we travel a lot, mostly abroad, for our work. But 17 years ago, I stayed in St Jude's church in Plympton for a short while, mainly to assist the parish. There aren't enough priests to go round. People are not coming for God's work."

Mathew remained silent.

"On that day, I said my morning mass. I changed my vest in the sacristy and went to lock the church front door and turn off the lights in the hall. Normally, the mass boys or girls do these things. Or the assistants show up.

Normally, six or seven elderly people attend a midweek morning mass, and they are out even before the mass finishes. There is no heating in the church, honestly speaking, to reduce the expenses wherever possible. I came up to the church hall, locked the front door, and then went back to the sacristy door where the switches for lights were. And then I saw a girl in one of the back pews."

Mathew opened his mouth to ask whether it was Abigale. Nonetheless, he waited for the priest to continue.

"I stopped at the end of the row, looking at her."

"She didn't say hello to you?"

"No. And I don't think she even knew I was there."

Without saying anything, Mathew looked at him intently.

"The girl was praying on her knees. She was slightly stooping forward with her face in her hands and her elbows on the back of the pew in front of her. 'Are you alright, my dear child?'

She didn't reply.

"I went further to her through the front row. 'Are you alright, dear child?'"

This time, she raised her face from her hands. Her eyes were wet with tears, and the tears were trickling down on her face. She didn't speak yet, but she simply nodded her head for an answer that she was fine.

"I take it that you're fine?"

She nodded her head again, catching my eyes.

I went next to her and stood facing her. "But the tears in your eyes and face are telling me something different."

"I was praying for my husband."

"Husband? What's the problem?"

"He is in prison."

"In Plymouth?"

"No, Father. He is in Atlantica."

"Good Lord! You had a coup lately?"

She beckoned her head for a response as if she was too shattered to speak.

"Now a new government run by a military regime?"

She repeated her beckoning.

"I don't think I've asked your name yet."

"Abigale."

"And the last name?"

She waited uncomfortably. "I'm very sorry. Shall I keep it to myself for the time being, please?"

"Of course. Any reason for it, if dare ask?"

"He's a popular man. Very rich and powerful. I can't humiliate his name."

"Well, I can appreciate your thinking on it. You're a fine reason. But whatever you do, please don't go back."

She shook her head strongly. "I have a murder case against me, Father. And, besides, I'm pregnant for five months."

"You've to be very careful now, Abigale."

"I know, Father. I won't do anything that harms my child."

"Mathew knows about the baby?"

"Yes, Father. He sent me here for the baby's safety. And, of course, to escape from the murder charge on me."

He stared at her caringly. "You look tired. I don't think you had your breakfast yet?"

She didn't reply immediately. "I don't eat breakfast these days, Father."

"Why? You're supposed to eat for two people now, aren't you?"

She glanced away without replying.

"That's good for me," he chuckled pleasantly. "I don't eat breakfast before the mass. And when I eat, I'm normally alone. Today, I'm glad I got company."

"Isn't it too much for you, Father?"

"Not at all, dear, when God is willing."

"We went to the priest's house which is at the back of the church. The dining room and kitchen were together in one room. She sat on a chair at a small table, and I checked the snacks in the fridge and on the shelves. "I've got more choices than normal."

Without replying, she smiled.

"You can have egg on toast or toast with egg."

She laughed amusingly. "It's the same thing, Father."

I watched her laugh before I replied. "Well, it sounds plenty!"

I toasted the slices of bread. She fried the eggs. I normally take the tea, but she preferred the coffee. We made the toast and the drinks. Then she sat down on the same chair. I sat on the opposite. "It's all okay. Where are you staying?"

She didn't answer as if she didn't understand.

I changed the subject. "This is your first baby, I take?"

"Yes, Father."

"And the baby is fine."

"Thanks God. It's fine."

"You check?"

"Not yet."

"You've a GP?"

"No."

"Why?"

"I haven't got a stable accommodation yet, Father."

"Your accommodation isn't okay?"

"It's not all that okay, father."

"What do you mean?"

"It's very difficult to get a room."

"Don't you look at the housing advertisements?"

"I do, Father. But everybody doesn't want to give me room." She chewed the food in her mouth and swallowed slowly down the throat. "Can I talk frankly, Father?"

"Of course!"

"I don't think I am not very welcome here."

"I'm sorry to hear it. You may find some people not very friendly."

"It's my colour." She took another bite and started to chew on it. "And money," she said while chewing. "They ask me more money than what they are advertising for."

"You are managing alright with money?"

"Not really. I am trying to work. I need it desperately now. My few pounds are going out faster than I can think."

Michael finished his toast and tea. She finished her food as well. "Please wait for a moment." He went up to his room and returned. "I've few pounds. Nine pounds, in fact. Please keep it with you."

"I'm alright, father, at the moment. Anyway, thank you so much for your kindness."

"You ought to have it. I insist, please."

She accepted it reluctantly. "I'll pray for you, I promise."

"Thank you for that. And see me on Thursday, the day after tomorrow. Hopefully, I will have some good news. And see me in the morning."

Without speaking, she looked at him. "My surname Hollings. There are a few Hollings in the South West, and mostly in Cornwall and Devon counties. Some run businesses. Probably, one of them can give you work."

"Thank you, Father," she replied, suddenly feeling uneasy. "I pray for you."

"You've to forgive me for now. I have an appointment. A very elderly lady is poorly and at home all alone. I've to hear her confession and give her the Holy Host."

"Oh, I'm sorry!"

"Please see me on Thursday."

"Father, I can't come out as I wish."

"What do you mean?"

"Someone is following me."

"Is it true?"

"She nodded. "And I'm in two police cases. One serious assault and one attempted murder case."

Michael sighed heavily. "Okay, I come and see you. You don't come."

"Thank you."

"And you don't go yourself. The church secretary, Joyce, is here. She will drop you at your address."

"Oh, Father. You're ever so kind."

On Thursday at 10.30, Father Michael Hollings turned up at her doorstep with his cousin brother, Simon. Simone had a chain of pharmacy stores, and its head office was in Plymouth. He gave Abigale a bookkeeping job in the office above the Plymouth store. In her duties, she didn't need to deal with outsiders. Another beauty of this job was that it came with accommodation facilities in a two-bedroom flat just above the office. The other room had been occupied for the last two to three years. It was a young woman who had been the resident there, and her name was Margery Wilcots.

A FEW TALES

At this juncture, Mathew interrupted quietly by saying, "Father, I thank you for everything you have done. But I couldn't do what I had wanted to do. The speed of political changes was so furious and fast, and my intentions for her slipped away even before I realised them."

Without speaking, Michael sat quietly and listened to him.

"The military coup of 1969 overran the democratic government at about 3.30 on August 19th. The news of it reached across the country at the 4.30 news bulletin on the national radio, which was also confiscated by the junta and produced its own political propaganda. The country gripped on its core existence. Atlantica had seen several coups in the past, but it had a system of leaks in drips and drabs before it hit the powerhouses. This time, no news was received. Even the news leakers were frightened to death because the fearful force destined to take on the crown was Field Marshall General Thylakoid Thaman Thirona, in short, Triple T.

When he was a teenage boy, he used to sell water on the Atlantic Ocean front for the farmers to drink. A year or two later, he started selling fish to the households along the lanes in the nearby villages. In a short period, he opened up a fish stall in the market. When he was 19, he organised a labour union, first in the market and then in the city. The rules and regulations of the union were not adequately thought about or logically put together, but not everybody questioned them because he was 6 foot 5 inches tall and hugely built. When he was 21, he joined the army, and the rest of his career was open to anyone's imagination. When he was 27, he became field Marshall general of the army, which controlled the National Air Force and the Navy. On Friday, 19th of August, 1969, he had an appointment to see the State President. He marched into the presidential Palace, saluted the present, and then asked, "Mr President, you want to quit and leave the country alive?"

The terrified president chalked for air before he struggled to speak. "What you're talking about? This meeting is scheduled for funds for guns?"

The General became very irritant. "You can't understand a simple question. You are too old. You shouldn't sit on the president's chair." He suddenly drew his gun and fired. The president fell off his chair to the sumptuous carpet. Two of his bodyguards ran to him, reaching for the guns on their sides. Swiftly, the general shot them into their chests. The president and the two men died instantly.

And as this news came out, Abigale screamed, "Let's flee." But where could they flee to? The airport was ordered to close even if there were no flights coming in or going out. So was the story of the harbour. Closed. Roadblocks were everywhere. And checkpoints were at every junction. And the Atlis Bridge brought fully under the control of the army."

"Abigale said to me about your frantic escape through the country."

"Yes, Father Michael. It was frantic and very risky. And at several points, I honestly thought we'd never make it."

"And her stepbrother tried to harm you in his ferry in the Atlis River. But she killed him and saved you."

He looked at the priest steadily. "True, Michael. She loved me so much. I don't think I ever had the time to tell her."

"No, Mathew. She knew well you never took an easy breath until you got her safely in that ship."

"Oh! That ship, Atlantic Queen," he said, sighing. "It was sheer luck, Father Michael. It was a merchant ship that was scheduled to leave Maddanko on 18th August, two days before. But a fire broke out in the engine room on the 16th, delaying the departure. And Triple T didn't even know the Queen was still in his waters. Otherwise, he would have confiscated."

"Bit of luck for you at last."

"When the ship was in the international waters, I said to myself, 'At last, Abigale is free."

"Good luck, Triple T didn't know it. He would've confiscated the ship. And thrown Abigale into prison."

Mathew didn't say anything for a moment. "But I made a serious mistake when I look back."

The priest stared at him silently.

"I asked the ship's Captain, Lawrence, to send a telex to Richard when they reached Lisbon. But Mr. Triple T immediately disconnected all communication systems in Atlantica."

"Who is Richard?"

"Richard is my ex's cousin. I had to inform someone that Abigale is coming and take good care of her."

Without saying anything, the priest stared at him impassively.

He knew what the priest was thinking. "Well, Richard is a good friend of mine, too. And I was in Maddanko. I didn't have any other contact details. The coup news shocked the whole country. Our priority was to escape from the Triple T, also known as the Great Rabie. And we ran away from home in Atlantica City."

"Obviously, you couldn't imagine what would happen and what you would need!"

He was silent for another moment before he started talking, "I had always thought that Captain Lawrence had phoned but some wrong people picked up the message. I didn't mean my ex-wife directly. Maybe someone in her family got it."

Michael didn't speak.

"The day after Abigale left Maddanko, the military arrested me. I stayed in the Nagaland Prison for three years until the last day of Triple T, who was then killed in a shooting in the palace. Alunka Addai, another extremely violent and ruthless, took the power. Another eighteen months later, Alunka was killed in a ceremonial shoot out at the country's Independence Day celebration and…..."

Michael interrupted him. "Definitely, that was a great celebration!"

"Yes, because this killing made the way for independence."

Michael didn't speak.

"I was freed shortly. I met Abigale's relatives and asked about Abigale. All of them said that she had always been in the UK during the military rule. I phoned various people in the UK. None of them knew her or had heard anything about her. I rushed to the country and made all sorts of enquiries. Unfortunately, there was no news about her. Eventually, I came to believe that, somehow, I lost her forever."

Michael was quiet.

"And then, Mark Windrush turned up with the artefact of carving that I gave to her on her 21st birthday."

"I kept it safely for 15 years."

"Thank you, Michael. It opened up a new world for me. In fact, I found our daughter."

"I'm pleased to hear that."

"Mark is a clever boy. He did lots of searches to find Abigale and me."

"I like him very much. He's a very determined boy."

"Yes, Michael. He is. And we went back to the hospital. But the hospital changed. Gemma was born in the old hospital that was restored from a disused military barracks. And during the development changes, they lost most of the records, they said. But the records they had showed that Abigale suffered a kind of phobia during the pregnancy."

"I disagree with that. When I knew her, she was as good as anybody else."

"And after the childbirth."

"I don't believe any of these."

"And she jumped out of the window and killed herself."

Without saying anything, Michael stared at him for a moment before he said gently. "Don't believe any of that. She was too intelligent to do anything that nasty."

"And no parents around, they let the baby go for an adoption, as they did it on those days."

"That's true, Mathew. It's estimated about 500,000 babies were removed forcefully from their mothers and given them for adoption. The safety of the babies of single mothers or separated women was paramount. Unfortunately, the authorities took the law for their own interpretations. Thousands of mothers and babies would have been a lot happier and safer if the mothers and babies were allowed to stay together as the way nature had intended." The

527

priest paused, looking at him. "Anyway, you're lucky. At least, you got your child alive and well."

He didn't reply.

"When Gemma was born, I wasn't in the UK. I was in Jerusalem on a theological course. And when I came back, I saw my cousin, Simon, to find out about Abigale and her child. He said she stayed in a ground-floor flat before the baby was born, and then she moved out to a bigger flat for her child's convenience. Shortly after, Margery moved out to another flat. And he hadn't seen any of them since then. And gradually, I thought Abigale had gone back home."

"I wish that was true."

Michael waited thoughtfully for a moment. "Now, we know what had happened to Abigale. But we don't know why it happened. Probably, we will never know."

Mathew didn't speak. His face reflected the expression of distress surging inside him.

"It could be jealousy, selfishness, or racism. And they are still there, whatever may be."

Staying silent, he stared at the priest.

The priest caught his eyes steadily. "This is what I want to say. Please take good care of yourself. And in the case of Gemma, provide the best protection around her because her mother was Abigale. The forces against Abigale are still there. Remember this all the time."

"This has never been out of my mind, Father Michael," he said quietly. "The security around the house is unbreakable. The security guards are active everywhere in the building complex. The surveillance cameras are positioned in such a way that they can pick up any intrusion from any angle."

"That sounds good."

"She has a tennis court on the seafront. A lovely running track on the cliff side, she loves running a lot. And a hall for karate practises. She hopes to get the black belt title, hopefully soon. A piano hall where a teacher comes three days a week and teaches her. And 2 or 3 times a week, she goes for yachting. And she really loves it. "

"Good. You should have brought her with you."

"I would have, father. But she's taking a correspondence course in French. And next week, she is having some tests."

"Wonderful!"

"And I teach her Atlantis. She should know what her mother used to speak."

"I'm really happy now, Mathew."

Part 2: Taking to Aliesha

Aliesha Royle was in the meeting room when Mathew entered. He walked further and stood in front of a couple of chairs a few feet away from her. She looked about 40 years old and had a graceful appearance. However, he could tell she was nervous and frightful inside. She was standing still, and her scary eyes on him steadily. "Why don't you sit down," he said gently while he took a seat in one of the chairs behind him.

She didn't sit down. "Who are you, sir?" She asked, her voice heavily cracking with tension.

"My name is Mathew."

"Are you from the police department?"

"No," he said easily.

She interrupted him hurriedly. "From the legal department?"

"No." He stopped and noticed her standing nervously. "Why don't you sit down."

Aliesha waited a moment. "I don't know the difference between sitting down and standing up."

"No?"

"No, sir. Or day and night in my cell."

"Please sit down, Aliesha. We can have a talk."

"Are you from the media?"

He smiled faintly. "No. Perhaps you may remember Abigale Agu."

For a split second, her body shivered visibly. However, she didn't speak

"Abigale was my wife."

She stared at him all the more fearfully.

As if to reduce her tension, he said quietly, "In fact, she was my girlfriend. Because we weren't married."

This time, she sat down and cast her eyes on the floor. "I remember Abigale very well. To be honest, I remember her every day."

He didn't speak immediately. Instead, he looked at her studiously, "Do you remember Abigale, Aliesha?"

She scratched her neck, clearly anxiously. "She was a lovely lady. I liked her very much."

"I'm glad to hear that."

She raised her face and looked at him. "I can swear on my life that I have nothing to do with Abigale's death. And I didn't know a thing about this. My boyfriend did it. And I'm genuinely sorry. He was an evil."

He caught her eyes steadily for a moment. "But you loved him?"

"I did. And I loved him so much before I knew him. That's my mistake. And I feel terrible about it."

"Lots of people do that."

"But I loved the worst evil. I must have been absolutely stupid."

Silently, he looked at her calmly.

"I hadn't talked to Abigale a lot. I didn't get the chance."

"Why?"

Abigale was normally with Margery. Cyril introduced Margery to me as his workmate. I had known him for five or six years before that."

Mathew was quiet.

"And I had few lessons that I shouldn't believe everything he says."

"I like this conversation. It's helping me with my purpose."

"What's that? My God, I'm in more trouble?"

"I have no intention to give you trouble, Aliesha."

She stared at him frightfully. "What d'you want?"

"I want to ask him why he threw my wife out of the window." He paused rather sadly. "I will ask him this if I meet him. But that won't happen. He is under the ground."

She didn't reply. He cast her eyes on the floor and moved from side to side as if she was distressed. In the end, she said, "Can I talk to you in my own way?"

"Of course."

"My talking is not very good."

"My impression is just the opposite, Aliesha Royle."

Without replying, she continued to sit. Still, her eyes cast down and moving in her chair crazily. "I met him in 1965," she started to talk. "I was 17 years old then. And he was 26. He came to the accounts department where I worked. He went up the aisle to the manager's desk, and my eyes followed him almost eagerly. He stood in front of the desk and began whispering with the manager. I stared at him constantly, his back towards me. I don't think I had breathed until he left the office, but I knew I was in love with him. The shame about it all was that I didn't even know his name."

"A week later, I knew he worked in the building maintenance department. His name was Cyril Baker. Another week or two later, I bumped into him in the staff canteen. We were at a table, having lunch. I nervously looked at him, but he continued to sit, staring away as if there was nothing around him to look at. Ultimately, I decided to break the ice and start the conversation. I had a bite of toast in my mouth, and I chewed quietly and swallowed it absently. I wanted to talk to him. I'm not scared to talk to anybody. I'm from St Ives in Cornwall close to the Atlantic Ocean...."

"St. Ives, did you say?"

"Yes, Mr Atkinson. But not proper St Ives. I'm from a little hamlet behind it called St Helen. Strictly speaking, four or five houses in the middle of nowhere. There, we knew who the neighbours were, and were not scared of talking to anyone, and trusted each other. Anyway, that was my personal experience with people. Anyway, I swallowed down the food and looked straight at him gently. "How are you, Cyril?"

He had the cup of tea in his hand and slightly held it away from his mouth. Slowly, he brought the cup to his lips and took a sip gently, but he thoroughly ignored my question and didn't even turn his head to give me a casual glance.

I gently joked, 'Have you checked out your hearing aid lately?'

He didn't respond. Instead, he finished his drink and walked away quietly as if nothing had happened.

After this, I didn't see Cyril for some time. Because he was in jail."

"Why?" he asked.

"He had a fight with someone in the pub. In fact, he was helping a female friend of his. But his friend didn't back him up when the police questioned him. And Cyril ended up in jail. He didn't seem worried about it, though. I heard he had been in prison a few times."

"And again, I met him in the staff's canteen. We were sitting nearby at two tables, and I saw him looking at me every now and then. I took my food and went to him. "Is it okay if I share this table with you?"

He looked at me silently for a moment, then looked down and sliced up the steak on his plate.

I asked clearly annoyed, "Can I use the chair on this side?"

He shot an angry glance at me. To my surprise, he said, "Yes."

We had a little talk, which helped us to have a relaxed understanding. We agreed that we would meet frequently. A month later, I went out with him for a music show. We danced for hours, and while we danced, I kept whispering to his ears, "I've always thought about you."

Without replying, he smiled.

Two weeks later, she moved in with him. It was a nice cosy home on the slope of a hill, with the view of a tributary on the right, the woodlands at the front, and the blue waters of the Atlantic Ocean beyond. The master bedroom looked up the hill at the back, and the rising sun appeared through the foliage in the morning. He guided her to the master room, and she settled there, and he slept in the guest room. Days went one by one. Then, weeks rolled into months. Her private thoughts started to make her nervousness unbearabe. One night, she stormed into his room. "Why are you ignoring me?"

He didn't reply immediately. "Please go to sleep," he said quietly. "We will talk tomorrow."

"No," she retorted harshly. "Why can't we talk now?"

"Alright." He got up, grabbed the gown from the hanger, and slipped into it. "Come to the terrace. It's quite warm."

She followed him to the terrace at the back of the building, facing the east. They didn't switch on the light. The night wasn't very dark. Numerous stars shone from the cloudless sky. The eastern horizon was fairly bright over the hills. It wasn't midnight yet; maybe the moon was about to rise. She pulled her nightshirt tight around her body and sat down on a wooden chair. In fact, the night was warm and pleasant. He didn't take a seat. Instead, he stood by the side of a wooden pillar and leaned against it. He searched for a pack of cigarettes from his gown and extended it to her. She took a cigarette and placed it between her lips. He lit his lighter and held it close to her mouth. She drew on it, ignited her cigarette, and fumed on it. He leaned back to the pillar and lit a cigarette. The burning end of it glowed through the dark. "I know you want a relationship with me," she whispered softly, letting the smoke out through his nostrils.

"You took six months to find out that?"

"I saw you earlier than that."

Without speaking, she stared at him rather angrily.

"Everybody knows you."

"Why?"

"I don't know. Maybe the way you look."

"Oh! That's refreshing."

He took a deep puff and blew out. "I'm not ready for a relationship. Maybe I never will."

"Is it right? I hear you got other women?"

"You didn't listen. I don't have any relationship."

"What about the women."

"Yes, they are women. And they take the money and go."

She struggled to restrain her anger before she screamed, "What an evil you're?"

He fumed on his cigarette, casually staring over the hill. At a distance, a huge crescent of the moon was partially rising into the view from the back of a band of clouds. He fumed again, then said morosely, "I am enjoying my life."

She smoked her cigarette absently, but her eyes stared at him through the darkness. "What did I do to treat me without respect?"

There was a calmness for a short while as neither of them spoke a word. "I can't even remember my dad's face from when he joined the army in 1941. I was a boy of two years old. My dad joined the army and took on the Germans." He paused as if unsure of himself. "While my father was taking on the Germans on the battlefield, my mother started an affair with a grocer. She had run away with her new man when he returned after the war. My dad took the bottles to steady down his nerve and died in the end in his vomit."

She continued to sit silently, looking away at the horizon. The crescent moon rose further up and glowed through the trees' high foliage.

"I stayed with my granddad. But when I was 9, he died of a heart attack, and council authorities put me in a care home. Eventually, I was freed when I was 16. The memories of the treatment I had received there still haunt me. And I have no respect for anybody since."

She didn't say anything.

"As soon as I was free, I started working in a restaurant in Piccadilly in London and worked as a cashier. And I met Cynthia. She used to come for meals. She was a theatre dancer two doors away. She was an amazing girl. She said she always loved me from the moment she first saw me. She wanted to marry me but delayed it as if she couldn't decide on the time. In the end, she came up with a date. It was too quick for me, but I agreed it. I was 21, and she was 19. I organised a church wedding. And then, on the night before the wedding day, she ran away with her dancing choreographer. I spent every penny I had. And borrowed every penny I could get. But what do I have now? Shame! I left London immediately and lived in Cornwall with my dad's brother."

Aliesha stared at him silently. The cigarette between her fingers burned, and smoke rose untraceable in the dark.

"On the night my finance left, I decided – no more woman in my life."

"I'm sorry to hear all this."

He didn't speak.

"If you don't mind, can I ask you a question?"

His cigarette was in his mouth. He drew deep on it and blew out the smoke through his nostril. He replied, "Yes."

The moon came over the hill, and its light swelled cosily into the terrace. She could see him meeting her glance. "What's your relationship with Margery Wilcots?"

He steadily met her eyes as if recollecting the past. "Nothing special. Her husband, Jack, and I were friends. We worked together in the Atlantic Hotel. I met them occasionally in their house, or maybe in nightclubs, before Jack died in a car accident." He finished the cigarette and threw the butt away. "You've seen her. She is a great lady. Why can't I continue my friendship with her?"

Suddenly, a petrifying thought flashed across her mind. Had Cyril played any part in his car accident? She didn't ask. She was too scared.

He turned and sat down on a chair close to her body. "It's getting cold," he said, putting his arms around her body and holding her even closer. "Why can't we go in and sleep together? I know you like it."

537

She was so scared to say anything but nuzzled in his arms breathlessly.

On that night, they slept together.

Mathew didn't speak. To be honest, he was feeling completely disgusted with Aliesha's words. She feared whether Cyril had a hand in the accidental death of Margery's husband, and at the very same moment, she was getting cuddled by the suspected killer and sleeping with him for the first time in her life. Finally, he asked, respectfully, "How did you manage to sleep with him that night?"

"I wasn't thinking straight."

"And you continued to stay with him?"

"I said I wasn't thinking straight. Or that he spent so much money on me."

He waited silently for her to speak.

"He used to give me stylish clothes. And expensive pieces of jewellery! He took me on holiday to different countries every two to three months. He had no care for money. Or short of money."

"Where did he get his money, if I may ask?"

"Of course, sir," she said. She stopped talking as if bringing the past into her thoughts. "He had contacts with rich, influential people like our financial director, Miss Isabella Roscoe."

He moved back in his chair, rest on the back, and looked at her with fixed eyes. "How do you know Isabella Roscoe?" He asked cautiously. "Did you work in her department?"

"Yes and no."

"What do you mean?"

"I worked in finance as a junior clerk. But I don't see Isabella at all in my daily routine. But I saw her in the staff meeting, and she used to give us small speeches about efficiencies in businesses and the importance of accounting." She stopped again.

"If the businesses are operated shrewdly, everything will collapse as they happen in Africa."

Silently, he waited for her to continue.

"She used to laugh and say, 'Africans walk on gold and diamonds, and also on empty stomachs. In another language, she says they are rich and stupid."

Mathew hesitated patiently. "I was born in Africa. And I grew up in Africa."

"Really?"

"They are not stupid. The problem is they are too innocent. Yes. They are poor because the political situation is not fair to the countries and people. Their own leaders abuse them. And foreign powers exploit them, too."

"That's what I had heard. But Miss Isabella Roscoe hates the African."

He waited briefly, rather uneasily, before he asked, "How do you know Cyril Baker had contact with Miss Isabella Roscoe?"

"Well, it must have been more than contacts. He used to drive her home in her car. I've seen that. And there were whispers that they were having an affair. But other rumours were also there that her affairs last only for a short while." She was silent as if unsure of herself. "But I don't know anything about these. I left that job in 1968."

"You left the job one year before we divorced."

539

Suddenly, she fell silent as if focusing on his words. "Divorced who?" she asked nervously. "You didn't mean Isabella Roscoe?"

"I'm her ex."

She was petrified. "Oh my God," she exclaimed breathlessly. "Was I too blunt? Am I going mad?"

"You've nothing to apologise, Aliesha," he replied gently. "I've heard a few episodes like this when she was legally my wife." He was silent, obviously lost for words. "But it didn't matter to me now. We had divorced a long time ago."

"Oh, thank you. I thought I said something stupid."

After a brief silence, he asked softly. "Can I ask you something? Just to understand about different lives."

"Of course, sir. Please do!"

"What kept you loving him all this while."

She smiled, somewhat confused for a moment. "First of all, sir," she said, casting her eyes on the floor. "I didn't have anyone to call my own. I don't know who my father is. My mother never talked about him. I gather it vaguely that she was raped. The name Royle is my mother's. When she fell pregnant, her parents chucked her out of home. It was too humiliating for them." She stopped talking for a brief while. "When I was sixteen, I started to work. I couldn't get a good job. I'm young and inexperienced. It was mostly housework. Cleaning the kitchen, washing the clothes, or shopping for the householders! And no decent wages for women. But the greatest danger was the men in the houses, and they would grab me when their women were away."

"Very difficult life you had!"

She didn't speak for a moment. "And then I got the job in Atlantic Hotel as an office cleaner and an account payable clerk. And I met Cyril. He could have abused me and then chucked me. He didn't! He was always graceful with me, gave money and gifts, and took exotic holidays. I saw him several times with Margery, an attractive lady – she was. But it didn't bother me. What he does is his business. And what I do is mine. That was our clear understanding. Anyway, we are not married."

He picked up a packet from his jacket pocket and handed it to her. She took a cigarette, and he struck his lighter and held it for her. She lit her cigarette and drew a deep puff. "But I can tell this honestly," she said while he was fuming his cigarette, "I never knew Abigale closely."

"No?" He asked, blowing the smoke from his mouth.

She shook her head with her cigarette in her mouth. She removed it and blew out the smoke. "I heard about Abigale when he was burying Margery in the Dartmoor Forrest."

"You were there?"

"She nodded heavily, smoking. "It was midnight. I was holding the light for him. He said to me Margery committed suicide. And he can't go to the police."

"Why?"

She smoked nervously. "He said the police are suspecting him with Abigale's death."

"Anything more?"

"I didn't ask. He was in a violent mood. I feared he might kill me as well if I asked." She drew her cigarette slowly for a moment. "When the police questioned Cyril about Margery's death, I knew he was lying."

"How?"

"He said to them she ran away."

"Did the police believe him?"

"I suppose so."

"Why didn't you tell the police the truth?"

"I was scared of him. And that he was looking after me well."

Mathew didn't speak for a while.

"But I confirmed to the police."

"What?"

"Whether Margery ran away. And when she ran away."

Mathew didn't speak.

"I continued to be as friendly as possible. But to be honest, I was scared of him." She waited to continue, seemingly trying to remember what had happened between them thereafter. "I pretended to be ill of something and kept a safe distance from him. But his new woman, Claudia, was very jealous of me. She wanted me to vacate the property where I lived for years and called my own home, though Cyril paid for it. Cyril also backed her up and insisted I should vacate for her to move in. I couldn't fight with him. He's a killer. And Claudia appears to be more dangerous than even Cyril. I saw the police and told them where Margery was buried. Or where her body was hidden."

Mathew continued to sit silently but watched the teardrops bubbling up in her eyes and then dripping down on her cheeks. She let it drip briefly, then cast her face down and said, "Okay, Margery made two mistakes. The first, she loved him. Second, she asked him to confess to the police that he killed Abigale and serve his time in jail for his punishment. And for that, he strangled her to death."

He hesitated before he spoke in the end, "I didn't bring my daughter with me because I don't want her to hear the cruelties her mother had suffered."

Without saying anything, she stared at him with tears still blubbing in her eyes.

"I know how Abigale died. She was pushed down from the third-floor window." He fell silent while struggling to restrain his emotions. "When she fell down and died, there were two men in a jeep in the car park. Do you know anything about them?"

Her face was blank before she shook her head, saying, "I'm sorry, sir. I know nothing about this incident or the men."

"I wish I had given her a respectable send-off. But I'm not lucky for that either."

"No hospital records?"

"Yes, there is. Abigale abandoned the child and ran away."

She wiped her tears with the back of her hand. "Margery may have known about it – I don't know. Cyril may have organised the men – I don't know. They are both not around. There was another woman who was around Cyril at the time. Her name was Lizzy Logan. Have you heard about her?"

He was quiet for a moment, apparently helpless. "Lizzy had gone out of the country using somebody else's passport."

"That's very depressing. But I had heard she had a brother in London."

"He had gone with her."

She fell silent briefly. "Have you heard a priest called Father Michael?"

He nodded gently. "I've talked to him. But he doesn't know much. He was in Israel when Abigale gave birth to Gemma, our daughter, and the subsequent tragedies."

"I'm so sorry I couldn't help you. Cyril ran his show very secretly." She stopped talking, seemingly trying to remember the days and years that had passed by. "If I come to know anything, which is unlikely, but how do I inform you if it happens, sir?"

He waited. "Tell the prison manager, and he will contact me."

She nodded for an answer before she said in a wearing voice. "Please let me repeat it again, sir?"

Confused, he looked at her.

"While Abigale was alive, I never saw her or heard of her. And this is the truth."

He didn't say anything.

"He came to my house and asked me to go with him for a drive. He drove to Devon Forrest, and I wondered why. It was already very late in the night." She hesitated for a short while. "He said to me, Margery's body is in the boot. I wanted to scream, but I had no voice or energy. Every bit of me froze to stiff. What can I do? Middle of the night, and inside the forest. And this was the moment I heard about Abigale."

He sat back in his chair calmly, his eyes steadily on her face.

"Here, I made the mistake. I should have reported to the police straightaway at my first opportunity I had."

"You should have. Cyril would have been thrown behind bars forever."

For a long time, neither of them spoke. A very uneasy tension engulfed them. In the end, she whispered, obviously remorsefully, "I made the mistake. I was young and stupid."

He got up to his feet. "I will talk to my solicitor about your situation," he said, looking down at her. "Maybe he can get your sentence reduced, hopefully."

"Thank you, sir."

Silently, he began walking out. At the door, he turned back. She was still sitting in her chair, her eyes tearfully following him. He waved at her before turning back and exiting the meeting room.

Part 3: Talking to Father

Mathew was in the study room, slumbered back in his chair in the view of the television set. He wasn't watching what was screening. On the side of his chair, a whiskey bottle and an empty glass were on a coffee table at a convenient distance. He hadn't bothered to pour the drink into the glass. His eyes were partially open, but they were seeing nothing. And Gemma arrived at the doorway and silently stood there looking at him. "Papa," she called gently. "Are you alright?"

He continued to stay immobile. "Yes, love?"

She stepped forward and sat on the arm of his chair, leaning sideways to face him. She put her hand on his shoulder, saying, "What's the matter, Papa?"

He didn't reply immediately. And when he replied, it was more like a question, "I thought you were playing?"

"I was. And, now, Tanya took my position."

"How was in the office?"

"She didn't say anything. She was impatient to get into the court."

"You should've been playing with her. You have a lot to catch up."

"Papa, I am not going to Wimbledon. Neither is Tanya. But I admit she is very good."

"She plays every evening."

"I know. But I've other things to do. My A-level exams are coming. I am training every day for the black belt tournament. And the French and Spanish foreign correspondence course......"

"I know."

She stared at him, smiling. "Why are you quiet these days?"

"Am I?"

"You're."

"A little tired, I suppose?"

"Is that right? Usually, 24 hours is not enough for you. Now tired by four o'clock?"

He didn't reply.

"Where did you go this morning, papa?"

He caught her gaze. "I went to see somebody."

"About Mama, isn't it?"

"How did you know?"

She didn't reply. Instead, she asked, "Why didn't you take me with you?"

"You never know what they will say."

"Say what?"

"Something your Mama went through. It will hurt you."

She didn't reply.

"She came here for safety, but what happened?"

This time, she spoke. "I look at the pictures you two are together. There are several other pictures, especially the ones where she is on Plymouth Beach with Margery and Lizzy. She was elegant and stunning. I'm very proud of being her daughter. And you know that I'll love her all my life."

Without saying anything, he stretched his hand around her and held her warmly to him.

She kissed his cheek again before saying gently, "But Papa.........." She stopped without completing the sentence.

"Yeah?"

She waited one more moment and said, apparently calmly, "Nothing's going to bring her back."

He didn't speak, and neither did she continue. An uneasy calmness engulfed them. Ultimately, she continued slowly, "Since the moment you found me, your mind was set on finding Mama. And then on, finding what they had done with her body."

He put his palm over her hand, which was holding his shoulder. "If we find, we'll give Mum the best send-off. Otherwise, we take it as fate, and we can do nothing further."

"I'm also coming around to that verdict."

Another uneasy silence ticked away.

"Now, you've to decide what you want to do with the Atlantic Hotel. If you don't want it, sell it. If you want it, get rid of the other shareholders. We can't work with them."

"I've already spoken to Stuart Armour, our solicitors, about it."

"You've been thinking about it?"

"Yes. Isabella and her family got a hand in Abigale's death. I am absolutely convinced about it, though we do not have physical proof."

"All the physical proof had gone down with Cyril Baker. And also, with Margery."

"Baker was also behind when Steve Coogan tried to kill you."

"And he was also behind when I was attacked in the prison by the guard and the inmate."

"Cyril was heavily paid by Isabella to kill the woman I loved and the daughter she had given to me."

Gemma didn't speak but analysed the thoughts that surged in her mind.

"Once they cleared my heirs, the Atlantic Hotel is theirs. Devilish dream!"

She was still silent.

"Now, I clear them out of their dream."

"Will it be easy?"

"Not that easy. But we own 65% of the shares. Isabella's family holds 25%. We have another family, Pattinson, and they own the rest, 10%. Andrew Pattinsons has been a good ally to us. And therefore, let him stay on. Now you see here, 75 against 25. They have no choice and will be forced to sell when we dictate the terms."

"I hope it won't cause further violence."

"Now they're learning soon that the violence can't win anything."

She sighed rather nervously.

"Twenty minutes before you came, I was talking with Stuart. He'll be sending official papers this week."

"You had already thought about it."

"Of course! I've been talking to Stuart about our assets in Atlantica."

"What have you decided?"

"Nothing finalised. But we better give everything to Abigale's relatives. Abigale has three sisters and two brothers, 16 half-sisters and 21 half-brothers."

"I don't think I met them all when I was there. And I was there six times."

"Some of them are in other provinces. And you know travelling up there is not that straightforward."

"Next time when we go, we stay longer."

He nodded lightly before he said, "I'll set up an office for you, I think. Maybe tomorrow. You can take over some of my duties."

"Papa, I'm only 17."

"Good. Juniors are paid very little. And you are getting nothing."

She smiled, "Now I know how you massed your millions."

He pulled a funny face.

The next day, Mathew took Gemma to his office. She had been there before on numerous occasions. She knew the layout of this executive wing very well. Mathew had a massive office at the centre with other dignitaries along the oval floor. His secretary Kathrine was next door with a private gliding door on the parting wall. Next door to Kathrine was his PA Trevor's office. Sales director Andrew Pattinson, also a major shareholder, occupied the next office. And then came the office of the finance director, Paul Fullaway. However, this office was empty for a while now as Paul took an office in the accounting Wing Upstairs, and it was ideally suited for Gemma to commence her profession in the hospitality industry. It was a spacious office with engraved oak panels covering the walls and a huge window overlooking the view of the blue waters of the Atlantic Ocean caressing the sandy beaches. Mathew and Kathrine took her into this room. She slowly glanced around, then stared back at them. "It's beautiful. I like it."

Mathew shot a glance at his secretary before she caught her stare. "Kathy is excellent for training."

Gemma caught Kathrine's eye. "Thank you. I can assure you I need you."

They laughed lightly before he said jokingly, "She is helpless without us."

Kathrine looked at her pleasantly. "When you'd like to start, Monday? In four days?"

As if unsure of herself, she glanced at her father. "That sounds fine," he said. "What do you think?"

"Monday is fine."

"That's good. The maintenance staff will have some time to give a thorough clean-up. It's been shut for a while since Mr Fullaway took his office in the accounting department."

"I'd like to start part-time, Papa. And as I cope well, I can think about taking full time."

"Of course, lazy," he replied, smiling, then turned to the secretary. "Now you can inform the personal department. And also tell them to put Gemma in the lowest pay scale."

"I don't think that's necessary. The Atlantic Hotel is known for paying no decent wages."

"And yet, you worked here for ten years."

"No 10. Actually, 15 years." She caught his eyes, then turned to Gemma, and then turned back to him. "And I've been here ever before you came here."

"No. My dad used to bring me here since I was five."

"I don't talk about toddlers," she said, laughing.

They also joined in laughing.

Just then, Tanya Roberts walked in quietly. "Hello, everybody," she addressed warmly, giving a pat on Gemma's cheek. "I was looking for you."

"You knew it," she replied, giving the pat back. "I told you this morning."

"You're staying back all day?"

"Mr Atkinson decides," she chuckled wittily. "I've no freedom."

"That's right. Freedom is no good. I'm going to take her home and lock her in."

"Good," Kathrine said. "She has nothing to do. So, let her watch the Wimbledon."

"Can I go as well?" he asked with a false nervousness. "Or any papers to look in before we go."

"No need. In fact, we manage better than when you are in."

"Thank you for your honesty. Alright, Gemma. We better go. I know when I'm not wanted."

They laughed again.

Gemma was holding Tanya's hand. "Don't be late," she said, letting her hand go. "Pamela and Brenda will be upset if we don't start tennis on time."

"It's not them," Tanya said, grimacing her face jokingly. "It's you, Gemma. Alright, I won't be late."

The other two smiled without speaking.

"Good, Tanya," she chuckled. "I won't beat you tonight."

"Thank you. Anyway, are you seeing Mark now?"

"He's a busy man. Again, he is on the other end. Better I talk with him when he phones in the evening."

However, Mark was outside and coming in. "I heard some non-staff are here," he said as he came further in.

"Not long," Gemma replied, moving towards him. "I'm forced to work here." She kissed him on the cheek and threw her hand around his back. "Job description has not been announced yet."

Tanya answered, giggling. "It's clear. Apprentice!"

"Better than I thought. What about salary?"

"I can speak for Mr Atkinson," Kathrine replied. "He doesn't pay them. Training time has to be free. Am I right, Boss?"

He smiled for an answer.

Nonetheless, Mark spoke, holding her closer. "She is a business dynamo. She is worth at least 10p per day."

They laughed to their offices. And Mathew and Gemma walked down to their car porch. The driver was already outside the car and ready to open the door. They sat in the back seat, and the driver shut the door. The Abigale House was only 15 minutes' drive away. In fact, there were two roads - Marine Drive and Ocean View Parade.

On Monday morning, Mathew was somewhat restless, and it was actually quite unusual for him. But in the back of his mind, he could see why he was restless. When Abigale found out that she was pregnant, they were not prepared for it, to be honest. However, they were both absolutely thrilled with the news and simply couldn't wait to see the baby born. And then, the political stability changed, and they had to part.

Every day and night, he wondered where the mother and baby were and of course, whether the baby was a boy or girl. About three years ago, he met his baby, a girl who is now 14 years old, and met her in the dirty cubical of a prison cell. He had also found out that Abigale died tragically, but what they did with her body. Today, happily, their daughter was about to go out to start a new career in life along his side and under his wing. How great it would have been if Abigale had also witnessed this special occasion.

Just then, the voice came from his daughter who was standing beside him. "What are you thinking, Papa? We're getting late."

"I just thought of Abigale."

The girl turned and hugged him, her face resting over his shoulder. "Kim Teo, my Chinese karate teacher used to say…."

"What?"

"We know we've life today. But we don't know what we've got tomorrow. And yesterdays are already dead."

"Yes, love. But he is wrong on fact."

"What's that, Papa?"

"About yesterday."

"What?"

"Yesterday's give us memories. And memories are more stable than lives."

She was quiet for a moment except for her sob that pierced through the stillness. In the end, she said, "Let's go, Papa."

On the car porch, the driver was waiting.

When they arrived at the office, Kathrine escorted Gemma to her office. Mathew also followed her. Her office was completely refurbished with a new carpet that reached out wall to wall and a new rug in the centre. Fancy curtains and swags were hung on the window. The wood panels on the walls were freshly varnished, and the ceiling was painted white. She stared at the place slowly once again, then turned to him. "Thank you, Papa." And then she looked at Kathrine. "I know it's your work. And thank you!"

They looked back as they heard the footsteps. Tanya and Mark were there, holding a bouquet of flowers for her. "Congratulations, Gemma," Tanya said as she handed the flowers.

Gemma put the bouquet on her table. "Oh, Tanya. You're not as bad as I thought."

Mark moved closer to her and, giving the bouquet in her hand, kissed her on the cheek. She also put his flowers on the desk before she held him with both hands and held him closer to her. "Thank you," she said, staring into his eyes. "And thank you for everything. I mean everything."

He held her gaze steadily for a moment. "You're welcome," he replied with a tinge of emotion in his voice.

"And if you're free at lunchtime, I could get you a meal. But I should say it's not as good as your prison meal."

Others all laughed. In the end, she also joined in rather spiritlessly.

A few minutes later, Mark and Tanya left.

Mathew gave a pat on his daughter's face. "Enjoy your day. And I see you later." He turned to Kathrine. "Keep an eye on my daughter, dear. She's not very clever." And he left to his office.

Gemma took her seat behind her desk.

"You like a drink? Tea – coffee?"

She got her eyes. "I don't drink much tea or coffee, Kathrine."

"What about a glass of juice."

"Alright."

"What do you prefer?"

"Anything."

"Pineapple?"

"Okay."

Kathrine ordered a cup of coffee, tea, and a glass of pineapple. Shortly, an office girl brought a small trolley with the drinks. She picked up the pineapple and placed it in front of Gemma. "Enjoy it."

She smiled back. "I will. Thank you."

Kathrine collected the coffee cups. "Thanks, Muriel."

The office girl nodded for an answer, and pushing the trolley, she went back.

"You know I'm next door."

She nodded, sipping on the juice.

"I always come and see you. And you can do the same, Gemma."

"Thank you. I will."

"And especially when you need help."

Gemma giggled. "You can bet I will."

"Please come and see me."

"Coffee getting cold. Let me take it your Papa."

"Thanks."

Katherine went around the desk and kissed her. "Wish you a great career in the hospitality industry."

"Thank you, Kathy."

She left.

It was a busy day, but not based on work. Numerous well-wishers literally queued up to meet her and introduce themselves. And the day rolled over even before she had realised it. And that was the pattern on Monday and Tuesday. But, by Thursday, she realised that there were three companies under the parent company Atlantic View Hotel (PLC), and Mathew Atkinson was its lifetime chairman. There were four subsidiary companies under its control, and The Atlantic Great Hall, which was available for political meetings, wedding celebrations, and musical performances and held under the auspicious of Isabella, Atlantic Cafeteria, which provided quality breakfast, dinner, and lunch for the locals and travellers, and managed by Jacob, Isabella's son and the Atlantic Bakery Products which produced and supplied through chain stores goods such as Cornish bakeries, Patties, and the like and this company chaired by Berney Atkinson, a cousin of Mathew Atkinson. However, she didn't see any documents to know the bankers who operated behind the subsidiary companies or any other investors and their security arrangements with the parent company. Even if she had seen, she wouldn't have acquired much knowledge on the subject. It was too complicated for her. Getting into the meticulous layout of various arrangements would take a life. Luckily, she had the time. Her life was only beginning.

The first week passed pleasantly, thanks to Kathrine, who was always on her side. Mark visited her when he had a few free minutes, and so did Tanya. Mathew had been busy with meetings of one kind or another. So passed the

557

second week. And she felt more confident than the last and felt relaxed. She hadn't met Isabella yet, and neither did she talk to.

Part 4: The Crash

It was the third week, and the day was Thursday, and it was about five-thirty when their car had an accident. They went down the Ocean View Parade, then turned to the Marine Drive. In this T-junction, a jeep flew off unexplainably and crashed onto their vehicle. Mathew and Gemma stared at each other as they jostled in their seat, but they remained in the car for the driver to handle the situation. And the driver, Jayson, got out and looked at the front where the Jeep crashed. Two men stepped out from the other vehicle and approached Jayson. He was examining the damages on the bonnet and the grilled front. Suddenly, one of the two men punched the driver's face. He was a big man, too. Suddenly, springing up straight, he hit the other man's eyes. This time, the second man got into the action and started striking the driver from his back.

Mathew glanced at his daughter. "You stay in." And even before she could reply, Mathew quickly got out and tried to separate the men away from his driver, shouting, "Move off and behave yourself."

That made the two men apparently very angry, and one turned to him and started punching. He stepped back and stayed outside his reach. This time, three men got out of the jeep and joined in the fight. And Mathew and Jayson were taking more attacks. Gemma kicked her shoes off her feet and rushed out. "

Two of the three men saw her coming and turned to her, one swearing mouthfuls and the other acting obscene, and the men were huge. Hurriedly, she put together a few steps and, rising to the air as if in a summersault, turned her body downwards. At the same time, her one foot landed heavily on the neck of the man who was swearing, and the other foot landed on the crocheter of the man who was acting dirty. They stubbled momentarily, agony surging on their faces before they fell on their backs. She swung around and touched the shoulder of the man who was next to her and exchanged punches with the driver. And as he twisted towards her, a foot of her fell heavily on his face.

He staggered violently, then tumbled to the floor. The man who was fighting with her Papa was almost blind by then, with the blood pouring out from his face. Suddenly, he took another punch and, reeling mechanically, fell on top of a man who was already there. The last man was standing on frozen legs and unseeing eyes but ran away limping painfully.

As if unable to stand on his feet, Mathew sank to the floor and sat leaning against the car. Jayson sat near to him, also leaning against the car. Gemma kneeled in front of them and looked at her father's face studiously, then at their driver's, and then back at her father's. "Shall we go to the hospital?" She asked anxiously.

Mathew caught her eyes. "Nothing bad, I hope? I only had a couple of soft punches."

She turned to the driver. "You want to go the hospital, Jayson?"

"No darling? We are okay."

"Why are you sitting like this?"

They stared at her. "Like what?" Jayson asked finally and humorously.

She didn't reply straight away. "Breathing heavily?"

"We are a little tired, that's all," her father chuckled. "And getting ready for the next round if they are coming back for more."

She looked over their car across the road. "They are not coming back."

"What do you mean?"

"The jeep was on the other side. And a little behind from us."

"Where is it now?"

"It's gone."

"Gone."

"Without exchanging the insurance details?" Jayson asked. "And who are they?"

Silently, father and daughter shot a knowing glance. "The car is okay. Can we go home?"

"Yes, we can get home."

They got in, and the car moved slowly. They didn't need a long drive. The Abigale House was about 200 yards down the road.

Mathew called the police and explained what had happened. An hour later, police inspector George Milburn and his assistant Kevin Stratford arrived for a sympathy call. However, they promised they would always be on the hunt for the violent thugs and that they would be available 24 hours a day for their personal protection if he preferred. Another hour later, Detective Inspector Stuart phoned him, saying that the police would be mingling around this location more frequently and that Mathew should be thinking of using bulletproof cars as soon as possible. Hopefully, these culprits will be behind bars very soon.

A FEW TALES

Mathew didn't go to his office on Thursday and Friday and for two more weeks. With the help of other senior staff, his secretary Kathrine and PA could manage and supervise the administration department efficiently. Mathew was only a phone call away for advice if a crisis arose. Gemma didn't go either. She preferred to stay with her father. One day, he asked her, "Why don't you go to Paris for a week or two?"

"No. I stay here with you, Papa."

"My sister will take you for a nice ride around the country."

"No, Papa. I'm not going anywhere away from you. And also, don't forget Pamela's 18th birthday is coming on Tuesday."

"You can go after that, love. She wants to see you, as well."

"I know, Papa," she insisted stubbornly. "But I just want to stay with you."

He smiled happily, "That makes me a proud father." He moved closer to her and put his hands around her, hugging her. "And happy father."

She smiled gladly. "I love you, Papa."

"And I love you, too."

A moment later, he asked, "Who else is coming on Tuesday for the yachting?"

"Tanya and Brenda are excited about the trip. And Pamela and myself! That makes four of us."

"What about the skipper Josh and the mechanic Barry?"

"Of course, they are with us."

"Where are you going?"

"Isles of Scilly. And exactly where we went to Tanya's birthday a couple of months ago."

"Nice place?"

"Very nice. A small guesthouse called 'Sealord.'"

"I know it. I've been there with Isabella sometime before our marriage."

"Did you like it?"

"We were on the main island, St. Mary's. And a hotel called St. John's. And it was absolutely fantastic."

She stood silently as if she were in the grip of a beautiful memory. "Good food, mostly fish. And the staff are so friendly and kind. And all on the fantastic sea view. I loved it. Everybody loved it. Pamela has been talking about it ever since. She wanted to go for her birthday."

"Are you all staying there for a couple of days?"

"No, Papa. We go about 3 and be back about 10 or 11."

"Bit late?"

"It's okay, Papa. It's summer time."

"Please be careful."

"Of course, Papa. You want to come with us, Papa?"

"No, love. I'm sure you can manage for a few hours with your friends."

She laughed. "I try. If I can't, I will scream."

"That's fine. Anyway, I will be on our seafront."

On Tuesday morning, Tanya fell ill with terrible tummy upset. "I've been there in May," she said while holding her tummy with both hands in an attempt to restrain the discomfort. "You better take, Pam. She's been dreaming for this day."

"We go next week."

"Not right, darling. Please take her. And others. Let them all have a nice day."

By 2 o'clock, they had taken some light food and drinks into the Princess Atlantica yacht and were ready for the sailing. The skipper was already behind the steering wheel, and the mechanic once again finished checking the overall performance of the yacht in general. Pamela and Brenda were in the saloon, choosing their favourite music records. Gemma was on the quayside behind their garden fence, and saying reluctantly byes to her father. "Aren't you getting in? They are waiting."

She hesitated. "You sure you don't want to come, Papa?"

He caught her eyes steadily. "You know I can't. My doctor is coming at one to check on me. My physio at 3. And you know that?"

"The housekeeper will cancel them."

"No, it's important they need to examine me." He paused. "But even if I can," he added smiling, "I won't come. You must learn to live on your own. I won't be always around."

She smiled, turning back to the steps to the yacht. She moved up a few steps, then she stopped, turning back to him. This time, the sweet smile on her face wasn't there. "You sure you don't want to come?"

"Go, dear. And I will be here waiting for you."

She steadily caught his eyes. "I love you."

"Please go. And enjoy yourself."

She entered the yacht and, standing on the deck, she stared at him. "Bye, Papa."

"Bye, my love."

"I love you, Papa."

"I love you, too."

The yacht started moving away from the quayside, while everyone shouted back, "Bye, bye, bye."

He shouted back, raising his hand. "Bye-bye!"

Pamela and Brenda moved off to the saloon. However, Gemma stayed on the deck and waved back at him, shouting, "I love you, Papa."

The yacht began to pick up speed, splitting the waves that were furiously surging against its way. It was a beautiful day; the air was fresh under the blue sky that spread out towards the western horizon. The sun was descending towards the midway of the western sky, though it wasn't hot at all against the embracing breeze that slipped over the rolling waves. Her voice dried up, and the yacht started to appear smaller as it sailed further out into the sea. It completely disappeared at times when large waves rose and burst into the air.

Mathew searched for a cigarette and tucked it between his lips, then struck a lighter and lit it. He drew a deep puff and blew out the smoke through his nostrils. The smoke quickly dissolved in the breeze and disappeared. He wasn't aware of it, as his eyes got stuck on the yacht. A fire broke out, lightening a space of horizon into a glowing shade, and the fragments of the yacht rose into the air and gleamed against the skyline.

Chapter 13

It All Ends

Part 1: Emma or Gemma

The fog shrouded the trees into the shapes of white cliffs, and in between, it drifted lazily over the shrubbery. The dense mist obscured the vision, and anyone would struggle to see beyond a few feet. The moistness of the air made the face feel cool and wet, especially in late December on the seafront. The silence was eerie and deafening. The sound of her footsteps on the ground and the rustling of leaves underfoot amplified, creating an almost supernatural atmosphere. She lost her bearings on and off. The roars of the sea waves ought to have kept her direction correct, but on the banks, it was everywhere. And then came a soft, cautious voice, "Gemma?"

It was the voice of Mathew, who was at the garden wall before the beach below. "It's cold," she said rather concernedly.

"Waiting for you, Gemma, my darling."

She chuckled deliberately to reduce the tension. "I'm Emma, Mathew."

She walked through the fog, coming to his sight.

He stared at her first, as if unsure of himself to believe, and then the expression in his eyes changed slowly to a calmer look. "You sounded like Gemma."

Without saying anything, she caught his eyes gently.

"And through the mist, you appeared as Gemma."

Emma moved closer and hugged him. "Let's go inside."

He waited. "How did you know I was here?"

He turned away to the wall, looking in the direction of the sea. "When I get a few minutes away from my daily schedules, I come here. And look over the sea."

"But what can you see tonight, Mathew? The fog is like an impenetrable mountain."

"Very true! But I don't see any fog, Emma, dear. I can always see the horizon in my mind where my daughter died two years ago and see the sea where my wife's body was dropped with weight tied to her neck about 20 years ago."

"Let's go in the house. It's cold."

Mathew ignored her words. "Sometimes, I see them rising over the water at the distance and looking at me as if they want to speak with me."

"I don't think so, Mathew," she replied politely. "But I think it may be the rolling waves, surging up into the air, then exploding into different shapes."

He looked at her face through the wisps of mist flowing idly. However, the expression in his eyes didn't agree with her completely.

A moment or two ticked away silently and uneasily before she said quietly, "Let's go in."

They shuffled towards the house. He walked in front as if he was guiding her. "We don't get this kind of fog normally. In fact, I've never seen it at all."

"Well, it's a norm since I've been here."

"You're right on that," Mathew said slightly humorously. "Looks like you brought it over."

Emma was about to laugh quietly, but she restrained herself. The occasion wasn't right for laughing.

"This is to me like whitish darkness," he said, again humorously. "I can't see a thing. We need lights with special effects to go through this darkness."

"I agree with you, Mathew," Emma chuckled quietly.

A big pear tree sprang up through the fog in front of them. He stopped walking and held her hand as if to protect her, then walked around it. "I still don't know how you found me when you came."

"I possess special power, Mathew."

He stared at her through the vapour while walking. "Let's share this power. I could do a little bit of it."

"Alright, I will consider it."

Silently, Mathew smiled faintly before he said, "We do get fogs and mists on the beach below and over the sea to the distance. But they seldom appear over here. Our ground is quite high from the beach. Especially, it never happened thick like as it is now."

"I like thick fogs," she said, slightly giggling. "And, maybe the fogs like me, too."

Eventually, they arrived at the terrace on the back. They went up the corridor and entered the study.

"You like a hot drink, Mathew? Or something strong?"

"Strong will be nice. Tell the butler. What about you, Emma?"

"I like a nice cup of tea."

Shortly, the butler came in, rolling a trolley with a glass of whiskey and a cup of steaming hot tea. A choice of nuts was also in it. "Enjoy it," he said politely. "And you don't want anything else."

"We're okay," he replied, equally politely.

The butler left the trolley nearer the low table in between them and crossed the room, saying, "If you need me, I'm in my room."

"Okay!"

Mathew stared absently at his drink for a moment. "How was your day?" he asked softly, his eyes returning to her slowly. "The preparations are getting to their final stages, I suppose?"

Emma sipped on her tea, meeting his eyes. "Looks like that way," she replied, putting her cup on the table. "Well, it has to be. Not even 24 hours are left before the wedding and the ceremonies." She paused, seemingly unsure of herself, before she added rather frustratedly. "They don't speak to me a lot."

He stared at her. "What makes you think so?"

Emma picked up her tea and sipped. "They keep me mainly in the hall where everybody seems busy with one thing or another. Like hanging flowers from the ceiling or pictures on the walls. Or table decorations. But none of them say to me what's is coming or happening next."

"Why do you think so?"

Emma sipped quietly. "They know I'm staying with you."

"They had known it even before you came here." Mathew paused and drank a mouthful of his whiskey. It went down his throat, warming up his body. "When you applied this job for your university project, the personal

568

department got a real shock when they saw your picture. And you know why?"

"Of course," she answered, quickly smiling. "They thought I was your daughter."

"And I thought the same when I saw the picture."

"I hope I reminded her."

"Yes. You could say that." He swallowed another mouthful of his drink. "But the fact is I remember Gemma here every hour and every day."

"Anyway, what a coincidence!"

"And when I phoned you, it was much more than coincidence." Mathew stopped talking and stared at her face in complete bewilderment. "Your voice was exactly like hers. And the words. And the laughs. And thank you for the feeling that my daughter, Gemma, came back alive."

Emma had the urge to laugh, but she resisted it. "If I have made you happy in any way, Mathew, I'm very happy too."

"You have indeed. And thank you!"

Emma waited while she sipped her tea. "And this is why, Isabella or Helena, or anyone else, doesn't tell me much. They think I'll tell you." She hesitated as if unsure of herself. "What happened between you and Isabella? I hope you don't mind me asking this question."

Without speaking, Mathew caught her gaze steadily, drinking a mouth full of his whiskey. He put his glass back on the table. "There was nothing in between us," he said finally, his eyes still meeting her gaze. "I suppose that's the honest answer I can give." His eyes drifted from her face and moved out of the window. It passed the cliff on the lefthand side of the garden and struggled to go ahead. But he didn't see anything. The fog heaved up higher than the cliff and obscured the world outside.

Emma was silent as she wanted him to continue.

Slowly, Mathew turned his face to her. "Yes, what I said was right, I think," he continued, remembering the past as it appeared in his mind. "She wasn't keen on foreign countries neither did she appreciate foreign people. She had her own valid reasons for it. She didn't understand any foreign languages, nor understood any other cultures, nor religious worships."

Emma picked up her cup of tea and held it in her hand, sipping slowly.

"On the other hand, I was born in Africa. In Atlantica, precisely. And I spent most of my childhood up there. And I studied there until the end of my primary education."

"Did you have good schools there?"

"Of course, there are! And the school I attended was run by catholic missionaries and regarded as one of the best schools in the world." He drained his whiskey glass and put it down on the table. "Anyway, I didn't stay long enough in Cornwall to get to know Isabella well."

"Who made the big decision to tie the knot?"

"Well, frankly speaking, none of us!"

Silently, she looked at him.

"Our families had known each other for centuries. And, more than that, our parents were very close friends. So, they made the decision."

"That says you had all the blessings. And then what happened?"

A FEW TALES

"Everything went wrong from the beginning. Even the honeymoon trip ended up in complete disaster. Or shall I say, put the nail on the head?"

As Mathew said, his mind clouded with the pictures of memories of the honeymoon. The wedding was on the 7th of August 1965. It was a beautiful day, warm and bright, with not a cloud in the sky. The wedding was held at the Cornwall Catholic Cathedral Church in the Lands End, and the reception was at the Great Atlantic Hall, which was then owned by Isabella's father, Lloyd James. There was super food and a super party, and everyone enjoyed every minute of the reception. In the evening, everyone gave a big send-off to the newlyweds. They flew from Newquay Airport to London and then in the morning to Atlantica City.

Now, Atlantica City was significantly calmer and struggling to generate a new image of peace and love, as well as cooperation and development. It wasn't an easy dream to achieve as the histories of killing and kidnapping scared everyone whether they were the natives or foreigners. After the independence of 1961, violence erupted four times, and several thousands of people were murdered, displaced, or made homeless. However, in 1963, Gundagai Amulet became the president through a bloody military coup, but he chose the path of reconciliation with all races and creed in the country and engaged in negotiations with foreigners, especially Europeans for cultural understandings and financial cooperations. By 1965, new roads were built across Atlantica City and extended or being built to the other provincial cities. New properties were raised for banks, schools, shops and petrol stations and the likes. And Mathew was always engaged in construction as his father before him.

When Mathew and Isabella arrived at the airport, he recognised some local boys and girls outside the check-out gate. He cheerfully waved at them.

They waved back as if greeting him and his wife. Isabella stared at them as they were moving forward. "I hope they're not going to mug us," she said in a mixed voice of fear and sarcasm.

Mathew watched them over the heads of co-passengers, still waving happily, but whispered into her ear, "Careful what you're saying."

"Who are they?"

"They are my friends and staff members."

"Hell. What am I supposed to talk to them?"

"Talk to them as you talked to me."

"I hadn't talked to a black man or woman."

"A start for anything! And you are here. You can talk to them."

They came near the exit door, and the number of people around the queue area increased. Mathew and Isabella moved slowly forward. "I don't feel comfortable with them, Mathew."

"We're in the midst of them. You've to talk to them when necessary, at least."

"Oh! You don't make my life easy, do you? You bring me for honeymoon. And you know well I don't even go for holidays here."

Well, Isabel. This is not a honeymoon as such or a holiday. This is where I was born. And my home is here. And I have brought you home!" He stopped whispering as a group of people mingled around them. And when it was safe, he added gently, "These people are my fellow citizens. We've to live with them."

Isabella didn't reply.

After twenty minutes or so, they came out. His friends came to them, rushing. Some took his hands or hugged him. Others stood around her in an act of respect. "Welcome home," they shouted in unison and warmly. "Did you have a nice flight?"

He chuckled happily, "Okay. Not worse than before!"

They laughed. "Anyway, thank God," Mrs. Chikuta prayed happily. "You're here."

He shot a glance at Isabella and realised that she wasn't enjoying a moment of it at all. "Isabella is a bit tired," he said. "Let's go home, Aunty Chikuta."

Part 2: Arriving in Atlantica

The airport was fifteen miles outside the city. The dusty road that linked to the city went ahead, winding and bumpy under the scorching sun. On the way, Isabella felt nauseous twice, but she managed without vomiting. Obviously, she didn't want to create a scene of embarrassment. When they arrived at the colonial district and then the Colonial House up on the hill, it took about one and half hours. A group of men and women were waiting in the forecourt. Mathew guided her into the house quickly, saying to people, "Thank you all," he said happily, "for welcoming us."

"Congratulations," they shouted back cheerfully. "And all the best!"

"Thank you. Isabella and I, we're grateful for your greetings." Mathew shot a glance at her, then told them, "Isabella had a rough flight. She must go in and need a little rest. We will see you tomorrow. And thank you again."

Mathew took her to his bedroom, turned on the ceiling fan, and opened the windows. A cool breeze swung around in the room. She lay in the bed with her body up against the leather headboard. Chikuta walked into the door space. "Did you have something in the plane?" she asked. "Or shall I get something to eat?"

"We're okay. But something to drink, please."

"What would you like? Pineapple, orange, or mango? With ice?"

Without replying, he looked at his wife, hoping she would answer. A couple of seconds ticked away silently, and he replied in the end, "Okay, Aunty. Bring pineapple drink. And for me as well, please."

"Any slices of cakes? Or fruits? Nuts?"

Again, he waited for her to speak, but he replied in the end, "Not now, Aunt."

A few minutes later, Chiku brought the drink in a stainless jar and two long glasses, and all in a steel square tray, which she held carefully. She was wearing a white skirt that went down below the knees and a half-sleeve white blouse that hung on her body smartly. "This young lady is Aunty Chikuta's daughter."

Isabella didn't respond to meet her.

"We call her Chikku. But her proper name is Abigale."

"I just want complete rest," Isabella retorted quietly, avoiding her eyes from the other two.

Mathew shot a glance at Chikku with a sympathetic expression. "Chikku, please put them there," he said, gesturing to a coffee table.

She smirked with an awkward expression, putting the tray with the drinks on the table. "The men put your luggage in the visitors' room. You want them here now?"

"Not now, Chikku."

"Okay," Abigale went.

"Drink it," he said, handing a glass of drink to her. "Nothing stays cold too long in this heat."

She took it from his hand and started sipping.

He sat down on her side and put his hand on her. "I know, love, you're not used to this sort of weather. But, you're okay?"

"I never been in Africa," she whispered listlessly. "And you know it."

"I will install air conditioning soon, love."

"But it's not going to help now, is it?"

"We've air coolers in the storeroom. I can get a couple of them here now."

Aunty Chikuta appeared outside the door. "How are you, Isabella darling? Would you like some cakes for the 4 o'clock tea?" She asked slightly nervously. "Or Isabella darling, do you like anything particular?"

Isabella finished sipping and put the glass back on the table but didn't answer. He turned his eyes to the butler. "We'll tell you later, Aunty. But tell Stefan to bring up a couple of air coolers."

"Okay, son."

"Tell him to leave them in the visitors' room,"

"Okay, son."

"Thank you!"

She replied and then walked away.

"Shut the door. I don't want them all coming here."

"It will be hotter. We better keep it open."

"No. The windows are open. That's enough."

Obediently, he shut the door.

Without replying, Isabella moved back and leaned against the headboard heavily.

"Have a rest. And I go and see the domestics. Also, some of the guests are still here."

Isabella didn't speak. Slowly, she fell into a doze. When she woke up, it was tea time. She went to the dining room with him. Dishes of fruits, cakes, and biscuits were clustered on the table, in addition to various juices in crystal jars, plus, of course, coffee and tea. Abigale was present to serve if they wished. However, none of them eat anything to mention. Isabella drank a glass of mango juice, and Mathew just had a coffee. After the tea, they went to the back of the house, where a stunning garden stretched to a large space. They walked around while he talked about the history of some trees or the origins of certain bushes and plants. They returned to the front of the Colonial House through the right side of the garden. She viewed the building for a few minutes. He briefly described when it was built, and when it was updated to the present style and who took the leadership to bring this amazing façade.

"It is lovelier than you said," Isabella said briefly.

Mathew smiled tactfully. "But, sorry, I forgot to tell.......," he paused without completing what he had intended to say.

"What did you say?"

He chuckled, "That this is your house now."

"Thank you," she said casually.

They continued to walk towards the sea. They didn't have much of a beach of their own, but the Atlantic Ocean caressed their land on the west side. There was a small quayside where small barges or ships used to harbour in the colonial days. Locals used to jump into the sea from the quay for swimming and fun. On the left side of the quay, the ground was sloping gently into the water, and the waves rolled in endlessly. As recently as 1960s, Mathew built an offshore barrier for ladies' bathing and washing. Abigale frequently used this facility for swimming and bathing, and eventually known as Abigale Jetty.

Mathew and Isabella came to the shore and stood there silently, watching the waves surging up into the air before they burst into droplets and fell while gleaming in the slanting sunlight. "The sea is all over," she remarked quietly.

"This the widest part of the Atlantic Ocean," he said as if he couldn't think of anything else to say.

"Maybe so! But wide or narrow, you can only sea to the horizon."

"That's true."

"Let's go back to the house."

He looked at her silently for a moment. "We've another hour or so of daylight left. Would you like to go up the beach for a walk?"

"Why? You want to get killed?"

"But it's completely deserted, other than the fishermen at the peninsula further up."

"Deserted? That makes it more frightening."

"What makes you believe these things?"

"Didn't you hear people talking on the plane?

Without speaking, Mathew stared at Isabella with a confused expression.

"That a bloody coup happens on average in two years. And it's about time for the next mass murder and confiscating foreigners' assets."

"They can happen. Because they always happen in Africa. But don't forget that Atkinsons have been here for over two hundred years. We have benefited from this country. And this country has also benefited from us enormously. And the people know that."

"What do they know?"

"They know that we've built schools, hospitals, communication systems, and roads here. And we built even the parliament building." He vaguely paused before he continued quietly. "And for our huge investments and risks, we also shared a healthy profit. After all, it's not all our money. We loan it from London banks."

She stared over the wavy waters. The sun was edging towards the horizon.

"Can we go in?"

"Of course," he said, walking with her by his side. "Take a bath in the cool water. It helps."

When they were indoors, Mathew suggested politely, "Like to see the house around?"

Isabella snapped quietly, "What's the rush? Maybe tomorrow!"

About 7 o'clock, she took a shower in the mild water and wore a matching blouse and skirt. However, the temperature was unbearably high. She sat under the fan and drank a glass of ice-cold coconut water. He went to the bathroom and stayed under the spray of cold water. The water hit on his face and then ran down his body. He was physically having an enjoyable cooling sensation, but his mind was stagnant with the thoughts that the staff wouldn't tolerate her behaviour and probably leave.

8 o'cAt lock, the d She ate a small piece of lamb with a few slices of potatoes and finished the meal. He looked at her calmly before he asked quietly, "What's the problem?"

Isabella shot a glance at Abigale, who was right outside the door and appeared to be ever ready to serve. Her eyes returned to the dishes in front of her, cleverly avoiding his eye contact. "I don't like them."

"What's wrong?"

"Wrong ingredients!"

"They are the fresh ingredients plucked from the bushes."

"And wrong proportions!"

He waited impatiently for a moment, staring at her face. "Aunty Chikuta came here when I was two," he answered calmly. "And she made the food here ever since. And everybody always loved her food."

"I appreciate that. But I don't like it."

"They made it specially for you."

"I can't eat anymore. I feel sick."

He looked at her without knowing what to say.

Abigale discreetly watched everything that was happening around the dining table. He came closer to the door. "Can I make something else for you, Ms Isabella?"

She answered tersely, "I'm okay."

Mathew turned and caught Abigale's gaze. "We finished, dear. And thank you."

"My mum has put juices in flasks in your room," she said politely. "Ms. Isabella may need it in the night."

"Thank you, Chikku."

Abigale stayed back in the dining room to clear up the table while they got up and went to their bedroom. Suddenly, they spotted mosquitos flying in the room. Mathew drew the canopy around the bed and shut the windows so these nasty flies wouldn't enter from outside. He also turned off the lights to ward off the flies from swelling into the light. "We've a generator. It's on a building site, shame."

"It's alright," she said in an obliging tone. "I hope we can manage it."

However, the breeze was not getting in since the windows were shut, the air inside the room was motionless, and the temperature was rising all the while. And Isabella began to sweat badly. The porter, Gary, who stayed in the staff house on the garden side, grabbed his bike, rushed to the building site, and returned with the generator an hour later. And, another thirty minutes or so later, they managed to produce enough power for a few lights in the house and the fan in Mathew's bedroom. Isabella didn't like at all the scenario she had to face, but she slowly fell asleep.

In the morning, they flew off to Durban in South Africa, which was only an hour's flight away, and the temperature was much cooler than in Atlantica

City. A day later, they flew off to Johannesburg, again in South Africa, for a day and returned to Atlantica City on the third morning, with the decision that Isabella couldn't live in this sort of primitive conditions. At lunchtime, they were in the Colonial House, and Chikuta served the meal. It included duck stew, beef roast, fried salmon, and three vegetable dishes. Isabella didn't like any of these. The duck stew was watery and had no flavours, and the beef was burned. She shouted at Chikuta, "Why did you make this mess?"

Mathew looked at Chikuta apologetically. His wife's tone was rude, and content was unwanted. "Sorry, Aunty," he said. "Isabella didn't mean that. But she is very tired after three days' travel."

His words made her absolutely annoyed. Isabella got up and left the dining room in a seething anger. "Sorry, Aunty," she said again. "Let me go and see her."

Isabella was standing by the window, looking over to the forecourt and the sea beyond. "Darling, what's bothering you?"

She didn't reply. Instead, she looked away into the sea.

"She came here when I was two. And she spent more time with me than my mum."

"I'm sorry."

"You better apologise to her?"

"You are joking, aren't you?"

"You've been rude."

"I think you've been right."

"What's that?"

"I'm tired. And I want to go home."

"This is your home."

"Never! Great Brittan is my home. And I want to go home as soon as possible."

"Darling, don't make hasty decisions," he said reassuringly. "I was born here in this house. I grew up here and live here. And I am an Atlantican citizen. "

"Everyone appreciates it?"

"Of course not! Everyone never appreciates everything due to political teachings. But I see every Atlantican as my fellow citizen."

Isabella looked at him and was about to say something. But, without saying, she turned back to the window.

"There is a popular saying here. 'This is Africa.'"

"Meaning?"

He waited. "Here, anything can happen against your expectations."

She smirked, "Don't I know it now?"

"Then you also know that the continent is coming out of the colonial ages." He paused thoughtfully. "And now the progress is taking place, but it is having its own early problems, like anywhere else...... "

Her voice interrupted him. "I understand, Mathew. But I don't want to jeopardise my life."

"What do you mean?"

"I'm going back to my home."

In a gentle but firm voice, he said, "Now, Isabella, this is your home, too. And your country, too."

She turned back and caught his eyes constantly. "I'm British. And I'm flying back tomorrow."

Part 3: The History

"Your wedding was not even a week old," Emma said rather hurriedly and puzzled. "And Isabella flew back alone?"

Emma's voice jolted his mind to the present moment. He picked up the whisky bottle from the trolley and poured the drink into his empty glass. He took the glass and, holding it in his hand, he looked at her cup of tea and then at her face, "I'm sure your tea must be cold. What about a drop of whisky?"

Emma touched the glass before she took it. "It's gone cold, but I like it cold, Mathew."

"You sure?"

"Absolutely!"

He waited for a moment. "I didn't let Isabella fly back alone. I travelled with her."

Emma didn't speak.

"We went straight to her parents' house in Falmouth. That's how she wanted it. And, in the evening, she put up an argument for only Heaven's sake why, and I left her and came here, then known as Atkinson Manor."

"Have you met her again?"

"Two months later, I came back from Africa mainly to see her."

"Did you see her?"

"Yes. But she wasn't happy with any of my suggestions. Isabella doesn't want to live in poor Africa. She didn't like any of the people I socialised with." He paused, took a mouthful of whiskey, and put the glass back on the trolley. "And a year later, I tried to see her again."

"Did you see her?"

"No. She was pregnant for five months."

Without speaking, Emma looked at him, somewhat bewildered.

"The child's father was called Carlos, a ballet dancer from Argentina. He used to stay in our hotel on and off. Helena was born when they were in Buenos Aires, in the Argentinian capital."

"Where is Carlos now?"

"He left Isabella a year after Helena was born and married his leading lady in the ballet."

Emma didn't say anything.

"Isabella settled here, and her father gave her the Atlantic Great Hall. And when her father died, she became its Managing Director."

"Did you divorce her properly?"

"No. Legally speaking, she is still my wife."

"Why didn't you do it?"

"She wanted big shares in anything I owned, even this house, Atkinson Manson. My great-great-grandfather built it. Or even the Colonial House. And everything else."

"Do you still love her?"

"I loved her when I married. And when she left me, the love for her also left me."

Emma didn't ask anything.

But Mathew asked calmly. "How's the Great Hall look after the final touches of decorations and the rearrangements of seatings."

Emma suddenly appeared overwhelmed with happiness. "To be honest, I 've never seen an auditorium as stunning as this Great Hall," she answered in clear gladness in her voice.

He smiled lightly. "I'd like to hear your findings. I know you've been in other entertainment halls."

"Yes, I've been to several places in London, Manchester, and Birmingham." She paused as if setting all her studies against his question. "But Great Hall is outstanding in structure and appearance. How do I say," she stopped talking and rolled her eyes enthusiastically around the room as if searching for the right words to say and say in the right order. And she said suddenly, "I don't know, but to me, it looks very special – a magical hall, and designed in a magical way."

Mathew caught her eyes silently.

"I don't think there are any metal beams in the structure."

"No"

"Any stones?"

"No! All made out of African teak, rosewood, and oak," he explained slowly. "And all the edgings or carvings or features you see on the panels are all handmade."

"Good Lord, there are thousands of panels."

"Yes, thousands! Because the ceiling is completed and finished in panels. And so are the walls and columns. And if you look at the legs of tables and chairs, you can see them uniquely carved as well."

"Amazing. Absolutely amazing!" Emma paused almost speechlessly for a moment. "Africans, when Isabella's great grandfather held them here as slaves."

She paused again. "It's worth some money, I supposed."

"I don't know the real value, Emma. But I insured the Great Hall and its contents for ten million pounds."

She finished her tea and put the cup on the trolley. "Mathew, Helena has invited me for her do tonight. I like to go."

"Of course, you should! You'll have something for your project."

"Thank you!"

"One of our drivers will take you."

"Don't stay very late. You're going for the bride's dressing, aren't you?"

"I know. What time are you meeting me in the reception hall?"

"We will talk when you come back."

"If I am late?"

"Then, in the morning."

"Okay."

An hour later, she went for the stag night.

Mathew stayed awake for a while in the family lounge. Though known as the family lounge, he didn't have any relatives to accompany him. Isabella, his estranged wife, was busy organising her daughter Helena's wedding the next day. Abigale, the love of his life, died a long time ago, and even the memories faded out of shape and clarity except for the aches in his heart that surged up erratically. He met his child, Gemma, unexpectedly, and dreams came alive in his life, and he embraced a new world. However, the world didn't keep him happy much longer as Gemma died in the sea in front of his own eyes. In the centre of all the wealth and comfort, he was struggling to get a wink of sleep.

Barry, the butler, came to the lounge. "Are you waiting for anybody, Mathew?"

"No, Barry."

"Is Emma coming back tonight?"

"Yes!"

"That's okay, Mathew. One of us will open the door."

"She can be quite late."

"It's already quite late, Mathew. Aren't you going to sleep?"

He waited nervously. "Sleep is not something I can easily grab, Barry."

"I know what's going through your mind now, Mathew."

"Do you?"

"And I also know you need a good sleep."

"Do you?"

Without answering, he went away through the side door. A couple of minutes later, he returned with a glass in his hand. "Drink this, sir. It's a strong dot of whisky. And go to sleep."

Mathew picked it up from the butler's hand, drank it in one mouthful, and swallowed it down.

"Please go to sleep."

He got up slowly and headed down to his bedroom. The butler followed him. He pushed the door open and entered. The butler stayed behind at the doorstep. "Have a good sleep sir."

"I'll, Barry."

"Please don't shut the door fully, sir."

"Why not?"

"Maybe I want to see you sleeping," he replied, shutting the door for him.

"Barry."

The butler looked in through the narrow gap. "Yes, Mathew?"

"Tell Emma I want to see her in the morning before she goes to the wedding."

"I'll do that, sir."

In the morning, it was raining, and he sensed it in his half-sleep half-awake from the dropping sound on the window panes forced by the irregular gust of wind. According to the weather forecast, the weekend should be dry and relatively mild, especially on Saturday, which would be bright and sunny and absolutely gorgeous. And the Saturday was dawning up, but the spectrum of colours of dawn was invisible behind the layers of clouds. It might be the answer was to wait and see.

Precisely at 5.30, Barry came softly into the room, rolling a small stainless-steel trolley with steaming coffee in a jar, three saucers with different biscuits, another saucer with fried cash nuts, and a plate with slices of fresh pineapple and spare cups and saucers. Coming close to the side of the bed, he poured a cup of coffee and, placing it in a saucer put them on the top shelf. "Against the forecast, it is another winter's day, Mathew."

He smiled causally. "It's still raining, Barry?"

"Not raining now, Mathew. It's more like drizzling at the moment with flakes of tiny snowflakes," he replied, pushing the trolley even closer for his mater's easy reach. "It's freezing outside."

He raised his body gently and rested against the headboard. He took his coffee and sipped on it.

"The coffee is okay, sir?"

"Great as usual," Mathew sipped again, then, holding the coffee in his hand, he turned to the butler. "Any further news about the storm?"

"Nothing, sir, which means the storm will rage through the northern regions of France and then to Germany and Russia."

"It will cause so much destruction and disasters for them."

"We pray God will have His mercy on them."

He finished his cup and put it on the trolley. "Lucky, we escape again?"

"I also hope, Mathew," the butler said, filling the cup with more coffee from the jar. "Do you know what they call this storm?"

"I don't think I heard a name."

"It's called 'Melody'."

"Wonderful. Very musical!"

"Thanks. And the weathermen predict that the northern fringes of Melody will pass through southern England. But it's not going to harm anybody."

"Good," he said, sipping the drink. "The Southern wind will lift up the temperature high."

"That's marvellous for the wedding, isn't it, Mathew? And for the reception."

"It's supposed to snow. That's what I heard last night. But it's raining now. That means the temperature has picked up nicely."

The door behind them opened, and Emma walked in wearing her nightgown. "Good morning, gentlemen," she said cheerfully.

"Good morning, Emma," they said in unison, then Mathew added gently, "You went to bed late?"

"Emma went to bed about three, Janice told me."

"And she got up early as this!" He exclaimed. "Where do you get this energy?"

Emma giggled quietly, "Today is my last day here. And I want to spend every minute of it with you, Mathew."

"I know you're not a coffee admirer," the butler said, turning to go. "I get the tea for you."

"Don't go. I like coffee as well, Barry."

Barry turned back to the trolley.

"The party went alright, Emma?"

"Very lovely," she chuckled. "About 50 guests! And lots of fun and laughter. Everybody thoroughly enjoyed it."

"Have you met Adam Aylesbury?"

"No. Do you know him?"

"Not Adam, personally. But I know his parents. Do you know the family, Barry?"

"Not personally, Mathew," the butler answered, pouring the drink into a cup. "Very reputable family, and made lots of money from the slave trade."

"Atkinsons also made lots of money," she said, picking up her cup.

"But Atkinsons never bought or sold humans as commodities. They did decent business, and all credit goes to them."

"How did the Roscoe family make their money?" Emma asked causally. "I mean Isabella Roscoe's ancestors?"

"Roscoe Family hasn't got a clean name either, like the Aylesbury. They went all over, including Africa, America, and the rest. But they made money mostly through dirty deals and running a slave trade." He paused and looked at her, "Shall I get something to eat for you?"

"Not now, Barry," she said gratefully. "I must go to my room now."

"What for, Emma?"

"I've been here a week now. I've seen lots of materials for my thesis. But I never made proper notes of them yet. I must do some in this morning. If not, I'll forget everything when I'm in London tomorrow."

"I can make a couple of steak sandwiches. It won't do any harm."

"Alright, Barry. I will have them. I can eat it in my room."

Barry went to the kitchen.

"I must say we didn't spend much time together."

"I know. I'm sorry about that. I spent most of the time with Helena for my course."

"Can't you go next week?"

"Next week, I'm in Manchester. And that will be my final fact-finding for my project."

"Aren't you going to the dressing up the bride and church wedding?"

"Now, it's not important to me, Mathew, because I know about the dressings and church rituals. And I told Helena that I will only come for the reception."

Part 4: Showing Off

Without saying anything, Mathew looked at Emma.

"Today, I want to spend all day with you. And don't forget we've to be there at least by four for the reception."

"Sorry, Emma. I don't think I want to come."

"Oh, Mathew, why not?" She asked, her voice clearly encouraging.

He didn't answer.

"Isabella invited you personally."

He was silent.

"Helena gave you the invitation card and then insisted you attend."

This time, Mathew spoke, "These are hollow actions. There is no honesty in them."

"What do you mean?"

He waited a moment. "They're showing off."

"What's that?"

"They've a great boy for Helena."

"That's okay if they want to feel like that."

Emma didn't say anything.

"And I failed completely to protect her." He paused as if the emotions of hurt were overpowering his gentle composure. A moment later, he managed to add, "She ended up at the bottom of the sea floor."

A silence erupted uncomfortably. Emma finally said, obviously trying to ease Mathew's mind, "I don't want to go alone. Please come with me, for my sake. And I want to spend every moment with you today."

Barry was returning at the time with steak sandwiches wrapped in foil paper and carried in a plate. "You must stay with us one more week at least. Mathew is delighted since you came."

Emma gratefully accepted the plate of sandwiches and, picking up the jar with the other hand, poured the coffee into her almost-finished cup. She put the jar back on the trolley, then took her drink and straightened up her body. "We've plenty of time," she answered, slightly giggling. "We'll talk."

"That means you're staying?" The butler chuckled rather leisurely.

She was about to start walking but stood, halfway-turning back to them. "When a lady has to go, the lady has to go."

The men laughed, and she went to her room.

The weather forecasters proved themselves correct slowly. At about eight o'clock, the rain stopped completely, and the morning turned bright with the sunlight. Only the gust of wind persisted stubbornly for half an hour or so before the weather changed yet again. This time, it was the snow, and it snowed heavily. The land and sea disappeared out of existence. Only the front garden and the driveway through the middle of it were partially visible to a fair distance. Gradually, it lessened to random flakes by midday before the wind caught speed and turned to gale-force. And the gale lashed onto anything in its way, howling, trembling, and devastating. Now and then, it had gone off on its fury slightly, but then it came back more ferocious than before. Three pine trees, which stood along the side of the driveway, uprooted and felled in front of Mathew's very own eyes. The conditions changed again by one o'clock, and it changed to a dry, calm afternoon. However, the meadows, the shrubs, and everything else that dared to stand up were shrouded in brilliant white and remained undisturbed.

"What a day?" The butler said, absolutely bewildered. "We've seen sun and storm. What else is there we haven't seen?"

"In several places," Mathew said, smoking on his cigarette, "the people have no electricity. The trees fell on the electric lines. I heard it on the radio. But television services cut off."

"And worst to come, there are a few major accidents in motorway 5. About 28 vehicles collided, and several drivers seriously injured. And motorway closed from both ends."

"And most of the roads are closed in Cornwall. Trees are blocking them."

"I hope the wedding will go ahead alright."

The wedding went well, and they returned for the reception at about 4 pm. Mathew and Emma got in 20 minutes before them. The balloons and glittery decorations that had been fixed on the fences along the private driveway were smashed up or destroyed by the storm, and the flower plants and bushes in the fancy pots in front of the main entrance were scattered into the snow on the floor.

The driver stopped the car right outside the car porch. It was drizzling with snowflakes and fine drops of rain through the light fog. The weather was freezing. Mathew and Emma stepped out of the car and walked under the cover of the porch. They went to the entrance door, which was partially closed, and door guards were attending the area. The guard in the front asked politely, "Can I help you, lady and gentleman?"

Mathew looked at him and realised that they were new staff members. "I am Mathew Atkinson, and this is my friend Emma ……"

"I am sorry, sir. We all are agency staff. Names don't help us. I believe you're the guests for the reception?"

Mathew and Emma shot a glance at each other before he replied, "Yes, we are."

"As you see, we are having serious problems. No electricity is here due to the storm. Believe you me, what a storm it was."

"Very dangerous," Emma said.

"And the generators are on, but not good enough. The place is very dark. And we've set up gas cylinders, but the hall is still freezing."

The guard looked at her quietly before he continued concernedly, "Most of the guests were redirected to other hotels and venues. Here, we have only the bride and groom and their close families and friends."

"We are the relatives of Helena, the bride."

The guard passed the other guards and went to a table. He took a folder that was resting on the top and ran down the list of guests. He left it where it was and came back, "I'm sorry. Your names are not in it."

"Anyone else you can ask here?"

"Not really! Due to the wedding, most of the staff are either off or gone to other avenues. But, after saying that," he paused as if unsure of himself. He walked a few steps out into the open and, raising his one hand, pointed along the side of the building. "If you walk up about hundred to there, you will see a door. A few regular staff are there. And they will help you."

Mathew and Emma thanked him and went up in that direction.

Part 5: The Reception

It was an average size door with an enquiry window on its side. Behind the window was a small office with a few chairs and tables along the wall. Mathew tapped on the window and stood back. One of the three men who were inside the office moved forward in his chair and opened the pane, "Good evening. Can I help you, sir?"

"We're invited for the reception."

"Oh, sorry for the inconvenience," he said apologetically. "The hurricane created so many problems here. And your names?"

"I am Mathew Atkinson. And this is Emma Willford."

One of the men at the table got up hurriedly, turning his head towards the window. "Thank you so much. We were waiting for you." He rushed out of the office and then to the door. The door was opened in front of them. "Please come in. It's not a nice day to stand outside."

They entered, and he shut the door behind them. "Please follow me," he said as he headed them through an inner door to the lobby. The lefthand side of it had an end-to-end glass partition and viewed across the Great Hall and a huge stage on the far end where the newlyweds couple would take their seats. There were another three exits in different directions. The other two guards also joined them with two men, and one of the new men locked the inner door from behind. Mathew stared at Emma rather tensely, and she, in turn, watched the men cautiously. One of the guards pointed her to a row of chairs and said in an uncaring tone, "You sit there."

Mathew asked quickly, "What do you mean?"

Another man answered in a cold voice, making a gesture towards one of the doors, "We go there. We've something to discuss."

Emma moved closer to Mathew. "I'm coming with him."

Mathew said politely, "We are here to attend the reception. And nothing more."

"Please cooperate with us. We are not looking for trouble."

Mathew quickly glanced into the Great Hall. The seats were filling in the front rows. About fifteen to twenty guests were on the stage, but no signs of Adam Aylesbury and Helena Roscoe were there. He turned back his head and stared at them, "Why can't we talk here?"

"You have to come with us. We've some papers to show you."

"No tricks. Okay?"

"No. And the lady can stay here."

She said quickly, "I am coming."

"That's your decision."

A man went and opened a door. "Yes, you can go in."

They went in as instructed.

The men came in behind and locked the door hurriedly. It was quite a spacious room with a look at the seawater in the distance. There was a desk in between two chairs, but the rest of the space remained empty. The fat man approached the table and stood behind there.

"What's all this suspense, men? I'm the chairman of this building and the business."

"Not for long, Mr Atkinson." He said. "Everything belongs to Mrs Isabella Atkinson."

"Is that right?"

"Now, I recognise you. It's you men who banged into our car and then started a fight?"

"Your memory is still good. We would have killed you, but your daughter saved you."

"You better sign these documents and transfer all the British assets to Isabella."

"I'm signing nothing."

The fat man moved closer to him, with an angry face and holding a knife. "You better sign the documents."

"Move away from Mathew," Emma shouted angrily. "And put away your knife."

The bald man laughed sarcastically, "Careful, babe. He can slice your neck and his in one second."

Neither Mathew nor Emma replied to him. He was focussing on the knife that was in the man's hand. But she said to the fat man. "You better move back with your knife. You don't want to hurt yourself. "

The three men and the guards laughed cynically. And the tall man snapped rudely, "Don't be a prat like his bastard daughter."

"Is that so?"

"We buried her in the sea. Our bomb exploded her into bits."

"What's wrong with you? Why are you telling him all this? Let's get on with our task."

"Let him understand we've always been in control."

"How did you know Gemma was going in that yacht?"

They laughed triumphantly. "Tanya, of course. She told me you'd be in the yacht as well."

"Tanya stayed with you while she was working for Isabella."

"Shame we couldn't kill you with your daughter. Please forgive us."

"Anyway, we drowned your daughter exactly where we buried your African bastard, Abigale. In the sea!"

"You sure you did that, too?"

"Of course, your wife paid us good money."

"Your wife, Isabella, always paid us good money."

"Why are you talking to him? Let's finish him and get our rewards."

The fat man with the knife started to square Mathew. The bald man moved up closer in case the fat man needed help. Mathew's total concentration was on the knife and the hand holding it while the man's face grew with an expression of evil determination. Emma sensed that the man would swing with the knife at any second, besides the fact that the bald man was also gearing up for the killing. She tiptoed and sprung up instantly onto the table on their side before she made a summersault through the air. The fat and bald men stared at her breathlessly in complete amazement and bewilderment. Her one foot stretched onto the knife, and it went into the fat man's chest instantly. He swung momentarily on his feet, but he fell on his back. Her other foot stretched onto the bald man's neck with full force, and he staggered onto the window. The glass shattered, and his head stuck out through a hole. A large piece of glass slipped out of the frame and fell on him, slitting his neck almost thoroughly. The young man became furious and ran to Emma as if he was ready to rip her into bits. Mathew, grabbing a chair, smashed it across his face. The man staggered on his feet momentarily, then turned to Mathew. He used the chair again, smashing him on his head and chest. The man stood up mechanically, without breathing, before he tumbled down to the floor.

The guards stared at each other, clearly experiencing mixed feelings of anger and fear. Their three men were on the floor, either already dead or dying in seconds. "Let's go to the gas room," one of the guards murmured fearfully. "let's get the cylinder and attack them."

As if the other two already had the same conclusion, they and the other man dashed out to the lobby. They then, opening one of the other doors, entered a corridor and ran towards the other end where the large heating room was situated, and next to it was the stage of the hall and hall beyond. About 70 gas cylinders were on fire, which sent the warm air through hefty pipes into the stage that was next to it and then the hall past the stage. "Will they escape?"

"Good. We burn them."

Each man grabbed a bulky burning cylinder and, holding them high over their shoulders, turned back, obviously in a hurry to get to Mathew and Emma. Petrified, the men stopped swiftly and, seemingly motionless, as they saw the latter right in front of them. Nonetheless, it was momentously risky as anybody could throw the fatal attack. And Emma was fully aware of it. Her leg rose at lightning speed, and her feet landed below the belt of the man who was close to her. He stooped backward and, dropping the cylinder, held his belly button while gasping for air. In the next split second, he dropped to the floor in extreme agony.

One of the other two had a ferocious kick on his tummy, while the last guard received a lefthand chop on his neck. The cylinders fell to the ground and crashed while their nozzles broke off. The gas escaped freely through the nostrils while the flames of fire grew more extensive and the agonising hot air increased. Suddenly, those three cylinders started to crawl aimlessly as if haunted before they gained enormous power and rolled over the floor. Immediately, they were nearer to the numerous cylinders that were providing warmth at the stage and around the hall. "Emma, they'll explode now," he said fearfully. "Maybe all of them will explode."

"Nobody knows, Mathew," she replied hurriedly. "Anyway, all your problems are over."

"What do you mean?"

"Time will tell you. Let's run out, quick."

They ran down the corridor, past the lobby. The exit door was locked. She rose to the air and produced an aerial jump with both of her legs. The door burst open, and they rushed out through. Exactly this time, one cylinder soared up with heat and fire, broke through the wooden wall, and exploded with unimaginable force, arriving under the zenith of the stage. The generator that produced electricity was lost immediately, and darkness instantly filled the air with a vengeance of its own. And more cylinders landed repeatedly, with massive fire and heat blazing through the murkiness, and ignited the ceiling structure. People on stage screamed with fear and cried for help. Mathew dashed to the guards at the main entrance. "Call the fire station and for the ambulance," he said to the doormen behind the counter. "People must be dead up there."

The uproar inside kept going on as burning beams and fragments of ceiling collapsed through the night. Various people were weeping and shouting out of sheer fear and screaming out for help while they were trying to get out of the hall in sheer panic.

"We're trying to phone, sir," one of them answered politely. "But no telephone lines are working."

"No telephone lines?" Mathew asked quickly, without realising himself.

"No, sir," a second man explained nervously. "The lines are broken. The storm smashed the trees on them."

"Who got the bikes?" Emma asked. "Tell them to go to the stations, please."

"We can go, sir. But it's not safe to go. Roads are full of snow. And the fallen trees."

"Please try."

"Okay, sir."

"And be careful."

"Okay." Two doormen got out and dashed to their motorbikes on the roadside.

A few more cylinders shot to the sky and exploded violently, spreading fire and sparkles and columns of smoke around. The fire on the roof rose high and burned in the foggy sky, creating a spectrum of colours and silhouettes. Below the burning roof, the smoke merged with the growing fog and limited the visibility into feet. Few guests struggled to get out, coughing badly and wheezing terribly, and their expensive clothes soiled with ashes and dirt all over. One who came out among them was his driver, Jose. "My God, I found you at last," he said, gasping for air. "I was walking over dead bodies looking for you."

Mathew turned in the direction of the voice and found him in the light that flashed from the fire on the roof or falling wood. "I am glad I found you, too. A few casualties, I fear?"

Before Jose could answer, Kathrine turned up on his side. She hugged him, obviously in tears, and said in an aching voice, "I thought you were in the seats on the stage."

"No, dear. Those were meant for Isabella's family and friends. I don't belong to that privileged class."

"That's good."

"Is that so?"

"You're lucky. Everyone up there is dead."

"Isabella?"

"Died."

"Francis?"

"Helena and Adam?"

"Died."

He waited. "Very sad! But I don't want to admit it."

Kathrine didn't say anything.

"Isabella killed the lady I loved. And she killed our daughter. Now, God's giving her reward."

The wall behind the stage exploded loudly as the flames of fire scorched out into the very old timber panels. "It's not safe here," Emma said. "Let's go to the other side of the road."

A FEW TALES

They walked across the road through thick fog; the fresh snow cracked under their feet. They got on to the payment and turned back to the hall. Mathew was holding Kathrine with his left hand, and Emma was inside his right arm. The fire was blazing from the entire roof, and the columns of black smog billowed, slitting the towering cliff of haze into two zones, and the flashes of blazes brightened the front of the hotel. Emma looked at Kathrine with a concerned expression. "It's not safe here," she said, coughing. She narrowed her eyes against the burning debris, ashes, and the sweltering heat from the fire. "We must move back."

Kathrine readily agreed. "The air is full of rubbles from the fire. If you're not careful, you'll lose your eyes."

"Yes," Mathew said. "We go back to the oak tree on the other side of the road. Surely, it's better than here."

Just then, sirens of the fire engines filtered through the layers of fog and mist and through the sounds of burning woods and falling roofs. Suddenly, besides the sirens, the flashes of emergency lights started to illuminate the area. And, in no time, the onlookers ran out of the yards, and fire engines, ambulances, and police vehicles hurried in as close as possible to the Great Hall. Some of these vehicles, such as police cars and health and safety vans, were parked near the hotel, allowing more space for the fire engines nearer the burning Great Hall. And all the officers and staff rushed out from their vehicles and engaged in actions. 'Lifesaving' was their motto. Police officers shouted to the crowd loudly, "Move away, as far as you can. Poisonous gas is everywhere."

"Mathew can't manage by himself," Kathrine said. "His leg is hurt."

"I'm okay," he said quickly. "But I like to sit for a few minutes."

Mark showed up breathlessly. "Oh God! You're here. I have been looking for you."

"Where were you?" Emma asked with a sigh of relief. "You are okay?"

He nodded for an answer. "I knew you were here."

Emma went near to him. "Please help Mathew towards the oak tree up there. He ought to sit down."

He looked at her quizzically.

"There was a fight."

"Why didn't you tell me?"

Some more emergency vehicles hurried into the yard. They silently watched them for a moment before she turned to him. "We came for the reception."

"And?"

"They gave us some reception, Mark!"

"What do you mean?"

"Big fight!"

"You got bad?"

"We got."

"Where are they now?"

"Oh! Don't worry about them. When we finished with them, they were burning in the fire."

He stared at her studiously. "You fought as well?"

"No problem. I enjoy it."

He looked deeply confused. "You sure you are Emma?"

She smiled faintly. "After staying with you one week, you still don't know me."

Mark stared. "Not Gemma? She was a great karate fighter."

"Well. We didn't miss her today. And let her have a day off."

The dust and ashes were increasing in the air, with the choking smell of smoke that was swelling minute by minute. Mark approached Mathew. "I can help you, Mathew. Let's go to the other side of the road."

He glanced across the yard and the road and then to the open park. "Better than here, Mark – I suppose."

"Shall I help you? I heard you hurt yourself."

"I had a few kicks on my legs. And that's nothing. Luckily, Emma was there."

"She helped you?"

"Very much so. And she destroyed them!"

Mark stared into his eyes. "I am getting worried. Who is this, Emma?"

Mathew caught his eyes steadily. "I know what you are thinking, Mark."

"And I know Mathew exactly what you are thinking, too."

Kathrine came closer to them. "Difficult to breathe this air," she said. "Let's go."

They crossed the yard and the road and then walked into the park with the oak tree. Mathew sat down on a stone bench. Kathrine sat next to him. Mark and Emma stood a few feet away from them. "I am not feeling well, Mark," Emma said uneasily.

607

"What is it?" He asked anxiously. "You want to sit down."

She didn't speak but nodded lightly for an answer. He held her firmly in his hands towards the side of Mathew. She sat down by the side of Mathew and leaned over lap and chest. "Emma?" Mathew called, clearly worried.

Kathrine leaned over and, holding her shoulder, called gently, "Emma, you okay?"

"Emma, Emma," Mark called.

She didn't respond.

Mark looked at Mathew. "Looks like she got hurt badly. Let me go and get some paramedics from the ambulance."

A few more fire engines and ambulances arrived and joined with their colleagues. However, there was no sign of the fire getting diminished. The three-hundred-year-old wooden structure of the hall was like an oil depot, fiery beyond imagination.

"Emma?" Mathew called in a mixed voice of fear and sadness.

"Did they harm her very badly?" Mark asked, kneeling down close to her.

Mathew didn't answer but asked her all the more lovingly, "Emma, you alright?"

Slowly, Emma opened her eyes and caught Mathew's gazing eyes. "Papa!"

All the other three fell silent breathlessly. However, in a moment or two, Mathew managed to speak. "Papa?"

"Yes, Papa. I'm Gemma?"

Mathew raised her body slightly and held her tightly close to his chest. Tears gushed out of his eyes and trickled down onto her face.

Just then, a view of the sea near the horizon zoomed into their direction.

They stared through the drifting ashes, smoke, and fog and tried to see into the distance. In their view, a section of the sky opened up, allowing them to see a large landscape. "That's the colonial districts in Atlantica City we are seeing," Mathew cried out. "And the building on the slop is my house, the Colonial House!"

A young lady appeared on the terrace while they were staring at the landscape and the house.

"Who is she?" They all wondered in delight.

"That's Abigale," Emma answered easily.

Abigale stood naturally and looked back at them.

"Do you know Abigale, Emma?"

Emma moved in his hold and stared into the distance. "Yes. Papa. Abigale is my mama."

He waited for a moment as the surging memories settled down a little.

"Of course, I know," Mathew replied rather easily. "Abigale, the lady I loved?"

She said, "Yes, Papa?"

Surged with more emotions, he turned to Gemma. Obviously, he was confused.

"You okay, Papa?"

Without answering, he turned and looked into the distance. Abigale was still there on the terrace. She raised her hand and waved at them, "Goodbye.'

Waving back, they all whispered, 'Goodbye, Abigale.'

A wasp of fog drifted into their view. Slowly, it grew larger and thicker.

Abigale disappeared out of their eyes, but a female voice came loud as thunder.

It was Abigale's voice, and it said, "I love you, Mathew."

The End

www.ingramcontent.com/pod-product-compliance
Lightning Source LLC
Chambersburg PA
CBHW070855120626
46546CB00001B/13